CAMBRIDGE TEXTBOOKS IN LINGUISTICS

General Editors: B. COMRIE, C. J. FILLMORE, R. LASS, D. LIGHTFOOT,
J. LYONS, P. H. MATTHEWS, R. POSNER, S. ROMAINE, N. V. SMITH,
N. VINCENT

TYPOLOGY AND UNIVERSALS

In this series:

TYPOLOGY AND UNIVERSALS

WILLIAM CROFT

PROGRAM IN LINGUISTICS
UNIVERSITY OF MICHIGAN

The right of the
University of Cambridge
to print and sell
all manner of books
was granted by
Henry VIII in 1534.
The University has printed
and published continuously
since 1584.

CAMBRIDGE UNIVERSITY PRESS

CAMBRIDGE
NEW YORK   PORT CHESTER
MELBOURNE   SYDNEY

Published by the Press Syndicate of the University of Cambridge
The Pitt Building, Trumpington Street, Cambridge CB2 1RP
40 West 20th Street, New York, NY 10011, USA
10 Stamford Road, Oakleigh, Melbourne 3166, Australia

First published 1990

Printed in Great Britain by The Bath Press, Avon

British Library cataloguing in publication data

Croft, William
Typology and universals. – (Cambridge textbooks in
linguistics)
1. Languages. Typology
1. Title
415

Library of Congress cataloguing in publication data

Croft, William
Typology and universals / William Croft.
    p.   cm. – (Cambridge textbooks in linguistics)
Includes bibliographical references.
ISBN 0-521-36583-X. – ISBN 0-521-36765-4 (pbk.)
1. Typology (Linguistics) 2. Universals (Linguistics) 1. Title.
II. Series.
P204.C7   1990
415 – dc20   89-36872 CIP

ISBN 0 521 36583 x hardback
ISBN 0 521 36765 4 paperback

BS

FOR JOSEPH GREENBERG

CONTENTS

Contents

Contents

PREFACE AND ACKNOWLEDGMENTS

This volume is an introduction to the concepts and methodology of linguistic typology. It complements other introductory volumes on typology, particularly Comrie 1981a and Mallinson and Blake 1981, in that the material is organized by theoretical concept (implicational universal, markedness, prototype) rather than by topic area (word order, grammatical relations, relative clauses, animacy). Also, the range of concepts covered is somewhat broader, mostly because of the need to describe developments in functional-typological explanation and diachronic typology in the last decade. Needless to say, there is some overlap with the aforementioned volumes. From a pedagogical point of view, however, this volume is intended to complement, not supplement, the more "topic-oriented" introductions. In particular, breadth in theoretical coverage has meant that detailed examples of typological generalizations, complete with qualifications, possible counterexamples and explanations for those counterexamples, could not always be included (though I have tried not to oversimplify examples without at least citing more detailed studies). The material in this volume has been used in courses in conjunction with Comrie 1981a, Greenberg 1966a (the original article on word order), Greenberg 1966b (the monograph on markedness) and other articles on more specific topic areas.

I believe that an essential part of any linguistics class, and above all any class on typology, is for the student to encounter one or more "exotic" languages. For practical reasons, in an introductory typology class this encounter must be somewhat limited. In my course, each student is required to "adopt" a grammar of an exotic language, from a list of grammars that I considered particularly detailed, careful and thorough (though not always easy to use!). Each student then writes short papers describing a particular aspect of the grammar, such as negative constructions or word order in the noun phrase. Some of these assignments include group efforts in order to give the students a chance to compare languages on their own.

These essentially descriptive assignments are not as easy as they may seem, as anyone who has actually done typological research using grammars and other descriptive materials can attest. (They can be supplemented with problem-solving assignments that more directly relate to the concepts discussed in the textbook and the readings.) Their value is to expose the students to the full richness and variety of human languages, which any linguistic theory tends to oversimplify in the name of creating order from data. If all goes well, this encounter engenders a fascination with ways of speaking (and perhaps of thinking) that are different from ours, and functions as an antidote to reductionist theorizing; and this is all for the best.

First in order of acknowledgment is the redwood country of the California Northcoast, in whose peaceful presence this book was largely written in the summer of 1988 (thanks to my family and to the University of Michigan, the latter through a Horace H. Rackham summer fellowship). Joseph Greenberg, Bernard Comrie, Keith Denning and three anonymous reviewers from the Cambridge Textbooks Series editorial board provided valuable comments on the earliest drafts. Special thanks go to Penny Carter of Cambridge University Press; Elizabeth Traugott of Stanford University; and Tom Toon of the University of Michigan. Pam Beddor exposed me to current work on phonological typology and phonetic explanation, some of which made its way into this volume. Four classes of typology students at Stanford and the University of Michigan contributed immeasurably to what ultimately became the organization of this volume. John Myhill read and commented on the penultimate draft, and used it in his typology course; Myhill's students gave important feedback on the manuscript, considerably improving the final version. Trisha Svaib assisted in preparing the final manuscript. Keith Denning provided valuable advice and invaluable moral support throughout the time that I wrote this volume.

Above all, I have benefited enormously from two of the leaders in the field of typology and universals. Bernard Comrie, whose research and whose own volume on typology set an excellent example for me, oversaw this project from the earliest drafts to the final manuscript and provided extensive comments and general support for my efforts. Finally, I must express my deeply felt appreciation to my teacher, Joseph H. Greenberg, whose erudition in human languages, language universals, historical linguistics and the history of linguistics is unequalled. I dedicate this volume to him with affection and respect.

ABBREVIATIONS

Á   adjective
abs.   absolutive
acc.   accusative
adv.   adverb
agt   agent
al.   alienable (possession morpheme)
ant.   antecedent (of conditional)
antipass. antipassive
art.   article
asp.   aspect
assoc.   associative
aux.   auxiliary

ben.   benefactive
buff.   buffer

caus.   causative
class.   classifier
CM   class marker
comp.   complement form
con.   construct (form)
cons.   consequent (of conditional)

dat.   dative
def.   definite
dem.   demonstrative
det.   determiner
dir.   direct
DO   direct object
DS   different subject
du.   dual
dur.   durative

emph.   emphatic

erg.   ergative
eval.   evaluative

f.   feminine
fut.   future

gen.   genitive

H   human

impf.   imperfective
incl.   inclusive
indef.   indefinite
indic.   indicative
inf.   infinitive
inst.   instrumental
interr.   interrogative
inv.   inverse
IO   indirect object
irr.   irrealis

lig.   ligature
link.   linker
loc.   locative

M   marker (of comparison)
masc.   masculine

N   noun
neg.   negative
N/F   nonfuture
NH   nonhuman
nom.   nominative
nontop.   nontopic
nt.   neuter
num.   numeral

$O_{nom.}$ nominal object

Abbreviations

O_{prn}	pronominal object	Q	interrogative particle
obj.	object		
obl.	oblique	redup.	reduplicative
oblig.	obligatory	rel.	relative (clause)
Ocomp.	object of comparison		
opt.	optional	S/sbj.	subject
		sent.	sentence
part.	participle	sg.	singular
partv.	partitive	SO	secondary object
perf.	perfect(ive)	SS	same subject
pl.	plural	std.	standard (of
PO	primary object		comparison)
poss.	possessive	subord.	subordinate
postp.	postposition		
pot.	potential	tns.	tense
pre.	preposition(al)	top.	topic
pres.	present	trans.	transitive
pro.	pronoun		
prt.	particle	uns.	unspecified
punct.	punctual	V	verb

Language examples have generally been presented in standard orthography (if there is one), or in the orthography used by the source. In some instances, orthography has been adjusted where no confusion would arise.

I
Introduction

1.1 Definitions and scope of typology

The term **typology** has a number of different uses, both within linguistics and without. The common definition of the term is roughly synonymous with "taxonomy" or "classification," a classification of the phenomenon under study into types, particularly structural types. This is the definition that is found outside of linguistics, for example in biology, a field that inspired linguistic theory in the nineteenth century. We will not be concerned with this definition except insofar as any scientific inquiry involves the classification of the phenomena under examination.

The broadest and most unassuming linguistic definition of "typology" refers to a classification of structural types across languages. In this second definition, a language is taken to belong to a single type, and a typology of languages is a definition of the types and an enumeration or classification of the languages into those types. We will refer to this definition of typology as **typological classification**. The morphological typology of the nineteenth and early twentieth centuries is an example of this use of the term. This definition introduces the basic connotation that "typology" has to contemporary linguists: typology has to do with **cross-linguistic comparison** of some sort. This chapter will discuss some methodological issues in cross-linguistic comparison, while chapter 2 will be devoted to the notion of a linguistic type, including morphological typology, and its refinements in twentieth-century research.

A more specific definition of "typology" is that it is the study of linguistic patterns that are found cross-linguistically, in particular, patterns that can be discovered solely by cross-linguistic comparison. The classic example of typology under this third definition is the implicational universal. Let us consider, for example, the implicational universal, "if the demonstrative follows the head noun, then the relative clause also follows the head noun." This universal cannot be discovered or verified by observing only a single language, such as English. One has to do a general survey of languages to observe that the language type excluded by the implicational universal, namely a language in which the demonstrative follows the head noun and the relative clause precedes it, indeed does not exist. (This requirement raises the problem of a typological language sample, which will also be discussed in this chapter.) Under this definition, typology is a subdiscipline of linguistics – not unlike, say, first-language acquisition – with a particular domain of linguistic facts to examine: cross-linguistic patterns. Typology in this sense began in earnest with Joseph H. Greenberg's discovery of implicational universals of morphology and word order, first presented in 1960 (Greenberg 1966a). We will use the simple term **typology** to refer to the subdiscipline. The primary purpose of this volume is to discuss the kinds of cross-linguistic patterns that have been discovered and the methodological and empirical issues raised by the study of these patterns. Chapters 3–6 are devoted to discussing these patterns and the empirical and methodological issues that their discovery raises. The organization of the material in chapters 3–6 reflects the thesis that the kinds of cross-linguistic patterns actually found represent a coherent set of patterns which should be central phenomena to be explained by any linguistic theory.

There is a final, still more specific definition of "typology." In this view, typology represents an "approach" to the study of language that contrasts with prior approaches, such as American structuralism and generative grammar. In this fourth and last definition, typology is an approach to linguistic theorizing, or more precisely a methodology of linguistic analysis that gives rise to different kinds of linguistic theories than other "approaches." Sometimes this view of typology is called the "Greenbergian," as opposed to the "Chomskyan," approach to linguistic theory (after their best-known practitioners; see, for example, Smith 1982:256). This view of typology is closely allied to **functionalism**, the hypothesis that linguistic structure should be explained primarily in terms of linguistic function (the Chomskyan approach is contrastively titled **formalism**). For this reason, typology in this sense is often called the **(functional-)typological approach**, and will be called so here.[1] The functional-typological approach became generally recognized in the 1970s and is primarily associated with Talmy Givón, Paul Hopper and Sandra Thompson, though it has well-established historical antecedents (discussed in Haiman 1985 and in chapter 9 of this book).

This volume explicates the functional-typological approach to language in the final three chapters. Chapter 7 discusses external explanations of typological patterns and the typology of form–function relations, an area in which typological research fits into the functionalist model. Chapter 8 describes diachronic typology, a central facet of many of the functionally inclined typologists (including Greenberg, Givón, Hopper, Bybee and the typologists associated with the Cologne Universals Project). Finally, chapter 9 describes the functional-typological approach to linguistic explanation. These topics only describe how typology relates to, and contributes to, functional approaches to linguistic theorizing, however. It is not our intention here to explicate functional approaches to language, a task which would take up another volume.

It is worth stating that despite claims that the "Greenbergian approach" and the "Chomskyan approach" to linguistic analysis are diametrically opposed to each other in every respect, there are several fundamental characteristics that the two approaches share (albeit with different emphases). Both approaches begin with the analysis of language structure, though the Greenbergian explains those structures in terms of function and the Chomskyan seeks "formal" explanations in harmony with the autonomy of language hypothesis. Both approaches consider the central question of linguistics to be "What is a possible human language?" and believe that there are universal constraints that define the answer to this question, though the Greenbergian uses an empiricist method and the Chomskyan a rationalist one to discover those constraints. And both approaches utilize a considerable amount of abstraction, though the Greenbergian abstracts patterns across languages and the Chomskyan abstracts patterns within languages. So it cannot be said that functional-typological theory is totally revolutionary (or counter-revolutionary, depending on one's point of view).

Not surprisingly, these differing definitions of typology – typological classification, typology proper and the functional-typological approach – have led to some confusion about what typology is, or is supposed to be. For example, it is frequently charged that typology is "solely descriptive" or "taxonomic"; that is to say, it does not provide a means for developing theories of language which can function as an alternative to, for example, generative linguistic theory (to which it is frequently compared).[2] This represents a confusion between typological classification with typology proper and the claims of the typological approach to grammar. Typology proper represents a well-established method of analysis, and the typological approach is by now a well-articulated theory of language.

The emphasis on theory and methodology in this volume should not be interpreted as minimizing the descriptive work necessary to develop

3

typological analyses. The descriptive work which has been and, I hope, will continue to be done on the tremendous number of languages in the world is absolutely essential not just to typological theory but to all linguistic theories. Unfortunately, typological studies have often had to withhold or remove their data sections upon publication due to size limitations,[3] while many good descriptive works such as the University of Hawaii Press PALI series of Micronesian language grammars rapidly go out of print. The attitude that descriptive work is not valued (it is "just" descriptive or "descriptivist") must be abandoned for there to be progress in linguistic theory.

This matter becomes even more urgent because of the alarming loss of the empirical data base for linguistic theory. Hundreds of languages have become extinct in this century or will by the end of the century. Hundreds of others no longer survive in viable speech communities; the languages are dying and there are often serious consequences about grammatical structure and stylistic characteristics (see Dorian 1981; Schmid 1985). This situation is getting worse, not better. The empirical problems with language research parallel the problems in biological research, in particular in evolutionary theory and ecology: the extinction of languages and the loss of the linguistic communities is like the extinction of species and the loss of their habitat (ecosystems), and in both disciplines it threatens theoretical progress.

1.2 Cross-linguistic comparison

The first question that may be asked of typology is, what is the role of cross-linguistic comparison – the fundamental characteristic of typology – in linguistic analysis? In this section, I will argue that cross-linguistic comparison places the explanation of intralinguistic phenomena in a new and different perspective.

Let us use as an example the distribution of the definite and indefinite articles in English:

(1a) He broke **a vase**.
(1b) He broke **the vase**.
(1c) The concert will be on **Saturday**.
(1d) He went to **the bank**.
(1e) I drank **wine**.
(1f) The French love **glory**.
(1g) He showed **extreme care**.
(1h) I love **artichokes** and asparagus.
(1i) Birds have **wings**.
(1j) His brother became **a soldier**.

(1k)   **Dogs** were playing in the yard.

The eleven sentences given above characterize eleven types of uses of the articles (or their absence) in English, given as follows:

  (a)   specific (referential) indefinite;
  (b)   specific and definite;
  (c)   proper name;
  (d)   nonspecific reference to a habitually frequented place or institution; [4]
  (e)   partitive of a mass noun;
  (f)   generic mass noun;
  (g)   specific manifestation of an abstract quality (mass noun);
  (h)   generic of a count noun;
  (i)   generic of an indefinite number of a count noun;
  (j)   predicate nominal;
  (k)   specific but indefinite number of a count noun.

Let us assume that we have an analysis that predicts exactly the distribution of the two articles (including their absence) in English. Such an account may be syntactic, semantic or pragmatic, or a combination of all three; whatever is the case, it will have to be a fairly complex and subtle analysis, especially since the eleven different construction types given here do not exhaust the possibilities. At this point, the typologist will ask: what is the significance of the analysis for the class of natural languages as a whole? Examining even a relatively closely related language, French, produces difficulties. In the exact same contexts, illustrated here by translation equivalents of the English sentences, the distribution of definite and indefinite articles *le/la/les* and *un/une* respectively (and their absence) is quite different:

  (2a)   Il a cassé **un vase**.
  (2b)   Il a cassé **le vase**.
  (2c)   Le concert sera **samedi**.
  (2d)   Il est allé à **la banque**.
  (2e)   J'ai bu **du vin**. (du = de + le)
  (2f)   Les Français aiment **la gloire**.
  (2g)   Il montra **un soin** extrême.
  (2h)   J'aime **les artichauts** et les asperges.
  (2i)   Les oiseaux ont **des ailes**. (des = de + les)
  (2j)   Son frère est devenu **soldat**.
  (2k)   **Des chiens** jouaient dans le jardin.

It is quite likely that the analysis of the distribution of the English articles would have to be drastically altered if not abandoned and a new one developed for the distribution of the French ones, in order to account for the more widespread use of the French definite article, the appearance of the partitive marker *de* plus the definite article, and the indefinite article, as well as the absence of the French indefinite article in the predicate nominal constructions. One cannot be certain how much we would have to start all over again, of course, since to the best of my knowledge no such analysis has been worked out. However, an analysis of a subset of three of the eleven contexts has been proposed: the generic count nouns in (h) and (i) and the indefinite number of count-noun usage in (k). Carlson (1977) proposed a unified analysis of the bare plural construction used in both situation types, in which both are of the same semantic type and the differing interpretations are attributed to the type of the predicate. But in comparing the English and French examples, we see that in fact two different types of NPs are found, and so a unified interpretation may not be desirable.[5]

The fact that analyses of linguistic phenomena "one language at a time" cannot be carried over from one language to the next is somewhat disturbing for the search for language universals. Intricate interactions of internal structural principles are proposed by linguists to "predict" grammatical patterns that do not apply to even the neighboring languages. This is true not only in structuralist-generative analyses; functionalist analyses, which invoke external (semantic or pragmatic) factors to account for the distribution of phenomena like the articles of English, often have the same problems:

Volumes of so-called functionalism are filled with ingenious appeals to perception, cognition or other system-external functional domains, which are used to "explain" why the language in question simply has to have a grammatical particularity that it does – when a moment's further reflection would show that another well-known language, or even just the next dialect down the road, has a grammatical structure diametrically opposed in the relevant parameter. (DuBois 1985:353)

Again, I must emphasize that these criticisms are *not* intended to denigrate detailed analyses of single-language phenomena; they remain the essential basis of *all* linguistic research. The issue is, to what level of generalization should such an analysis be developed before taking into consideration cross-linguistic patterns? The typologist essentially takes the position that cross-linguistic patterns should be taken into consideration at virtually every level of generalization (see chapter 9 for further discussion).

A cross-linguistic comparative approach, that is a typological approach in the third sense described in the previous section, allows us to make progress on universal characteristics of the distribution of articles, for example, and in turn causes us to reassess the single-language analyses.

There are certain generalizations that cut *across* the two languages that are very likely to be characteristic of language in general. For instance, the first four uses, (a)–(d), are identical in the two languages, and it is only in the following seven that there is substantial variation. With the exception of the (d) use (which is rather unusual and has not been well documented) and the (k) use, all of the typologically variable uses concern generic and mass-noun contexts of various sorts. This suggests that there may be some uniformity across languages in specific NP contexts that does not exist in generic and mass NP contexts.

There are two important points implicit in this suggested reanalysis which summarize the argument for cross-linguistic comparison. The first is that this generalization could not be made without looking at more than one language. (Examining still more languages would, of course, refine the oversimple generalization that we have made.) That is what makes this analysis of the phenomenon "typological." The second, stronger claim, characteristic of the typological approach, is that this generalization ought to be *part of* the language-specific analysis of the distribution of articles in both French and English, in fact of any language that has articles. That is, the analysis of the distribution of the articles in both English and French ought to characterize the distribution in specific NP contexts as "typical" or even "universal" (if that turns out to be the case), and the distribution in generic and mass NP contexts as arbitrary and language-specific, or perhaps subject to other conditions that would be revealed by further cross-linguistic analysis. In this view, the linguistic analysis of the articles in French or English would be incomplete, and therefore an inadequate explanation of the phenomenon, if its position in the universal, cross-linguistic distribution of articles is not taken into account. The reason for this is that the generalizations revealed by examining more than one language at a time are the only ones which can be said to hold of natural languages in general, and our analyses of particular languages must be done in terms of how the particular language manifests the characteristics of language in general.

It is true that some universal characteristics of language can be observed in just one language; these are called **unrestricted** universals, such as the presence of vowels and consonants and the existence of nouns and verbs. However, the number of unrestricted universals is fairly limited. There are many other generalizations that hold over all natural languages that are not unrestricted universals; they are patterns which are manifested only across languages, and can only be discovered by examining more than one language. (The validity of even unrestricted universals can be supported only by the inspection of other languages, indeed a large number of other languages.)

Another illustration of the need for a cross-linguistic approach to linguistic analysis and the difference between a cross-linguistic approach and a "one language at a time" approach is found in syntactic argumentation. Perhaps the central means of syntactic argumentation on the status of a particular linguistic category is the presentation of a series of different constructions all of which behave in the same way with respect to the category. For example, in arguing the case for the category "subject" in English, one would present the following examples as evidence that the immediately preverbal NP is the subject:

(3) He congratulated him/*he.
     (Nominative case of the pronoun *he* as opposed to *him*.)
(4) Teresa likes/*like horses.
     (Agreement of the verb with *Teresa*.)
(5) Jack wants to leave.
     (The person understood to be leaving is Jack; *Jack* controls the subject of the infinitive following *want*.)
(6) Take out the garbage.
     (Absence of the NP in the imperative construction.)
(7a) John found a ring and took it home with him.
(7b) *John found a ring and was gold. (the ring was gold)
     (Deletion of shared NP in a conjoined sentence.)

In terms of traditional syntactic argumentation, I have just presented five independent pieces of evidence for identifying the immediately preverbal NP as the "subject" of the sentence.

A typological analysis, on the other hand, would not present the preceding facts as "arguments" for a category subject, and in fact this style of argumentation is generally not found in typological studies (another reason for their being perceived as "descriptive" or "atheoretical" by some linguists). Instead, the typologist would say that the preceding examples demonstrate a correlation among several grammatical categories and constructions – word order, case, agreement, imperatives, control with *want* and one type of coordination – in a single language, English. For the typologist, the significant questions all refer to the status of this correlation cross-linguistically. What elements of this correlation are accidental, a peculiarity of English? What elements of this correlation are universal? What correlations systematically vary across languages, and why? (See 6.5 for further discussion.)[6]

The other side of the coin in invoking cross-linguistic comparison is that by examining a number of diverse languages, one will find striking, fascinating and sometimes mysterious connections between certain linguistic structures that one would not have imagined if one's attention were restricted to one language or a few typologically similar languages. This may take the form of a peculiar fact of one language which turns out to be widespread, or of a connection between two linguistic phenomena that is widespread but not manifested in one's own language.

An example of the former is that the apparently arbitrary irregularity of the "objective" forms of the English pronouns (*me, us, him, her, them*) is actually a manifestation of an extremely widespread pattern of relationship between case and animacy, namely that direct objects that refer to "more highly animate" beings (see chapters 5 and 6) are more likely to have distinct object case forms.[7] Another example is the variety of uses of the preposition *with* illustrated in the following sentences:

(8)   I went to New York with John.   ("comitative")
(9)   He opened the door with a crowbar. ("instrument")
(10) He swims with ease.   ("manner")

Intuitively, there seems to be little if any semantic connection between these three distinct uses of the same preposition, but a typological study of the distribution of adposition/case uses reveals that the subsumption of these and certain other uses under the same adposition or case marker is actually quite common. Consider for example Hausa *dà* and Classical Mongolian *-iyer ~ -iyar* in the following examples.

Hausa (Abraham 1959:22; Kraft & Kirk-Greene 1973:85)
(11) nā   hàrbē shī dà   bindingà
      1SG.COMP shoot 3SG with gun
      'I shot him with a gun.'
(12) mun   ci àbinci tàre   dà   shī
      1PL.COMP eat food together with 3SG
      'We ate food with him.'
(13) yā   gudù dà   saurī
      3SG.COMP run with speed
      'He ran fast ("with speed").'

Classical Mongolian (Poppe 1974:153–4)
(14) küol -iyer giški-
      foot -with tread.on-
      'to tread on with the foot'

9

(15) manu   morin tegün   -ü   morin -iyar belčimüi
      1SG.GEN horse that.3SG -GEN horse -with grazes
      'Our horse grazes with his horse.'

(16) türgen -iyer yabumui
      speed -with goes
      'He goes fast.'

Investigation of this cross-linguistic phenomenon suggests that the connection between these three uses and certain other uses can be defined in terms of causal relations between participants and properties of an event (Croft, forthcoming).

An example of two apparently unrelated constructions in English hiding a cross-linguistically evident connection is Haiman's examination of the relationship between the antecedent (protasis) of a conditional sentence, marked with *if* in English and a sentence topic, marked in English, if at all, with *as for* or *about* (Haiman 1978a):

(17)   If you eat that, you will get sick.

(18)   As for Randy, he's staying here.

Beginning with the Papuan language Hua, in which a suffix *-mo* is attached to both (potential) sentence topics and conditional protases, Haiman notes that Turkish *-sA*, the conditional marker, can also mark the contrastive topic, and the Tagalog word for "if," *kung*, can mark contrastive topics in conjunction with the preposition *tungkol* "about" (Haiman 1978a:565–6, 577). This somewhat mysterious connection between conditional protases and sentence topics found in several languages – though not in English – led Haiman to the discovery that the two are actually quite closely related in semantic and pragmatic terms.

Finally, cross-linguistic examination may also suggest that a certain type of phenomenon found in well-known languages is actually extremely unusual if not unique in the world's languages and thus may be a rather "peripheral" linguistic phenomenon from a cross-linguistic perspective. For example, the use of the indefinite article in predicate nominals illustrated in (1j), and the phenomenon of "stranding" prepositions as in *the book that I told you about* are extremely rare among the languages of the world. This is not to say that such phenomena do not need to be explained, of course.[8] It is just that they are perhaps not of as great importance to the study of language universals as the more widespread or universal phenomena, such as the extremely widespread use of the bare noun for predicate nominals and the subsumption of certain case roles under the same adposition or case affix.

1.3 The problem of cross-linguistic comparability

The characteristic feature of linguistic typology, in any of the senses given in the first section, is cross-linguistic comparison. The fundamental prerequisite for cross-linguistic comparison is cross-linguistic comparability, that is the ability to identify the "same" grammatical phenomenon across languages. One cannot make generalizations about subjects across languages without some confidence that one has correctly identified the category of "subject" in each language and compared subjects across languages. This is a fundamental issue in all linguistic theory, in fact. Nevertheless, this problem has commanded remarkably little attention relative to its importance.

Greenberg's original paper on word order offers one of the earlier discussions of the problem in the typological literature:

It is here assumed, among other things, that all languages have subject-predicate constructions, differentiated word classes, and genitive constructions, to mention but a few. I fully realize that in identifying such phenomena in languages of differing structure, one is basically employing semantic criteria. There are very probably formal similarities which permit us to equate such phenomena in different languages ... The adequacy of a cross-linguistic definition of "noun" would, in any case, be tested by reference to its results from the viewpoint of the semantic phenomena it was designed to explicate. If, for example, a formal definition of "noun" resulted in equating a class containing such glosses as "boy," "nose," and "house" in one language with a class containing such items as "eat," "drink," and "give" in a second language, such a definition would forthwith be rejected and that on semantic grounds. (Greenberg 1966a:74).

These brief remarks summarize the essential problem and a general solution. The essential problem is that languages vary in their structure to a great extent; indeed, that is what typology (and more generally, linguistics) aims to study and explain. But the variation in structure makes it difficult if not impossible to use structural criteria, or only structural criteria, to identify grammatical categories across languages. Although there is some similarity in structure ("formal" properties) that may be used for cross-linguistic identification of categories, the ultimate solution is a semantic one, or to put it more generally, a functional solution.

Greenberg's remarks are echoed by Keenan and Comrie in their analysis of relative clauses in their pioneering work on noun-phrase accessibility:

> We are attempting to determine the universal properties of relative clauses (RCs) by comparing their syntactic form in a large number of languages. To do this it is necessary to have a largely syntax-free way of identifying RCs in an arbitrary language. Our solution to this problem is to use an essentially semantically based definition of RC. (Keenan & Comrie 1977:63)[9]

In the case of relative clauses, the variation of morphosyntactic expression is such that a number of languages use morphological rather than syntactic means for forming what we would intuitively, that is semantically, identify as "relative clauses" (Comrie 1981b:136).

The term "semantic" probably implies a slightly narrow view of what the relevant factors are that have been used for cross-linguistic identification of morphosyntactic phenomena. Various pragmatic features, such as discourse structure (for comparing everything from forms of greeting to discourse-defined connectives such as "anyway" to the information structure of clauses) and conversational context (as in expressions of politeness and interlocutor status) also play a role in determining the cross-linguistic identity of the morphosyntactic phenomena that linguists are concerned with. These parameters are all essentially **external**, that is outside the structure of the language itself.

The typological studies of linguists such as Keenan, Comrie, Downing and Stassen have demonstrated the formulation of a standard research strategy for the typological study of some grammatical phenomenon: (1) determine the particular semantic(-pragmatic) structure or situation type that one is interested in studying; (2) examine the morphosyntactic construction(s) used to express that situation type; and (3) search for dependencies between the construction(s) used for that situation and other linguistic factors – other structural features, other external functions expressed by the construction in question, or both.

This solution to the problem of cross-linguistic comparability implies a close relationship between functional approaches to linguistic explanation and cross-linguistic analysis. Doing a typological classification, the descriptive prerequisite to typological analysis, requires a cross-linguistic analysis of the relationship between linguistic form and external function. Since this is a controversial point, it is worth examining the problem more closely.

First, it should be pointed out that many grammatical categories are identified cross-linguistically by semantic means without significant objections. For instance, if one is trying to find out if a set of verbal suffixes represents tense or aspect, one examines their meaning and use, not any formal properties. In these categories, difficulties in cross-linguistic comparability arise chiefly when a single form combines multiple functions (as often happens, in fact). The main problematic categories for cross-linguistic identification are the fundamental grammatical categories: noun, verb and adjective, subject and object, head and modifier, main clause and subordinate clause, etc. Needless to say, these categories are central to linguistic theory. On the one hand, these categories do not have an obvious functional (semantic and/or pragmatic) definition. On the other hand, these grammatical categories and the categories defined by them do vary considerably in their structural expression across languages – once we have identified the categories cross-linguistically by semantic-pragmatic heuristics.

The problem of cross-linguistic identification should not be overstated. In most cases it is not difficult to identify the basic grammatical categories on an intuitive basis. To a great extent this is accomplished by examining the translation of a sentence and its parts, which is of course based on semantics and pragmatics. On the other hand, the weaknesses of an intuitive cross-linguistic identification of categories become apparent when one focuses on an example which is not so intuitively clear after all (for example, is the English gerund form, in *Walking the dog is a chore*, a noun or a verb?).

To give an idea of how unavoidable considerations of external function are, we will briefly discuss some of the problems involved with a cross-linguistic identification of "subject." First, across languages, the grammatical relation of "subject" is expressed structurally in several different ways: by case/adposition marking, by indexation or agreement, by word order, or by a combination of both of these. Yet, how does one "know" this in the first place? Only by using a heuristic definition involving external function, including some notion of "agent of an action" and "topic of the sentence," among other things, to determine what is a "subject" in each language.

Now one must have a cross-linguistic means to identify case/adposition, indexation/agreement and word order. Word order appears to be the easiest, since it is clearly based on a physical property of the utterance, the sequence of units, which can be directly observed. However, the correct word-order statement requires that the grammatical category of each unit be identified. For example, the assertion that Yoruba subjects can be identified by their position before the verb requires the identification of verbs in Yoruba, not to mention the category "noun phrase" or at least "noun," which the subject is assumed to fall into (and not to mention a cross-linguistic means of individuating syntactic units, a problem that we will not deal with here).[10]

A cross-linguistic definition of case/adposition and indexation/agreement on a structural basis seems difficult as well. Case/adposition markers can be attached to the NP argument, or be independent particles, or even be attached to the verb in some cases, so syntactic position and dependency cannot be suitable criteria for a cross-linguistic definition.

Attachment to subject: Russian

(19) pis'm -o   lež -it   na stol   -e
      letter -NOM.SG.NT lie -3SG.PRES on table -LOC.SG.MASC
      'The letter is lying on the table.'

Independent particle: Japanese (Kuno 1972:3)

(20) John **ga**   Mary o   but -ta
      John NOM   Mary ACC hit -PAST
      'John hit Mary.'

Attachment to verb: Mokilese (Harrison 1976:164)

(21) ngoah insingeh   **-ki**   kijinlikkoau -o   nah pehnn -o
      I   write.TRANS **-with** letter   -DET his pen   -DET
      'I wrote that letter with his pen.'

Indexation/agreement markers are syntactically at least as variable: they can be affixes to the verb, independent particles, or attached to other constituents of the sentence, even affixed to the noun phrase it putatively agrees with.

Attachment to verb: Hungarian (Whitney 1944:15)

(22) áll   **-unk**
      stand **-1PL.INDEF**
      'We are standing.'

Independent particles: Woleaian (Sohn 1975:93)

(23) sar   kelaal **re**   sa   tangiteng
      child those 3SG ASP cry.REDUP
      'Those children over there cried and cried.'

Attachment to other constituents: Ute (first constituent; Givón 1980a:311)[11]

(24) kavzá -yi -**amṳ** -'ura maĝá -x̂a -páa-ni
      horse -OBJ -**3PL** -be feed -PL -FUT
      'They are going to feed the horse.'

Attachment to any constituent, including noun phrase: Bartangi (J. Payne 1980:163, 165):

(25) āz -**um** tā -r kitob vuj
      I -**1SG** you -to book bring.PERF
      'I have brought you a book.'

Thus morphosyntactic dependence – e.g., case marking on subjects, agreement on verbs – will not provide an unproblematic cross-linguistic definition, at least not by itself. A more suitable definition would be that a case marker/adposition is a morpheme that refers to the grammatical relation that holds between the noun phrase and the verb, while indexation/agreement is a morpheme that refers to ("indexes" or "cross-references") the subject itself. This definition is essentially a semantic one, referring to reference and subject–verb relations (though it is not clear what semantic/pragmatic relation underlies a case marker for subject).

If we assume a cross-linguistic definition for case marking and agreement that fits our intuitions, then we encounter a larger problem. Our intuitive notion of "subject" is based on English subjects (or "Standard Average European" subjects, to use Benjamin Whorf's [1956:138] term), specifically, on the semantic relation between the event denoted by the verb and the participant denoted by the English subject. Examining more "exotic" languages, we find that what we have identified as the "subject" by the use of a particular case-marking or agreement form does not correspond to English subjects, or the English subject does not conform to the "exotic" subject. For example, in Chechen-Ingush (Nichols 1984:186), the English-translation "subjects" of the following three examples display quite different case-marking and agreement patterns (CM is a class marker that agrees with a verbal argument).

(26) bier -∅   d- ielxa
      child -NOM CM- cries   (CM agrees with "child")
      'The child is crying.'

(27) aːz   yz   kiniška -ø   d- ieš
     I.ERG this book   -NOM CM- read   (CM agrees with "book")
     'I'm reading this book.'

(28) suona   yz   kiniška -ø   d- iez
     me.DAT this book   -NOM CM- like   (CM agrees with "like")
     'I like this book.'

If we identify the "subject" with the nominative noun phrase that the verb agrees with, then "this book" in the second and third sentences becomes the "subject." If we treat the ergative and/or dative noun phrase as "subject," then the first sentence appears not to have a "subject." Whatever solution is taken to this problem must refer at some level to the actual semantic relations that hold between the "subject" and the verb. Thus, a cross-linguistically valid definition of "subject" referring extensively to external properties appears to be unavoidable. (See chapter 6 for a discussion of the typological analysis of "subject," "noun" and "verb.")

Many grammatical constructions are defined in terms of the basic categories whose difficulties in cross-linguistic identification we have discussed – "subject," "noun," "verb," etc. If one simply assumes that these basic categories can be identified across languages without major difficulties, one may develop "derived" structural definitions for the construction in question. For example, the passive construction can be defined as one in which the subject of the passive verb is the object of the counterpart active verb. This is a structural definition of the passive that can be used for cross-linguistic identification – once one has already identified subject, verb, object and the active construction.

However, the functional definition may not lend itself to as many useful typological analyses as a "derived" structural one. A significant part of typological research is devoted to determining which cross-linguistic definitions lead to fruitful cross-linguistic generalizations. For example, we may propose two candidate cross-linguistic definitions for the subjunctive. The first definition is a semantic one: the situation denoted by the subjunctive clause is "irrealis" (not factual). The second definition is a "derived" structural one: a subjunctive clause is a clause which (1) expresses the subject and the object of the clause in the same way as an ordinary declarative main clause does, but (2) whose verb inflections differ from those of the verb in an ordinary declarative main clause. Condition (1) is intended to distinguish the subjunctive from various types of nonfinite clauses; and condition (2) is intended to distinguish the subjunctive from the indicative. The derived structural definition of the subjunctive may turn out to be more useful than the semantic definition, because the types of linguistic structures used to express irrealis situations vary too greatly (see Givón 1980b). Indeed, the very purpose of the typological study may be to determine what functions the subjunctive (second definition) plays across languages. Significant typological generalizations can be found by examining what functions are expressed by a given form just as much as by examining what forms are used to express a given function. The central issue in all of these cases is the relation between linguistic form and linguistic function; this underlies most typological analysis, not just that described in chapter 7.

Not all externally based definitions are created equal. For example, in seeking a cross-linguistically valid definition of "subject," one would not use translation equivalents of expressions such as "The lightning struck the tree" or "I like bananas"; one would more likely use expressions like "I broke the stick" or "John killed the goat." *A priori*, there is no reason to select the latter two as better for defining "subject" than the former two; in either case, one determines the grammatical relation of the relevant argument and declares it to be the "subject." However, our pretheoretic intuitions about grammatical categories strongly suggest that some external definitions are better cross-linguistic criteria than others, and detailed analysis of the relevant linguistic phenomena generally bears out those intuitions. Hence, we use physical actions with animate agents for defining "subject," the relationship of ownership for defining "(alienable) possession," and so on. These definitions are called "prototype definitions," and their typological properties will be discussed in chapter 6.

It is crucial to remember that these choices are based on pretheoretic intuitions concerning the "prototypical" or "core" examples of the linguistic categories in question and may turn out to be incorrect. For example, many linguists, e.g. Faltz (1978), use the recipient of the verb "give" as the defining environment for the dative, but others have argued that "in many languages . . . 'give' is syntactically a very atypical ditransitive verb . . . selection of 'give' always requires cross-checking with a variety of other verbs of similar valency" (Borg & Comrie 1984:123). Reliance on single exemplars can lead to building a typological generalization on too narrow an empirical base. The interplay between our pretheoretic notion of the nature of the category and the actual cross-linguistic variation found in that category determines what is the "best" or most useful cross-linguistic definition for typological analysis.

It may seem that in phonology, the problem of cross-linguistic comparison would not be so intractable. Presumably, the cross-linguistic identification of English /p/ with Russian /p/ is based primarily on their articulatory–acoustic similarity – that is, their external (phonetic) values. Also, to argue that a category [p] participates in a typological pattern involving a hierarchy of stops including [t], [c], [k] and [q] presumably means that the articulatory gestures and/or acoustic features involved in [p] are related to those involved in [t] in such a way as to manifest the linguistic behavior which led us to postulate the hierarchy in the first place. It is difficult to see how one could use any other criterion, because there may be no obvious way to identify anything in the alternative phonemic system with English /p/, because of differences between the other phonemic system and the English system. For example, if the language is Hindi, which distinguishes between aspirated /pʰ/ and unaspirated /p/, the whole phonemic system is different and so it would be impossible to identify English /p/ with Hindi /p/ on the basis of the phonemic system.

The problem is, it is extremely difficult to gauge which Hindi phoneme the English /p/ should be identified with phonetically. Most allophones of English /p/ are quite aspirated; but most linguists would hesitate to associate English /p/ with Hindi /pʰ/, chiefly on phonemic grounds. Most phonological typological studies have involved the analysis of phoneme inventories, making generalizations based, for example, on five-vowel systems vs. seven-vowel systems. However, phonetically, not all seven-vowel systems are alike; the individual vowels differ acoustically. In a typological approach to phonology, one will also have to do cross-linguistic comparison on the basis of the relationship between the linguistic system and its external (phonetic) manifestation.

1.4   Nontypological factors and the sampling problem

The cross-linguistic resemblances that the typologist seeks to explain, in structural or functional terms, may actually be due to other interfering factors that must be avoided or at least accounted for in analysis. The need to account for these other possibilities leads us naturally to issues in the construction of a linguistic sample.[12]

The first possible source of nontypological linguistic resemblance is pure accident. For example, Spanish has a three-way distinction among demonstrative modifiers: *este* (near speaker), *ese* (near hearer) and *aquel* (away from both speaker and hearer). Spanish also lacks the uvular stop [q]. Ponapean, a Micronesian language spoken in Oceania, also has a three-way distinction among demonstrative modifiers, -e(t), -en and -o respectively, and no [q] (Rehg 1981:144, 34). On the basis of these observations, one could propose the universal that languages have a three-way distinction among demonstrative modifiers if and only if they lack [q]. This is, however, just an accidental coincidence between Spanish and Ponapean, as can be seen from the examination of other languages: English has no [q] and only a two-way distinction between *this* and *that*; and Quiché Mayan has [q] and a three-way distinction among the demonstrative modifiers *wē*, *lē* and *rī* respectively (Mondloch 1978:82). The obvious solution to this problem is to increase the number of languages examined with the properties in question until one can be confident that one is not dealing with a coincidence. The next question is, how large should that sample be?

First, one must take into consideration the population size, that is the total number of languages which exhibit the linguistic phenomenon under study. If one is examining a phenomenon which is exhibited in only a relatively limited number of languages, such as implosives or numeral classifiers, then a complete or nearly complete sample is advisable. For example, in his study of glottalic consonants, Greenberg (1970) used a sample of 150 languages which was virtually exhaustive at the time for implosives (though not for ejectives). In these cases the typologist is examining a single linguistic type or strategy as thoroughly as possible.

On the other hand, if one is examining some feature that is universal or almost universal, such as the comparative construction (Stassen 1985), or a particular type which is extremely widespread, such as the passive (Siewierska 1984), sampling becomes a practical necessity. In these cases, the sample size thus becomes a significant question (as well as sample distribution; see below). Of course, there is no definitive answer to such a question (Bell 1978:142). The most important criterion is that the sample should be large enough so that the results will be statistically significant, but that cannot be determined beforehand (i.e. it cannot be determined until some results are gathered).[13]

However, in surveying past typological research, one is impressed at how thorough a typology can be developed on the basis of a well-selected sample of about forty to fifty languages. Increasing the sample size beyond perhaps a hundred languages for the formulation of initial hypotheses is probably too unwieldy for the potential analytic returns. On the other hand, it is probably best to treat a sample of 40–100 languages as a pilot study. Once the initial hypotheses are formulated, then a thorough examination of a considerably larger sample (over 100 languages) on the narrower topic of the hypotheses in question can be useful for examining quirky aspects of the phenomenon and for refining the hypotheses. Or – as is more common – the results of the study of 40–100 languages can be published, and the linguistic community as a whole is thus invited to contribute information on the phenomenon in question from additional languages. The point remains that although a sample size of under 100 languages, even under fifty languages, can be extremely productive, it probably will serve only as an impetus to further research, not as a definitive cross-linguistic survey of the phenomenon.

A major problem with sample size is the rarity of the phenomenon in question. If crucial subclasses of the phenomenon are present in, say, only ten languages, then a larger sample is necessary (or at least a larger sample of languages with those crucial elements). Finally, it should be noted that phonological typological studies generally use much larger samples than morphosyntactic ones (see for example Maddieson 1984).

The two other important nontypological sources of cross-linguistic resemblance besides accident are genetic descent from a parent language and areal contact. For example, in both Russian and Czech, there is an interesting construction for distinguishing expressions of location and expressions of motion. The same preposition is used for motion and location, but the locative case is used for location and the accusative case for motion.

       Czech
(29) pokládám knihu   na stůl
       I.put   book.ACC on table.ACC
       'I am putting the book on the table.'
(30) kniha   leží na stol -e
       book.NOM lie on table -LOC
       'The book is lying on the table.'

       Russian
(31) on položil   knigi   na stol
       he put.3SG.PAST books.ACC on table.ACC
       'He put the books on the table.'

(32) knigi   ležat na stol -e
     books.NOM lie   on table -LOC
     'The books are lying on the table.'

On the basis of this evidence, one might propose that if a language uses both adpositions and case affixes for indicating grammatical relations, then the case affixes will be used to distinguish motion from location. However, the resemblance between Russian and Czech illustrated here is almost certainly the result of common inheritance (the actual morphology is cognate, and the same distinction is found in Old Church Slavic, generally considered to be close to the Common Slavic parent language of Czech and Russian; see Schmalstieg 1976:180, 183). Thus, the occurrence of the phenomenon in both Russian and Czech is not truly "cross-linguistic." In ontogenetic terms, it is just a single occurrence in a single language (Common Slavic) that happens to have survived into the daughter languages (Czech and Russian). To develop this as a truly cross-linguistic hypothesis, one would have to examine non-Slavic and also non-Indo-European languages.

Genetic relatedness through common descent is not the only way a putatively cross-linguistic resemblance could turn out not to be truly cross-linguistic. Areal contact could result in a borrowing of the resemblance, a phenomenon that can be illustrated by structural resemblances found in languages of the Balkans. Languages in this area include Bulgarian, Rumanian and Albanian (see Sandfeld 1930; Comrie 1981a:199; Campbell, Kaufman & Smith-Stark 1986:559–60) which are all Indo-European languages but from different branches of Indo-European. These languages have developed certain structural features which are not characteristic of their parent languages or of their sister languages outside the Balkan area. For example, these languages have for the most part eschewed the use of infinitival verbal forms for complements, any infinitive present in the parent languages being lost. In addition, these languages have also developed a pattern of a definite article suffixed to the noun. One would not want to propose a typological connection between these two features on the evidence of these three languages alone because these two developments are probably historically the same phenomenon, resulting from a contact situation in the Balkan area. Thus, it only represents one instance of the correlation of absence of the infinitive and postposed definite article, and if one wanted to pursue this correlation, languages from outside the Balkan area of linguistic influence would have to be examined.

The possibility of genetic and areal sources for cross-linguistic similarities requires a wide distribution for the typological sample. The essential idea is to take a classification of languages by genetic affiliation and geographical location, and use that to develop an unbiased sample. This has turned out to be a more controversial topic than the size of sample issue. First, it should be pointed out that the areal–genetic distribution problem is different for small samples than large ones. In small samples, the problem is the possibility of excluding from consideration large linguistic families or large areas which may be of potential importance for the phenomenon in question. In large samples, the problem is how to avoid having subsets of the sample "clustered" together areally and/or genetically (e.g., a large cluster of European languages is undesirable; see Dryer 1986:98). In the latter case, that means obtaining a proportional distribution for each areal and genetic group – for example, making sure the proportion of Indo-European languages in the sample is equal to the proportion of Indo-European languages in the world (see Bell 1978:138; Tomlin 1986:24–9).

Examining the latter problem, the one which has attracted most debate, reveals a fundamental problem which has not been addressed in the sampling literature.[14] In order to determine the proper distribution of languages in the sample, we have to know the distribution of languages in the world – how many are Indo-European, how many are Austronesian and so on. But we do not know the distribution of languages, because the definition of a language is itself problematic. How do we know that the "Swabian dialect" of German is just a dialect of German and so should not be counted in the total number of Germanic and Indo-European languages; but that the five lects Bierebo, Baki, Mari, Bieria and Lewo on the small island of Epi in Vanuatu, totalling altogether 1,640 speakers, are all distinct languages (as claimed by Wurm & Hattôri 1981) and should be included in the count for Austronesian? The answer is, we don't, and probably never will, since the definition of "language" as opposed to "dialect" involves nonlinguistic as well as linguistic factors (see, e.g., Chambers & Trudgill 1980:3–4).

This appears to cast grave doubts on the sampling criteria, but it need not do so if we keep in mind the genuine reason for doing an areally and genetically distributed sample. This is to obtain **historically independent** instances of the linguistic phenomenon in question, in order to make sure that we are dealing with a typological pattern that is a result of general principles, not of historical accident (common descent or contact; see Bell 1978:141). Since the historical development of most languages is unknown (there being a lack of written records and of historical linguistic and demographic research) the safest way to guarantee the historical independence of the instances of the phenomenon under examination is to obtain a wide areal and genetic distribution.

Unfortunately, wide areal and genetic distribution is neither a necessary nor a sufficient condition for historical independence of the instances of the phenomenon. First, two phenomena in genetically closely related languages, even if they use cognate forms, may be historically independent. Consider the use of the reflexive morpheme as a "middle voice" marker of verbs of certain semantic classes and as a marker of generic passives and other construction types in Spanish and Russian. These two instances appear to be historically independent: the Slavic development was largely completed by the time the Romance development began, and the two language groups were not in contact at the time of the Romance development. Thus we may consider the Spanish and Russian instances of the reflexive as a middle-voice marker independent occurrences of the phenomenon, even though both languages are Indo-European and are located in Europe, and even though the morpheme in question (*se/sja*) is cognate.

Conversely, genetic and areal distance may not be a guarantee of historical independence. Fula is in the West Atlantic group of the Niger–Congo branch of Niger–Kordofanian, found in the northwest portion of sub-Saharan Africa. Kinyarwanda is a Bantu language, a tenth-degree subgroup of the Central Niger–Congo branch and thus genetically quite distant from Fula, and is found in East Africa in the area of Rwanda. It is quite plausible that both Fula and Kinyarwanda could be found in an evenly distributed sample of about a hundred languages. The unmarked word order of both Fula and Kinyarwanda is SVO. It is quite possible that the SVO word order of these two languages is a common retention from proto-Niger–Congo; the vast majority of all Niger–Congo languages are SVO, and the few Niger–Congo SOV languages that are found occur sporadically across the whole group (see the extended sample description in Hawkins 1983:283–7).[15] Hence, a hundred-language sample for the purposes of examining the word order of subject, verb and object may quite likely be dealing with historically the same phenomenon in the vast majority of Niger–Congo languages.

This problem varies depending on the degree of stability of the phenomenon in question, of course; highly unstable phenomena are much less likely to turn out to be common retentions from the parent language. Unfortunately, very little is known about the relative stability of different types of linguistic structures, and it appears that even flexible phenomena such as subject–verb–object order can be quite old.

This discussion of the sampling problem should make clear to the reader how diachronic considerations enter typology even at its methodological foundations.[16] It also leads to two important methodological points. Beyond taking a reasonable amount of care in drawing up an areally and genetically well-distributed sample, refining the sample for the sake of distribution may be missing the point of doing the sample in the first place. For example, given a fifty-language sample that is areally and genetically well distributed, adjusting it to avoid a bias towards well-described languages in each group will probably not affect the degree of historical independence of the construction in question among the languages in the sample. Second, one must address the diachronic dimension directly in analyzing cross-linguistic patterns (see chapter 8 for further discussion). In the meantime, however, it is still necessary to take care in developing an areally and genetically distributed sample.[17]

A final difficulty is the distribution of the sample over other typological features of language structure, such as major word order. Since one does not know in advance what the cross-linguistic generalization will be, the linguist may inadvertently leave out languages containing the relevant structural types for the generalization. Generally, typologists try to include a distribution of languages by major word-order type. Since major word order is frequently correlated with particular structural features, this often has the effect of bringing most of the structural types into the sample. For example, in his study of comparative constructions, Stassen (1985) had a 150-language sample with each of the major word-order types well represented. He discovered that word-order types correlated with the comparative construction types, but later concluded that the reason for this was that the major word-order types correlated with the major types of clause-chaining constructions, which was the true determinant of the distribution of comparative types. We may note, however, that the distribution of word-order types created a reasonably good sample of clause-chaining types due to their correlation of word-order and clause-chaining type, and so Stassen's sample was adequate for revealing the correct analysis.

A good typological sample should attempt to achieve a balanced distribution of major word-order types, not just subject–object–verb order but also genitive and adposition order as in the types defined in Greenberg 1966b.[18] It must also be distributed among the basic morphological types as described in chapter 2, since the use of morphological vs. syntactic strategies may turn out to be significant in many cases, and grammaticalization may play a major role in the analysis (see chapter 8). The sample, of course, should also be genetically and areally well distributed. The current state of genetic classification is discussed in Ruhlen (1987). There is no presentation of the current state of areal classification, so I list here a number of linguistic areas that do not coincide with genetic groupings that have been noted in the literature: the Balkans (Sandfeld 1930); northwest Europe (suggested in Chambers & Trudgill 1980:184–9); sub-Saharan Africa (Greenberg 1959, 1984); South Asia, extending possibly further into Asia (Masica 1976; Dryer 1986); the Caucasus (Catford 1977; the languages there may constitute a single genetic group); Southeast Asia (Henderson 1965); Papua New Guinea; Arnhem Land (Heath 1978a, 1981); the northwest coast of North America; and Mesoamerica (Campbell, Kaufman, & Smith-Stark 1986). This list is certainly not exhaustive, and also the status of these geographical regions as linguistic areas varies greatly (see the useful discussion of defining linguistic areas in Campbell, Kaufman & Smith-Stark 1986: 530–6).

1.5   Data sources

Finally, there remains the problem of the quality of the actual data used in typological research. This is an extremely important issue, since no one typologist can achieve the level of knowledge of all of the languages in his or her sample that a specialist in each language, let alone a linguistically trained native speaker, has. For this reason, the typologist has to rely on faith in the qualities of the materials at hand.

Unfortunately, most of those materials do not inspire faith, for various reasons. Descriptive research is not generally a means to achieve recognition in the field and so it is poorly funded or just not done. Those linguists who do fieldwork are not always the best-trained in linguistic analysis. However, primary grammatical sources, written by native speakers or fieldworkers, are superior to the use of secondary sources, in which data from primary sources is gathered together. The selection and interpretation of the data in secondary sources is often biased by the hypothesis of the analyst, whose knowledge of the language(s) is at best indirect. Secondary sources must always be confirmed by the primary sources they cite (see Mallinson & Blake 1981:14–15; Holisky 1987:106–8, 122).

One alternative is for the typologist to rely on native speakers. Reliance on native speakers, in general a much better expedient, is unfortunately impractical if a large and diverse sample is desired, and also has its difficulties. The process of eliciting grammatical information is not a natural language situation, and so the data provided do not always accurately represent actual language use. In particular, the informant does not report actual usage, but instead an unsystematic perception of usage, colored by social attitudes towards the speech form and even towards the interrogator (e.g. a desire to give the interrogator an agreeable answer). As Comrie puts it: "elicitation techniques and the elicitation situation impose a number of intermediary stages between the structure of a language and the eliciter's perception of it" (Comrie 1983:909).

In order to avoid this problem, a number of linguists have turned to using textual data for analysis. This has the advantage of being data of actual language, unfiltered by artificial elicitation situations or by informant's self-perceptions. Also, texts provide quantitative data, which play an important role in typological analysis (see chapters 4, 7, 8). However, even textual data have their difficulties. Most texts are narratives, sometimes literary in origin, and there are very few available texts of face-to-face spoken conversation. It may be difficult, if not impossible, to find the relevant data in a given set of texts, if the phenomenon is rare. Finally, the proper interpretation may not be adequately captured by the morpheme-by-morpheme gloss and free translation. Consultation of an informant is often necessary, but is often impossible (e.g. with extinct languages). Even if possible, it would produce results about as accurate as the consultation of a literary critic – or better, a person in the street – for the interpretation of a Shakespeare or a Pinter play.

These considerations, pro and con, on the sources of linguistic data apply to all linguistic analysis, not just typological analysis. They have particular importance for the typologist because the typologist must handle a large amount of data for a large number of languages, for most of which he or she must rely on indirect knowledge. No source of data – primary grammars, native informants or actual texts – is perfect; but any and all sources can provide the relevant data when used judiciously.

2
Typological classification

2.1 Introduction

Typological classification is the process of describing the various linguistic types found across languages for some grammatical parameter, such as grammatical number or the formation of relative clauses. Typological classification is historically the first manifestation of typology in modern linguistics, starting with the morphological classification of languages in the nineteenth century. The notion of a linguistic type has changed somewhat since that time, particularly under the impact of structural linguistics (the term "typology" was first used in linguistics in 1901; von der Gabelentz 1972 [1901]:481). The following section will describe the current concept of a linguistic type, or **strategy** as it is sometimes called, while the concluding section will discuss morphological typology and the major conceptual changes that occurred in the evolution of the concept of a linguistic type.

2.2 The concept of a linguistic type (strategy)

The usual procedure for initiating a cross-linguistic comparison of a particular grammatical phenomenon for the purposes of a typological analysis is to survey the range of structures used for the phenomenon in question. In morphosyntax, the phenomenon is generally a grammatical construction, which is usually defined on an external basis precisely because of the degree of structural variation actually found in languages (see 1.3). Thus, given a particular external definition of a category, such as that proposed for the relative clause, one may then classify the linguistic structures found across languages to express or manifest that external definition. These structures are called **types** or **strategies**. This is typology in the second sense, a cross-linguistic structural classification.

In order to illustrate the most important issues of the classification of cross-linguistic structural types, we will use the example of the genitive construction, defined as the semantic relationship of ownership as used

27

when the speaker intends to refer to the possessum (possessed item) – i.e. the possessum is the head of the genitive noun phrase. This example, though not as well explored as others in the typological literature, has the virtue of being relatively simple (compared to clause-level constructions such as relative clauses and comparatives) and relatively uncontroversial (compared to the example of grammatical subjects). On the other hand, the genitive construction displays the range of problems that we wish to address here. Also, the typology of genitive constructions displays practically the full range or morphosyntactic strategies used to relate two morphemes or syntactic elements, and thus serves as a useful introduction to the basic grammatical structures that will appear throughout this volume.

The typology of genitive constructions provided here is not exhaustive, for reasons that will soon become clear. We will begin by enumerating a variety of what we may call the basic genitive constructions.

A. *Fusion*: a rare type is the use of a single morpheme that expresses the entire genitive construction, fusing the possessor and the possessed into one unit. This is found with basic kin terms and pronominal **possessors** (i.e. genitive modifiers) in some languages.

> Lakhota (Buechel 1939:103)
> (1) ina/nihu/huku
>   'my mother/your mother/his, her mother'

B. *Special form*: a special form for either the genitive modifier or the head noun is used. The special form may involve outright suppletion, that is, a completely different form, as is commonly found with independent pronominal possessors:

> Yoruba (Rowlands 1969:46)
> (2) ilé   wa
>   house our (cf. a 'we')
>   'our house'

However, the special form may be only a morphologically irregular (or morphologically conditioned) version of the standard word form. For example, a special **construct form** is found for the possessum noun in the Semitic languages:

Syrian Arabic (Cowell 1964:163)
(3)   ʔəṣṣeṭ   haz- zalame
story.CON that- fellow (cf. ʔəṣṣa 'story')
'that fellow's story'

C. *Affixation* or *compounding*: the possessor is morphologically an affix on the head noun (possessum). This is most commonly found with pronominal possessors:

Tigre (Raz 1983:37)
(4)   səʔli   -hom
photograph -3SG
'his photograph'

However, it is occasionally found with nominal possessors, in which case it may more appropriately be called "compounding" since it involves two roots of major syntactic categories:

Kiowa (Watkins 1984:107)
(5)   nɔ́:- tɔ̀:   -cègùn
my- brother -dog
'my brother's dog'

D. *Juxtaposition*: the simplest syntactic strategy is to simply juxtapose the possessor and the head noun, in one order or the other, without any morphological fusion or alteration of either constituent. This strategy is quite common:

Yoruba (Rowlands 1969:44)
(6)   fìlà Àkàndé
cap Akande
'Akande's cap'

Kobon (Davies 1981:57)
(7)   Dumnab ram
Dumnab house
'Dumnab's house'

E. *Case*: The genitive construction may be expressed by a bound morpheme on the possessor that contrasts with other bound morphemes that are used to indicate spatial and nonspatial grammatical relations. This morpheme is called a **case marker**:

Russian
(8) kniga Ivan -a
book Ivan -GEN
'Ivan's book'

F. *Adposition*: The adposition is simply the independent counterpart of the case marker, an independent particle that contrasts with other particles that indicate grammatical relations. The case and adposition strategies are generally used for verb–argument relations as well as for noun–noun relations such as the genitive:

Bulgarian (Scatton 1983:317)
(9) nova -ta kniga **na** majka mi
new -the book **of** mother my
'my mother's new book'

G. *Agreement ("adjectival" agreement, concord)*: The genitive may be expressed by morphemes found on the possessor and usually also on the head noun that inflect for the number and sometimes the gender and/or other characteristics of the head noun. This strategy is commonly used for adjectival modification (including demonstrative and other modifiers), and is occasionally used for the genitive:

Russian
(10) mo -**ja** knig -**a**
my -FSG book -FSG
'my book'

This form of agreement is also known as "concord," because in most of the familiar European languages agreement morphemes are found on both the head and the modifier, and they must match in grammatical features (gender, number, and/or case).[1]

H. *Indexation (" person" agreement, cross-reference)*: Another strategy commonly found for the genitive construction is also often called "agreement," but it differs from strategy G in that the agreeing constituent is the head noun instead of the possessor, and the agreement marker inflects for person (though it usually also inflects for number and sometimes also for gender). Other terms, "indexation" and "cross-reference," have been proposed to distinguish this sort of agreement from concord; we will use the term "indexation."

Mam (England 1983:142)
(11) t-   kamb' meeb'a
      3SG- prize orphan
      '(the) orphan's prize'

I. *Classification*: A rare genitive strategy, found commonly among Micronesian languages and occasionally in neighboring Melanesian languages and a few languages in North and Central America, is classification. In this strategy, the possessor is a dependent of the additional morpheme, called a **classifier**, which is in apposition to the head noun and indicates the class of objects that the head noun belongs to. The **possessive classifier** strategy is syntactically identical to the much more common **numeral classifier** strategy for expressing modification of numerals. However, the possessive classifier classifies the head nouns by the type of relation between the possessor and the head noun, whereas the numeral classifier classifies the head nouns by various inherent properties of the head noun alone (Lichtenberk 1983a).

The possessive classifier is itself related to the possessor and/or the head noun by one or more of the strategies already illustrated for expressing grammatical relations between elements:

> \+ affixation: Kosraean (Kusaiean; Lee 1975:117)
> (12) mos   sᴀnᴀ -k
>   breadfruit CLASS -1SG
>   'my breadfruit tree'
> \+ indexation: Kosraean (Lee 1975:112)
> (13) pinsᴧl fototo soko nætᴧ -l   Sepe
>   pencil short one CLASS -3SG Sepe
>   'Sepe's short pencil'

In some modern Arabic dialects in North Africa, there is a genitive construction resembling the possessive classifier, using a word that formerly meant "possession" or "property":

> \+ affixation: Tunisian Arabic (Harning 1980:103)
> (14) el- ḥōš   mtāʕ- i
>   the- house POSS- my
>   'my house'

In this case, it is difficult to distinguish a one-classifier system from a linker (see below).

J. *Linker*: A rare strategy, found chiefly in adjectival, genitive and other noun–noun constructions, is to use an additional morpheme called a "linker." The linker is a normally invariant marker used for modifiers in noun phrases but not in predicate–argument (verb–noun-phrase) relations in clauses. The linker is invariant or contrasts only with simple juxtaposition, and functions merely to link the possessor and head noun grammatically. The linker may be bound to one (or both) of the constituents, or function as an independent particle:

> Persian (Mace 1962:19)
>
> (15) asb   -é-   mard
> horse -LINK- man
> '(the) man's horse'

If the morpheme is used *only* for the possessive relation, and not for either predicate–argument relations or any other modifier–noun relations, then it is difficult or impossible to distinguish a linker from a case marker, an agreement marker, or a one-class possessive classifier. The reason for this is simple: a unique morpheme indicating possession can be historically derived from a case marker, an agreement (indexation) marker, a classifying word (as in example 14), or even a demonstrative element, as in the following example (see Harning 1980:112–13 for discussion of the etymology of the possessive):

> Moroccan Arabic (Harrell 1962:202)
>
> (16) ž- žmel   dyal had r- ṛažel
> the- camels POSS this the- man
> 'this man's camels'

The English -'s genitive clitic is a unique possessive morpheme. However, it would probably best be analyzed as a linker, because it contrasts primarily with noun–noun juxtaposition, it does not occur in the same syntactic position as the English prepositions, and is not used for verb (predicate)–argument NP relations.

Finally, we find various combinations of the different strategies involving additional morphemes, some of which are illustrated here:

> case + indexation: Turkish (Lewis 1967:42)
>
> (17) uzman -ın   rapor -u
> man   -GEN report -3SG
> '(the) man's report'

linker + adposition: English
(18) a book **of** John's
suppletion + adposition: English
(19) a book **of mine**

We have now illustrated the basic morphosyntactic means for expressing grammatical relations of any sort between two (or more) grammatical elements, all of which happen to be used for the genitive relationship. All of the basic genitive types have been described, although there are variants that have not been illustrated. In addition, some of the more complex genitive types, involving combinations of the basic strategies, have been given to demonstrate that the typology must be extended beyond what we have provided here. But this will suffice to make two important refinements to the classification of structural types, "typology" in the second sense described above.

Typology, in the sense of a cross-linguistic classification of types, is often considered to be a classification of languages into types, that is, a classification of **language types**. For example, Mam is an indexing genitive language type, Bulgarian is an adpositional genitive language type, etc. The notion of a "language type" originates in the nineteenth-century view of the morphological typology of languages (see 2.3). In the vast majority of cases, however, a classification of language types is difficult, if not impossible. Most languages have at their command several different structural types for a given construction, such as the genitive. For example, English has many different constructions, all of which are genitive constructions on the basis of our external definition, that represent several different types and combinations of types:

(20a) *suppletion*: my house
(20b) *linker*: Jan's house
(20c) *adposition*: the library of Boston
(20d) *linker+adposition*: a book of Jan's
(20e) *suppletion+adposition*: a book of mine

Instead, we can say the particular genitive *construction* illustrated by *the library of Boston* belongs to the adposition type. This is our first refinement of the notion of a type in typology: *a structural type is represented by a particular construction in a particular language*. We will call this a classification of **linguistic types**. A language may have more than one construction representing more than one linguistic type. Technically, therefore, one cannot say that languages are of one type or another, or that languages use one strategy or another. This point is crucial in evaluating claims concerning entities like "OV languages" or "ergative languages" (see chapters 3 and 5 respectively). In most cases, such claims must be identified with the actual constructions in which OV word order or ergative morphology are used.

Although it is impossible to say in general that a language belongs to a particular structural type, such as the adpositional genitive type, it is very often possible to determine which of the many structural types a language uses is the **basic** type. A language's basic type may be useful in making typological generalizations; for example, there has been a good deal of success in making typological generalizations on basic word-order types. Thus, there may be a legitimate sense in which we may be able to speak of a language belonging to a "language type," as opposed to a construction belonging to a structural type. This raises the question of determining which of several structural types a language uses for a given function is the basic one. Here we will describe three factors which can be used to determine the basic type. We will continue using the example of English genitive constructions.

First, certain structural types of a phenomenon such as the genitive construction may be restricted to one subclass of the phenomenon, and the other types to another subclass. The English genitive strategies can be divided into those used with pronominal possessors and those used with nonpronominal possessors, since the suppletions are the English possessive pronouns:

> *Pronominal possessor genitives*: suppletion, adposition + suppletion
> *Nonpronominal possessor genitives*: linker, adposition, linker + adposition

In many languages, the pronominal possessive construction(s) is/are quite different from the nominal possessive construction(s). In general, one frequently finds that the phenomenon under study is partitioned into subclasses that have their own distinctive structural types. Having discovered those subclasses, one can choose the one which appears to be the most common or representative in some fashion as the "basic" one, if possible. In this case, we will examine the nonpronominal possessor genitive.

Second, if two structural types are used in the same class or subclass of the phenomenon, one type may represent the **primary** strategy while the other type(s) constitute **secondary** strategies. This is usually taken to mean that one type may be more frequently used than another type, or is the "normal" way of expressing the external function associated with the phenomenon. In English, the genitive strategies that combine *of* with a suppletive possessor or the linker *-'s* (*the book of mine*, *the book of Jan's*) are clearly secondary, and therefore do not represent the basic English genitive type. In so doing, it must be noted that we must restrict our concept of the genitive construction again, this time to definite-head genitive constructions. When the head noun is indefinite, the strategies that are used are represented by *a book of mine/John's* or *one of my/John's books*. In this case, it is reasonable to conclude that the definite-head genitive is more "basic" than the indefinite-head one.[2]

Lacking other more specific structural evidence, simple text frequency is sometimes used as an indicator of basicness. For example, in Derbyshire and Pullum's survey of languages with object before subject, they frequently had to resort to this criterion (Derbyshire & Pullum 1981). Although this appears to be the weakest of the requirements for determining basicness, text frequency does play an important role in typological analysis (see chapters 4 and 7).

This leaves us with the linker (*Jan's house*) and the adpositional (*the library of Boston*) strategies as candidates for the basic English genitive type. The third and final factor in finding a basic type or strategy is that strategies may have distinct semantic or pragmatic functions associated with them. This allows one to divide the strategies and possibly determine one to be more "basic" than the other(s). The linker strategy is primarily used for the relationship of ownership. The adpositional strategy is almost never used for ownership except when an institution such as the city of Boston can be construed to own the possessum – and even in that case, the primary strategy is simple juxtaposition (*Boston library*). If we restrict the basic genitive to the relationship of ownership, as we suggested at the beginning of this section, then the linker strategy is the basic English genitive strategy. If, however, we do not make such a semantic restriction, then the adpositional strategy is probably more basic, since it is used in a wider range of semantic relations than the linker, including ownership if, for example, the possessor NP is heavy (*the car of the man sitting between the speaker and the master of ceremonies*).

A much more common example of a semantic distinction between genitive constructions is the division into **alienable** and **inalienable possession** types, each using its own strategy for the genitive. This can be illustrated with examples from Kosraean, which uses a classifier construction for alienable possession but not for inalienable possession (Lee 1975:117, 104):

(21) mos   sᴀnᴀ   -k
     breadfruit plant.CLASS -1SG
     'my breadfruit tree' (alienable)

(22) siyᴀ -k
     belly -1SG
     'my belly' (inalienable)

Note that at each step of our analysis of the basic English genitive type, we had to make assumptions regarding basicness that could be contested. We have had to assume that the "prototypical" English genitive construction has a nonpronominal possessor, a definite head noun and represents the relationship of ownership, and restrict ourselves to just that type. Some linguists may quite justifiably argue that the adpositional strategy is just as basic as the linker strategy regardless of semantic distinctions between the two, or that pronominal possession is no less basic than nominal possession (see note 2 of this chapter). It is not always possible to determine the basic structural type for a given phenomenon in a given language. Ultimately, however, the classification of structural types into primary and secondary, the specification of the subclasses that each type applies to and its semantic/pragmatic function is crucial to typological analysis, even if it does not result in the discovery of a basic language type. That is because these properties of structural types are themselves susceptible to typological analysis, as are generalizations based on "basic" language types.

The second important refinement of the cross-linguistic classification of structural types has to do with the structural analysis of the types themselves. The structural types themselves are morphosyntactically complex and subject to analysis. The simple enumeration of the ten or so genitive types given above will not suffice for typological analysis. Each genitive type or strategy possesses a number of morphosyntactic features, most of which are logically independent of each other. For example, the relative order of the possessor and the head noun (abbreviated "G" and "N" respectively) is independent of any of the enumerated genitive types: any of the types could have GN or NG word order. The classification of genitive types offered here is based on morphological and syntactic relations, not word order. The morphological and syntactic relations can themselves be divided into independent factors as well, of course. A more thorough analysis of the genitive construction types would involve the following morphosyntactic features:

1 *Word order of G and N*: GN, NG
2 *Degree of morphological fusion of G and N*: none (juxtaposition), compounding/affixation, fusion
3 *Additional morpheme*:
   (a) *Existence*: absent, present
   (b) *Type*: case/adposition, agreement, index, classifier, linker, combinations thereof
   (c) *Constituent of*: G, N, neither (i.e. ternary branching structure)
   (d) *Word order*: precedes, follows, between (if not a constituent of either)
   (e) *Degree of morphological fusion to G or N*: juxtaposition, affixation, suppletion

The following represents an analysis of some of the genitive constructions used to illustrate the types into structural features:

Yoruba
(6) filà Àkàndé
     cap Akande
     'Akande's cap'

NG; juxtaposed G and N; no additional morpheme

Bulgarian
(9) nova -ta   kniga **na** majka mi
     new -the book **of** mother my
     'my mother's new book'

NG; additional morpheme is case/adposition, is constituent with G, and precedes G (preposition); all three morphemes juxtaposed

Persian
(15) asb -é   -mard
      horse -LINK -man
      '(the) man's horse'

NG; additional morpheme is linker and is between N and G; all three morphemes affixed

Mam

(11) t-   kamb' meeb'a
3SG- prize orphan
'(the) orphan's prize'

NG; additional morpheme is an index, is constituent with N, is affixed
to N and precedes N (= prefix)

On the basis of the analysis of factors given in the above table, one
can readily see that there are far more than ten or so genitive constructions, that is the space of possible genitive-construction types is much
larger than ten.[3] The structural analysis therefore forces us to redefine
the notion of a linguistic type. The final definition of a linguistic structural
type is *a particular structural feature associated with a particular construction in a particular language.* A particular construction will normally
have several structural features associated with it, each representing
a different structural type in the final sense of this term. For example,
the Bulgarian adpositional genitive construction belongs to the NG word-
order type, the case-marking genitive type, and the "analytic" genitive
type (i.e. all morphemes are juxtaposed, not affixed).[4]

Linguistic types based on individual structural features form the foundation of most typological analysis. Each structural feature represents
the independent variables on which cross-linguistic generalizations are
based. This is not to say that there are not interdependencies among
the different structural features of a given construction, or that a more
holistic view of constructions may not reveal important typological generalizations that call for explanation. However, the analysis into structural
features allows us to use the same method in all of these cases. For
example, the separation of the structural feature of word order allows
us to construct implicational universals such as "SOV word order implies
GN word order." If it turns out that within the genitive construction
there is a dependency between word order and the type of additional
morpheme such that there do not exist languages with NG order and
adjectival agreement, then we can easily construct an implicational
universal linking these two features: "adjectival agreement in genitives
implies GN word order." And if it turns out that a more holistic analysis
of the construction is necessary, that is, that a combination of structural
features plays a role in an implicational universal, then we may construct
the universal using a conjunction of the relevant structural features:
"If the genitive construction is GN, with an agreement prefix, indexing
G, then ... "

Thus, the structural analysis of types is essential to typological analysis. The necessity of the structural analysis of the types in order to do a proper typology demonstrates the debt that typology, like other modern approaches to language, owes to the structuralist (and generative) approach to linguistic analysis.

2.3 Morphological typology[5]

The first typological classification of languages (i.e. classification by structure rather than by genetic affiliation) is the so-called **morphological typology**, developed in the nineteenth century (for a fuller historical discussion, see Greenberg 1974a, chapter 3 and references cited therein). The original formulation, by Friedrich von Schlegel, divided languages into two types: affixal and inflectional. Although it is not clear what criteria Schlegel used, the distinction may be characterized roughly as the simple combination of morphemes vs. the phonological alteration of morphemes in combination. Schlegel's brother, August, added a third type: languages with "no structure" (i.e. no affixation or inflection), with modern Chinese being the paradigm example. Wilhelm von Humboldt added a fourth type, "incorporating," to designate languages such as those of North America that treated the verb and the object as a whole word. The incorporating type did not figure in the "classical" formulation of the morphological classification, by August Schleicher, into the three types isolating, agglutinative and inflectional, corresponding to August von Schlegel's "no structure," affixal and inflectional respectively. Under the classical formulation, isolating languages did not use affixes at all; agglutinative languages used affixes that denoted single grammatical categories (such as number), and were concatenated with relatively little phonological alteration; and inflectional languages used affixes which often fused together several grammatical categories (such as number, gender and case) into a single morpheme, and which often underwent major phonological alterations when combined with roots.

The typological classification of languages at the time differs from the modern concept of typological classification in two important respects: first, the classification recognized only a single parameter on which languages varied, the morphological structure of words; second, it was a classification of languages as a whole, not parts of a language. Both of these characteristics can be attributed to what is called the neo-Humboldtian view of language. In this view, each human language has its organic unity which manifests an "inner form" (a point of view which at the beginning had clear connotations of cultural superiority). The morphological type of a language was a manifestation of its organic character. For that reason, the morphological classification was a classification of a language as a whole because it reflected the inner form of the language as a whole. Also, it was the only typological parameter used for classification (genetic classification was, of course, a distinct enterprise), because a cross-cutting classification by type would mean that a language could belong to two different types and thus have two different "inner forms." Thus, the concept of typological classification in the nineteenth century was in harmony with the philosophical view of language held by many nineteenth-century linguists. Greenberg (1974a) called this view, that languages as a whole had an organic, even unique, character, the **individualizing** approach to typological classification.

The structuralist movement in linguistics altered the view of the morphological typology of languages. By postulating that languages had a synchronic structure, it made it possible to examine parts of language in isolation and make a typological classification of various features of language.[6] Thus, one could typologize different parts of language, and one could typologize languages in different ways, as we have done with the example of genitive constructions in the preceding section. Edward Sapir's revision of morphological typology illustrates the possibility of typologically classifying languages in different ways. Sapir divided the morphological properties of the nineteenth-century classification into two independent parameters: the number of morphemes per word and the degree of phonological alteration of morphemes in combination. Sapir distinguished three language types in terms of the number of morphemes: **analytic** (one morpheme per word); **synthetic** (a small number of morphemes per word); and **polysynthetic** (a large number of morphemes, particularly multiple roots, per word). He then distinguished four types in terms of the degree of alteration of morphemes: **isolating** (no affixation at all); **agglutinative** (simple affixation); **fusional** (considerable morphophonemic alternation); and **symbolic** (suppletive).

Sapir also developed a complex typology of languages in terms of the ways that a language expressed different types of concepts, not unlike modern concerns with the typology of form–function relations (see chapter 7). Sapir classified concepts into four types: "concrete," the basic lexicon; "derivational," as traditionally defined; "pure relational," used to indicate grammatical relations; and "concrete relational," also used for grammatical relations but still containing some concrete meaning (the example Sapir uses is gender). The types are ranged from "most concrete" to "most abstract":

Type I	concrete
Type II	derivational
Type III	concrete relational
Type IV	pure relational

According to Sapir, all languages must have concrete and pure relational concepts, while they may do without either derivational or concrete relational concepts. This leaves four possibilities:

Language Type	Occurring Morpheme Types
A Simple pure-relational	I, IV
B Complex pure-relational	I, IV, II
C Simple mixed-relational	I, IV, III
D Complex mixed-relational	I, IV, II, III

Greenberg (1954) took the morphological typological classification one step further in developing the concept of a linguistic type. He observed that there were no clear boundaries between the analytic, synthetic and polysynthetic types, because the number of morphemes per word was a quantitative value that was for all practical purposes continuous. Greenberg made a quantitative index, M/W (morphemes per word), which one could measure using text counts. The significance of this representation of language types for typological classification is that languages (or constructions) need not be classified into **discrete** types, or to put it differently, languages could be **ranked** on some structural parameter relative to other languages. Greenberg also quantified the degree of phonological alternation, that is, the degree of allomorphy, and a host of other structural parameters, including some functional parameters reminiscent of Sapir's Types I-IV, as follows:

1	M/W	morphemes/word
2	A/J	agglutinations/morpheme junctures
3	R/W	morphemes/word
4	D/W	derivational morphemes/word
5	I/W	inflectional morphemes/word
6	P/W	prefixes/word
7	S/W	suffixes/word
8	O/N	word order used to indicate grammatical relations/total grammatical relations
9	Pi/N	pure inflections used to indicate grammatical relations/total grammatical relations
10	Co/N	concordial inflections used for grammatical relations/total grammatical relations

The first two indices correspond to Sapir's two morphological parameters and hence the original morphological classification. The next five indices typologize words by the type of morpheme (root, derivational, inflectional) and by affix position (prefix, suffix). The last three indices typologize grammatical relations (taken in the broadest sense of any grammatical dependency, not just subject and object) by the means of expression of the relation – word order, "pure" inflections (not involving agreement, i.e. usually case marking), or concordial inflections (agreement, including indexation).

The idea that typological classification involves a particular construction, not the language as a whole, is a more recent one, though there is some presentiment of this in some Prague School work (see Greenberg 1974a:46, n.9). It is found, for instance, in the syntactic typology of Keenan and Comrie (1977) on relative clauses, in which they describe languages as having both "case" and "noncase" strategies for forming relative clauses (see chapters 5 and 6). Although the traditional morphological typology is generally applied to a language as a whole, it could just as easily be applied to different parts of the linguistic system. For instance, the nominal system of a language may be agglutinative while the verbal system is inflectional. Also, Greenberg's first seven indices could be computed separately for words of different categories, so that, for example, one might discover that nouns in a single language (or perhaps in languages in general) are more likely to be suffixing than verbs.

The primary interest for morphological typology in current typology, however, is in its role in diachronic typology, the typological study of language change. August Schleicher was the first to propose that language could change from one morphological type to another. He conceived of the change as unidirectional and acyclic; that is, languages proceeded from isolating to agglutinative to inflectional but not in the reverse order and not from inflectional back to isolating. (Schleicher also had a cultural valuation associated with his stages, with the final, inflectional stage the most superior.) Sapir rejected both the cultural valuation of the morphological types and the "progressive" evolution, but without denying that languages do change morphological type. As we will see in chapter 8, languages do appear to shift morphological type unidirectionally and cyclically, and this change is associated with particular morphosyntactic and functional changes that go under the name of "grammaticalization."

The current concept of a linguistic type is a characteristic of what

Greenberg (1974a) called the **generalizing** approach to typological classi-fication, the classification of languages, or more precisely elements of a language, by structural features of maximal generality. The individua-lizing approach, taken to its extreme, defines languages by their indivi-dual and perhaps unique combination of grammatical features. The truth has to be somewhere in between, since languages are different structur-ally, though not so different as to be incommensurable. However, the individualizing as well as the generalizing approach contains the seeds of modern typology, the study of cross-linguistic patterns of variation. If language as a structure does hang together in a certain way, then the identification of one structural feature – the feature defining the linguistic type – would imply the presence of certain other structural features: "Type is for me a collection of grammatical characteristics, which are close to each other, such that if one of them is in a given language we expect that the second will be present also, as well as the third, and so on" (Skalička 1941:4, cited in Greenberg 1974a:46). The individualizing intuition expressed in this quotation has a genuine basis in empirical fact, as modern typology demonstrates. The generalizing approach to typological classification, with its emphasis on single mor-phosyntactic features rather than the language as a whole, also contri-butes to modern typology. It does so by separating the typological classification of **logically independent** grammatical properties of lan-guages from the discovery and explanation of relationships *between* fea-tures *across* languages. The latter is the topic of the next four chapters.

3
Implicational universals

3.1 Restrictions on possible language types

The first step beyond typology as the classification of types and towards the explanation of the cross-linguistic variation that classification describes is the discovery of restrictions on possible language types. As was stated in chapter 1, linguistic theory of any approach, "formalist" or "functional–typological," has as its central question, what is a possible language? This question can in turn be paraphrased as: of the logically possible types of languages, how do we account for what types actually exist?

As was also stated in chapter 1, one of the features that distinguishes the typological method of discovering constraints on possible language types is the strongly empiricist method applied to the problem. If a typologist wants to find restrictions on possible relative-clause structures, for example, he or she gathers a large sample of languages and simply observes which of the possible relative-clause types are present and which are absent. That is, the restrictions on logically possible language types are motivated by the actually attested language types. If there is a gap in the attested language types, then it is provisionally assumed that the gap represents a constraint on what is a possible language, and explanations are sought for the gap.

There are a number of objections that have been raised to the empiricist method of determining gaps in logically possible language types. The first is that there may have existed languages that represented the unattested language type, or there may come to exist languages that do so. Virtually all linguists, however, use a working hypothesis of linguistic uniformitarianism. That is, it is assumed that the rules that govern language structure today are the same that governed language structure yesterday and will be the same that will govern language structure tomorrow. Although human language arose from some prelanguage in perhaps some gradual way, those steps in the evolution of language are unattested, and the oldest records of human languages display the full range of structural complexity and the same kinds of structural types found in modern languages. Typologists frequently avail themselves of extinct languages in their sample, both ancient literary languages and recent aboriginal languages that have disappeared.[1]

A second objection is that an unattested language type is not necessarily an impossible language type. This fact cannot be denied, of course; it can only be mitigated. The primary mitigation is to have a language sample that is much larger than the space of possible language types. For instance, let us consider a typological study of the word order of demonstratives, numerals, genitives and adjectives relative to the head noun. Each element may precede or follow the head noun; hence each parameter has two possible values (modifier precedes or modifier follows). There are four logically independent parameters corresponding to the four kinds of modifiers. Multiplying together the number values on each independent parameter yields $2 \times 2 \times 2 \times 2 = 16$ logically possible types. For this study, a sample of fifteen languages is simply inadequate. Even if every language was of a different type, one type would be unattested just because the number of logically possible types is one more than the number of languages in the sample. A much larger sample, such as fifty or a hundred languages, is necessary to avoid this problem. And there still remains the possibility that our sampling procedure may have missed an actually attested language type.

One might still object that even if we examined every existing human language, that still does not guarantee that unattested language types cannot ever come to exist. This objection to the empiricist method applies to any other method, however. Any method for proposing constraints on possible language types can only be verified by the examination of actual languages. In those cases one cannot be absolutely certain that one has verified the proposed constraint, any more than one can be certain that an empirically arrived at typological universal is absolutely valid.

Another important point about the empiricist method that should be mentioned here is that theoretical significance also accrues to the *frequency* of a language type, not just to whether it is attested or unattested. If one language type is extremely rare and another type extremely common, this distribution merits explanation even though both types are classed as "attested." For example, the first universal listed in Greenberg's original paper on implicational universals is "In declarative sentences with nominal subject and object, the dominant order is *almost always* one in which the subject precedes the object" (Greenberg 1966a:77; my italics). As the italicized words indicate, Greenberg was aware of exceptions (Greenberg 1966a:105, n. 5); a later statistical sample indicated that the exceptional languages numbered approximately 5 percent of the total (Tomlin 1986). Although Greenberg's universal turned out to have exceptions, it still remains to be explained why 95 percent of the world's languages have the subject preceding the object in normal declarative sentences, whereas only 5 percent have the opposite order.

3.2 Unrestricted and implicational universals

Greenberg's first universal on the order of subject and object is an example of an **unrestricted universal**. An unrestricted universal is an assertion that all languages belong to a particular grammatical type on some parameter, and the other types on the same parameter are not attested (or are extremely rare). Unrestricted universals characterize the distribution of languages along a single parameter – for example, the order of subject and object, or whether or not a language has oral vowels. The parameter allows for the logical possibility of more than one type, but only one type is attested (or is extremely common, in the case of unrestricted universals with exceptions). This is illustrated here with the unrestricted universal "all languages have oral vowels" ("X" indicates that languages of that type exist, " – " that no language of that type exists):

Oral vowels	No oral vowels
X	–

In other words, there is a gap in the logically possible language types, and the unrestricted universal states the restriction on language types along the relevant parameter.

The number of unrestricted universals is relatively small (though the validity of some unrestricted universals, such as "All languages have nouns and verbs," is sometimes questioned; see chapter 6). Most unrestricted universals are built into the frameworks of linguistic theories because they are true of all languages. Nevertheless, unrestricted universals require deeper explanation just as much as implicational universals or other more complex cross-linguistic patterns do. For example, why do all languages distinguish consonants and vowels, and nouns and verbs, apparently without exception? Why do virtually all languages appear to have words, phrases and clauses, have subject and object in that order, the protasis and apodosis of conditionals in that order, etc.?

Although the subject–object order question has been discussed extensively (see e.g. Tomlin 1986: Chapter 3), and the noun–verb question has been addressed recently (Hopper & Thompson 1984; Croft forthcoming; Langacker 1987a; Wierzbicka 1986), many of these other questions could be investigated much further.

Implicational universals differ from unrestricted universals in that they do not assert that all languages belong to one type. Instead, they describe a restriction on logically possible language types that limits linguistic variation but does not eliminate it. We may illustrate this with a simple implicational universal, "If a language has noun before demonstrative, then it has noun before relative clause" (Hawkins 1983:84, Universal XI'). This implicational universal covers the following four logically possible types:

1 demonstrative and relative clause both follow the noun (NRel, NDem);
2 relative clause follows the noun and demonstrative precedes the noun (NRel, DemN);
3 relative clause precedes the noun and demonstrative follows the noun (RelN, NDem);
4 demonstrative and relative clause both precede the noun (RelN, DemN).

The implicational universal restricts language variation to three types (1, 2, 4) by excluding the third type (3). Thus, implicational universals capture a pattern in language *variation*, and differ from unrestricted universals, which account for uniformity, not variation. As such, implicational universals cannot even be discovered without cross-linguistic comparison. One can examine a single language alone, such as English, and observe properties such as the presence of oral vowels that turn out to manifest unrestricted universals. However, one could not guess from looking at English alone, which is of type (2), that types (1) and (4) are attested but type (3) does not exist. One must look at a large sample of languages to determine the range of possible variation. This is what makes implicational universals the paradigm example of a typological generalization: they represent the simplest form of pattern in language variation, and they can only be discovered through cross-linguistic comparison.

What makes implicational universals more interesting than unrestricted universals above all, however, is that they state a dependency between two logically independent parameters. The four logically possible language types described in the preceding paragraph actually represent two independent parameters, demonstrative–noun order and relative clause–noun order. Each parameter has two values: the modifier precedes or the modifier follows. We may construct a table, called a **tetrachoric table**, that displays the two parameters as two dimensions:

	DemN	NDem
RelN	X	–
NRel	X	X

The tetrachoric table is simply a useful means of displaying the data of attested and unattested language types. An implicational universal is a rule that characterizes the distribution of attested and unattested language types. The pattern in the tetrachoric table basically matches the pattern of values for "true" (T) and "false" (F) in the truth table for implication found in propositional logic:[2]

Distribution of attested types				Truth table for implication		
Type	NDem	NRel	Attested	P	Q	$P \supset Q$
1	yes	yes	yes	T	T	T
2	yes	no	no	T	F	F
3	no	yes	yes	F	T	T
4	no	no	yes	F	F	T

Thus, we may retitle the column "attested" by the implicational universal "NDem $\supset$ NRel," changing the values "yes/no" to "T/F." The implicational universal characterizes the gap in attested language types as a dependency between values on two logically independent parameters, in this case, NDem and NRel. Unlike unrestricted universals, implicational universals begin to assemble the independent parameters of a grammar together into an integrated whole. Since implicational universals do this only a few parameters at a time, they have been set aside for more complex tools, which will be described in this chapter and the following three chapters. Implicational universals remain central to typological analysis, however, because they are the lowest-level link between grammatical parameters.

Another important feature of both unrestricted and implicational universals is that they are universal, not language-specific. Unlike assertions of dependencies between grammatical properties in individual languages, unrestricted and implicational universals hold, or are intended to hold, for all languages (setting aside exceptions for now). In the case of implicational universals, the universal dependencies between grammatical properties may not even be apparent in individual languages taken one at a time, because they are patterns of variation. Even so, since implicational universals cover all human languages, the forces that account for their existence must be operating in the grammars of individual languages (we will return to this point in 6.5 and chapter 9).

Implicational universals represent an application of propositional logic to typology. For that reason, we have the full power of propositional logic at our disposal, and we now use it to try to further illuminate the dependencies among grammatical parameters. First, propositional logic asserts that for every universal of the form $P \supset Q$, there is an equivalent universal, $\sim Q \supset \sim P$, called the **contrapositive**. We may illustrate this with the truth tables for the contrapositive of "RelN $\supset$ DemN":

Type	NDem	NRel	NDem $\supset$ NRel	$\sim$NRel	$\sim$Ndem	$\sim$NRel $\supset$ $\sim$NDem
1	T	T	T	F	F	T
2	T	F	F	T	F	F
3	F	T	T	F	T	T
4	F	F	T	T	T	T

One can observe that the truth values for the columns headed by "NDem $\supset$ NRel" and "$\sim$NRel $\supset$ $\sim$NDem" are identical, demonstrating their logical equivalence. Since the opposite of NDem is DemN and the opposite of NRel is RelN, we may replace "$\sim$NRel" with "RelN" and "$\sim$NDem" with "DemN." This yields RelN $\supset$ DemN, which is equivalent to NDem $\supset$ NRel. This is possible because each parameter has two values, and each value can be treated as the opposite of the other value. This is not possible, however, if there are more than two values for a parameter. Consider Greenberg's Universal 3: "Languages with dominant VSO order are always prepositional" (Greenberg 1966a:78), and the table that is derived from:[3]

	VSO	SVO	SOV
Prep	6	10	0
Postp	0	3	11

In this example, the parameter of declarative-clause word-order has three values: VSO, SVO and SOV. Greenberg's universal can be restated as the formula VSO $\supset$ Prep, but its contrapositive is simply Postp $\supset$ $\sim$VSO, since languages that are not VSO can be either SVO or SOV.

A standard implicational universal is a generalization over a tetrachoric table in which three types are attested and one type is not. It is important to remember that the pattern of attested and unattested language types in a tetrachoric table (or larger table) is the central fact, and that an implicational universal is only a convenient low-level description of that pattern. There are other possible patterns of attested lan-

49

guage types in which only two types are attested, or even just one type is attested. If just one type is attested, then one is dealing with two unrestricted universals, such as "All languages have consonants" and "All languages have vowels":

	Consonants	No consonants
Vowels	X	–
No vowels	–	–

If two types are attested and two are unattested, there are two possible patterns. In one pattern, the unattested types are in the same row or column (it doesn't matter whether it is a row or a column, since a table can always be inverted). In the vast majority of cases, this represents an unrestricted universal on one parameter, and a second parameter in which both types are attested:

	Uvular consonants	No uvular consonants
Vowels	X	X
No vowels	–	–

The unattested types in the second row are accounted for by the unrestricted universal, "All languages have vowels," while the two columns simply note that some languages have uvular consonants and some languages do not. This does not indicate any relationship or dependency between the presence or absence of uvular consonants and the presence of vowels, since all languages have vowels anyway.

This is not true in all cases, however. Greenberg describes a case regarding oral vowels and nasal vowels:

	Nasal vowels	No nasal vowels
Oral vowels	X	X
No oral vowels	–	–

This table may be accounted for by an unrestricted universal that states "All languages have oral vowels." However, there is another possibility. The unattested type with no oral vowels or nasal vowels can be accounted for by the already-existing unrestricted universal "All languages have vowels," and the unattested type with nasal vowels but no oral vowels can be accounted for by the implicational universal "If a language has nasal vowels, then it has oral vowels." Normally, this alternative hypothesis would be rejected on the grounds of simplicity. However, other evidence would suggest that the alternative hypothesis is the correct one. First, there is additional evidence having to do with the markedness of nasal vowels with respect to oral vowels (see chapter 4) that implies that a dependency holds between the two of the sort described by the implicational universal. Second, the unrestricted universal "All languages have vowels" can be explained by the impossibility, or at least extreme difficulty, of articulating speech without vowels, whereas the unrestricted universal "All languages have oral vowels" cannot be accounted for in the same fashion, since a language with only nasal vowels does not have the same articulatory restrictions. The lesson to be drawn from this example is that unrestricted and implicational universals cannot be mechanically read off tables of attested and unattested language types. Both wider typological patterns and deeper explanations of what is going on must be appealed to in order to yield the best combination of unrestricted and implicational universals to account for the data. Above all, the choice of the correct generalization(s) to account for the constraints on possible language types is determined by the hypotheses of relationships between parameters.

The other pattern of two attested and two unattested types is much more straightforward, and can be illustrated by Greenberg's Universal 2: "In languages with prepositions, the genitive almost always follows the governing noun, while in languages with postpositions it almost always precedes" (Greenberg 1966a:78):

	NGen	GenN
Prep	X	–
Postp	–	X

In this universal, which is not without exceptions (see chapter 8), the unattested types are found on a diagonal in the tetrachoric table. Greenberg phrased his universal as two opposite implicational universals: Prep $\supset$ NGen and Postp $\supset$ GenN. These can be combined to a **logical equivalence**: Prep $\equiv$ NGen (and its contrapositive, Postp $\equiv$ GenN).

A logical equivalence is not the same as an implicational universal. For example, RelN $\supset$ DemN is not equivalent to DemN $\supset$ RelN; in fact, DemN $\supset$ RelN is *false* (look at English, for example). The true equivalent to RelN $\supset$ DemN is its contrapositive, ~DemN $\supset$ ~RelN, or NDem $\supset$ NRel, as we saw above. An easy way to remember this is that the tetrachoric table for a genuine logical equivalence will have two gaps in it, whereas a tetrachoric table for a regular implicational universal will have only one gap in it. The distinction between a logical equivalence and an implicational universal, and the equivalence between an implicational universal and its contrapositive, will turn out to be important in the next section.

In this section so far, we have discussed universals that involve only one typological parameter (unrestricted universals) or two parameters (simple implicational universals of the form "If P, then Q"). It is quite possible to combine three or more parameters into implicational universals involving the full power of propositional logic. Some of these universals can be rephrased as sets of simple implicational universals. For example, Greenberg's Universal 18 is a complex implicational universal that can be reduced to two simple implications using standard methods in logic: "Universal 18. When the descriptive adjective precedes the noun, the demonstrative and the numeral, with overwhelmingly more than chance frequency, do likewise" (Greenberg 1966a:86).

Propositional representation: A ⊃ (DemN & NumN)
Decomposition: AN ⊃ DemN (see Hawkins 1983:81, Universal v')
AN ⊃ NumN (see Hawkins 1983:82, Universal vi')

In general, an implicational universal of the form P ⊃ (Q & R) can be decomposed into P ⊃ Q and P ⊃ R. However, an implication of the form (P & Q) ⊃ R (such as Greenberg's Universal 5, equivalent to Hawkins' (1983) Universal I, (SOV & NG) ⊃ NA), cannot be decomposed into P ⊃ R and Q ⊃ R. Also, implications with disjuncts in either the antecedent or the consequent – (P ∨ Q) ⊃ R and P ⊃ (Q ∨ R) respectively – cannot be decomposed into simple implications. (The value of decomposing complex implicational universals will be discussed in the following section.)

John Hawkins has been a strong proponent of complex implicational universals (Hawkins 1980, 1983). There are two major arguments for using complex implicational universals instead of simple ones. The first is that adding further conditions on a simple implicational universal can remove exceptional cases, making the universal into an exceptionless universal. This process can be quite useful, because it may turn out that the further condition can contribute to the correct explanation for the exception to the simpler version. For example, consider a candidate universal, "If a language is SOV, then the genitive precedes the noun" (SOV ⊃ GN). (This simplified version has indeed been used by some linguists working in word-order typology.) However, there are a number of languages which are SOV and NG. It turns out that in all of those languages, the adjective follows the noun. Thus, we may modify this universal to read, "If a language is SOV, then if the adjective precedes the noun, then the genitive precedes the noun" (SOV ⊃ (AN ⊃ GN); Hawkins 1983:64). This universal is now exceptionless. Since one has to include adjective–noun order in the universal in order to make it exceptionless, it implies that genitive–noun order is somehow dependent on adjective–noun order as well as declarative clause order. This seems to be a reasonable explanation for the exceptional cases (see chapter 8 for a historical interpretation of these cases).

On the other hand, adding conditions to make an implicational universal with exceptions into an exceptionless universal may turn out to be unproductive if the additional conditions do not help to account for the exceptions. To take an extreme example, let us assume that it turned out that all the exceptions to the simple universal SOV ⊃ GN lacked the phoneme /ü/. Changing the universal to SOV ⊃ (/ü/ ⊃ GN) would make it exceptionless but it would not help to account for the exceptions, since it is highly unlikely that the presence of the phoneme /ü/ has anything to do with genitive–noun order. The logical structure of the implicational universal implies a deeper set of dependencies between the grammatical properties found in the universal. For that reason, it is worth complicating implicational universals to make them exceptionless only if there is reason to believe that the additional complications play a role in explaining the exceptions that are removed.

The second reason that Hawkins has argued for more complex implicational universals is that by combining individual universals, one can discover larger patterns that underlie individual implicational universals, as Hawkins does in his book on word-order universals. These larger patterns, which can be found with sets of simple implicational universals as well, will concern us for the rest of this chapter and most of the following chapters.

3.3 Deeper explanations for word-order universals

Implicational universals first reached a wide linguistic audience in Joseph Greenberg's influential paper, "Some universals of grammar with particular reference to the order of meaningful elements" (Greenberg 1966a), first presented in 1961. Greenberg enumerated forty-five universals based on a thirty-language sample and on informal observations of a much larger number of languages. Only the first twenty-eight universals dealt with word order; the remaining seventeen dealt with inflectional categories (most of those will be discussed in chapter 4). Greenberg's word-order universals were incorporated in much linguistic work, and considerable effort has been expended to try to explain the universals. We will discuss the more significant attempts to explain the universals, concentrating on those which proposed deeper typological patterns and beginning with Greenberg's own explanations.

If one examines all of Greenberg's universals that refer to adjective–noun order, a striking pattern emerges:

(SOV & GN) ⊃ NA	Universal 5
VSO ⊃ NA	Universal 17
NDem ⊃ NA	
NNum ⊃ NA	(both derivable from Universal 18)

In all of the implicational universals involving adjective–noun order, one finds the order noun–adjective in the implicatum of the universal. If the contrapositive of these universals were taken, they would all have the order adjective–noun in the implicans:

$$AN \supset \sim(SOV \ \& \ GN)$$
$$AN \supset \sim VSO$$
$$AN \supset DemN$$
$$AN \supset NumN$$

The generalization that covers these universals is, "All implicational universals whose implicatum involves the order of noun and adjective will have the order NA as the implicatum" (with a complementary statement for the contrapositives following logically). Greenberg called this pattern **dominance**: the dominant order was the one that always occurred in the implicatum. To say some word order P is dominant is to say that implicational universals involving P will be of the form $X \supset P$ (or the contrapositive $\sim P \supset X$), and never of the form $X \supset \sim P$ (or $P \supset X$). Intuitively, the dominant order can be thought of as the preferred order of elements, other things being equal.

Dominance can be read directly from a tetrachoric table. Consider the table for $AN \supset DemN$:

	DemN	NDem
NA	X	X
AN	X	–

The dominant order is the order that occurs with either possible order of the cross-cutting parameter. Thus, NA is dominant because it occurs with either DemN or NDem, whereas AN can occur with DemN only. Likewise, DemN is dominant (note also that with the universal RelN ⊃ DemN, DemN order is dominant as expected). The orders that are not dominant, AN and NDem, are called **recessive** by Greenberg.

The other pattern that Greenberg discovered in his universals is **harmony**. This pattern is also derivable directly from the tetrachoric table, though it is less obviously manifested in the implicational universal. A word order on one parameter is harmonic with an order on the cross-cutting parameter if it occurs *only* with that other order. In the preceding example, AN is harmonic with DemN and NDem is harmonic with NA. Harmony defined in this way is not reversible: DemN is not harmonic with AN because it also occurs with NA, and NA is not harmonic with NDem because it also occurs with DemN. Harmony is always defined with respect to the recessive orders: the recessive order is harmonic with the order that occurs with it, and not the other way around.

Harmony is only reversible in a tetrachoric table with two gaps, expressible by a logical equivalence, such as is the case with genitive–noun order and adposition–noun order:

	NG	GN
Prep	X	–
Postp	–	X

In this example of a logical equivalence, Prep is harmonic with NG and vice versa, and Postp is harmonic with GN and vice versa. Also, in a logical equivalence there is no dominant order, since each word-order type occurs with only one word-order type on the other parameter. (Conversely, in an unrestricted universal like "Subjects almost always precede objects," there is a dominant order, SO, but no harmonic orders.)

From the implicational universals discovered by Greenberg and later researchers, dominant orders (where they exist) and two major harmony patterns have been found (see table 3.1). The first column lists the dominant pattern for each word order. The second and third columns list word orders that are harmonic with each other. The first harmonic pattern is often called the **OV pattern**, based on the order of nominal object and verb, and the second is often called the **VO pattern**.

Greenberg's analysis illustrates the next step in a typological analysis. Whereas an implicational universal describes a relationship between just two parameters (or maybe three or four, in the case of complex implicational universals), concepts like dominance and harmony describe a relationship between a large number of parameters in a single stroke. The concept of dominance, for example, defines a relationship between a particular word-order type and any other parameter that is involved with it. Many of these deeper and broader typological concepts can be recast in terms of a generalization over implicational universals. In some cases, however, they cannot be described in terms of implicational universals very easily (if at all). However, they can of course be directly read off tetrachoric tables or other descriptive representations of the

Table 3.1 *Dominance and harmony patterns for word-order universals*

Dominance	Harmony (1)	Harmony (2)	Universals
SV	SV	VS	(3/4), 5, (12), 17
VO$_{Nom}$	O$_{Nom}$V	VO$_{Nom}$	5, (12), 13, *17*, 21, 25
O$_{Prn}$V	O$_{Prn}$V	VO$_{Prn}$	25
SO	–	–	1
Prep (?)	Post	Prep	(2), (3/4), (22), 24, (27)
GN (?)	GN	NG	(2), (23), IX′
PossN	PossN	NPoss	XXI, XXIII
DemN	DemN	NDem	V′ (=18), XI′
NumN	NumN	NNum	VI′ (=18), XII′
NRel	RelN	NRel	24, IX′, XI′, XII′, XXIII
NA	AN	NA	5, 17, 18, 21, 24, *40*, XXI
AdvA	AdvA	AAdv	21
–	StdMA	AMStd	22
VComp	CompV	VComp	15
–	VAux	AuxV	(16)
–	SentQ	QSent	(9)
AntCons	–	–	14

Universals supporting hypotheses: Greenberg 1966a (Arabic numerals), Hawkins 1983 (Roman numerals). Universals in parentheses are logical equivalences which support harmony but not dominance. Universals in italics are counterexamples to the proposed dominance pattern.

distribution of attested language types. As more of these broader concepts have been discovered and employed, they have replaced the implicational universals as typological generalizations.

Greenberg considers both dominance and harmony to operate in explaining word-order patterns. He proposes the following generalization: "A dominant order may always occur, but its opposite, the recessive, occurs only when a harmonic construction is likewise present" (Greenberg 1966a:97). The concluding section of Greenberg's original word-order paper is devoted in large part to using the interaction of dominance and harmony to explain some subtle and apparently inconsistent word-order patterns. For example, the logical equivalences Prep ≡ NG and Postp ≡ GN have some exceptions: there exist languages with prepositions and genitive–noun order and languages with postpositions with noun–genitive order. However, in almost all of the languages in which the genitive–noun order is disharmonic with the adposition order, the genitive–noun order is harmonic with the adjective–noun order, which suggests that the genitive–noun order is influenced by the adjective–noun order.[4]

Greenberg's analysis is one of the earliest examples of an important type of explanation of cross-linguistic variation, the concept of **competing**

motivations. Competing-motivations models describe the interaction of universal typological principles in order to account for the existence of variation in language types. In a competing-motivations model, no one language type is optimal (wholly motivated) because the different principles governing the existence of language types are in conflict (competition). In Greenberg's word-order analysis, dominance favors some word orders, such as NA, absolutely, while harmony will favor an alignment of the adjective with other modifiers. Since for some modifiers, modifier–noun order is dominant, and for others, noun–modifier order is dominant, a language cannot be harmonic without having some recessive orders. However, an order cannot be both recessive and disharmonic at the same time. This is the interaction between dominance and harmony that Greenberg described with his principle, and which accounts in a single stroke for the unattested types in the tetrachoric tables for word-order types. The general principle behind competing-motivations analysis is: attested types must be motivated by at least one general principle; the more motivated a language type is, the more frequently it will occur; and unmotivated language types should be unattested, or at most extremely rare and unstable (see 7.4 for more detailed discussion). The value in competing-motivation models for typology is that they can account for both variation in language types and also frequency of language types across the world.

Word-order typologists immediately after Greenberg focused almost exclusively on harmony. The two harmonic types were named "OV" and "VO" after the declarative-clause order type. Harmonic patterns were treated as reversible: AN, DemN and NumN were harmonic with each other regardless of whether the order was recessive. The major drawback of this approach is that it is empirically less adequate than Greenberg's original formulation. Although many languages fit one or the other of the two harmonic types, many other languages do not, having instead one, or more, dominant word order that is disharmonic with the overall pattern of the language. Harmony is only one half of the picture.[5]

The most important word-order work since Greenberg is that of John Hawkins (Hawkins 1980, 1983). Hawkins used a sample of over 300 languages and thus brought in a much greater range of data, especially data for the various noun modifiers (demonstrative, numeral, adjective, genitive and relative clause). Hawkins introduces two competing motivations for noun–modifier order, similar to Greenberg's concept of dominance. The first concept is **heaviness** (Hawkins 1983:90). Certain types of modifiers tend to be larger grammatical units, in terms of number of syllables, number of words and syntactic constituency (relative *clauses* vs. genitive *phrases* vs. single-*word* demonstratives and numerals), and could be ranked in order of heaviness as follows:

$$Rel < Gen < Adj < \{Dem, Num\}$$

Hawkins interprets this as a preference for heavier modifiers to follow the head noun, and lighter modifiers to precede. This concept resembles Greenberg's concept of dominance in its effect of complementing harmony: heavier modifiers follow the noun even if the harmonic order is modifier–noun, and lighter modifiers precede the noun even if the harmonic order is noun–modifier. Since demonstrative and numeral are lighter, and adjective and relative clause are heavier, they correspond roughly to Greenberg's dominant orders DemN, NumN, NA and NRel.

Hawkins also introduces the concept of **mobility** to account for a number of exceptions in which neither harmony nor heaviness could be the operating factors (Hawkins 1983:92–4). The notion of mobility is that certain modifiers are more variable in their word order within single languages, and so are more likely to switch from a harmonic order to a disharmonic one. Specifically, Dem, Num and Adj are more mobile than Gen and Rel. Hawkins uses this principle to explain why some "lighter" modifiers such as Dem, Num and Adj, are (rarely) found to follow the head noun while "heavier" modifiers such as Rel precede. The assumption here is that the original harmonic order was modifier–head, including RelN and AdjN, but historically the adjective shifted to NA order while the relative clause did not.[6] Thus, the mobility principle, unlike the heaviness principle, has an essentially diachronic dimension to it, as Hawkins notes: "We are, in effect, claiming that constraints on diachrony are an important part of the explanation for synchronic universals" (Hawkins 1983:108). We will encounter mobility again in the guise of "stability" in chapter 8.

Hawkins' heaviness principle, if it is indeed equivalent to Greenberg's dominance, can be thought of as an explanation of dominance. The dominant order is that which places the lighter element before the heavier element. This explanation actually represents a putative relationship between one grammatical parameter – word order, taken in general – and another, independent grammatical parameter – the length (in phonological and syntactic terms) of the grammatical element. This relationship has a plausible and well-supported functional explanation: order of con-

stituents reflects ranking in size for processing reasons (see Hawkins
1983:98–106 and references cited therein).

Hawkins proposed his heaviness principle only for noun modifiers,
whereas Greenberg's concept of dominance applied to word order in
general (and, possibly, to implicational universals in general). It is worth
examining the dominant orders other than those for noun modifiers
to see if the heaviness explanation is at least a plausible one. There
is some limited evidence (Universal 24) that prepositions are dominant
over postpositions. This is quite reasonable from the heaviness principle:
adpositions are generally smaller constituents than the noun phrases
they govern. In the case of object–verb order, it seems likely that objects
are heavier than verbs when they are full noun phrases, but not when
they are pronouns. Greenberg has a universal, Universal 25, which states
that if the nominal object precedes the verb, then the pronominal object
does also – which gives evidence that the dominant order for pronominal
objects is before the verb, but the dominant order for nominal objects
is to follow. This suggests that heaviness is a major factor in determining
object position typologically, since pronouns are also smaller than full
noun phrases.

The dominant subject–verb order may also be accounted for by heaviness. Recent text studies have demonstrated that across languages subjects, especially transitive subjects, tend to be pronominal, and nominal
subjects when they occur tend to follow the verb cross-linguistically
(DuBois 1985, 1987; Lambrecht 1987). Thus, with subjects as well, heaviness may be a contributing factor to the dominant word order, though
DuBois and Lambrecht emphasize iconic principles of information flow.
Iconic principles may also be involved in the unequivocal dominance
of subject–object order and antecedent–consequent order in conditionals
(see chapter 7).

A number of hypotheses have been proposed to account for harmony.
Greenberg suggests that harmony represented an analogical relationship
between the harmonic orders, placing all of the modifiers on one side
of the head. This account held for nominal modifiers, but it remains
to include the adposition and declarative-clause patterns. Greenberg
suggests an analogy between genitive constructions and adpositional constructions, for example between "the inside of the house" (NG) and
"inside the house" (Prep). Greenberg also proposes an analogy between
the ordinary genitive and the subjective and objective genitives, that
is, the genitive of subjects and objects of nominalized verbs, so that
the following analogy holds: genitive is to noun ("John's house") as

subject and object (genitive) is to (nominalized) verb ("Germany's conquest of Europe"; Greenberg 1966a:99). These analogies account for the harmony of SV/OV/Postp/GN and VS/VO/Prep/NG, which otherwise appear to be a rather mixed bag of word orders.

Greenberg's hypotheses also have diachronic importance, since adpositions frequently evolve from genitive constructions and finite declarative-clause constructions also commonly evolve from nominalizations with genitive arguments (see Aristar 1987; chapter 8). This can be observed directly in many languages, in which the genitive and adpositional constructions and/or the genitive and declarative constructions are similar or identical. Greenberg cites Berber as a language in which the genitive form of the noun is the same as the subject form (provided the subject immediately follows); thus the VS construction is very close to the NG construction (Greenberg 1966a:99). In many languages, the genitive form of the noun is identical with the subject form (especially transitive subjects; Allen 1964), and/or the object form. In many more languages, the adposition construction is transparently a genitive construction, with the adposition the head. A good example of the constructional similarity of VS, PrepN, and GN can be found in Quiché (Mondloch 1978:195, 24):

(1) šaq si   š-   ∅-   aʔiʔ   kān rī xun čicop
     just really PAST- 3SG.B- became.sunned left the an animal
                                V   S

     č-   u-   či   rī   mār
     at- 3SG.A- edge the sea
               Prep N

     'And the animal was left sunning (= dead) at the sea shore.'

(2) u-   ḉiʔ lē   ala
     3SG.A- dog the boy
            N   G

     'the boy's dog'

Quiché has two agreement prefix sets, A and B. Set B is used for intransitive subjects; set A is used for transitive subjects, prepositions and genitive constructions. The general construction is: "prefix-head dependent," a structure that includes VS, PrepN and NG.

The explanations for harmony based on analogical head–modifier relations are more successful than the various attempts to account for the harmonic patterns in semantic terms, since the variety of semantic relations that hold between harmonic types is too great to subsume under a single semantic generalization (e.g. verb and object, adposition and noun, adjective and noun, adverb and adjective).[7] Moreover, evidence that the same construction is used for the more diverse word-order types, or is the historical source for those word-order types, strongly suggests that the head–modifier analysis is essentially correct at some level of explanation (cf. Hawkins 1983:93–8).

The examination of morphosyntactic constructions and word order can also account for anomalous word-order patterns. In Mandarin Chinese, one finds prepositions and **circumpositions**, adpositional constructions with one element preceding the noun and one element following:[8]

(3)   Wǒ bǎ shuǐ dào dào guàn lǐ
      I   BA water pour to can in(side)
      'I pour the water into the can.'

Mandarin has a basic word order of SVO, but is GN. It turns out that the prepositions and the prepositional element in the circumpositions are verbal, and the postpositional elements in the circumpositions are nominal. In this case *dào* is also a verb meaning "arrive," and *lǐ* has a nominal source not unlike English "inside." Thus, the PrepN construction is derived from the VO construction, and the NPostp construction is derived from the GN construction. It may turn out that these constructional parallels underlie many of the harmonic patterns, particularly the semantically less tractable ones for adpositions and declarative-clause elements.

All of the discussion in this section so far has assumed that implicational universals, and the deeper concepts, such as harmony, dominance/heaviness and mobility, capture only cross-linguistic variation. As we noted in chapter 1, however, there is actually a good deal of *intra*-linguistic variation in the expression of particular constructions, and word order is no exception to this phenomenon. Word order is particularly variable at the clause level and somewhat less so at the phrase level (in fact, one could propose the generalization that the lower the morphosyntactic level, the more rigid the word order). Of course, word order is never entirely free, and constraints on the variation can be found. Several of Greenberg's original word-order universals refer to flexibility (or inflexibility) of word order. Universal 6 states that all VSO languages have at least SVO as an alternative order, while universals 7, 13 and 15 state that in SOV languages with at most OSV as an alternative order (the **rigid** SOV type), then neither adverbial modifiers of the verb nor subordinate verbal forms can follow the main verb. The most thorough study of word-order variation in the declarative clause is Steele 1978. Steele discovered that certain alternative word orders were more likely to be found than others. In particular, VSO and SOV are most likely to have VOS and OSV respectively as alternative word orders. In other words, the most likely alternative orders kept the verb in the same position and reversed the position of subject and object. SVO was also a very common alternative order to both VSO (note Universal 6) and SOV (this is the nonrigid SOV type). This phenomenon can be accounted for by the dominance of SV and VO orders: nonrigid VSO languages allow subjects to shift to their dominant position and nonrigid SOV languages allow objects to shift to their dominant position. Languages with basic SVO order are the least likely to have any alternative word orders; i.e. they are the language type that is most likely to have rigid declarative clause word-order.

More detailed investigation of actual texts in many languages has revealed that word order is more flexible in more languages than was previously imagined. Close attention has been paid to "free word-order languages," by which is meant "purely discourse-determined" clause-constituent order and sometimes also free noun-phrase constituent order (Hale 1983; Heath 1986; Mithun 1987; D. Payne 1987). The study of typological patterns of word-order variation is a relatively new area, and will turn out to be increasingly important in typological word-order research.

The concept of an implicational universal has had its greatest impact in the area of word order. Although broader theoretical concepts have been invoked to account for typological patterns of word order, implicational universals still remain a basic unit of typological analysis. Implicational universals of word order illustrate the basic elements of the typological method in their simplest form. The first step is the enumeration of logically possible language types by the structural parameters involved, illustrated by the tetrachoric table. The second step is the discovery of the empirical distribution of attested and unattested types, illustrated by the pattern of gaps in a tetrachoric (or larger) table. The third step is developing a generalization that (1) restricts variation in language types without eliminating it – i.e. allows for the various attested types while excluding the unattested types, and (2) reveals a relationship between otherwise logically independent grammatical parameters – in this case the implicational relationship. At this point, typologists from Greenberg onward have observed more far-reaching relationships between the word-order parameters, such as harmony and dominance, than could be captured by simple implicational universals. The final step in the analysis is to seek a deeper (possibly external) explanation for the relationship, such as heaviness, mobility and the various proposals for explaining the existence of harmony. The following chapters will introduce other typological concepts that are like harmony and dominance in that they are much broader than implicational universals; but the discovery and explanation of cross-linguistic patterns follows this same basic methodology.

4
Markedness in typology

4.1 Introduction

The concept of markedness was first developed in the Prague School of linguistic theory. The notion of marked and unmarked values of a category was first developed for phonological systems by Nicholas Trubetzkoy (1931, 1969 [1939]) and first applied to morphosyntactic categories and semantics by Roman Jakobson (1984a [1932], 1984b [1939]).[1] Markedness has since been adapted by both the generative and the typological approaches to linguistic theory, not surprisingly in rather different ways. As a consequence, markedness in generative grammar is considerably different from markedness in typology (for an analysis of markedness in generative grammar, see Battistella, forthcoming). This chapter will be restricted to the role of markedness in typology.

Like implicational universals, markedness is a fundamental concept underlying much contemporary work in typology, even though it is not overtly referred to very often. Much current typological work, particularly work on grammatical hierarchies and prototypes, is supported by evidence that is largely evidence of markedness; this will be discussed in chapters 5 and 6.

The essential notion behind markedness in typology is the fact of asymmetrical or unequal grammatical properties of otherwise equal linguistic elements – inflections, words in word classes and even syntactic constructions. The typological concept of markedness is based on several specific types of grammatical asymmetry, the description of which is the topic of this chapter. However, it is useful to keep in mind the more general notion of markedness as a type of asymmetry, since that is what links markedness conceptually to implicational universals, hierarchies and prototypes.

Markedness is an important tool for the typologist because it provides a means to directly link formal (structural) linguistic properties across languages. In chapter 1 it was argued that it is difficult, if not impossible, to compare formal categories of natural languages discovered by internal structural analysis because of incommensurability: structural variation from one language to another in, for example, the category "adjective" or the "genitive" construction is simply too great. The discovery of markedness patterns demonstrated that certain properties of linguistic structure which were basic and general enough to be directly compared across languages do display significant cross-linguistic patterns. In particular, markedness patterns can be used to account for phonological, morphological and syntactic irregularities. One need not succumb to the temptation to "regularize" irregular grammatical patterns, because the irregularities themselves are manifestations of regular typological patterns. This is true of syntax as well as morphology and phonology, although markedness has been applied mainly to the latter two levels of grammar.

Markedness is also of theoretical interest because it is a significant cross-linguistic pattern that cuts across the traditional stratification of linguistic analysis into grammatical levels. If, for example, we find a markedness relationship between /p/ and /b/ in allophonic variants, so that /p/ is the unmarked member of the pair, we would also expect to find /p/ unmarked in phonological patterns, segment inventories and morphophonemic patterns. Likewise, if we discover that in the grammatical category of number, morphological evidence indicates that the singular is unmarked as opposed to the plural, we would expect to find that the singular is unmarked in syntax and the lexicon as well. In fact, it is a primary hypothesis of marking theory that markedness patterns are consistent across these different "levels" of grammar. There is a diachronic reason for this: the different levels can be identified with different historical stages in the conventionalization and grammaticization of a linguistic pattern, proceeding from allophone to phoneme to morphophoneme, and from syntactic construction to morphological inflection to lexical subregularity. If that pattern involves a markedness relation, there is no *a priori* reason to believe that markedness of the categories or constructions should change over the historical process (assuming that no other factors, such as semantic change or some conflicting historical process, interfere). The role of markedness in diachronic typology will be discussed further in chapter 8.

Typological marking theory consists of two parts. The first part is the kinds of evidence for markedness patterns. This chapter deals exclusively with the evidence for markedness, presenting a new classification of Greenberg's and later researchers' markedness criteria. Most of the markedness criteria, with certain important qualifications, have stood the test of time and data.

The second part of typological marking theory are the actual markedness patterns. What we may call "**classical**" (i.e. Prague School) marking theory allows for only one sort of pattern: an absolute relationship between the two values of a binary-valued category, such as singular and plural, so that one value (singular) is unmarked and the other value (plural) is marked. This part of typological marking is inadequate almost from the start. The extensions to marking theory that are necessary to capture the data will be discussed in the following two chapters. However, in order to use actual examples in this chapter, we must introduce the basic concepts of a hierarchy and a correlation or prototype here.

First, many grammatical categories have more than two values. For example, grammatical number, the main category described in this chapter, includes not only singular and plural but also **dual** and **trial** (or in some languages, **paucal**, that is a small number greater than two). Markedness is altered to a concept of **relative** markedness, so that plural is marked relative to singular but unmarked relative to dual, etc. This yields a **hierarchy**: singular < plural < dual < trial/paucal. It will be argued in the following chapter that most if not all the evidence for grammatical hierarchies is the same evidence used for markedness that is discussed in this chapter.

Second, the markedness of grammatical values turns out to be dependent on other categories that intersect with it. Continuing with the example of number, it turns out that for subclasses of nouns in many languages, the singular form is the marked one (in which case it is called a **singulative**), and the nonsingular form (usually called a **collective**) is unmarked. This phenomenon is called a **markedness reversal** or **local markedness**. It turns out that cross-linguistically the subclass of nouns which displays this reversal is more or less the same across languages, generally objects that naturally occur in groups or are difficult to individuate, such as oats (see 6.3.4). Thus, there is a pattern to the reversal, and we may say that the singular is marked or unmarked depending on the noun class it is applied to. This correlation between the category of number and the noun class represents a **prototype**: most object classes are prototypically singular, but some objects are prototypically nonsingular (collective). It will be argued in chapter 6 that most, if not all, grammatical prototypes, like hierarchies, are based on markedness evidence. (Hence, the rather involved discussions of the markedness criteria in this chapter are necessary for understanding how hierarchies and prototypes are uncovered in typological research.)

Since even the simplest examples of markedness tend to involve multi-valued categories such as noun class, we will not be able to avoid some reference to hierarchies and prototypes in this chapter.

4.2 **Markedness and implicational universals**

In the preceding section I referred to several different types of evidence for the markedness of a particular linguistic category, mentioning explicitly the presence vs. absence of a morpheme indicating the category value. This is a convenient example to use in illustrating the relationship between markedness and implicational universals.

For example, plurality in nouns is expressed by a nonzero morpheme /-S/ in English, whereas the singular is characterized by the absence of a morpheme indicating number. This evidence from English cannot alone provide the argument for the cross-linguistic markedness of the plural as opposed to the singular. One must demonstrate that in general, the category "plural" is marked and "singular" is unmarked, in their expression. A plausible starting point is to take the structural pattern of English – a nonzero morpheme for the plural and no morpheme for the singular – and propose the following universal: the plural is marked and the singular is unmarked if and only if the plural is marked by a nonzero morpheme and the singular is marked by the absence of a number morpheme. This statement, a logical equivalence, is too strong. There are many languages in which both the plural and the singular are "marked" by the absence of a number morpheme, for example Mandarin Chinese (see Li & Thompson 1981:11–12; these languages are commonly said not to possess the category of number). There are also languages with a rich system of nominal morphology in which both the singular and the plural have nonzero morphemes that indicate number, for example Latvian (see Lazdiņa 1966:292–3). On the other hand, there are almost no languages in which the singular is expressed by a nonzero number morpheme and the plural is expressed by the absence of a number morpheme.[2] The non-existence of this type is the significant fact for the singular–plural markedness relationship. It can be illustrated with the tetrachoric table familiar to us from implicational universals:

	Absence of *singular morpheme*	*Presence of* *singular morpheme*
Presence of *plural morpheme*	English	Latvian
Absence of *plural morpheme*	Mandarin Chinese	–

Thus, the markedness pattern illustrated by the presence or absence of a (nonzero) morpheme indicating the category value in question is of the classic implicational universal type: only three of the four possible types are found in natural languages. Thus, it is not the case that languages such as Mandarin and Latvian are exceptions to the markedness of plural and the unmarkedness of singular. Rather, the status of Mandarin and Latvian with respect to the cross-linguistic concept of the markedness of plurality is exactly parallel to the status of English and Japanese with respect to the implicational universal "if a language has VSO word order, it has prepositions": they do not offer a counterexample, since the antecedent of the conditional does not apply to them. The only genuine counterexample to the markedness of plurality would be a language in which the singular required a nonzero morpheme while the plural was characterized by the absence of a number morpheme.

Thus, we may formulate the markedness relationship of singular and plural in the following implicational universal: "If the plural is expressed by the absence of a morpheme, then so is the singular." More generally, the implicational statement capturing the marked–unmarked relationship for morpheme structure would be: "If the marked category value is expressed by the absence of a morpheme, then so is the unmarked value." This can also be expressed in the contrapositive form, "If the unmarked category value is expressed by a nonzero morpheme, then so is the marked category value."

In the preceding chapter, it was stated that an implicational universal describes a relationship between two otherwise logically independent types. For example, the main word-order type VSO exhibits a relationship to the otherwise logically independent adpositional word-order type Prep so that one can construct the implicational universal "VSO implies Prep." In the markedness example used here, the two types are the singular and the plural, or more precisely the form of expression of the singular and the form of expression of the plural. These two types are independent in that there is no logical constraint on the number of morphemes used to express the singular that is imposed by the form of expression of the plural or vice versa. Hence these two types can be treated as the implicans and the implicatum of an implicational universal even though they are both values in the same grammatical category, i.e. "number."

This immediately raises the question, however, of what combinations of two values can be related in such a way. It does not make sense to ask which is the marked value, passive or glottalized. The two values that can be related by a markedness pattern must in some sense be **paradigmatic alternatives**. Singular and plural are an example of a low-level pair of paradigmatic alternatives for the higher category of number. Paradigmatic alternatives exist at higher levels of abstraction in the grammar; for example, noun, verb and adjective are comparable members of the higher category "major syntactic category," although they are not normally paradigmatic alternatives in a sentence. The notion of paradigmatic alternatives, of course, presupposes certain hypotheses concerning the organization of linguistic categories. These hypotheses must be valid across languages, so that we may say the singular–plural paradigm in English is comparable to the singular–plural paradigms in Mandarin, Latvian and any other language. Thus, we must have cross-linguistic comparability of the organization of grammatical categories into paradigms as well as comparability of the categories themselves. Without delving into this thorny question any further, we may simply say that (classical) markedness is restricted to asserting a relationship between two paradigmatic alternatives: "the concept of marked and unmarked is a relation between features which are mutually exclusive where they are the source of minimal contrast between two phonemes or two lexemic units" (Greenberg 1966b:57).

If we examine more closely the distribution of attested and unattested language types, we find that classical markedness does differ from implicational universals. Consider, for example, the markedness relationship between the predication of a simple adjective and the predication of a comparative adjective, that is, between *John is tall* and *John is taller than Fred*. One would want to say that the English data supports the markedness of the comparative degree and the unmarkedness of the simple degree. However, the comparative degree involves the presence of not one but two non-zero morphemes over and above the simple degree (the suffix -er and the particle *than*). This contrasts with the Yoruba construction in which only one additional morpheme, *jù*, is involved (Rowlands 1969:124):

(1) ó tóbi jù mí
     he big exceed me
     'He is bigger than me.'

One might propose that there are now three different language types: those in which the grammatical category is expressed by no morphemes, those in which it is expressed by one morpheme and those in which it is expressed by two morphemes. However, there is theoretically no end to the number of language types that could be described in this way: one would have to add a type for constructions expressed by three morphemes, four morphemes, etc. A better way of classifying language types for the purpose of markedness patterns is necessary. (Incidentally, this also demonstrates that the first step in typological analysis, defining the logically possible language types, is not a mechanical process.) The intuition behind markedness is that what is relevant is whether or not the plural, the comparative degree, etc., are expressed by *more* morphemes than the singular, the simple degree, etc. The relevant logically possible language types therefore number three:

1 the number of morphemes for the marked value exceeds that for the unmarked value;
2 the number of morphemes for the marked and unmarked values are the same;
3 the number of morphemes for the unmarked value exceeds that for the marked value.

The third type is the type excluded by a markedness relationship.

In this formulation of the markedness relationship, the basic resemblance to implicational universals still remains. That is, although more than one language type is possible, at least one type is not attested. As with implicational universals, this fact can be confirmed only by cross-linguistic comparison. Nothing about the expression of English singular and plural tells us that the expression of singular and plural by the same number of morphemes is possible but expression of the plural by fewer morphemes than the singular is not. In fact, however, the simpler formulation of markedness in terms of an implicational relationship between the presence vs. the absence of a relevant morpheme will suffice for the majority of cases encountered, and it will only be in the case of complex syntactic constructions that use of the more complex but more accurate formulation of markedness will be necessary.

4.3 Criteria for markedness

The preceding section illustrated some basic characteristics of markedness as it is used in typology: the cross-linguistic basis of typological markedness, and the constraint on attested language types. The cross-linguistic pattern represents a relationship between the values "singular" and "plural" in the grammatical category of number and the relative number of morphemes used to express those values. Markedness, like harmony, dominance/heaviness and mobility in word-order universals, is a much broader and deeper pattern than the one implicational universal we have used suggests. First, the same constraint applies to many more categories than that of number. Marking theory hypothesizes that the marked–unmarked relationship holding for any grammatical category, say active vs. passive, is of the same type as that holding for singular vs. plural – that is to say, we are dealing with the same typological phenomenon in every grammatical category in which it is manifested. More important, markedness is a broader concept, because it links together several other cross-linguistic patterns in addition to the relative number of morphemes. To say that one value in a grammatical category is marked and the other is unmarked subsumes a whole set of cross-linguistic patterns which (should) all behave in the same way, that is every pattern should select the same value as the unmarked value. These patterns are the **criteria** of markedness.

The most exhaustive summary and discussion of the linguistic properties found by linguists to be relevant to markedness in both phonology and morphosyntax is a monograph by Joseph Greenberg (1966b). He enumerates thirteen criteria for markedness: five for phonological categories and eight for morphosyntactic categories. The markedness properties discussed there are as follows (page references are in parentheses):[3]

Phonology

P1   In neutralized contexts, the unmarked value is realized, not the marked one (12–13).

P2   In text counts, the unmarked value has at least as great frequency as the marked value (14).

P3   The unmarked value has at least as wide a distribution across phonological environments as the marked value (21).

P4   The unmarked value has at least as great a variety of allophonic variants as the marked value (21).

P5   There are at least as many phonemes with the unmarked feature as the number of phonemes with the marked feature (21–2).

Morphosyntax

S1   The surface realization of the unmarked vs. marked value is frequently that of zero vs. nonzero morpheme (more generally: the realization of the marked value will involve at least as many morphemes as the realization of the unmarked value) (26–7).

S2   The marked member will display syncretization of its inflectional possibilities with respect to the unmarked member (that is, there will be at least as many distinct forms in the paradigm with the unmarked value as in the paradigm with the marked value) (27).

S3   The form that normally refers to the unmarked value will refer to either value in certain contexts ("facultative" use); the "par excellence" use of the unmarked term for the supercategory including the marked and unmarked term, e.g. *man*, may also be included here (28, 25).

S4   In certain grammatical environments, only the unmarked value will appear (contextual neutralization) (28–9).

S5   An unmarked form will have at least as many allomorphs or paradigmatic irregularities as the marked form (29).

S6   An unmarked form will display at least as great a range of grammatical behavior as that of the marked form (defectivation) (29–30).

S7   (Grammatical number only) The plural form of the unmarked gender is used to refer to collections consisting of objects of both genders ("dominance") (30–1).

S8   In text counts, the unmarked value will be at least as frequent as the marked value (31).

Some of these criteria cluster together, as Greenberg himself noted in a number of places in his monograph. In this section, I will argue that they fall into four broad criteria, three of which occur in both phonology and morphosyntax, as listed in table 4.1.[4]

Table 4.1 *Standard criteria for markedness (based on Greenberg 1966b)*

	Phonology	Morphosyntax
Structural	(see below)	zero value (S1)
Behavioral		
Inflectional	number of phonemes (P5); number of allophones (P4)	syncretization (S2); number of allomorphs (S5); defectivation (S6)
Distributional	number of environments (P3)	(not discussed by Greenberg)
Frequency	frequency (P2)	frequency (S8)
Neutral value	neutralization (P1)	facultative use (S3); contextual neutralization (S4); "dominance" (S7)

4.3.1   *Structure*

The structural criterion of markedness is the one referred to by S1 in the preceding list. It is the best-known criterion for markedness in typology. Nevertheless, it is actually of somewhat limited application – for example, we cannot say which of the word orders RelN or NRel is marked on structural criteria – and possibly cannot be applied to phonology. Hence, it is a mistake to identify markedness solely with structural markedness.

The definition of the structural criterion of markedness is quite straightforward and has already been provided in the discussion of the relationship between markedness and implicational universals:

> *Structure*: the marked value of a grammatical category will be expressed by at least as many morphemes as is the unmarked value of that category.

This definition has a structure which will recur in the definitions of behavioral and frequency criteria. First, the markedness pattern is characterized as a relation between the two values, marked and unmarked. One cannot determine the markedness status of, for example, the singular in English without also examining the plural. Second, the actual linguistic phenomenon which is used to identify markedness is a relative measure of quantity. The actual process of determining the markedness patterns of values of a given category involves counting morphemes of the two values and comparing how many morphemes are involved. These features will be crucial in the extensions to classical marking theory to be described in chapters 5 and 6.

The important and sometimes difficult question that must be answered in finding evidence for structural markedness is whether or not the morphemes being counted really are there to signal the category whose markedness is under examination. For example, in comparing the simple and comparative degrees of adjectives, we counted the suffix *-er* and the particle *than* but not the copula verb, thus arriving at the total number of morphemes signalling the comparative construction as two. The decision regarding the comparative suffix should be uncontroversial, while the choices for the other two morphemes require some additional argument. The copula is not a signal of the comparative construction, but rather a signal of the predicative function of the adjective (and indeed it demonstrates that words denoting properties are marked in that function compared to words denoting actions; see chapter 6). The comparative construction can occur with a modifying adjective, and in that case the copula is of course absent but both of the other morphemes are present: *a man taller than John, a taller man than John.* The argument for including the particle *than* depends on the status of the additional noun phrase governed by *than* which is added by the meaning of the comparative. The Yoruba example illustrates that it is not necessary to have a particle or adposition when the additional noun phrase is introduced, hence I take the particle as helping to signify the comparative construction rather than (or as well as) introducing the additional noun phrase. Needless to say, fairly sophisticated argumentation is required to determine exactly what a morpheme signifies in many cases, and in a number of cases the answer is controversial, or perhaps simply indeterminate (for example, does the auxiliary verb in the English passive help to signal the passive construction, or is it just a copula verb as with adjectives?).

In addition to the problem of determining what the functions of the morphemes in a construction actually are, there are also difficulties in counting how many morphemes are involved due to processes that have obscured or eliminated morpheme boundaries. These processes are fusion, suppletion, ablaut and reduplication.

Fusion occurs when a single morpheme denotes several different values from several different categories. For example, in the Spanish form *habló* 'he, she spoke,' the suffix *-ó* indicates third person (vs. e.g. first person *hablé* 'I spoke'), singular (vs. plural *hablaron* 'they spoke'), past (vs. present *habla* 'he speaks'), aorist (vs. imperfective *hablaba* 'he was speaking') and indicative (vs. [past] subjunctive *hablara* '(if) he had spoken'). If one were, for instance, attempting to determine the markedness of past as opposed to present, how many morphemes would be counted here? The solution is to count one morpheme, because one is evaluating the markedness of just one category, that of tense, and the other values associated with the morpheme in question are not relevant to that category. In the Spanish example, all of the contrasting forms involve nonzero morphemes. Frequently, however, there is a "zero form" which involves more than one category. For example, in Ngalakan, an Australian language of Arnhem Land, there is a zero form for third-person singular animate (masculine or feminine) subject (Merlan 1983:82):

(2) ŋugu- jawoṇ -ṇowi ∅-   ṛabo   guṇmąṇ? yukaji?
     MASC- friend -his 3SGMASC- went.PAST-PUNCT maybe   forever
     'Maybe his friend went away forever.'

Should this be taken as evidence for the unmarked status of third person, singular, animate, or all of the above? The answer is all of the above: when evaluating one category, the other categories are not relevant to the one in question. In fact, in the Ngalakan case the only opportunity for zero expression is when all three of the categories fused in the morpheme have their unmarked values;[5] this is a common phenomenon.

74

Suppletion occurs when there is no relation between the two forms related in a morphological paradigm. For example, the comparative degree of the English adjective *bad*, *worse*, cannot be related synchronically to the simple degree form. Hence, it cannot be treated as a combination of the simple degree form plus some additional morpheme. Both the comparative and simple forms involve one morpheme. There is a temptation to subsume this instance of suppletion under the vast number of English adjectives in which a second morpheme indicating comparison is added to the adjective (either a suffix *-er* or the particle *more*). However, this kind of one-for-one suppletion cannot be used to add to the evidence provided by regular forms, since the number of morphemes in both present and past tense forms is the same: one.[6]

In ablaut, as in suppletion, one cannot identify an "additional" morpheme. However, the two forms are closely related in that one is the same as the other except for some internal phonological alternation. The question that must be answered is whether or not one can say that a morpheme was *added* to one form to yield another form. In the case of ablaut, this cannot generally be asserted: synchronically, it is impossible to say that *sang* involves the addition of something to *sing*, or that *mice* involves the addition of something to *mouse*.[7]

Reduplication involves the addition of phonological material to a morpheme, but by copying some or all of the original morpheme in a more or less predictable manner. Reduplication shares some features with independent morphemes, namely that it represents a continuous piece of phonological material that is outside the root. For that reason, a reduplicated form may be considered to involve two morphemes, the root and the reduplication. On the other hand, the reduplication is by no means an independent morpheme from the root, and it does not occur separated from the root by any other morpheme. Finally, it may be that the phenomenon of reduplication ought to be given a direct external explanation in iconic terms (see chapter 7), not related to the phenomenon of markedness at all.

The question arises as to whether the structural criterion of markedness can be applied in phonology. This was indeed one of Trubetzkoy's original criteria for phonological markedness. The argument for structural markedness was that the production of the marked phonemes involved more articulatory gestures than the production of their unmarked counterparts. The difficulty here has been that to argue that a phonetic feature has been "added" means decomposing the articulation of a phoneme and its acoustic structure in such a way that one can assert that an articulation and/or an acoustic feature is really *not there*, rather than simply being different. This seems to be possible, since producing a phoneme clearly involves many articulatory gestures, but considerably more phonetic research is necessary to establish this fact for specific phonemes.

A more serious problem is whether the number of articulations for a phoneme is the proper analogue for zero morphosyntactic expression. Greenberg did not think so:

Zero expression involves the relation between content, the grammatical or semantic category involved, and expression, in this case the lack of overt sound sequences. At this point the fundamental difference between the phonological and grammatical level asserts itself, the sound–meaning relationship which is absent in the former and present in the latter. (Greenberg 1966b:62–3)

Jakobson's extension of Trubetzkoy's model assumes that the proper analogy is: the number of morphemes is to the concept expressed as the number of articulations is to the phoneme expressed. This analogy suggests some sort of mental reality to the phoneme, and also ignores the acoustical aspect of the structural complexity of phonemes. It seems that although the concept of structural markedness in phonology may make sense, it will require the resolution of a number of controversial issues.

In conclusion, it is worth noting that the difficulties with determining formal aspects of the structural criterion of markedness are a greater problem in morphological categories, while the difficulties in determining the function of morphemes is a greater problem in syntactic constructions. Finally, one must note that the structural criterion is founded on the linguistic structure of the phenomenon in question – the number of morphemes – and not the physical structure – the length of the morphemes. One cannot extend the structural criterion to the physical length of morphemes (beyond zero, of course). Although there is a general tendency for morphemes indicating unmarked values to be shorter forms than those indicating marked values, many examples demonstrate the mismatch between physical length and markedness. For example, the Spanish first-person plural agreement morpheme as in *hablamos* "we speak" is longer than the second-person form *habláis*, but this does not fit in with most other evidence for person markedness, by which first person is less marked than second person.

4.3.2   *Behavior*

The behavioral criteria, along with the frequency criteria, are the most general and important criteria for markedness. The behavioral criteria are the primary source of evidence for markedness within the language structure, and are of universal applicability in both phonology and morphosyntax. Half of the criteria from Greenberg 1966b can be described as behavioral, and even some of the neutral-value criteria may turn out to be behavioral ones (see 4.3.4).

The behavioral criteria are any sort of evidence from the linguistic behavior of the elements in question that would demonstrate that one element is grammatically more "versatile" than the other, and hence is unmarked compared to the other. The universal applicability of behavioral criteria follows from the fact that any linguistic element has a linguistic behavior – in fact, at a very general level the goal of linguistics is to characterize the behavior of linguistic elements.

The behavioral criteria can be divided into two general types, roughly the morphological criteria and the syntactic ones; there are phonological analogues to both of these types. The morphological criterion, which I will call the **inflectional** criterion, pertains to the number of morphological distinctions that a particular grammatical category possesses. The phonological analogue is the number of phonemes or allophones that a phonological feature is found in. The syntactic criterion, which I will call **distributional**, pertains to the number of syntactic contexts in which a grammatical element can occur. The phonological analogue is the number of phonological environments in which the phoneme or feature can occur.

4.3.2.1   Inflectional behavior

The inflectional criterion can be illustrated for the categories singular and plural with the third-person pronouns of English (Greenberg [1966b:27] calls this "syncretization"):

	Singular	Plural
Masculine	he	they
Feminine	she	they
Neuter	it	they

This chart is intended to represent the expression of particular combinations of features of number and gender, and lists all of the logical possibilities. There is a clear asymmetry in the chart in that the singular has three distinct forms for the three genders, whereas the plural has only one form covering all three genders. In other words, the category "singular" manifests a three-way morphological distinction of gender but the category "plural" does not. The singular has a greater number of distinctions than the plural, and hence is unmarked; conversely, the plural has fewer morphological distinctions and is therefore marked.

There are a number of observations that can be made about the information in the chart. First, the inflectional-behavioral criterion provides us with evidence for the markedness relationship between singular and plural that is not evidence under the structural criterion, since the plural forms are suppletive. This demonstrates the greater power and applicability of the behavioral criteria. Second, this pattern is only one of the language types allowed by the inflectional criterion. The inflectional criterion allows for languages in which the same gender distinctions are found in both singular and plural. The language type predicted not to occur is a language with gender distinctions in the plural but not in the singular.[8] Third, this evidence agrees with the structural evidence for the markedness of the plural in common nouns. The concord between structural and behavioral (and also frequency) criteria illustrates the pervasive nature of markedness patterns in the grammar.

Finally, the evidence here does not tell us anything about the markedness relationship of gender, only of number. In order to find behavioral evidence for markedness patterns among the gender categories, one would compare the rows rather than the columns. However, in every row there are two distinct forms, the singular and the plural form. Each gender has the same number of singular–plural distinctions (namely two), hence the inflectional-behavioral evidence is neutral with respect to the markedness of any gender category. In addition, the singular gender forms are all suppletive, and so one cannot use the structural criteria to determine markedness either.

The difference between structural and (inflectional-) behavioral evidence for markedness is straightforward, at least in theory. If one is looking for structural evidence for the markedness pattern of values in a grammatical category, one must compare the values to each other and count morphemes. If one is looking for inflectional-behavioral evidence for the markedness pattern of values in a grammatical category, one must look at other categories orthogonal to the category in question and count morphological distinctions.

The use of the inflectional criteria for markedness involves the comparison of the number of morphological distinctions found for two related categories, for example singular and plural. Given that many morphological categories are multivalued, for example the many case or tense inflections found in natural languages, the definition of the inflectional criteria will require the relative quantitative language that we used in defining the structural criteria:

> *Behavior (inflectional)*: if the marked value has a certain number of distinct forms in an inflectional paradigm, then the unmarked value will have at least as many distinct forms in the same paradigm.

An example of an inflectional behavioral distinction that is *not* evidence for the markedness of one category over another is the use of distinct inflectional sets for distinct classes of words. For example, as table 4.2 shows, the masculine nouns *tēvs* 'father' and *brālis* 'brother' in Latvian fall into two different declensional classes, each taking different inflections in some or all of the cases (Lazdiņa 1966:292).

Table 4.2 *Declension of Latvian* tēvs *'father' and* brālis *'brother'*

Singular			Plural		
Nom.	tēvs	brālis	Nom.	tēvi	brāļi
Gen.	tēva	brāļa	Gen.	tēvu	brāļu
Dat.	tēvam	brālim	Dat./Inst.	tēviem	brāļliem
Acc./Inst.	tēvu	brāli	Acc.	tēvus	brāļus
Loc.	tēvā	brālī	Loc.	tēvos	brāļos

However, one cannot argue that the *tēvs* declension class is more (or less) marked than the *brālis* declension class, because, although the inflectional forms are distinct, the number of inflectional distinctions remains the same. Distinct inflectional forms do not imply any grammatical asymmetry, and asymmetry is the source of markedness patterns.

An intermediate case between the legitimate criterion of lack of inflection and the illegitimate one of two separate but equal inflectional patterns is a distinction between a morphological and a syntactic expression of the category. For example, one may contrast the inflectional (morphological) passive of Latin, found in the present system of tenses, to the periphrastic (syntactic) passive, found in the perfect system, as in the first-person singular indicative forms of the first conjugation verb *amāre* (Gildersleeve & Lodge 1895:74–5):

79

Present system		*Perfect system*	
Present	amo-r	Perfect	amātus sum
Imperfect	amāba-r	Pluperfect	amātus eram
Future	amābo-r	Future Perfect	amātus erō

In this case, the same grammatical distinction is made (active vs. passive), but in the present system it is made morphologically and in the perfect system it is made syntactically. The distinction between morphological and syntactic expression of a relevant construction can be taken as evidence in favor of the unmarkedness of the form taking the inflection, because the form taking the periphrastic can be considered to be inflectionally defective (i.e. the perfect tenses do not inflect themselves for passive, instead they take an auxiliary).[9]

A similar argument may be used to consider a root that has suppletive inflectional forms to be less marked than a root which takes regular inflections. For example, one can state that the English pronouns (other than *you*, which is an exceptional case) are less marked than the nouns, since their plurals are suppletive.[10] This can be generalized to the assertion that greater allomorphy or morphological irregularity of any type, not just suppletion, is evidence for the unmarkedness of the category in question (see Greenberg 1966b:29).

The phenomenon corresponding to inflectional behavior in phonology is the occurrence of gaps in segment inventories at the phonemic or allophonic level. A typical example of this is that the number of nasal vowels is always smaller than the number of oral vowels (Ferguson 1966:58). A brief glance through Ruhlen's catalogue of segment inventories (Ruhlen 1976) strongly suggests that the number of nasal consonant phonemes is always smaller than the number of oral consonants, yielding the hypothesis that nasality is marked overall in comparison to orality. The greatest problem in determining markedness patterns by gaps or irregularities in segment inventories is determining what type of segment to include. For example, in a number of languages the velar nasal η is considered to be absent from a segment inventory because it is not a phoneme of the language, but it may actually be present in the language as an allophone. The probable solution to this problem is carefully to separate phonemic from allophonic inventories in evaluating gaps in segment inventories. Presumably phoneme inventories will display more gaps than allophone inventories but those gaps that do exist in allophone inventories will not contradict the markedness evidence from phoneme inventories. This, of course, requires that we can distinguish phonemes from allophones, that is separate the "basic" allophonic forms that will be used in the phoneme inventories from the "nonbasic" ones that will be discarded.[11] This problem will arise again with the distributional criterion.

4.3.2.2   Distributional behavior

The second type of behavioral criterion is the distributional criterion.[12] This involves determining the number of environments in which the linguistic elements in question occur. The element which occurs in a larger number of constructions is the less marked one. We can illustrate this with a well-known example concerning the category of voice in English. Most transitive verbs occur in both the active and the passive voice. However, there are a number of verbs which occur in the active voice but do not occur (at least not without some degree of unacceptability) in the passive voice; and there are certain constructions which occur with the active voice but not with the passive voice:

(3a)   My brother bought this cabin.
(3b)   This cabin was bought by my brother.
(4a)   That cloud resembles a fish.
(4b)   *A fish is resembled by that cloud.
(5a)   Fred killed himself.
(5b)   *Himself was killed by Fred.

If we consider co-occurrence with *buy*, co-occurrence with *resemble* and co-occurrence with a reflexive object as three contexts for the active and passive voice, then we find that the active voice occurs in all three contexts while the passive voice occurs in only one. On that evidence, we would consider the passive voice marked and the active voice unmarked.

Of course, a proper analysis would examine the full range of contexts in which the active and the passive are found. This process is quite difficult in syntax, but if we can make the stronger claim that the contexts in which the marked member is found is a (possibly proper) subset of the contexts in which the unmarked member is found, then an exhaustive enumeration of contexts is not necessary.

However, there do exist examples of passives in English without obvious active counterparts (*be rumored*, *be born*, if one does not accept *bear* "give birth"). These examples suggest weakening the distributional criterion to merely "no more contexts than" instead of "a subset of." This renders the criterion too weak in at least one important respect. Let us say that we allow this weaker version. The extreme case of that would be complementary distribution. The major difficulty is determin-

ing how to count contexts so that we could say that the number of contexts
in which one element is found is more than the number of contexts
in which another element was found. Some independent means for individuating and counting morphosyntactic contexts is required. This may
be possible, though it does not yet exist. On the other hand, if one
set of contexts is a proper subset of the other, then it is clear that the
former set of contexts is smaller in number than the latter, no matter
how one counts contexts.

The strong version of the distributional criterion is as follows:

> *Behavior (distributional)*: if the marked value occurs in a certain
> number of distinct grammatical contexts (construction types), then
> the unmarked value will also occur in at least those contexts that
> the marked value occurs in.

The phonological counterpart to the distributional behavioral criterion
is the distribution of sounds in phonological environments. This is a
syntagmatic property, concerning the collocations of sounds, in contrast
to the paradigmatic one of gaps in segment inventories. Phonotactics
is an important source of data for distributional phonological markedness. For example, in Wintu plain (unglottalized) stops occur in word-
and syllable-initial and final positions, but glottalized stops and fricatives
occur only in word- and syllable-initial, prevocalic position (Pitkin
1984:26–7), supporting the general pattern that stops are less marked
than fricatives and unglottalized consonants are less marked than glottalized ones.[13]

There are two basic reasons why the distribution of a marked category
value would be more limited (or "defective") in comparison with the
corresponding unmarked value. The first is no obvious reason at all;
it just appears to be an arbitrary fact about the language. For example,
in Quiché there is distributional evidence that a process verb is unmarked
compared to a stative verb. Process verbs take the tense–aspect inflectional prefixes *k-* and *š-* and stative verbs do not. There is no apparent
reason for this, since there is no semantic incompatibility between the
inflectional prefixes (which denote "present" and "past" respectively)
and stativity, and in fact in a language like English stative predicates
do inflect for tense. It is simply a grammatical fact regarding the expression of stative predicates in Quiché. As such, it provides very strong
evidence for the markedness of stative predicates compared to process
predicates.

The second reason is that there is some semantic incompatibility
between the grammatical category in question and the construction in

which it is not found. In English, for instance, stative predicates are
not found in the progressive construction, because the latter construction
requires process predicates.[14] Another example of defective distribution
due to semantic incompatibility is the inability of mass nouns to occur
in plural constructions in English and other languages.[15] Although these
are irregularities in distribution due to semantic factors, this type of
evidence still supports the markedness of stative predicates and mass
nouns, if one accepts the external basis of cross-linguistic comparison.

A brief digression into the functional explanation behind markedness
patterns is necessary here. Behavioral markedness involves irregularities
in the interaction of morphosyntactic categories and constructions. The
unmarked values in those categories are the prototypical members of
those categories. The constructions that act as indicators of markedness
of categories (e.g. the progressive construction and the inflectional category of number) pertain to the unmarked members of the categories,
and may not be semantically compatible with the marked members of
the category. The constructions were, so to speak, "designed" for the
unmarked members of the categories, in this case process predicates
and count nouns. If one accepts this functional explanation, then the
cases of semantic incompatibility are perfectly acceptable evidence for
markedness.

In addition to these intralinguistic means for using behavioral criteria
to evaluate markedness patterns, there is a cross-linguistic technique
as well. We may define the cross-linguistic technique by substituting
the phrase "language types" for "construction types" in the definition
of the distributional criteria:[16]

> *Behavior (cross-linguistic)*: if the marked value occurs in a certain
> number of distinct language types (represented by some orthogo-
> nal typology), then the unmarked value will occur in at least the
> language types that the marked value occurs in.

For example, the dual number is marked in contrast with the plural
since the number of languages that have a dual number category is a
proper subset of the number of languages that have a plural number
category. This fact can also be phrased as an implicational universal:
"If a language has the category of dual, then it also has the category
of plural." This is Greenberg's Universal 34 (Greenberg 1966a:94). In
fact, virtually all of Greenberg's universals that do not have to do with
word order (Universals 29 through 45), are markedness relationships
among morphological categories.

Returning to the word-order universals, it can be seen that the cross-linguistic behavioral criterion is simply the concept of dominance in another guise. Consider the implicational universal "NDem implies NRel." This can be described by the following tetrachoric table, in which "X" indicates there are languages of this type and " – " indicates that no languages of this type occur.

	NRel	RelN
DemN	X	X
NDem	X	–

The dominant types in an implicational universal "P implies Q" are ~P and Q, in this case, DemN and NRel. Those are the two types which have exactly the wider distribution in terms of language types. DemN occurs in languages with both RelN and NRel word orders, while NDem occurs only in languages with NRel word order. Likewise, NRel occurs in languages with both DemN and NDem word orders, while RelN occurs only in languages with DemN word orders. Thus, the cross-linguistic distribution of DemN by relative-clause order-type is wider than that of NDem, and so by the distributional criteria DemN is unmarked and NDem is marked; likewise for NRel and RelN. This is exactly the same pattern as dominance, and demonstrates that the concept of dominance can be subsumed under markedness (harmony will be discussed in chapter 6).

4.3.3 *Frequency*

The frequency criteria are straightforwardly taken here from Greenberg's work. They require measuring the frequency of occurrence of the value in question in actual language use ("textual") and across language. Like the behavioral criteria, the frequency criteria are of universal applicability: the frequency of any linguistic element can be determined. Unlike behavior, however, frequency is not found in language structure. The textual-frequency criterion, in particular, demonstrates the important role of quantitative text analysis in providing evidence for linguistic analysis and in corroborating (or questioning) linguistic patterns that can be arrived at by internal structural means. The textual-frequency criterion shows a direct connection between properties of language structure and properties of language use (or, as some put it, "competence" and "performance"), and strongly suggests that these two should not be separated as much as they are in most current theories.

The statement of the textual-frequency criterion follows the same pattern as the statement of the structural and behavioral criteria:

> *Frequency (textual)*: if a marked value occurs a certain number of times in frequency in a given text sample, then the unmarked value will occur at least as many times in a comparable text sample.

Greenberg's monograph on marking theory (1966b) contains many text counts of both phonological and morphosyntactic categories to corroborate the markedness patterns of those categories found by structural and behavioral criteria. For example, in 1,000-phoneme text counts of glottalized vs. unglottalized consonants in Hausa, Klamath, Coos, Yurok, Chiricahua and Maidu, Greenberg found that the percentage of glottalized consonants ranged from 7.8 to 19 percent – clear textual evidence for the markedness of glottalized consonants (Greenberg 1966b:15–17).

Before turning to text sampling and counting issues, it should be pointed out that just as with the behavioral criteria, there is a cross-linguistic version of the textual-frequency criterion, which can be phrased as follows:

> *Frequency (cross-linguistic)*: if a marked value occurs in a certain number of languages in a given language sample, then the unmarked value will occur in at least as many languages in a comparable language sample.

In other words, the absolute cross-linguistic frequency of a linguistic type will provide evidence for the markedness of that type. Examples of this are the dominance (heaviness) word-order patterns found by Greenberg and Hawkins. In the last section, I pointed out that the dominant word order is the unmarked word order. If this is true, then the unmarked word order (the dominant one) should also be the more frequent one in absolute cross-linguistic terms. This is generally true, as is illustrated for selected word-order patterns in table 4.3 (however, the figures for VO, NA for Hawkins, and GN are probably not statistically significant).

It is important to note that the behavioral unmarkedness of these word orders, which states that the unmarked orders occur in a larger number of language types, does not logically imply that the behaviorally unmarked word orders will necessarily occur in more languages. Consider again the example "NDem implies NRel," which means that DemN will occur in both RelN and NRel languages, but NDem will occur in only NRel languages. NDem languages could still outnumber DemN languages if the following situation held:

Table 4.3 *Cross-linguistic frequency of dominant word orders*

Dominant word order	Frequency (dominant) (%)	Source
SV	86	Tomlin 1986 (n = 402)
VO	54	Tomlin 1986 (n = 402)
SO	96	Tomlin 1986 (n = 402)
DemN	63	Hawkins 1983:96, 100 (n = 158)
NumN	68	Hawkins 1983:96, 100 (n = 147)
NRel	69	Hawkins 1983:96, 100 (n = 163)
NA	55	Hawkins 1983:96, 100 (n = 350)
	64	Dryer 1988 (n = 287)
GN (?)	53	Hawkins 1983:96, 100 (n = 348)

	NRel	RelN
DemN	30	30
NDem	80	–

In this situation, NDem occurs in eighty languages and DemN occurs in only sixty languages (see Greenberg 1966a:97). This example demonstrates that this situation can arise even when the intersecting order, NRel/RelN, does obey the cross-linguistic frequency criterion: NRel occurs in 110 languages while RelN, the marked order, occurs in only thirty. Hence the fact that DemN is indeed more common than NDem is an independent piece of evidence supporting the unmarkedness of DemN.

The question now arises, does every implicational universal represent an instance of markedness? This is equivalent to saying that the dominant categories in an implicational universal will always turn out to be more frequent, since dominance itself verifies the behavioral unmarkedness of the categories. This is also a plausible conjecture which requires more studies for confirmation.

Of course, in doing cross-linguistic frequency tests the issue of a large, unbiased sample, discussed in chapter 1, becomes much more acute. Hawkins' samples are large but biased. Tomlin's study is large and well distributed, but, by virtue of its size, there are many instances of non-independent phenomena. Nevertheless, Tomlin's percentages corroborate well with what other, smaller studies have indicated. Dryer (1985) has attempted to correct for bias in his study of adjective order, arguing that previous studies suggesting that there is no dominance relation for adjective order (e.g. Ruhlen 1976) reflected an Asian areal bias. Dryer counted low-level language families (equivalent to the level of Romance) as well as individual languages. The word-order percentages for families are 47 percent NA, 33 percent AN, and 20 percent both orders. Ironically, examining Dryer's individual language numbers yields a stronger bias towards NA order (64 percent). This is especially impressive since Dryer's sample has a disproportionately large number of individual languages that are SOV; this would be expected to bias his study towards AN, not NA order. In sum, most of the figures given in table 4.3 must be taken with a grain of salt, but they represent first steps in a potentially powerful area of confirmation or disconfirmation of cross-linguistic generalizations (see Schwartz 1980).

The correspondence of the results of the frequency criteria and the behavioral criteria provides further evidence that the phenomenon of dominance is actually a markedness pattern. This result is important for two reasons. First, it demonstrates a strong connection between implicational universals of word order and markedness. In fact, it suggests a relationship between all types of implicational universals and markedness, in that any universal "P implies Q" will yield a dominance pattern of "not P" and "Q" and hence the hypothesis that "not P" and "Q" are unmarked. Second, it demonstrates a way in which markedness can be extended to characterize relationships among linguistic forms in which the structural criterion of markedness can play no part. There is no way in which AN word order can be said to be more or less structurally marked than NA word order, and this is in general true of word-order facts. The behavioral and frequency criteria of markedness are more important than the structural criterion precisely because they are universally applicable.

There are some precautions that must be heeded in establishing the textual-frequency criterion. A good text-sample must be obtained, one that is large and representative of the textual styles used in the language. Generally, one attempts to use the "unmarked" text style, that is, conversation or oral narrative, rather than written genres. One reason for doing this is that studies (e.g. Greenberg & O'Sullivan 1974) have indicated that the textual frequencies for certain "marked" categories increase in formal and written styles, and hence, they are not such reliable indicators of correlations between text frequency and other markedness criteria. (Actually, what this really indicates is that there is a correlation between informal, oral style and some, if not all, unmarked categories.)

Another important question that must be addressed is how exactly to count the linguistic elements or constructions in question. This can be illustrated by a problem manifested in Greenberg's text counts for the category of person (Greenberg 1966b:45). The text counts indicate that the third person is of much greater frequency than first or second person, while the first person is of greater frequency than the second person. This would yield a relative statement of markedness that third person is less marked than first person which in turn is less marked than second person, or in shorthand third < first < second. Other data, to be presented in chapter 5, imply a hierarchy first < second < third. If this is the case, how does one account for the frequency data? A possible answer to this is that Greenberg's count of third-person forms included a large variety of third-person subjects: pronouns, proper names and common nouns. This is simply a count of all third-person forms regardless of word class. We could instead count all occurrences of individual words, that is count all occurrences of "I," "you," "he," "John," "the dog," etc. separately. Then it will in all probability indicate a higher frequency of the first- and second-person *pronouns* over any single third-person form, even if all the third-person forms added together outnumbered "I" and "you."

The next question, then, is when to count what. In the preceding example with the category of person, it is most plausible to count individual words when determining the markedness of the independent pronouns, since in so doing one is actually counting occurrences of those pronouns. If, on the other hand, the markedness of verb agreement is being examined, then counting all third-person subject noun-phrases together is more plausible, since the third-person agreement marker does not distinguish between pronouns and common nouns, or between occurrences of tokens of pronouns and common nouns. As such, the frequency data would be in harmony with the structural evidence that third-person (singular) agreement is zero.

A comparable problem in counting units in phonology would be the following hypothetical example: in counting glottalized vs. unglottalized consonants, should one use the total frequencies of all the glottalized consonants as against the unglottalized ones, or should one examine the frequencies of each glottalized consonant against its unglottalized counterpart? The former method will probably suffice to capture the relationship between "glottalized" and "unglottalized," whereas the latter would be useful in examining possible correlations between glottalization and specific places and manners of articulation.

Unfortunately, most available text-frequency counts are not adequate to a proper study. One problem is that they are generally based on written rather than oral language. Their main problem is, however, that they give the frequencies of forms but not functions. For example, one will not be able to distinguish the passive as opposed to the predicative uses of English *be* since the same form is used. Some frequency counts do not give the different inflectional forms of words, rendering them useless for studying the markedness of those inflectional categories. These shortcomings limit their usefulness but do not entirely eliminate them as tools, depending on what phenomenon is under examination (see Schwartz 1980).

Finally, it should go without saying that the relative frequencies of forms should be demonstrated to be statistically significant. In the case of simple markedness patterns within a single grammatical category this is fairly straightforward; but in the case of the cross-categorial correlations described in chapter 6 the statistical tests will be more complex.

4.3.4   *Neutral value*

Although the neutral-value criteria are among the original criteria cited by Trubetzkoy and Jakobson, their status in the modern typological version of marking theory is not entirely clear. The neutral-value criteria are different from the structural, behavioral and frequency criteria in nature. The latter three all involve a relative quantitative measure of the grammatical properties of the marked and unmarked term: the unmarked member of the category has relatively fewer morphemes, relatively more versatile inflectional and distributional behavior and relatively greater text frequency than the marked member. The relative quantitative character of the three primary criteria is crucial in extending the applicability of markedness to hierarchies and cross-category correlations. The neutral-value criteria, on the other hand, cannot be so relativized. Either the neutral value is the unmarked one or not. These differences in theoretical structure suggest that the neutralization phenomena, or at least some of them, may actually be different from the markedness phenomena. Let us consider each of them in turn.

The one phonological criterion described by Greenberg that falls under the neutral-value criteria is the phenomenon of neutralized contexts, which dates back to Trubetzkoy's pioneering work (1969 [1939]). In neutralized contexts, only one of two possible feature-values is realized. The oft-repeated example is that of German word-final devoicing, in which *Bund* "bundle" is pronounced the same as *bunt* "colorful," namely, [bʊnt]. This criterion can be in part re-evaluated as a behavioral criterion of markedness. Essentially, the unmarked phonological feature is realized in more environments than the marked features, namely the contexts of neutralization. This is essentially the distributional type of behavioral markedness (see Gundel, Houlihan and Sanders 1986:114–16).

The difference between phonological neutralization and ordinary cases of behavioral markedness in phonological distribution is that a phonological alternation between two forms of the same word is involved: *Bund* [bʊnt] alternates with *Bunde* (plural) [bʊnd-ə]. This property defines the notion "neutralized context": in a context where the morphological form of the word suggests either phoneme may occur, in actuality only one does (in this case, [t]), even when the word form "requires" the other ([d]). In phonological theories allowing derivation from underlying forms, this alternation is captured by making the unmarked (non-neutralized) segment the underlying one and the marked one derived. We will leave aside the question of how the relationship between [d] and [t] in the inflection of *Bund* is to be captured in a thoroughgoing typological-phonological approach. What is of interest for us here is that the distribution of [t] and [d] in neutralized contexts is essentially a manifestation of the behavioral criterion.

The next criterion Greenberg discusses is the "facultative" use: the form that normally refers to the unmarked value will refer to either value in certain contexts. The common example is the use of English *man* to indicate either the male of the species or the species as a whole, including females. The facultative use does not always follow the markedness pattern, however. For example, English *they* is used to refer to unidentified individuals regardless of number, so that *They told me to sit down* can be used when only one individual told me to sit down.

This suggests that the plural is the neutral (unmarked) value, although the behavioral criterion (lack of gender distinctions) suggest that it is the marked value. However, this example can be explained in another way that suggests that at least some cases of facultative use are not part of a markedness pattern. The use of English *they* in question is an example of neutralization of gender as well as number. The English third-person plural, unlike the third-person singular, does not display a gender distinction. Hence, it is plausible to use *they* in this context because it is semantically the least specific of the third-person pronouns – in part precisely because it is the marked value.[17] Hence there are different reasons for the facultative employment of a form which are quite plausible explanations for its employment but go against the markedness pattern. Thus, it is likely that instances of facultative use must be evaluated separately before they can be determined to support (or undermine) a proposed markedness pattern.

Similar remarks apply to the phenomenon Greenberg calls "dominance" (not to be confused with the notion of dominance in implicational universals), in which the unmarked form is used in the plural to refer to collections consisting of objects of both the unmarked and marked type (usually two distinct genders). An example of this phenomenon is the use of the Spanish masculine plural pronoun *ellos* to indicate groups consisting of both men and women. This is another example of a form being employed for an intermediate category (e.g. masculine + feminine) for which there is no separate form. It probably ought to be interpreted behaviorally, in terms of distribution – a use which the unmarked form has but the marked form does not. It may, however, have to be interpreted with respect to the specific function it is used for.[18]

This leaves "contextual neutralization" in morphosyntax. This situation is exactly analogous to phonological neutralization: only one value occurs in some context, where both values are semantically and/or grammatically possible. The example that Greenberg gives is the use of the root (singular) form of the noun after all numerals in Turkish. On semantic grounds, one would expect singular after "one" and plural after other numbers, but in fact in this context only one form is found, the "singular." This example illustrates the morphosyntactic equivalent of the phonological neutralized context: semantics predicts that both forms should be able to occur, but there is only one form occurring, the "unmarked" form. This criterion can also be explained in terms of behavioral distribution in the same way, with the caveat once again that some sort of alternation or derivation is required when the marked form is expected (here, on semantic grounds) in the neutralized environment.

Thus, it appears that most cases of neutralization, in particular the classic cases of neutralization in certain phonological or morphosyntactic contexts, can be reinterpreted as examples of behavioral distribution. The remaining criteria, facultative use and "dominance," are perhaps distinct phenomena that often converge on the unmarked value but sometimes do not. More examples of these types of neutralization phenomena must be investigated in order to determine their relationship *vis-à-vis* markedness.

4.4 Conclusion

The many criteria for markedness proposed in the typological literature can be reduced to three general criteria (assuming that the elimination of the neutral-value criteria is valid), as follows:

1 *Structural*: number of morphemes used to express marked and unmarked values.
2 *Behavioral*:
   (a) *Inflectional*: number of cross-cutting distinctions/phonemes the marked and unmarked values contain;
   (b) *Distributional*: number of syntactic/phonological environments in which the marked and unmarked values occur;
   (c) *Cross-linguistic*: number of language types in which the marked and unmarked values occur.
3 *Frequency*:
   (a) *Textual*: number of occurrences of the marked and unmarked values in text;
   (b) *Cross-linguistic*: number of languages in which the marked and unmarked values are found.

All three of these criteria are phrased in terms of relative quantitative values, determined over morphemes to express the category in question, the morphosyntactic environments in which the values occur and the number of occurrences of individual instances of the category. The unmarked value has a smaller number of morphemes used to express the value and a greater inflectional range, grammatical and cross-linguistic distribution and textual and cross-linguistic frequency, than the marked value. Of these three criteria, the structural criterion is applicable to a subset of morphosyntactic phenomena only (albeit a large and important subset). The behavioral and the frequency criteria are the broadest, being applicable to the full range of both phonological and morphosyntactic phenomena, and hence are the fundamental manifestations of markedness.

We may summarize the basic markedness patterns of various grammatical categories enumerated by Greenberg, including hierarchies discussed by him but not correlations across categories:

Morphosyntactic features
Number (noun, pronoun, adjective, verb)
   singular < plural < dual < trial (31–7; U33–U35, U37, U45)
Gender (noun, adjective)
   masculine < feminine < neuter (38–40)
Grammatical relation (noun, adjective)
   subject < direct object < oblique (37–8, U38; see 5.3.2)
Degree (adjective)
   positive < comparative, superlative (40–1)
Size (adjective, noun)
   normal < augmentative, diminutive (41)
Numeral type (numerals)
   cardinal < ordinal (41; this is a simplification)

Numerals
  one < two < three < ... (42–4; excluding bases)
Person (verbal indexation/agreement)
  3 < 1 < 2 (42–4)
Tense (verbs)
  present < preterit < future (47–8; preterit status uncertain)
Aspect (verbs or verb phrases)
  imperfect < perfective (49)[19]
Mood (verbs or sentences)
  indicative < hypothetical (excluding imperative) (46–7)
Voice (verbs or verb phrases)
  active < passive, mediopassive (45–6)
Derivation (verbs)
  base < causative < other derivational forms (49–50)
Polarity (sentences or verbs)
  positive < negative
Direct speech-act type (sentences)
  declarative < interrogative[20]
Affix type (words in general)
  derivation < inflection (U29)
Inflectional categories (words in general)
  number < gender (U32, U36)
Inflectional categories (verbs only)
  tense–aspect–mood < person–number, gender agreement (U30)
NP type
  pronoun < common noun (51, U43)

Phonological features
Nasality (vowels)
  oral < nasal (18)
Length (vowels)
  short < long (19–20, but see 22 for exceptions)
Voice (vowels, sonants)
  voiced < unvoiced (24)
Voice (consonants)
  unvoiced < voiced (24)[21]
Glottalization (consonants)
  unglottalized < glottalized (15–17)
Aspiration (consonants)
  unaspirated < aspirated (15–17)
Palatalization (consonants)
  unpalatized < palatalized (20)

Notes: "X<Y" = "X is unmarked relative to Y"; "X<Y, Z" = "Y and Z are marked with respect to X but not with respect to each other." Page numbers refer to Greenberg 1966b; "U ... " to universals contained in Greenberg 1966a. The categories of case and person (agreement) will be discussed further in chapters 5 and

6. The phonological patterns are more tentative; for instance, a number of categories that Greenberg treats as binary are phonetically scalar. For evidence supporting these patterns, the reader is referred to Greenberg 1966a, 1966b.

Most, if not all, of these patterns are strikingly common and consistent in human languages (as noted above, the facts regarding certain patterns, particularly case and person, are more equivocal). Virtually every language has some irregularities or asymmetries in phonology and morphosyntax, and most of these irregularities can be attributed to markedness patterns. The primary value of markedness in typology is to explain asymmetries in linguistic behavior (including the asymmetric relationship of implicans and implicatum in implicational universals). Markedness also addresses the problem of the separation of language-universal from language-specific grammatical properties, demonstrating that many grammatical "irregularities" are actually manifestations of universal patterns. Some exceptions do occur, but a number of these can be accounted for by correlations across categories (see chapter 6). In fact, the extension of markedness to hierarchies and prototypes will allow a more complex interplay of different markedness patterns that will provide us with more subtle predictions of typological grammatical phenomena.

The final question is, why are the two phenomena of behavior and frequency (both intralinguistic and cross-linguistic), and in the case of some morphosyntactic categories, structure as well, correlated so strongly? Is there some explanation that we can offer which will link the markedness criteria together? This question will be deferred to chapter 7.

5
Grammatical hierarchies

5.1 Introduction

The notion of a grammatical hierarchy is conceptually quite simple, although it actually implies an important and fundamental change to classical (Prague School) marking theory. In the preceding chapter hierarchies were referred to on a number of occasions. In this section we will recapitulate the basic notion and describe the change in the concept of markedness it implies.

Consider the example used in chapter 4, the category of number. Typological evidence overwhelmingly indicates that the plural is marked while the singular is unmarked; for example, it is very difficult to find a language with a singular–plural distinction in which the singular is not expressed by a zero morpheme in contrast to a nonzero plural marker. The problem arises in the fact that the category of number involves not two values but three or more: singular, plural, dual and a trial or paucal (a small number). A language with the maximum number of number distinctions, including a paucal, is Manam (Lichtenberk 1983b:267; the -a- morpheme in the dual and paucal is a morphophonological "buffer"):

(1a) áine   ŋára -ø
      woman that -3SG
      'that woman'

(1b) áine   ŋára -di
      woman that -3PL
      'those women'

(1c) áine   ŋára -di -a   -ru
      woman that -3PL -BUFF -DUAL
      'those (two) women'

(1d) áine   ŋára -di -a   -to
      woman that -3PL -BUFF -PAUCAL
      'those (few) women'

If we examine the standard typological evidence for markedness, we find that in comparing the dual and plural, the dual is marked and the plural is unmarked (see 5.3.1). In the classical theory of markedness this leads to a paradox: on the one hand the evidence indicates that the plural is marked, but other evidence indicates that the plural is unmarked.

The solution to this problem is fairly obvious and quite simple. Instead of treating markedness as an *absolute* property of a value in a grammatical category, it is taken to be a *relative* property. The plural is marked relative to the singular, but unmarked relative to the dual; or as it is usually stated, the plural is more marked than the singular but less marked than the dual. Thus, the evidence for markedness implies the existence of a **scale** or **hierarchy** of markedness, not a set of two absolute values, "marked" and "unmarked." We will use the following notation for indicating hierarchies, seen already in the chart of markedness patterns at the end of chapter 4: singular < plural < dual < trial/paucal.[1]

The definitions of the markedness criteria in chapter 4 anticipated this extension of the concept of markedness to relative markedness. All of the criteria – structural, behavioral, frequency – were defined in terms of relative quantity: relative number of morphemes, inflectional distinctions, morphosyntactic environments, etc. Originally, however, the markedness criteria were not conceived of as quantitative scales. The evidence for markedness used by the Prague School was mostly binary: presence vs. absence of a morpheme, presence vs. absence of an inflectional distinction, presence vs. absence in a neutralized context.[2] However, in order to avoid the markedness paradox illustrated in the preceding paragraph, it is necessary to modify the definitions of markedness to represent scalar values, and this was done in chapter 4.[3]

The discussion of hierarchies in this section has presupposed that grammatical hierarchies are an extension of markedness patterns, not something conceptually different from markedness that happens to overlap with it to some extent. The rest of this chapter will investigate this hypothesis. The next section will analyze the relationship between grammatical hierarchies, implicational universals and markedness. The following sections will survey the grammatical and phonological hierarchies that have been discovered so far.

5.2 Hierarchies, implicational universals and markedness

Grammatical hierarchies in typology characterize patterns of cross-linguistic variation. That is, they predict or specify which language types do occur and which types do not occur. For example, the hierarchy singular < plural < dual < trial/paucal implies, among other things, that the following language types can be found:

1 languages with a single noun[4] form (which is used for singular, as well as everything else; these languages are said not to have the category of number);
2 languages with singular and plural forms for nouns;
3 languages with singular, dual and plural forms for nouns;
4 languages with singular, dual, trial/paucal and plural forms for nouns.

No other types should be found, according to this hierarchy.[5] This particular manifestation of the hierarchy can easily be expressed as a set of implicational universals, and in fact was so expressed as Universal 34 (Greenberg 1966a:94; rephrased here): If a language has a trial number, then it has a dual number. If a language has a dual, then it has a plural. (Also, if a language has a plural, then it has a singular.)

In general, a grammatical hierarchy covers a "chain" of implicational universals, so that the implicatum of the first universal is the implicans of the second, the implicatum of the second universal is the implicans of the third, and so on:

presence of trial/paucal ⊃ presence of dual
presence of dual ⊃ presence of plural
presence of plural ⊃ presence of singular

The various manifestations of grammatical hierarchies in typology can all be cast into the form of a "chained" set of implicational universals such as the one just given. Thus, a hierarchy, like dominance and harmony, can be thought of as a typological generalization over sets of implicational universals, that is, as a "broader" or "deeper" typological generalization than implicational universals. It allows implicational universals in one direction only, i.e. "trial/paucal implies dual implies plural implies singular." It also predicts the absence of implicational relationships in the reverse direction or in some scrambled order, such as "dual implies trial implies singular implies plural."

The chained set of implicational universals found in hierarchies causes a problem for the concept of dominance described in chapter 3. Dominance represents a generalization over implicational universals that the same grammatical property would be found in the implicatum, but not the implicans, of all implicational universals involving it. However, the very definition of hierarchies in terms of implicational universals means that the grammatical property in the implicatum of the first universal in the chain will be in the implicans of the next universal in the chain. Hence it appears to be dominant and recessive at the same time. This is exactly the same problem as we encountered with the plural being marked and unmarked at the same time. The solution is identical: alter the concept of *absolute* dominance to one of *relative* dominance. Indeed, this is exactly what we would expect if grammatical hierarchies were a species of markedness, since dominance is essentially another name for the cross-linguistic behavioral criterion for markedness. We now turn to the relation between hierarchies and markedness.

Normally, grammatical hierarchies in typology are represented as a scale of values in some grammatical category: singular < plural < dual < trial. One must translate this scale into a set of predictions about cross-linguistic variation in languages. That is, one must specify what sorts of grammatical properties, that is, what linguistic types, are predicted to occur and not to occur in human languages. This is the evidence for grammatical hierarchies. In the next section, we will see that the evidence for certain grammatical hierarchies is the same as the evidence for markedness (modified to account for relative markedness). The hierarchies that manifest markedness patterns include the most important grammatical hierarchies in terms of their basic and pervasive effects in the grammars of human languages: number, grammatical relations (accessibility), animacy and definiteness.

The first prerequisite that any markedness pattern must satisfy is that the markedness relationship holds between paradigmatic alternatives, that is the values of a single grammatical category (see chapter 4). We do not expect to find a markedness relationship between the values "passive" and "glottalized." Grammatical hierarchies also are defined among paradigmatic alternatives. We do not expect to find a grammatical hierarchy "passive < glottalized < dual." In fact, it is generally much easier to see the values on a grammatical hierarchy as paradigmatic alternatives than it is to see the implicans and implicatum of certain implicational universals as paradigmatic alternatives.

We now turn to the principal grammatical hierarchies that appear to have significant cross-linguistic evidence in their support.

5.3 The principal grammatical hierarchies

5.3.1 *Number*

Greenberg's research on the hierarchy of grammatical number was explicitly done in the typological-marking theory framework, and so it is not surprising that the evidence for the number hierarchy is amenable to markedness analysis. Since we have already discussed evidence in favor of the markedness of plural with respect to singular in chapter 4, we will restrict ourselves here to some examples of the markedness of the dual and the trial (or paucal) relative to the plural form.

Greenberg's frequency counts include counts of Sanskrit noun forms and verb-agreement forms that demonstrate the much greater frequency of plural forms compared to dual forms, and of singular forms compared to either (Greenberg 1966b:32, 37):

	Singular	*Plural*	*Dual*	*Total number*
Noun inflection	70.3%	25.1%	4.6%	93,277
Verb agreement	71.0%	23.4%	5.6%	29,370

It is also worth noting that although there are no text counts of languages including trial forms, Greenberg's counts of numerals, both cardinal and ordinal, exhibit a strict hierarchy (except for numeral bases like "ten"), with the lower numbers less marked (Greenberg 1966b: 42–4). In addition, occurrences of the number "one" (that is, singular) appear to outnumber occurrences of all other numbers put together (that is, plural).

In more common singular–dual–plural systems, there is structural evidence of the markedness of the dual. Structurally, the dual forms are frequently marked with a nonzero morpheme just as the plural is. However, one also finds examples of dual forms which consist of a morpheme added to the plural form, which in turn consists of a morpheme added to the zero-marked singular noun form. For example, in Kharia animate nouns have a plural in -*ki* and a dual in -*ki-yar*: e.g. *biloi-ki* 'cats'/ *biloi-ki-yar* 'two cats' (Biligiri 1965:36; cf. the Manam examples in [1b] and [1c] above). Another example of the dual added to the plural form is found in the Chumash verbal-agreement system (Kroeber 1904:33):

	Singular	*Plural*	*Dual*
1st person	k-	k-i-	k-i-s-
2nd person	p-	p-i-	p-i-s-
3rd person	s-	s-i-	s-i-s-

The markedness of the dual is also manifested in its marked inflectional behavior compared to the plural. For example, in Classical (Attic) Greek (see Goodwin 1892:36–7), the singular forms of nouns distinguish the following cases: nominative, genitive, dative, accusative and vocative (the number of case distinctions varies with declension to some extent). The plural forms do not distinguish the nominative and the vocative, thus demonstrating the marked inflectional behavior of the plural with respect to the singular. The dual distinguishes only two forms, collapsing

the nominative, accusative and vocative into one form and the genitive
and dative into the other form. Thus, the dual is more marked inflectionally than the plural (and, of course, the singular).

Most commonly, the dual is marked with respect to distributional
behavior. Frequently dual forms are found only with personal and
demonstrative pronouns, as in Wikchamni *maʔ/maʔan/maʔak̓* 'you
(singular/dual/plural)' vs. *pušun/pušun-hat* 'granary/granaries' (Gamble
1978: 94, 101). Also, in most of those few languages with trial or paucal
forms, those forms are generally found only with pronouns, while nouns
have only singular, plural and dual forms. Finally, the cross-linguistic
distribution of the higher-number forms fits with the number hierarchy:
"No language has a trial number unless it has a dual. No language has
a dual unless it has a plural" (Greenberg 1966a:94, Universal 34).

A very important question that arises at this point is how to apply
universal grammatical hierarchies to languages that do not appear to
have the categories described in the hierarchy. For example, in the
number hierarchy singular < plural < dual, it is assumed that the languages described have number categories defined as "one object"
(singular), "two objects" (dual) and "more than one/two objects"
(plural). In fact, the vast majority of languages do have number categories defined in just this fashion. However, there do exist other number
systems. For example, Chemehuevi does not have a separate plural category; instead, it has the categories "two or more" (glossed as "2+"
here) and "three or more" (glossed as "3+"; see Press 1979:54, 78):

> *Noun inflection (animates and some inanimates)*
>
> (2a) aipac
>   boy
>   boy (singular)'
> (2b) aipaci -w
>   boy   -2+
>   'boys (two or more)'
> (2c) a-   ʔaipaci -w
>   REDUP /3+- boy   -2+
>   'boys (three or more)'
>
> *Verb agreement (animates)*
>
> (3a) mam nukwi -ji   -ʔɨm
>   they run -PRES -2+
>   'they (two or more) are running'
> (3b) mam nukwi -ka -ji   -ʔɨm
>   they run -3+ -PRES -2+
>   'they (three or more) are running'

In these examples, the "three or more" forms consist of a morpheme (or stem reduplication) added to the "two or more" forms, which in turn consist of a morpheme (-*w* for nouns, -*ʔim* for verbs) added to the stem (the stem alone is the zero-marked singular). The "three or more" forms are therefore more marked structurally than the "two or more" forms.

The important fact to note here is that the "two or more" form is not a dual, since a dual form by definition is "only two." In a "standard" number system, the dual form is more marked than the plural ("three or more") form. This is supported by the frequency data cited in 4.3.3: the category "three or more" is more frequent than the category "only two." However, the category "three or more" is less frequent than the category "two or more," since it is a proper subset of the category "two or more." Thus, by the frequency criterion, the category "two or more" should be less marked than the category "three or more," and in Chemehuevi it is. This observation has important consequences for markedness and cross-linguistic comparison. It demonstrates that the frequency criterion can be used to make predictions of markedness for "nonstandard" grammatical categories such as the Chemehuevi category "more than two." Although the Chemehuevi category is extremely rare, the same method of using frequency to determine markedness patterns, can be applied to other grammatical examples, most notably the grammatical relations hierarchy, to be discussed in the next section.[6]

5.3.2 *The grammatical relations hierarchy and NP accessibility*

The **grammatical relations** (GR) **hierarchy** was described at the end of chapter 4 in the following form: subject < object < oblique. The GR hierarchy plays a much more important role than the number hierarchy in the organization of grammatical structure, since it is a ranking of grammatical relations between a main verb or predicate and its dependent arguments. The primary means by which grammatical relations are expressed in human languages is through one (or more) of three morphosyntactic strategies: word order, case marking and indexation (agreement) (see chapter 2 for definitions of these terms). The GR hierarchy is manifested in markedness patterns of all three of these strategies.

Before examining the GR hierarchy in case marking, agreement and word order, we must digress and outline some basic patterns of variation in the marking of grammatical relations in the clause. These patterns are manifested chiefly in the case-marking system, although they can be found in agreement and word order as well. We will illustrate these patterns using examples of case marking, and then proceed to determine how the GR hierarchy should be applied to these differing patterns.

In traditional grammatical terms, intransitive clauses have only a single argument, the "subject." Transitive clauses have two arguments, the "subject" and the "direct object"; and ditransitive clauses have three arguments, the "subject," the "direct object" and the "indirect object." Examples of each clause type in English are given below:

(4a)　*Intransitive*:　Marie slept.
　　　　　　　　　　　　　S
(4b)　*Transitive*:　Wally tickled　Sandy.
　　　　　　　　　　　　A　　　　　　　P
(4c)　*Ditransitive*:　Joan　sent　a　package　to　Paul.
　　　　　　　　　　　　A　　　　　　T　　　　　　G

Essentially, the variation is found in the relationship between the expression of grammatical relations in intransitive, transitive and ditransitive clauses. These will be illustrated below, but in order to talk about these distinctions clearly, it is necessary to introduce some distinctions not found in the traditional terminology, to be indicated by the letters below the argument phrases in the examples. The definitions of the letters are as follows:[7]

> S: intransitive subject ("subject")
> A: transitive or ditransitive subject ("agent")
> P: transitive direct object ("patient")
> T: ditransitive direct object ("theme")
> G: ditransitive indirect object ("goal")

In most Standard Average European languages, A is expressed in the same way as S, and T is expressed the same way as P. This is illustrated in the English examples: S and A are unmarked noun phrases that precede the verb, while P and T are unmarked noun phrases that immediately follow the verb. G is expressed as a prepositional phrase (i.e. a noun phrase whose grammatical relation to the verb is marked by a preposition).[8] This is encoded in the traditional grammatical terminology: S+A is the "subject," and P+T is the "direct object." However, other patterns are attested.

In many languages of the world, P (the transitive object) rather than A is expressed the same way as S (the intransitive subject), and A is expressed in some other way. The case marking associated with A is called the **ergative**, and the case marking associated with S and P is called the **absolutive**. Languages exhibiting this pattern are often called

ergative languages. An example of an ergative case-marking pattern is given below, for Yuwaalaraay (Williams 1980:36):

(5) ḍuyu -gu nama ḍayn -∅ yiː -y
    snake -ERG that man -ABS bite -N/F
    'The snake bit the man.'

(6) waːl ṇama yinar -∅ banaga ṇi
    NEG that woman -ABS run   -N/F
    'The woman didn't run.'

This pattern in the case marking of "subjects" is quite widespread, common in the languages of Oceania, the South Asian subcontinent, the Caucasus, Siberia and the Americas.

Equally widespread is a pattern of variation in the case marking of "objects." In many languages, G (the ditransitive indirect object) rather than T is expressed in the same way as P (the transitive direct object), and T is expressed differently. The combination of G+P is referred to as the **primary object**, and T is the **secondary object** (see Dryer 1986, which first describes this phenomenon in detail). The primary/secondary object distinction is most commonly manifested in agreement patterns, as we will see, but it is also found, rarely, in case marking, as in Yoruba and Yokuts:

Yoruba (Rowlands 1969:21; secondary object marked by locative preposition)

(7) a fẹ́ ówó
    we want money
    'We want money.'

(8) nwọ́n kọ́ wa   ní Yorùbá
    3PL.SBJ teach 1PL.OBJ LOC Yoruba
    'They taught us Yoruba.'

Yokuts (Newman 1944:198, 201; secondary object marked by -*ni*)

(9) kaːy̌u' teːw -a 'amin   xatta
    Coyote rabbit -PO 3SG.POSS ate
    'Coyote ate his cottontail rabbit.'

(10) 'ama' ṭan kay̌iw wanaː -'an   heẋaː -ni 'amin
    and DEM.PO Coyote give -DUR.PRES fat   -SO 3SG.POSS
    'And Coyote gives him his fat.'

Finally, English constructions of the form *I gave/sent her the book* suggest that English uses the primary–secondary object distinction as well as the direct–indirect object distinction found in *I gave/sent the book to her.*

We may summarize the patterns of variation in the expression of the major grammatical relations in Figure 5.1.

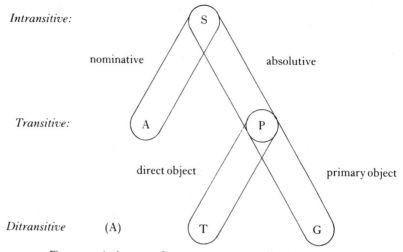

Intransitive:

nominative · absolutive

Transitive:

direct object · primary object

Ditransitive (A)

Figure 5.1 Assignment of arguments to grammatical relations

Now we may turn to the typological evidence for the GR hierarchy and its interpretation in light of these patterns of variation. The GR hierarchy is normally expressed as subject < (direct) object < oblique. The hierarchy, as traditionally interpreted, can be recast in our notation as $S+A<P+T<G$. If the case marking of languages with traditional subjects and direct objects is examined, there is very strong evidence in favor of this hierarchy. This can be illustrated by the structural criterion of markedness: if a grammatical relation on the hierarchy is zero-marked, then the grammatical relations above it on the hierarchy are also zero-marked. This is illustrated by the chart of case marking for selected languages that illustrate each predicted language type:[9]

	Subject (S+A)	Object (P+T)	Indirect object (G)	Gloss
Latvian	ruden-**s**	ruden-**i**	ruden-**im**	'autumn'
Hungarian	ember-∅	ember-**t**	ember-**nek**	'man'
Big Nambas	∅ dui	∅ dui	**a** dui	'person'

(Latvian: Lazdiņa 1966:302; Hungarian: Whitney 1944:18–19, 22; Big Nambas: Fox 1979:41,125–6)

However, this does not take into consideration languages which display the ergative/absolutive distinction or the primary/secondary object distinction. The structural-markedness criterion for case marking clearly indicates that the absolutive (S+P) is the zero-marked case:

	Absolute (S+P)	Ergative (A)	Gloss
Tongan	'a he talavou	'e ha talavou	'a young man'
Yup'ik	nuna-∅	nuna-**m**	'land'
Tzutujil	aachi-∅	aachi-∅	'man'

(Tongan: Churchward 1953:66, 68; Yup'ik: Reed *et al.* 1977:41; Tzutujil: Dayley 1985)

And the Yoruba and Yokuts examples indicate that the primary object is structurally unmarked compared to the secondary object:[10]

	Primary object (P+G)	Secondary object (T)	Gloss
Yokuts	hexa:-**in**	hexa:-**ni**	'fat'
Yoruba	∅ Yorùbá	**ní** Yorùbá	'Yoruba'
Tzotzil	ʔanȼ-∅	ʔanȼ-∅	'woman'

(Yokuts: Newman 1944:201; Yoruba: Rowlands 1969:21; Tzotzil: Aissen 1983:275)

These patterns, which are quite consistent, can be explained in the same way as the "nonstandard" number marking of Chemehuevi described in 5.3.1: the more frequent the category, the less marked it will be. The essential fact here is that in texts it appears that intransitive verbs greatly outnumber transitive verbs, which in turn greatly outnumber ditransitive verbs.[11] Thus, the combination S+A (subject) will always outnumber P+T (direct object) in text frequency, and P+T will outnumber G (indirect object). Hence, subject will be less marked than direct object, which will in turn be less marked than indirect object. However, S+P (absolute) will outnumber A (ergative) for the same reason, and P+G will outnumber T also. Hence, absolute is less marked than ergative, and primary object is less marked than secondary object. Finally, oblique cases other than indirect object are almost always structurally marked, with certain exceptions to be described in chapter 6.[12]

The GR hierarchy and its motivated exceptions are also found in verb-agreement (indexation) patterns. Agreement differs from case marking with respect to markedness patterns. Case marking indicates the case (grammatical) relation itself, and therefore the presence of case marking is an indicator of the structural markedness of the case relation. Verb agreement, however, indexes or cross-references the argument; it does not directly indicate the case relation. Instead, verb agreement is a behavioral property of case: an argument in a case relation that can trigger verb agreement is less marked than an argument in a case relation that cannot.

If we first restrict our attention to languages with traditional subjects (S+A) and objects (P+T), then we find that agreement fits the GR hierarchy: if the verb agrees with the direct object, then it agrees with the subject. This can be illustrated as follows:

> No agreement: Mandarin Chinese (Li & Thompson 1981:24)
>
> (11) tā néng shuō Zhōngguó -huà
> 3SG can speak China -speech
> 'He can speak Chinese.'

> Agreement with subject only: Spanish
>
> (12) Los soldado -s quebr **-aron** las ventana -s
> the.MASCPL soldier -PL break **-3SG.SBJ.PAST** the.FPL window -PL
> 'The soldiers broke the windows.'

> Agreement with subject and direct object: Kanuri (Hutchison 1981:135)[13]
>
> (13) **nzú-** rú **-kɔ́** -nà
> **2SG.OBJ-** see **-1SG.SBJ** Perf
> 'I saw you.'

In languages with the ergative/absolutive distinction, the frequency prediction holds: if the verb agrees with the ergative, then it agrees with the absolutive:

> No agreement: Tongan (Chung 1976:34)
>
> (14) 'e 'omi 'e Sione 'a e siaine ki -ate au
> UNS bring ERG John ABS the banana to -PRO me
> 'John will bring me some bananas.'

> Agreement with absolutive only: Chechen-Ingush (Nichols 1984:186)[14]
>
> (15) bier -ø **d-** ielxa
> child -NOM CM- cries   (CM agrees with "child")
> 'The child is crying.'

> (16) aːz yz kiniška -ø **d-** ieš
> 1SG.ERG this book -NOM CM- read   (CM agrees with "book")
> 'I'm reading this book.'

> Agreement with absolutive and ergative: Quiché (Mondloch 1978:46)
>
> (17) k- **at- in-** ¢ukū -x
> PRES- **2SG.ABS- 1SG.ERG-** look.for -TRANS
> 'I look for you.'

In languages with the primary/secondary object distinction, the frequency prediction again holds: if the verb agrees with the secondary object, then it agrees with the primary object. This is a very common (and apparently exceptionless) pattern, and is discussed extensively in Dryer 1986. The following examples illustrate the pattern:[15]

> No agreement with any object: Yoruba (Rowlands 1969:21)
> (18) nwón kó   wa   ní   Yorùbá
>   3PL.SBJ teach 1PL.OBJ LOC Yoruba
>   'They taught us Yoruba.'

> Agreement with primary object only: Huichol (Comrie 1928:99, 108)
> (19) Uukaraawiciizï tïïri   me-   **wa-**   zeiya
>   women   children   3PL.SBJ- **3PL.PO-** see
>   'The women see the children.'

> (20) Nee uuki uukari ne-   **wa-**   puuzeiyastïa
>   I   man girls   1SG.SBJ- **3PL.PO-** show
>   'I showed the man to the girls.'

Agreement and case marking are actually sensitive to a number of factors other than the GR hierarchy, even including the modifications given here for ergative/absolutive systems and primary/secondary object systems. These other factors do not replace the GR hierarchy, but rather supplement it, and will be discussed further in 5.3.3 and chapter 6.

All of the typological data supporting the GR hierarchy from case marking and agreement patterns are of the same type as the markedness data described in chapter 4. Turning to word order, one finds cross-linguistic evidence in favor of the GR hierarchy, but not of the markedness type. Instead, one finds the general pattern that basic word order in the clause follows the GR hierarchy, other things being equal. The fact that subjects generally precede objects is embodied in Greenberg's first universal: "In declarative sentences with nominal subject and object, the dominant order is almost always one in which the subject precedes the object" (Greenberg 1966a:77). Greenberg notes some exceptions to this pattern, the most common of which are VOS order (found in many Mayan and Austronesian languages) and OVS order (found chiefly in Carib languages; Pullum 1977, 1981; Derbyshire 1977; Derbyshire & Pullum 1981). Many of the VOS languages listed in Derbyshire and Pullum 1981 – the Mayan ones – are actually ergative languages, raising the possibility that their word order would better be expressed as V-Abs-Erg (see DuBois 1987:809, who calls this order "VOA"). In this case, the order is absolutive < ergative, as the frequency criterion would suggest.[16]

In general, objects also precede obliques.[17] However, the position of the indirect object (the G argument) varies. In many languages it precedes the direct object (T), as in the English so-called "dative shift" construction (*I showed the boy a butterfly*). However, most of these languages (including the English "dative-shift" construction) use the primary/secondary object distinction, so the order is primary object–secondary object, as the frequency criterion would suggest.[18]

The word-order patterns are not markedness patterns. Instead, one observes that the GR hierarchy "subject < object < oblique" (or its variants, "absolutive < ergative" and "primary object < secondary object"), is directly manifested in the linear order of the arguments of the clause. That is, the conceptual ranking of arguments as described by the GR hierarchy is directly mirrored in the physical sequence of arguments in the phrase. This type of cross-linguistic pattern is called "iconicity," and will be further discussed in chapter 7.

The first manifestation of the GR hierarchy based on typological evidence to come to widespread attention was the **NP accessibility hierarchy** of Keenan and Comrie (1977; first presented in 1972). The NP accessibility hierarchy was based on a cross-linguistic pattern of relative-clause behavior. Relative clauses come in a wide variety of forms, but can be generally characterized as a referent (noun phrase) being qualified (modified) by a proposition (clause, or verbal form plus its modifiers) in which the referent plays a role (has a grammatical relation). For example, in *the man that left the house*, the noun phrase *the man* refers to an individual who is being described or qualified by the relative clause *that left the house*, which describes an action in which the man participates. The relation that the head NP, called here the **relativized NP**, has to the relative clause is that of the subject.

English allows NPs of virtually any grammatical relation to the verb to be relativized:

> (21)   the man that _____ left the house
> the book that I read _____
> the woman that I sent the report to _____
> the party that I went to _____
> the person that I went to the party with _____
> etc.

Keenan and Comrie discovered that many languages were more restricted as to which NPs could be relativized or, as they put it, which NPs were **accessible** to relativization. (More precisely, every language has a primary relativization strategy which may be restricted in this fashion; other relativization strategies might exist to relativize NPs inaccessible to the primary strategy.) The general pattern that they

discovered for a large class of relative-clause types can be described
as follows:[19]

NP *Accessibility Hierarchy*
subject < direct object < indirect object < oblique

If an NP on the accessibility hierarchy is accessible to relativization
in a language, then all NPs higher on the hierarchy are also accessible
to relativization.

This is, of course, the GR hierarchy, manifested here in another grammatical domain.[20] The typological phenomenon on which Keenan and
Comrie based the relative-clause hierarchy is an example of the cross-
linguistic distributional-behavioral criterion of markedness, as applied
to grammatical relations. The following list gives the possible language
types that Keenan and Comrie's generalization allows:

1   Subjects only are accessible to relativization: Toba Batak (Keenan
    & Comrie 1977:68–9):[21]

(22) boru-boru na   manussi   abit   i
      woman   that wash.ACTIVE clothes the   (subject)
      'the woman who is washing clothes'

(23) *abit   na   manussi   boru-boru i
      clothes that wash.ACTIVE woman   the   (direct object)
      'the clothes that the woman is washing'

2   Subjects and direct objects are accessible to relativization: Persian
    (Keenan & Comrie 1979:343):

(24) John mard -i   râ ke zan   zad mišenâsad
      John man -the DO that woman hit knows   (direct object)
      'John knows the man whom the woman hit.'

(25) *Man zan   -i   râ ke John be (u) sibezamini dâd
      I   woman -the DO that John to potato   gave
      mišenâsam
      know
      'I know the woman to whom John gave the potato.'

                                                    (indirect object)

Persian has a secondary relative-clause formation strategy that is used
in the "lower" end of the GR hierarchy; this construction is represented
in (25) by the presence of the pronoun *u*. For languages of this type,
which is quite common, we may characterize relative clauses at the lower
end of the GR hierarchy as structurally marked compared to relative
clauses at the higher end, since the lower-end strategies always involve
the presence of a morpheme (anaphoric or relative pronoun) indicating
the case relation of the relativized argument to the verb in the relative
clause (see Givón 1979; Maxwell 1979; and chapter 7 for more discussion).

3   Subjects, direct objects and indirect objects are accessible to relativization. Tamil uses a nonfinite participial verb form for relative-clause formation at the upper end of the hierarchy (Keenan & Comrie 1977:73):

(26) Jāṉ puttakatt -ai(k) koṭi -tt   -a   peṉmaṇi(y) ai nāṉ kaṇ
      John book   -DO give -PAST -PART woman   -DO I   see
      -ṭ   -ēṉ
      -PAST -1SG
      'I saw the woman to whom John gave the book.'

However, Tamil uses a separate clause adjoined to the main clause to express relative clauses for oblique, a morphologically and syntactically more complex construction:

(27) eṉṉa(k) katti(y) -āḷ   koṟi(y) -ai   anta maṉitaṉ
      which   knife   -with chicken -DO   that man

      kolaippi -tt   -āṉ anta katti(y) -ai jāṉ   kaṇ -ṭ
      kill   -PAST -3SG that knife   -DO John   see -PAST
      -āṉ
      -3SG,MASC
      'John saw the knife with which the man killed the chicken' (lit. 'with which knife the man killed the chicken, John saw that knife')

4   Subjects, direct objects, indirect objects and obliques are accessible to relativization: English (see example [21]).

Thus subjects are accessible in all language types; direct objects are accessible in all but one language type; indirect objects are accessible in all but two language types, etc. Moreover, direct objects are accessible only if subjects are, indirect objects are accessible only if direct objects are, and so on.

The NP accessibility hierarchy is subject to numerous qualifications and has some exceptions (see Keenan & Comrie 1977; Maxwell 1979; Comrie & Keenan 1979; Comrie 1981a: chapter 7; and Lehmann 1986). We will simply note here that, not surprisingly, accessibility to relativization is based on the ergative/absolutive distinction in some languages, and in those languages the absolutive role is the least-marked role (i.e. the only one accessible to relativization). This phenomenon is found in the Mayan languages (Larsen & Norman 1979) and Dyirbal (Dixon 1979:127–8). Dyirbal, which uses a nonfinite verb form for relative clauses, is illustrated here (relative clauses in brackets):

(28) ŋuma -ŋgu yabu -∅ [duŋgara -ŋu -∅] bura -n
      father -ERG mother -ABS [cry   -REL -ABS] see -PAST
      'Father saw mother, who was crying.'   (S argument)

(29) ŋuma -∅ [yabu   -ŋgu bura -ŋu -∅] duŋgara -nyu
      father -ABS [mother -ERG see -REL -ABS] cry   -PAST
      'Father, who mother saw, was crying.'   (P argument)

(30) ŋuma -∅ [buṛal -ŋa   -ŋu -∅ yabu -gu] duŋara -nʸu
      father -ABS [see   -ANTIPASS -REL -ABS mother -DAT] cry   -PAST
      'Father, who saw mother, was crying.'   (A argument)

In order to make the A argument accessible to relative-clause formation, the verb must be antipassivized, thus placing the A argument in the absolutive case (and structurally marking the construction).[22]

Finally, it is possible that the Bantu languages, which are described as having only subject and direct object (P+T) NPs accessible to relativization, are better described as having only subject and primary object (P+G) NPs accessible to relativization (see Kisseberth & Abasheikh 1977). In these cases, the rankings absolutive < ergative and primary object < secondary object are confirmed, as the frequency criterion of markedness would predict.

We now turn to the most important other factors that influence the expression of grammatical relations in the clause: animacy and definiteness.

5.3.3 *Animacy, definiteness and hierarchy of features*

Number distinctions in nouns and pronouns are often restricted to a subset of forms. A typological survey of the restrictions reveals the following types.

1 First and second person pronouns have a number distinction not found in third person pronouns or common nouns. This is the case in Guaraní (Gregores & Suárez 1967:141), in which the pronouns are *šé* '1sg.,' *né* '2sg.,' *yané* '1pl. inclusive,' *oré* '1pl. exclusive,' *peẽ* '2pl.,' but *haʔé* '3sg./ pl.'

In Chrau (Thomas 1971:138), this is a matter of discretion: a plural prefix is not required for any of the personal pronouns, but the third-person pronoun is the most likely one to be used in the (unmarked) singular form with plural meaning. This example reveals an important methodological point regarding typological patterns: even if the grammatical distinction is not categorical, it supports the markedness pattern as long as the tendency is in the right "direction." Markedness, including hierarchies, is a matter of relative degree.

2 Pronouns (including third person) have a number distinction not found among common nouns. An example is Mandarin Chinese: *tā* 'he/she/it' vs. *tāmen* 'they,' but *shū* 'book/books' (Li & Thompson 1981:13).

3 Pronouns and nouns referring to human beings have a number distinction not found among common nouns referring to nonhuman entities; for example, Tiwi has *wuɹalaka* 'young girl'/ *wawuɹalakawi* 'young girls,' but *waliwalini* 'ant/ants' (Osborne 1974:52).[23]

4 Pronouns and nouns referring to animate beings (including human beings) have a number distinction not found among common nouns referring to inanimate things. For example, the aforementioned Kharia example *biloi* 'cat'/*biloi-ki* 'cats' contrasts with *soreŋ* 'stone/stones' (Biligiri 1965:36).

The same phenomenon is found in verb-agreement patterns. For example, in Takelma (Sapir 1922:160–1), one finds *yowo't'e* 'I run (aorist)'/*yowoyi'k'* 'we run,' but *yowo'* 'he, she, it, they run.' In Quiché, the verb displays number distinctions only for animate subjects and objects (more precisely, ergatives and absolutives); examples of absolutive-agreement prefix usage are given below (Mondloch 1978:42; note that nonhuman nouns do not indicate number):

(31) š-   ∅-   in-   ¢uku   -x   lē   ¢i?
     PAST- 3SG.ABS- ISG.ERG- look.for -TRANS the   dog
     'I looked for the dog.'

(32) š-   ē-   n-   ¢uku   -x   lē   ¢i?
     PAST- 3PL.ABS- ISG.ERG- look.for -TRANS the   dog
     'I looked for the dogs.'

(33) š-   ∅-   in-   ¢uku   -x   lē   laq
     PAST- 3SG.ABS- ISG.ERG- look.for- TRANS the   clay.dish
     'I looked for the clay dish/dishes.'

This phenomenon illustrates a behavioral-markedness criterion, the possibility of inflecting for number. The data given above indicate the following markedness relations:

1 first, second-person pronoun < third-person pronoun
2 pronoun < common noun
3 pronoun, human common noun < nonhuman common noun
4 pronoun, animate common noun < inanimate common noun

These are not independent markedness patterns. Each one can be appended to the preceding to form a hierarchy as follows:

> *Animacy*: first, second-person pronouns < third-person pronoun < proper names[24] < human common noun < nonhuman animate common noun < inanimate common noun

This combination of features has been named the **animacy hierarchy**. The most common representation of the animacy hierarchy is the one given above, found in Dixon (1979:85), though its first modern description is found in Silverstein (1976).[25] The animacy hierarchy actually involves several distinct but related grammatical dimensions. The first

is a **person hierarchy**, in which first and second person outrank third
person. The second is an **NP-type hierarchy**, in which pronouns outrank
common nouns (there is some evidence that proper names occupy an
intermediate position on this hierarchy). Finally, there is the **animacy
hierarchy** proper, in which humans outrank nonhuman animates, which
in turn outrank inanimates.

The dual and paucal noun forms (also used for verb agreement) in
Manam, described at the beginning of this chapter, represent an intermediate category between "human" and "nonhuman animate" on the animacy hierarchy: they are used only for humans and "higher animals":

The category of higher animals traditionally consists of human beings, pigs,
dogs and birds (including fowls), and now also goats, horses and other large
animals, which are of relatively recent introduction in New Guinea. However,
while humans are always considered higher animals, there is some variation
with the other members of the category: the latter are always considered higher
animals when domesticated but only optionally so when wild. (Lichtenberk
1983b:110)[26]

This example demonstrates that the animacy hierarchy (or other hierarchies, for that matter) is not an ordering of discrete categories, but
rather a more or less continuous category ranging from "most animate"
to "least animate."

The person hierarchy plays an important role in the expression of
subject and object in many languages, and it represents one of the most
striking differences between other languages and Standard Average
European languages, more striking even than the ergative/absolutive
system described in the preceding section. In a number of languages
found scattered around the world, the transitive verb agrees not with
the subject (A), or the absolutive (P), but whichever of A and P is
higher on the person hierarchy. In such languages, first and second person must be ranked with respect to each other in the person hierarchy.
An example of this system is found in Tangut (DeLancey 1981:631):

(34) ni   tın nga ın   ldıə   thı   -nga
      you if I ACC indeed chase -1ST
      'If indeed you are chasing me,'
      ku   that tsı   viə- thı   -na
      then her also   chase -2ND
      'then chase her too.'

(35) ni   pha ngi- mbın ndı- siei   -na
      you other   wife   choose -2ND
      'Choose another wife!'

(36) mei-swen manə   na   khe -na
     M.   formerly you hate -2ND
     'Mei-swen formerly hated you.'

A ranking based on animacy is also found in word order. In Navajo, the higher-animacy argument always precedes the lower-animacy argument in word order. If both arguments are third person and the higher-animate argument is the subject, then the verb uses the prefix *yi-*; if the lower-animate argument is the subject, then the verb uses the prefix *bi-* (Witherspoon 1977:65–6):

(37) hastiin łį́į́'   yi- ztał
     man   horse YI- kick
     'The man kicked the horse.'
(38) hastiin łį́į́'   bi- ztał
     man   horse BI- kick
     'The man was kicked by the horse.'
(39) *łį́į́'   hastiin bi- ztał
     horse   man   BI- kick

Changing the word order so that the "lower" entity on the animacy hierarchy precedes the "higher" one results in ungrammaticality. Just as in the case of word order and the GR hierarchy, we have an iconic pattern in which the order of arguments mirrors the ranking of the animacy hierarchy. From these examples, it is also clear that the ranking of arguments with respect to the GR hierarchy sometimes conflicts with the ranking of the same arguments with respect to the animacy hierarchy. We will address the interaction of GR and animacy in chapter 6.

The Navajo system is distinctive not only because word order rather than agreement is involved, but also because animacy distinctions other than person play a role in the system.

If we turn to case marking, we find that the major manifestation of animacy patterns is found in the case marking of objects, and that another important factor enters the picture. In many languages, objects that rank high in animacy have a nonzero case marker that objects lower in animacy do not have. For example, in Punjabi the object pronouns have a special marked direct object form using the dative suffix *-nū* (Shackle 1972:69):

(40) mɛ̃ tɛɛ-nū   pəɾàvaŋga
     1SG 2SG.OBJ will.teach
     'I will teach you.'

In Punjabi, an animate common-noun direct object also uses *nū* (as a postposition). An inanimate direct object uses *nū* only if it is definite (Shackle 1972:69–70):

(41) éo   nili   kitāb   nū   mez   te   rakkho
that   blue   book   to   table   on   put
'Put that blue book on the table.'

(42) koi   kitāb   mez   te   rakkho
some   book   table   on   put
'Put some book on the table.'

Other markedness evidence indicates that there is a hierarchy of indefiniteness: definite < referential indefinite < nonreferential indefinite. A referential indefinite stands for a specific individual (not known to the hearer), and a nonreferential indefinite is used when the speaker has no specific individual in mind. It can be illustrated by the following Spanish example.

(43) busc   -o   a   una   secretaria
look.for -1SG.PRES   to   a   secretary
'I am looking for a secretary (specific person in mind).'

(44) busc   -o   una   secretaria
look.for -1SG.PRES   a   secretary
'I am looking for a secretary (any secretary).'

The direct object in (43) is a referential indefinite and takes the case marker *a* "to," while the direct object in (44) is a nonreferential indefinite and does not take a case marker.

It can be seen here that animacy interacts with definiteness to constrain patterns of case marking of objects in Punjabi (which it also does in Spanish). The definiteness hierarchy is in fact closely related to the animacy hierarchy; this will be discussed in 6.2.2.

Michael Silverstein's original analysis of the animacy hierarchy (1976) differs from the more common representation of grammatical hierarchies that has been used in this chapter. The more common representation is a hierarchy of **values** in a single **category**, such as singular < plural < dual < trial, or subject < object < oblique. Silverstein represents animacy in terms of a hierarchy of binary **features**, with a "cascading" set of features, as in table 5.1 (Silverstein 1976:122).

This may appear to encode basically the same information in a different way. However, the alternative representation of a hierarchy of features does imply certain theoretical hypotheses and assumptions. The assumption is retained that all categories (i.e. features) are binary; that is, all categories have only two values. The consequence of this assumption is that a category such as "animacy" is divided into several distinct sub-

Table 5.1 *Hierarchy of features compared to hierarchy of values*

Hierarchy of features	Hierarchy of values
+tu	second person (pronoun)
−tu:	
+ego	first person (pronoun)
−ego:	
+pronominal	third person pronoun
−pronominal:	
+human	human common noun
−human:	
+animate	nonhuman animate common noun
−animate	inanimate common noun

categories, each of which is binary. The hierarchy is then no longer a hierarchy of grammatical values, but instead a hierarchy of grammatical features: SAP, pronominal, human, animate.

Animacy is not the only category that lends itself to formulation in terms of a hierarchy of features. Definiteness is also easily recast as a hierarchy of features:

Hierarchy of features	*Hierarchy of values*
+definite	definite
−definite:	
+referential	referential indefinite
−referential	nonreferential indefinite

The appeal of the hierarchy of features is that it captures the inclusiveness of terms such as "referential." There are a number of problems with attempting to represent all grammatical hierarchies as hierarchies of features, however. For example, it is virtually impossible to recast the number hierarchy (singular < plural < dual < trial/paucal) as a hierarchy of features with any natural set of features. In fact, the ability to formulate a hierarchy of features for categories such as animacy and definiteness may simply be a byproduct of the terminology applied to that category.

In the case of the animacy hierarchy, in which we argued there are three distinct hierarchies (person, NP type and animacy proper), these three parameters are not related in a hierarchical fashion. Specifically, both pronouns and common nouns may refer to human, animate or inanimate beings. Thus, for example, one cannot with certainty rank inanimate pronouns relative to human common nouns.

Another problem with hierarchies of features is that they do not directly characterize the relative nature of the markedness patterns that support grammatical hierarchies. This is most obvious in the matter of frequency. Frequency is clearly a unitary quantitative measure that is best interpreted as a simple ranking of values. For example, the sort of quantitative evidence from Sanskrit illustrated above for the number hierarchy is best represented by a simple ranking: singular < plural < dual, rather than by a hierarchy of features.

This is true for behavioral and even structural criteria of markedness. For example, as we noted above, the dual is often formed by adding a morpheme to the plural, which in turn is formed by adding a morpheme to the (zero-marked) singular. Thus, the singular is formed by zero morphemes, the plural by one and the dual by two. Grammatical behavior can also yield a straightforward ranking. In Quiché, only animate nouns have plural verb agreement, and only human nouns allow plural marking. Thus human nouns have two distinctive types of grammatical behavior (plural marking and plural agreement), nonhuman animate nouns have one (plural agreement) and inanimate nouns have none. In general, the quantitative formulation of the markedness criteria provided in chapter 4 – which is necessitated by the empirical data – is best represented by a ranking of values.

A final problem with the representation of grammatical hierarchies as hierarchies of features is that it breaks up the unitary character of the grammatical category in question. The criteria of markedness are based on the fact that markedness relations hold among paradigmatic alternatives. A unified category, with as many values as exist in the paradigm, captures this fact. The hierarchy of features, in addition to being more complex than a ranking of values in a single category, must be supplemented with some device that shows that all the values are paradigmatic alternatives. Other things being equal, it seems appropriate to prefer the simpler and more perspicuous representation of the typological facts, namely a ranking of values in a category.

5.3.4   *Bondedness (the modifier hierarchy)*

The GR and animacy hierarchies described in 5.3.2 and 5.3.3 are manifested in clause-level grammatical relations, that is between a main verb or predicate and its arguments (noun phrases, with or without case marking). It is reasonable to ask if there are hierarchical patterns operating within the noun phrase, among the modifiers of the head noun. William Foley (1980) proposes just such a hierarchy, which he calls "bondedness":

> *Bondedness*
> articles < deictics < interrogatives < quantifiers < adjectives <
> relative clauses

The evidence that Foley provides for this hierarchy is not universal, but is restricted to the Austronesian languages. Many Austronesian languages use a linker morpheme, called a **ligature** by Austronesianists, to link various modifiers to the head noun. The bondedness hierarchy captures the distribution of the ligature in those Austronesian languages that have it: if the ligature is used with a modifier in the bondedness hierarchy, then it is used with all modifiers below it in the hierarchy.

Austronesian languages that use the ligature vary as to the "cut-off point" at which the ligature is no longer used. Examples of each possible "cut-off point" are given below (all data from Foley 1980; in each case modifiers above the cut-off disallow the ligature and modifiers below require it):[27]

Palauan
(45) a   kliokl   (article)
      ART hole
      'a/the hole'
(46) ngikey 'l ?ad   (demonstrative)
      that   LIG man
      'that man'

Ilokano
(47) daytoy   (a)   balay   (demonstrative)
      this.near.me (LIG) house
      'this house'
(48) ania **nga** aso   (interrogative)
      what LIG dog
      'what dog?'

Toba Batak
(49) dija   baoa   (interrogative)
      which man
      'which man?'
(50) huta   **na** leban   (quantifier)
      village LIG another
      'another village'

Tolai

(51) tara   bul   (quantifier)
another child
'another child'

(52) a   gege   **na** davai   (adjective)
ART crooked LIG stick
'a/the crooked stick'

Wolio

(53) o   mia   mate   (adjective)
ART man   dead
'a/the dead man'

(54) wakutuu **na** a-   umba -mo   (relative clause)
time   LIG 3SG come -DEF
'the time he did come'

This evidence is of the form of presence vs. absence of a morpheme, the ligature, and hence an instance of structural markedness. As expected, in any given Austronesian language with the ligature, the higher modifiers on the bondedness hierarchy will be less marked than the lower modifiers on the hierarchy.

The bondedness hierarchy as described does not have universal cross-linguistic validity, since it is based only on Austronesian languages. Nevertheless, it does correspond to an intuition that the higher a modifier is on the hierarchy, the more "intimate" or closely bonded it is to the head noun in some semantic or pragmatic sense. As such, it is worth investigating the bondedness hierarchy from a wider typological perspective. For example, one of Greenberg's universals that pertains to the modifier hierarchy is Universal 20: "When any or all of the items (demonstrative, numeral and descriptive adjective) precede the noun, they are always found in that order. If they follow, the order is either the same or its exact opposite" (Greenberg 1966a:87). Later research has indicated that postnominal modifier order is more variable than Greenberg believed (see, e.g., Heine 1980), but the prenominal modifier order is almost always demonstrative – numeral – adjective – noun. This order mirrors the order represented in the modifier hierarchy, in the same way that the order of arguments in the clause generally mirrors the order represented in the GR hierarchy.

In fact, one of the reasons that the bondedness hierarchy or some comparable hypothesis has not been investigated is that little attention has been directed towards the typology of noun-phrase structure, compared to the tremendous amount of research on the typology of clause structure. It is to be hoped that future typological research will be directed to this comparatively neglected area of grammar.

5.4 Phonological hierarchies

Grammatical hierarchies supported by typological evidence occur in phonology as well. Most of the typological evidence regarding patterns as complex as hierarchies is in the form of **segment inventories**, an enumeration of the phonemes of the language. An example of the segment inventory of stop consonants is given here for Tigre (Maddieson 1984:311):

	Bilabial	Dental	Velar	Glottal
Voiceless plosive		t̪	k	ʔ
Voiced plosive	b	d̪	g̱	
Voiceless ejective		t̪̓	k̓	

The major source of typological patterns are in the "gaps" in segment inventories. Based on the pattern of features (in this case, place and manner of articulation) one can identify expected segments that in fact are not found in the language. For example, one would expect bilabial voiceless plosives (*p*) and ejectives (*p̓*) in Tigre, but they do not exist. A typological survey of gaps can reveal interesting patterns. These are markedness patterns of cross-linguistic distribution.

The Tigre voiceless bilabial ejective gap illustrates one of the better-explored patterns. Maddieson (1984), in a survey of the segment inventories of 317 languages found in the UCLA Phonological Segment Inventory Database (UPSID), confirms the following generalizations regarding gaps in the place of articulation of glottalized consonants (see also Greenberg 1970):[28]

(iii) If a language has /p̓/ it also has /*t̪̓/. 33/34 97.1%
(iv) If a language has /*t̪̓/ it also has /k̓/. 33/34 97.8%
(v) If a language has only one ejective stop, it is /k̓/. 5/5 100%
(Maddieson 1984:120)

From these universals, one can derive a hierarchy of place of articulation from the back of the mouth to the front, at least for the three most common places of articulation:[29]

Place of articulation
velar < dental/alveolar < bilabial

This hierarchy can also be applied to other consonant series – voiced implosives, voiced and voiceless plosives and nasals. However, complications arise in these cases; they will be discussed in 6.4.

In section 5.3, we observed that the GR, animacy and (possibly) the modifier hierarchies were supported by universal patterns of the linear order of arguments. A similar phenomenon is found in patterns of the linear order of segments in a syllable. It has been proposed that segments can be ordered in a **sonority** hierarchy from the edge of the syllable to its core as follows:[30]

Sonority
obstruent < nasal < liquid < glide < vowel

That is, the universal (or at least, unmarked) order of segments in a syllable is:

obstruent – nasal – liquid – glide – vowel – glide – liquid – nasal – obstruent

so that the order from the beginning of the syllable to the peak vowel is reversed from the peak vowel to the end of the syllable.

A typological study of word-initial and word-final consonant clusters by Greenberg (1978a) provides support for some, but not all, of the sonority hierarchy. The patterns in the data are somewhat obscured by other typological patterns of cluster dissimilation and voicing patterns. The universals that are relevant are as follows:

17. In initial systems [word-initial consonant clusters], the existence of at least one sequence containing a liquid, whether voiced or unvoiced, immediately followed by an obstruent implies the existence of at least one sequence containing an obstruent immediately followed by a liquid.

18. In final systems [word-final consonant clusters], the existence of at least one sequence containing a stop immediately followed by a liquid implies the presence of at least one sequence containing a liquid followed by a stop.

19. Voiced semivowels [glides] are not followed by obstruents in initial systems or preceded by obstruents in final systems.

20. Two successive voiced sonants [liquids, nasals and glides] are always followed by a vowel in initial systems and preceded by a vowel in final systems.

24. In initial systems the existence of at least one sequence consisting of a voiced liquid followed by a nasal implies the existence of at least one combination consisting of a nasal followed by a liquid.

25. In final systems, the existence of at least one sequence consisting of a nasal followed by a liquid ... implies the existence of at least one sequence consisting of a liquid followed by a nasal. (Greenberg 1978a:257–9, 261–2)

Universal 17 (and its mirror image, 18) demonstrate that the sequence liquid–obstruent at the beginning of a syllable, disallowed by the sonority hierarchy, does indeed occur, but only if the acceptable sequence obstruent–liquid is also present. The implicational universal indicates that the initial sequence obstruent–liquid is the dominant, that is unmarked, order, which is basically in keeping with the sonority hierarchy. Universal 19 demonstrates that the sonority ranking obstruent < glide is exceptionless in word-initial and word-final clusters, and Universal 20 lends support to the minimal sonority of obstruents and the maximal sonority of vowels. Finally, Universals 24 and 25 provide evidence that the ranking nasal < liquid is unmarked, as one would expect, though not absolute. This places nasals between obstruents and liquids in the sonority hierarchy, and since liquids can precede obstruents (as a marked cluster), it might be expected that nasals can precede obstruents. In fact, they often do, and Greenberg does not report any universals that would suggest that the combination nasal–obstruent is more marked than the combination obstruent–nasal (or vice versa for final clusters). Finally, Greenberg notes (1978a:258) that glides very rarely precede nasals or liquids, though without constructing any unrestricted or implicational universals. Thus, the typological data based on the distribution of initial and final obstruent clusters supports the following version of the sonority hierarchy (< means the order is absolute; ? < that the order is unmarked or dominant):

> *Sonority (revised)*
> obstruents, nasals? < liquids < glides < vowels

5.5 Conclusion

This chapter has described all of the major grammatical and phonological hierarchies found in the world's languages: number, GR, animacy, definiteness, modifiers, place of articulation and sonority. These hierarchies have been described in the typological literature and supported by two types of evidence. The first type of evidence is patterns of markedness, as described in chapter 4. The second type of evidence is linear order of constituents (or segments) mirroring the rank order of the hierarchy. This latter type of phenomenon is an iconic relation, and will be discussed in chapter 7.

In addition, we have observed that neither the evidence for a hierarchy nor the values in a hierarchy need be discrete. In some cases (as in animacy in Chrau), markedness is expressed by the more frequent use of, say, a plural form for first- and second-person pronouns than for third-person pronouns, rather than a sharp boundary between mandatory use and prohibited use. In other cases, the category itself may describe an "intermediate" category in the hierarchy, such as the category "higher animal" in Manam. In both the definition of the hierarchy of values and the typological evidence for the hierarchy, a continuum is necessary to account for the data. This is part of the reason for the relativized, quantitative definitions of the markedness criteria in chapter 4.

Although these are certainly not the only grammatical hierarchies to be found in cross-linguistic study, they play a major role in structuring clauses, noun phrases, segment inventories and syllables in the world's languages. In the next chapter, we will examine how grammatical hierarchies and other typological patterns interact with each other, resulting in typological patterns of still greater complexity.

6
Prototypes and the interaction of typological patterns

6.1 Introduction

The grammatical categories that we have seen to be organized into typological markedness and hierarchy patterns do not occur in isolation. Any given noun phrase has values for number, case and animacy/gender, for example, and any given verb has values for tense, aspect, modality and so on. In other words, grammatical categories always occur in combination in utterances. Hence it is reasonable to examine the possibility of grammatical interactions between categories, and seek typological patterns in those interactions. This chapter will explore these patterns.

6.2 Clusters and typological evidence for prototypes

The simplest pattern is one in which a certain combination of grammatical-category values will result in the least-marked form of a word or grammatical construction. This is most easily illustrated with the inflectional categories of nouns and verbs. For example, in Classical Mongolian (Poppe 1974:76), the unmarked form of a noun is the singular nominative form (there is no inflection for gender), such as *aqa* 'elder brother'; contrast the structurally marked forms *aqa-nar* (nominative plural), *aqa-yi* (accusative singular), and *aqa-nar-yi* (accusative plural). Likewise, the unmarked verb form in Ngalakan is present-tense positive, with a third-person singular "animate" gender subject, such as *ṛabo* 'he/she goes' – contrast *yiri-ṛabo* 'we (inclusive) go,' *ṛabo-gon* 'he/she went (subordinate form)' (Merlan 1983:154–5). This is a widespread typological pattern: the unmarked noun is nominative (or absolutive), singular, masculine (or animate) gender, normal size (i.e. not diminutive or augmentative); the unmarked verb is third-person singular, present, positive, realis modality and active voice.[1]

In other words, we may treat the actual unmarked word form in an utterance as representing a **cluster** of grammatical values on different

124

parameters. Such a cluster immediately evokes the image of a **prototype** category (e.g. Rosch 1978). A prototype category, loosely defined, is a category with a clear "core" or "central" members of the category, but fuzzy or variable boundaries. The core members have a cluster of properties, but the peripheral members of the category lack some of the core properties. To use an often-cited example: the category "bird" is said to be a prototype category (cognitively, not biologically), because there are central members of the category such as robins, and less central members, such as ostriches and penguins. Among the properties that define prototypical birds are that they have feathers, wings, two legs and can fly. Robins satisfy all of those properties, but neither ostriches nor penguins can fly, and penguins' feathers do not at all resemble proto-typical bird feathers. Hence, ostriches and penguins are peripheral members of the category. Properties such as "being able to fly" are what distinguish prototype categories from "classical" definitions of categories. Being able to fly is neither a necessary nor a sufficient condition for being a bird: some birds can't fly, and some things that can fly are not birds (e.g. flies). Nevertheless, psychological experiments indicate that these "typical" properties do play a role in categorization by human beings.

Since prototypes are a characteristic of human categorization, and human language involves categorization, prototypes have a potential explanatory value in linguistics. The prototype concept is applied to grammar in the following way. As we stated above, a particular word (or construction) expresses many grammatical categories at once. Some particular combination of those category values represents the "core" members of the category. If a word or construction lacks some of the category values of central members, then it is a peripheral member of the category.

The following sorts of typological evidence are used to determine that a particular member of a category is central or peripheral. First, the most frequently mentioned forms are commonly the central members of the category. Core members, that is, members that have all of the prototypical properties, are typical members. To be typical, they must be common, or at least commonly perceived and attended to by human beings. A textually frequent category member will satisfy the definition of (proto)typicality. For example, Greenberg (1966b:68) cites a study of the Rigvedic verb in which the "prototypical" verb form, third-person singular present active indicative, occurred 1,404 times, whereas a highly marked verb form, second-person dual mediopassive perfect optative, did not occur at all. This corresponds to the frequency criterion of markedness.

Another important piece of typological evidence used to support prototypicality in grammatical categories is the common zero (or minimal) marking of the core members of the categories. We have already observed this in the examples of inflectionally zero-marked nouns and verbs, and we will see more examples of this below with regard to transitivity, animacy and case. This is of course the structural criterion of markedness.

A third kind of typological evidence is loss of category behavior. A peripheral member of a category is not expected to display the full range of category behavior that a central member displays. This is, of course, the behavioral criterion of markedness. It is not always easy to apply, however. The behavioral criterion determines the markedness of an individual grammatical value (e.g. singular) by using variation on cross-cutting categories (e.g. person), and so cannot be used to find an unmarked cluster of grammatical values (number and person). Instead, one must rely on the behavior of cross-cutting categories not included in the cluster. For example, the third-person singular pronoun category in English displays the largest number of gender distinctions – *he, she, it* – and so that cluster of values is least marked, at least with respect to gender distinctions (see 6.4.2).

One of the more important or distinctive criteria for typological prototypes is outright **exclusion** of nonprototypical members from the prototypical category. For example, we will discuss the prototypical transitive construction in 6.2.2. Constructions missing one or more grammatical properties (e.g. completive aspect) of the transitive prototype appear as intransitives in many languages. That is to say, constructions lacking some prototypical transitive features no longer display transitive-clause behavior; in fact, they display no transitive-clause behavior, so that they are classified as intransitive constructions (see 6.2.2 for the definition of transitive behavior). This is essentially the behavioral criterion of typological distribution, taken to its logical extreme: the peripheral member displays no behavioral characteristics of the prototype category, and is instead classified as belonging to some other category. In fact, the evidence for grammatical prototypes is essentially the same as evidence for markedness patterns.

The examples of inflectionally unmarked nouns and verbs are not really ideal cases of prototypically organized categories. Lack of inflectional marking of nominative singular masculine nouns may simply result from the convergence of the unmarked categories "nominative" (case), "singular" (number) and "masculine" (gender). This is particularly obvious in a language like Classical Mongolian, in which each grammatical category is expressed in a separate morpheme. In this case, one need not hypothesize any grammatical interaction between case, number and gender to produce the unmarked combination "nominative singular masculine." This is because the combination "nominative singular masculine" is the *only* unmarked noun form.

6.2.1 Animacy and definiteness

In 5.3.3, the case marking of objects in Punjabi was described as an illustration of the animacy and definiteness hierarchies. In Punjabi, pronominal direct objects, animate nouns and definite inanimate nouns took the postposition *nū,* while indefinite inanimate nouns did not take any postposition. This evidence suggests that there is a clustering of animacy and definiteness, so that the higher a direct-object noun phrase is found on the animacy AND/OR the definiteness hierarchy, the more likely it is to be marked with a case marker. This evidence is also confirmed by the Spanish example of the preposition *a* before referential indefinites such as *secretaria* 'secretary': if the referential indefinite is nonhuman, the *a* is generally not used. In fact this is a typological pattern; Comrie (1979) examined a number of systems, including Turkish, Finnish, Persian, Southern Tati and Hindi, in which some combination of definiteness and animacy triggered case marking of the direct object.[2]

The explanation for the clustering of definiteness and animacy is relatively straightforward. The animacy hierarchy actually consists of three hierarchies, person, NP type and animacy proper. The first- and second-person pronouns are at the "top" of the combined hierarchy, because they are by definition human and pronominal. The first- and second-person pronouns are also definite by definition. Thus, definiteness should be added to the person, NP type and animacy proper hierarchies, since it is equally closely related to the personal pronouns:

Person:	first, second < third
NP type:	pronoun < proper name < common noun
Animacy:	human < animate < inanimate
Definiteness:	definite < referential < nonreferential (nonspecific)

Hence, there is actually a cluster of four hierarchies, with first and second person linking the other three together by virtue of their inherent human, pronominal and definite properties.

The implicational universal describing the cross-linguistic pattern is: "If a language uses a nonzero case marking for a direct object on the animacy/definiteness hierarchies, then it uses a nonzero case marking for direct objects higher on the hierarchies." The unusual aspect of this typological generalization is that relative rank is not absolutely predictable, since there is actually a cluster of four hierarchies. For instance, is a pronoun referring to an inanimate object higher than a common noun referring to a human? Neither is actually higher, and in fact there is typological variation as to the treatment of inanimate pronouns and human common nouns. For instance, in English the inanimate (singular) pronoun *it* does not have a distinct object form, unlike all of the other pronouns which have animate reference (except, unfortunately for markedness, *you*); but nor do human common nouns. In Punjabi, on the other hand, both inanimate pronouns and human common nouns require the object-marking *nū*. In general, it is a prediction of prototype analysis that combinations of prototypical and nonprototypical features such as ⟨inanimate, pronominal⟩ and ⟨human, common noun⟩ will be the most variable cross-linguistically, whereas the core members, possessing all of the prototypical properties and the extreme peripheral members, lacking all (or almost all) of the prototypical properties, will be treated consistently across languages.

The clustering of animacy and definiteness in direct objects is found in two related grammatical phenomena, noun incorporation and verb agreement. Noun incorporation is the phenomenon by which a noun is so closely bound to a verb grammatically that it is considered to be a part of it. It resembles noun–verb compounding, such as English *birdwatching,* but it is also found with finite verb forms, as in Ngandi (Heath 1978b:262; 3PL/3PL = "third plural acting on third plural"):

(1) barba-   ga-   miṛʔ- ñilʔ   -bo -m
     3PL/3PL- SUBORD- jail confine -AUX -PAST.PUNCT
     'they locked them up in jail'

The least-marked direct objects (with respect to case marking) are the least definite and least animate objects; these are also the ones that are most likely to be incorporated. Sadock (1985), using data based on Allen, Gardiner and Frantz (1984), describes the following incorporation options for direct objects in Southern Tiwa:[3]

	Plural, unmodified	Plural, modified	Singular, not modified by dem., num.	Singular modified by dem., num.
Human	oblig.	opt.	opt.*	opt.*
Animate	oblig.	oblig.	oblig.	oblig.
Inanimate	oblig.	oblig.	oblig.	oblig.

*Incorporation obligatory if subject is third person; see 6.3.2.

If we take singular number and modification (by demonstrative or numeral) to indicate a greater degree of definiteness of the direct object, the data here agree with the animacy–definiteness hierarchy: the more properties the direct object shares with the upper end of the animacy–definiteness cluster, the less likely incorporation will occur. This is illustrated by the obligatory incorporation found in the lower-left part of the chart and the optional incorporation found in the upper-right. This is part of a typological pattern in which incorporation of direct objects (and also of intransitive subjects) is found at the lower end of the animacy–definiteness cluster. Mithun (1984) describes four types of noun incorporation, based on discourse function (closely related to the phenomena described by the definiteness hierarchy). Simplifying somewhat, Mithun's types range from compounding, in which the noun plays a generic (nonreferential) function to a type of incorporation in which the incorporated noun plays an essentially anaphoric function. Based on a survey of over a hundred languages, Mithun found that languages form an implicational scale so that if a language allows incorporation of the highest type (the "anaphoric," or as Mithun calls it, "classifying" type), then it will allow incorporation of all the lower types.[4]

On the other hand, direct objects that are the most animate and definite are those that the verb will most likely agree with typologically.[5] For example, languages exist in which verbs agree with definite direct objects but not with indefinite ones, as in Amharic (Givón 1976:161–2; see Moravcsik 1974):

(2) Kasa   borsa -w   -ɨn   wässädä -w
     Kassa   wallet -the -OBJ took-he -it
     'Kassa took the wallet.'

(3) Kassa   borsa wässädä
     Kassa   wallet took
     'Kassa took a wallet.'

Givón also cites the example of Swahili, in which the verb agrees with all human and definite nonhuman objects (Givón 1976:159):

(4) ni- li- **mw-** ona yule mtu
ISG- PAST- OBJ- see the person
'I saw the person.'

(5) ni- li- **mw-** one mto mmoja
ISG- PAST- OBJ- see person one
'I saw one person.'

(6) si- **mw-** oni mtu yeyote
ISG.NEG- OBJ -see person any
'I didn't see any person.'

(7) ni- li- **ki-** soma kitabu
ISG- PAST- OBJ- read book
'I read the book.'

(8) ni- li- soma kitabu
ISG- PAST- read book
'I read a book.'

In addition, as Givón and Moravcsik note, agreement is frequently with the primary object, that is, with the G argument (see 5.3.2) of ditransitive verbs instead of with the T argument. Givón points out that the G argument, playing a semantic role of receiver or experiencer, is almost always human (in fact, by semantic necessity) and frequently definite, while the T argument, a possessed item or physical object, is almost always nonhuman. Thus, primary-object agreement has the effect of allowing agreement with the object that is generally higher in animacy. This argument is supported by languages such as Manam. In Manam, the verb may agree with the **benefactive,** a person for whom the action is being performed, as well as with the direct object (P argument). However, if the P argument is first or second person (a very rare circumstance), the verb will agree with it instead (Lichtenberk 1983b:165–6):

(9) nátu go- ruʔu **-í** -a -n **-a**
child 2SG.IRR- wash **-3SG.OBJ** -BUFF -BEN **-ISG.OBJ**
'Wash the child for me!'

(10) ŋáu -lo da-' uŋ -ʔo
ISG -for 3PL.IRR- beat -2SG.OBJ
'They will beat you up for me.'

The typological evidence indicates that the various animacy and definiteness parameters cluster in a universal way with respect to direct objects.[6]

6.2.2 *Transitivity*

The best-known application of prototype analysis to grammatical categories is Hopper and Thompson's (1980) study of transitivity.

This analysis has spawned intensive research on cross-linguistic manifestations of the transitivity prototypes and the search for other grammatical prototypes (see the collection of essays in Hopper & Thompson 1982).

The criterion that Hopper and Thompson used to define grammatical transitivity is the ability of the clause to display morphosyntactic transitive behavior. The following grammatical criteria were taken by them to define "transitive behavior":

(1) A morpheme, usually a verbal affix, that explicitly codes the transitivity of the clause.
(2) Evidence of the direct-object status of the P argument of the verb (see 5.3.2):
(a) the P argument does not have an oblique (dative, instrumental, locative, etc.) case marker;
(b) the P argument has a special direct-object (accusative) case marker, if such exists in the language;[7]
(c) the verb has object agreement with the P argument, if object agreement exists in the language.

In languages with ergative case-marking or agreement patterns, the criteria listed under (2) appear not to apply, since the language does not have a distinct "direct object" (see chapter 5). However, many of these languages have an **antipassive** construction which differs from the standard ergative construction in one or more of the following ways:

(1) the P argument of the verb is marked as an oblique;
(2) the verb does not agree with the P argument, if such agreement exists in the language;
(3) the A argument is coded in the same way as the S argument in intransitive verbs (i.e. it has absolutive rather than ergative case marking and/or verb agreement).

All of these properties indicate that the standard ergative construction is the analogue to the prototypically transitive construction in nonergative languages, and the antipassive construction is the analogue to an intransitive construction in those languages.

Hopper and Thompson's typological evidence for the prototype structure of the grammatical category "transitive" has already been mentioned in 6.2. For each of the prototypical properties of transitivity, there exist languages in which clauses possessing that property display transitive behavior; but clauses that differ only in lacking that property do not display transitive behavior, even if they possess other "transitive" properties (most importantly, if the verb has a P argument). The cluster of prototypically transitive properties are shown in table 6.1 (the terminology is theirs).

Table 6.1 *Prototypical transitivity (after Hopper & Thompson 1980:252)*

Grammatical category	Prototypical transitive feature
Participants	two or more
Kinesis	action (process)
Aspect	telic (bounded)
Punctuality	punctual
Volitionality	volitional
Affirmation	affirmative (positive polarity)
Mode	realis
Agency	highly agentive
Affectedness of object	totally affected object
Individuation of object	highly individuated

A highly individuated object is defined by Hopper and Thompson as itself constituting a cluster of grammatical properties (Hopper & Thompson 1980:253): proper name (vs. common noun), human or animate, concrete, singular, definite or referential and count (vs. mass). The concept "individuated object" is almost identical to the cluster of animate/definite direct objects described in 6.2.1, with the addition of singular number, concrete and count.

We will illustrate examples of the effects of presence/absence of the prototypically transitive properties, using examples of the different sorts of transitive constructions found in the world's languages. In Samoan, a transitive clause uses the ergative preposition for A and the absolutive (zero) for P. If a stative verb instead of a process verb is used, the construction is intransitive: A takes the absolutive and P is expressed with an oblique preposition (Hopper & Thompson 1980:270):

(11) na   fasi **e**   le tama $\emptyset$ le teine
TENSE hit ERG the boy (ABS) the girl
'The boy hit the girl.'

(12) na   va'ai $\emptyset$ le tama **i** le   teine
TENSE see (ABS) the boy OBL the girl
'The boy saw the girl.'

The clause with the stative verb *va'ai* 'see' can be made transitive by using a transitive suffix; but then the verb is in the perfective (telic) aspect, and is better translated as 'spot' (Hopper & Thompson 1980:272):

(13) na   va'ai **-a**   **e**   le tama $\emptyset$ le i'a
TENSE see -TRANS ERG the boy (ABS) the fish
'The boy spotted the fish.'

In Finnish, there is a special nonzero accusative case. In the telic (completed action) aspect, the P argument is expressed in the accusative. In the atelic (incompleted action) aspect, however, the P argument is expressed using the partitive case (Hopper & Thompson 1980:271):

(14) liikemies kirjoitti kirjee **-n** valiokunnalle
businessman wrote letter -ACC committee.to
'The businessman wrote a letter to the committee.'

(15) liikemies kirjoitti kirjet **-tä** valiokunnalle
businessman wrote letter -PARTV committee.to
'The businessman was writing a letter to the committee.'

Yucatec Maya uses "ergative" agreement affixes for transitive subjects (A) and "absolutive" affixes for intransitive subjects. If the object noun does not refer to a specific entity, then the object is incorporated, an antipassive suffix is added and the subject argument is expressed with the absolutive/intransitive subject affix (Mithun 1984:857):

(16) t- in- čak -ǿ -ah če?
COMP- ISG.ERG- chop -3SG.ABS -PERF tree
'I chopped a tree.'

(17) čak -če? -n -ah -en
chop -tree -ANTIPASS -PERF ISG.ABS
'I wood-chopped.' ('I chopped wood.')

Even verbs that have only one argument can display transitive behavior if other transitive prototype features are present. In addition to the case-marking patterns described in 5.3.2, there are languages in which the S argument of an intransitive verb is sometimes expressed in the same way as the A of a transitive verb ("active"), and sometimes in the same way as the P of a transitive verb ("stative"). Expression of the S argument as an A can be taken as the manifestation of transitive behavior (i.e. marking of S like A; in fact, this is frequently called the "ergative" in traditional literature). The "active" or "ergative" is generally found with semantically intransitive predicates indicating processes, particularly processes over which S has control (volition). Hopper and Thompson illustrate this with Eastern Pomo, in which the same verb may occur with active or stative prefixes, indicating controlled and accidental action respectively (1980:265):

(18) **wí** če:xélka
ISG.ACTIVE slip
'I'm slipping (controlled).'

(19) **haː**   čeːxélka
      1SG.STATIVE slide
      'I'm sliding (uncontrolled).'

In general, one can summarize the typological pattern found by Hopper and Thompson as follows: if clauses lacking X can exhibit transitive grammatical behavior in a language, then the clauses possessing X can also exhibit transitive grammatical behavior in the language.

This represents the classic prototype pattern: there is a set of grammatical properties which are associated with transitivity such that the absence of one or more of those properties in a clause may lead to the loss of transitivity of that clause. No single property is a *necessary* characteristic of transitivity, but every property *contributes* to the transitivity of the clause. This is true typologically, of course: within a particular language, the grammar has conventionalized the prototype so that some grammatical properties affect the transitivity of a clause and others do not.

6.3 Markedness reversals and complementary prototypes

Clusters or prototypes represent an unmarked combination of values from different grammatical categories that are found together in a single word, phrase or construction. The combination of values that define the cluster/prototype is unmarked, and any other combination of values is marked to a greater or lesser degree, depending on how close the combination is to a prototypical combination of values.

In many cases, however, there is more than one unmarked combination of values. In general, one finds two prototypes, which complement each other in their combinations of values. In other words, not only does a combination of values form a prototype, but the combination of exactly the opposite values also forms a prototype. We will begin by giving some simple examples of this from phonology.

6.3.1 *Some phonological examples*

In the first mention of this phenomenon in the typological literature, Greenberg writes, "It should be noted that in some cases we have what might be called conditional categories for marked and unmarked. For example, whereas for obstruents, voicing seems clearly the marked characteristic, for sonants [nasals, liquids, glides, vowels] the unvoiced feature has many of the qualities of a marked category"

(Greenberg 1966b:24). The phenomenon that Greenberg describes can be displayed in the following chart:

	Voiced	*Voiceless*
Obstruents	marked	unmarked
Sonants	unmarked	marked

The markedness pattern of voicing for obstruents is reversed for sonants. The phenomenon has been called "markedness reversal" for this reason (e.g. Witkowski & Brown 1983); it has also been called **local markedness** (Tiersma 1982) and **markedness assimilation** (Andersen 1968, 1972), because the markedness is "assimilated" to, or determined "locally" by, the cross-cutting category; and a **natural correlation** (Croft 1983, 1984), because it represents a natural (unmarked) correlation between values on different grammatical parameters. It is crucial to note here that markedness reversal is not random, but is consistent across languages: languages in general treat voiceless obstruents as unmarked but voiceless sonants and vowels as marked.

Instead of representing voicing as marked or unmarked relative to the manner of articulation, one can represent the correlation of unmarked values directly, as follows:

	Unmarked cluster	*Unmarked cluster*
Voicing	voiced	voiceless
Manner	sonants	obstruents

Markedness reversals represent two unmarked clusters or prototype categories that are organized around the opposite values of the same grammatical parameters (here, voicing and manner of articulation). The same phenomenon can easily be illustrated for grammatical hierarchies, using another phonological example, place of articulation and glottalization. In 5.4, a hierarchy of place of articulation for glottalized consonants was derived from phoneme-segment inventory data. The hierarchy mirrored the order of place of articulation in the mouth: labial, dental/alveolar, velar (the behavior of palatals and other less common places of articulation is complex, and will be ignored here). For implosives, the least-marked end of the hierarchy is the labial. For ejectives, however, the least-marked end of the hierarchy is the velar. This can be illustrated as follows:[8]

	Prototype		*Prototype*
Place	labial	dental/alveolar	velar
Glottal type	implosive		ejective

Reversals in grammatical hierarchies are, if anything, more orderly than simple markedness reversals. The ranking of values is the same in both cases; what differs is which end constitutes the least-marked value. Once again, this phenomenon is consistent across languages; we are not dealing with random effects.[9]

6.3.2 *Case, animacy and verb type*

In 5.3.3, it was observed that Navajo orders arguments of the verb by animacy and not by case, so that the higher-animacy argument precedes the lower-animacy one, regardless of whether it is A or P in a transitive clause. Instead, "who did what to whom" is indicated on the verb: the *yi-* prefix indicates that the higher-animacy argument is acting on the lower one, and the *bi-* prefix indicates the opposite situation.

A similar pattern is found with verb agreement in many languages, leading to a very un-English verb pattern. In these languages, the verb possesses agreement affixes for both the A and P arguments of the verb, but the agreement affixes do not indicate who is doing what to whom. Thus, an affix such as Cree *ki-. . .-in* "second-person singular and first-person singular" is used for both "you did it to me" and "I did it to you." Instead, some other verbal affix indicates who did what to whom. This affix is called **direct** if the animacy ranking matches the case ranking, so that the higher-animacy argument is A; and **inverse** if the opposite ranking is found. This system is found in Algonquian languages such as Cree, where the animacy ranking is second < first < third (Wolfart & Carroll 1981:69–70):

(20) ni-   pēh   -ā   -nānak
     1PL/3PL- wait.for -DIR -1PL/3PL
     'We (exclusive) wait for them.'

(21) ni-   pēh   -iko -nānak
     1PL/3PL- wait.for -INV. -1PL/3PL
     'They wait for us (exclusive).'

(22) ki-   wāpam -ø   -in
     2SG/1SG- see   -(DIR) -2SG/1SG
     'You (SG) see me.'

(23) ki-   wāpam -it   -in
     2SG/1SG- see   -INV -2SG/1SG
     'I see you (SG).'

This system is also found in Nocte, in which the verb agrees with only the higher-animacy argument, and the inverse suffix -*h*- indicates that the higher-animacy argument is P, not A (DeLancey 1981:641):

(24) nga -ma ate hetho -ang
      ISG -ERG 3SG teach -I
      'I will teach him.'

(25) ate -ma nga -nang hetho -h   -ang
      3SG -ERG ISG- -ACC teach -INV -I
      'He will teach me.'

(26) nang -ma   nga hetho -h   -ang
      2SG -ERG ISG teach -INV -I
      'You will teach me.'

(27) nga -ma nang hetho -e
      ISG -ERG 2SG   teach -IPL
      'I will teach you.'

In the Nocte version of the animacy hierarchy, unlike in Cree, first person outranks second person. This demonstrates that there is no universal typological ranking of first person relative to second person, and in fact many languages avoid the "problem" of ranking first and second person by using separate verb forms entirely.[10]

Our attention here, however, is on the direct–inverse verbal affix. Typologically, the inverse form is marked and the direct form is unmarked. In Nocte, for example, the direct form is zero, and one of the direct-form allomorphs in Cree is also zero. DeLancey (1981) interprets this as representing a parallel alignment of the animacy (specifically, person) hierarchy and the case hierarchy (specifically, subject < object):

1,2   → 3
subject → object

This correlation of the animacy hierarchy and the case hierarchy is typologically unmarked in the direct–inverse systems. It also represents a markedness reversal: first/second person are unmarked as subject and third person is unmarked as object. The markedness "reversal" is expressed directly in transitive clauses, because both subject and object are manifested.

DeLancey links the relatively rare (though geographically and genetically widespread) direct–inverse patterns with another, equally widespread and somewhat more common pattern of "split ergativity," analyzed by Silverstein (1976). In many languages, some pronominal and nominal arguments display a nominative (A+S)–accusative (P) distinction, and others display an ergative (A)–absolute (S+P) distinction, for instance in Dyirbal (Dixon 1979:87):

> *First-/second-person pronouns*: nominative -ϕ, accusative -*na*
> *Third-person pronouns*: ergative -*ŋgu*, absolutive -ϕ

Other languages display more complex splits in the case-marking of arguments, e.g. Cashinawa (Dixon 1979:87):

> *First-person singular/second-person pronouns*: nominative -ϕ, accusative -*a*
> *Third person pronouns:* "ergative" *habū*, intransitive subject *habu*, "accusative" *haa*
> *Proper names and common nouns:* ergative formed by nasalization (cf. *habū*), absolutive -ϕ

The typological pattern manifested in these two languages can be more easily observed if the data is displayed differently, so that the A, S and P arguments are listed separately and the zero-morpheme cells are left blank ("$\tilde{v}$" indicates nasalization; see Dixon 1979):

Dyirbal	A	S	P
1st/2nd pronouns			-na
3rd pronouns, nouns	-ŋgu		
Cashinawa	A	S	P
1st/2nd pronouns			-a
3rd pronoun	$\tilde{v}$		-a*
nouns	$\tilde{v}$		

*with truncation of *habu-* to *ha-*

There is a markedness reversal involved here: the transitive subject is less marked, the higher in animacy it is, but the transitive object is more marked the higher in animacy it is. This pattern was first discussed extensively by Silverstein (1976:123). DeLancey identified it as the same phenomenon as that found in direct–inverse systems. In fact, the transitive-object half of this markedness reversal is virtually identical to the high animacy-definite object cluster described in 6.2.1.[11]

DeLancey also links the markedness reversal to certain constraints on passive-voice forms. DeLancey notes that the second of the following two English passives is less acceptable (DeLancey 1981:638):

(28)   I was flunked by Prof. Summers.
(29)   ?Mary Summers was flunked by me.

The passive is acceptable if the passive subject is higher in animacy (specifically, person) than the passive agent. In fact, the effect of passivizing the sentence *Prof. Summers flunked me* is to have the animacy ranking correlate with the case ranking (first-person subject < third-person oblique); the marked passive morphosyntax indicates that the animacy–case ranking is the reverse of the semantic agent–patient relation.[12] On the other hand, the passive is questionable in just the situation that the passive agent is higher in animacy than the passive subject.[13] DeLancey argues that the reason for the unacceptability of example (29) is that the active counterpart *I flunked Mary Summers* already has the unmarked animacy–case correlation and is unmarked for voice, so it is paradoxical to use a marked voice construction for the unmarked correlation of the two hierarchies.

Finally, DeLancey examines another type of "split ergativity," in which nominative–accusative case marking is found in the incompletive (imperfective) aspect and ergative–accusative case marking and/or agreement in the completive (perfective) aspect. This is illustrated here for Gujarati (DeLancey 1981:628–9; see also DeLancey 1982):

(30) Ramesh   pen   khərid -t   -o   hə -t   -o
     Ramesh.MASC pen.F buy   -IMPF -MASC AUX -IMPF -MASC
     'Ramesh was buying the pen.'
(31) Ramesh   -e   pen   khərid -y   -i
     Ramesh.MASC. -ERG pen.F buy   -PERF -F
     'Ramesh bought the pen.'

Following the well-established criteria of marking patterns with agreement and case marking, the imperfective aspect is therefore associated with an unmarked A argument, and the perfective aspect is associated with an unmarked P argument. Combining this pattern with the previous ones yields an animacy–case–aspect correlation (see DeLancey 1981; 7.2.2):

first/second → third person
subject (A)   → object (P)
imperfective   perfective

The typological analysis of the expression of the arguments of verbs has revealed that no simple universal definition of "subject" and "object" is possible. Nevertheless, there is a rich and complex pattern of markedness, hierarchies, correlations and prototypes that does appear to have universal application and suggests several routes for a typologically valid explanation of the concepts "subject" and "object." This will be discussed in the next chapter.

6.3.3 *Nouns, verbs and adjectives*

In 3.2, it was mentioned that one of the relatively few unrestricted universals is that all languages have nouns and verbs. However, it is not entirely clear how one can define the category "noun" or the category "verb" in a universal sense. The methods of typological analysis presented so far allow one to make significant steps both in verifying the universality of nouns and verbs and in defining the two categories.

The first typological analysis of relevance to this problem was of a category whose universality has been repeatedly contested, however: adjectives (Dixon 1977). Cross-linguistically, the category identified with the label "adjective" varies much more than those labeled "noun" and "verb." In some languages, such as English, there is a large class of adjectives which can be added to quite easily; adjectives form an **open class.** In a number of other languages, such as Hausa, there is a small **closed class** of words, defined on internal grammatical criteria, which is generally identified with the category "adjective." In yet other languages, such as Chinese, it is claimed that "adjectives" do not exist, and the translation equivalents of English adjectives are assigned to the categories "noun" or "verb."

In a paper first circulated in 1970, R. M. W. Dixon (1977) made a typological study of languages with closed classes of adjectives, and compared them to languages with open classes and languages without adjectives. Dixon observed that languages with a small closed adjective class tended to include words referring to a specific set of concepts. An example of such a system is Igbo (Dixon 1977:21):

úkwú	'large'	ńtà	'small'
ọ́hụ̀'rọ́	'new'	ọ́cyè	'old'
ójí'í	'black, dark'	ọ́cá	'white, light'
ọ́má	'good'	ọ́jọ́'ọ́	'bad'

The basic adjective concepts included dimension, age, color and value ("good"/"bad"). Dixon formulated the following generalizations: If a language has an adjective class, it will include words referring to the basic adjective concepts (dimension, age, color, value) in that class. If a language includes nonbasic adjective concepts in the adjective class, then it will include basic adjective concepts in that class (see Dixon 1977:56, generalization (a)).

Evaluating these universals as typological distributional statements, it can be seen that concepts referring to dimension, age, color and value are unmarked as adjectives. Dixon provides additional evidence that suggests this is a markedness pattern. Rotuman has an open adjective class, but only the following have distinct singular and plural forms (Churchward 1940:39):

ti'u	'big'	mea'mea'	'small'
roa	'long'	luka	'short'
hepa	'broad'	jiakjika	'narrow, thin'
'atakoa	'whole, complete'		
		mafua	'old'
kele	'black'	fisi	'white'
		mi'a	'red'
		hạni	'female'

In Acooli, there is a closed class of about forty adjectives, only seven of which inflect for number (Dixon 1977:23, citing Crazzolara 1955):

dɪ̂t	'great, big, old (persons)'	tëdi	'small, little'
dwóò	'big, large (volume)'		
boòr	'long, high, distant'	ceèk	'short'
bɛɛ̀r	'good, kind, nice, beautiful'	raàc	'bad, bad tasting, ugly'

The markedness pattern that Dixon identified with adjectives, and which is found in nouns and verbs, represents a semantic class as unmarked with respect to a particular grammatical function, the adjectival function of modification or attribution. The use of a basic adjective concept in the nominal function of reference and the verbal function of predication is marked, in the standard sense of that term. English provides a good example of structural markedness patterns: adjectival nominals require a nominalizing suffix if they refer to the property they denote: e.g. *leng-th, red-ness*. When predicated, adjectives require a copula: *Emma is tall*. Basic noun concepts, words denoting persons and physical objects, are structurally marked as predicate nominals, requiring a copula in English and many other languages. Basic verb concepts, denoting processes and actions, are also marked when they serve as referring expressions (nominalizations, complements) or as modifiers (participles, relative clauses). In sum, structural markedness is manifested by the typological distribution of derivational morphology that does not also involve a major semantic change, across classes of concepts and grammatical functions (see table 6.2).

The correlations other than "unmarked nouns/adjectives/verbs" are structurally marked, using the derivational morphosyntax named in the relevant cells of the table. This is illustrated in the table 6.3 by English examples for each derivational type (nonzero derivational morphosyntax is indicated in boldface).

This is a typological markedness pattern of course, which implies that languages exist that use zero morphology to indicate the marked deri-

Table 6.2 *Derivational morphology indicating markedness of syntactic category types*

	Reference	Modification	Predication
Objects	**unmarked nouns**	genitive, compounds	predicate nominals
Properties	deadjectival nouns	**unmarked adjectives**	predicate adjectives
Actions	nominalizations, complements, infinitives, gerunds	participles, relative clauses	**unmarked verbs**

Table 6.3 *English derivational morphology indicating syntactic category markedness*

	Reference	Modification	Predication
Objects	dog	dog's	**be** a dog
Properties	happi-**ness**	happy	**be** happy
Actions	fly-**ing, to** fly, **that** ... fly .., fli-**ght**	fly-**ing**, fl-**own which** ... fly ...	fly

vational relations in the chart. For example, Lakhota inflects predicate nominals and adjectives directly (Rood & Taylor 1976):

(32) ni-   wašte
     2SG.PATIENT- good
     'You are good.'

(33) ma-   lakhota šni
     1SG.PATIENT- Lakhota NEG
     'I am not a Lakhota.'

Genitive constructions can also involve zero marking, as was illustrated in 2.1 with Kobon:

(34) Dumnab ram
     Dumnab house
     'Dumnab's house'

In addition to nonzero verb nominalizations, English has a large number of zero nominalizations, such as *march, fall* and *split*. The typological pattern, however, predicts that one will not find examples of languages in which words denoting actions require a derivational affix in order to be predicated, but words denoting objects or properties will not.

The marked cells in the chart also display behavioral markedness, both inflectional and syntactic. For example, in Quiché predicate nominals may agree with their subjects just as verbs do, but they may not take the tense/aspect prefixes (Croft, forthcoming):

(35) ?in (*k)-   in-   ačih
      I   (*PRES)- 1SG.ABS- man
      'I am a man.'

Such forms are marked behaviorally as lexical nouns, as well: they do not allow the full range of nominal inflections, such as the article, which is present in virtually all Quiché referring noun phrases (cf. Hopper & Thompson 1984:715–17). In other words, predicate nominals are marked relative to nouns used in referring, and marked relative to verbs used as predicates. In general, the marked combinations of semantic class and grammatical function (which may be identified with pragmatic function; see Croft, forthcoming) display this sort of two-way defective grammatical behavior.

The complementary counterpart to the marked category of predicate nominals are verbal nouns, gerunds and related forms. These forms are behaviorally marked both as verbs and as adjectives. For example, the infinitive verbal noun in Turkish does not allow subjects, while a verb functioning as a predicate does, of course; but as a noun the infinitive is behaviorally marked, since it does not allow the possessive personal suffixes or the genitive case. The infinitive does allow the accusative suffix (for definite direct objects), like nouns, and may govern direct objects, like verbs (Lewis 1967:167–8):

(36) ekmek al- mağ -ı   unuttu
      bread buy -INF -ACC he.forgot
      'He forgot to buy bread.'

The evidence given above demonstrates that the typological pattern of major syntactic-category membership is a set of markedness reversals that correlate grammatical function and semantic class for the three major syntactic categories.[14] These provide the basis of prototype definitions for noun, verb and adjective that can be applied across languages.[15]

6.3.4 *Other markedness reversals*

The relationships among animacy, definiteness, case and verbal aspect have received the greatest amount of attention in the typological literature, because they play such a dominant role in determining the structure of clauses. Nevertheless, there are a number of other typological patterns of interaction among parameters, and certainly many more that have yet to be discovered.

The animacy–case-hierarchy correlations described in 6.3.2 appear to pertain to subjects and objects (including the two "objects" of ditransitive verbs). One also finds correlations producing local markedness patterns in certain oblique phrases (Croft 1988:171; cf. Tiersma 1982:843, Principle 2). Deictic terms, proper names and common nouns referring to places and times are unmarked when occurring as locative or temporal expressions; compare Yoruba to English and Malay:

> Yoruba (Rowlands 1969:29)
> (37) mo rí i   l-   óni
>   I   see him LOC- today
>   'I saw him today.'

> English
> (38) George Washington slept ϕ here.
> (39) George Washington slept **in** this bed.

> Malay (Dodds 1977:13)
> (40) *kĕ-ϕ* 'to'/*dari-ϕ* 'from' + noun phrase denoting a place
>   *kĕ-pada* 'to'/*dari-pada* 'from' + noun phrase denoting a person

The structural-markedness evidence for the correlation between place terms and locatives is further supported by frequency data collected by Greenberg for Russian (1974b). Russian uses a construction of preposition + accusative case for directional phrases and preposition + prepositional (locative) case for locative phrases (see examples in 1.4). Greenberg computed frequencies for nouns of various classes in each case and states: "The place names ... may be characterized as having a low nominative, a high accusative and, as would be expected, a very high prepositional [case frequency], far higher than that in any other category" (Greenberg 1974b:26).

It has also been observed (e.g. Tiersma 1982) that certain noun classes tend to be unmarked in the plural instead of in the singular. Tiersma identifies this as a markedness reversal ("local markedness" is his term), and provides examples from diachronic processes in Frisian (his Principle 1; see chapter 8 for discussion of the relationship between diachronic process and markedness patterns). Evidence for this reversal is found in synchronic alternations as well, in which the unmarked plural is generally called a **collective** and the marked singular a **singulative,** a pattern particularly common among Semitic and Nilo-Saharan languages. The

typological generalization is that the same noun classes tend to have
unmarked collective–marked singulative forms:

(1)   small objects that tend to occur together, yet are distinct to the
      naked eye (especially foodstuffs): e.g. Russian *gorox* 'peas'/*gorošina*
      'pea,' *soloma* 'straw(s)'/*solominka* 'a straw' (Wierzbicka 1985:324);
      Turkana *ŋi-ɲa* 'grass'/*ɛ-ɲa-it* 'blade of grass' (Dimmendaal
      1983:228);[16] Syrian Arabic *šaʕr* 'hair' *šaʕr-a* 'a hair,' *xass* 'lettuce'/
      xass-e 'head of lettuce' (Cowell 1964:297);

(2)   animals, birds and people, which also tend to occur in groups: Tur-
      kana *ŋi-tyaŋì* 'wild animals'/*e-tyŋ-it* 'wild animal,' *ŋi-tùrkanà* 'Tur-
      kana people'/*e-tùrkanà-it* 'Turkana person'; Syrian Arabic *baʔar*
      'cattle'/*baʔar-a* 'a cow,' *badu* 'Bedouin'/*badaw-i* 'a Bedouin.' In
      some languages, the only collective–singulative alternation found
      is with the word for 'person,' e.g. Kanuri (Hutchison 1981) and
      Amharic (Leslau 1968). Finally, the unmarked English plurals for
      some wild creatures *(deer, moose, fish, trout, salmon)* is probably
      an instance of this same typological phenomenon;

(3)   body parts and other items that occur in pairs: Turkana *ŋa-kì* 'ears'/
      a-k-it 'an ear,' *ŋa-muk* 'shoes'/*-muk-àt* 'a shoe.'

Thus, one finds an unmarked correlation between nouns referring
to objects that normally come in groups and the plural. Presumably,
these nouns are those which are most likely to occur more frequently
in the plural than in the singular, although evidence for the frequency
criterion of markedness has not been gathered for this correlation.[17]

Tiersma (1982) provides one more example of local markedness. In
contrast to the general pattern of zero-marked agreement in the third
person (see 4.3.3 and 6.4.2), Tiersma suggests that for verbs of perception and emotion ("mental verbs"), the first person is the least marked
form (1982:846, Principle 3). Tiersma provides frequency evidence from
Spanish, and some unconvincing morphological evidence from Frisian
and French. However, the frequency pattern suggests that his Principle
3 may be valid. Another example of a third-person/first-person markedness reversal that has some typological support is the possession of kin
terms. In Lakhota, possession is usually expressed with a zero third-
person singular form (Boas & Deloria 1941:131):

(41)   **mi**   -tʼa woyuha
       1SG -AL household.goods
       'my household goods'

(42)   ∅-tʼa- ·sųke
       AL- horse
       'his/her horse'

However, with many kin terms, the first-person form is zero and a nonzero third-person possessive suffix found only with these terms is used (Boas & Deloria 1941:129):

    (43)   ∅-lekši
          mother's.elder.brother
          'my mother's elder brother'
    (44)   lekši   **-tku**
          mo.eld.bro.   **-3SG.POSS.KIN**
          'his/her mother's elder brother'

A similar phenomenon is found in Ngandi. A special set of possessive prefixes is used for kin possession; the first-person form of this set is zero (Heath 1978b:38):[18]

    (45)   ṇa-   ∅- guṛač
          F.SG-   elder.sister
          'my/our elder sister'
    (46)   ṇa-   **maṛ-**   guṛač
          F.SG-   **2ND.POSS.KIN-**   elder.sister
          'your elder sister'
    (47)   ṇa-   **roŋ-**   guṛač
          F.SG-   **3RD.POSS.KIN-**   elder.sister
          'his/her/their elder sister'

Finally, it is worth noting in this regard the use of the unmarked kin terms *mother, father,* etc., in English to refer to "my mother," "my father," etc.

The markedness-reversal patterns found for collective nouns, (possibly) mental verbs and kin-term possession are not manifested in every language, in the way that the markedness reversals described in 6.3.1–6.3.3 and the patterns described in chapters 4 and 5 are. Instead, they must be described in implicational universal form: if a language has any zero plural/nonzero singular forms, they will be found on collective nouns; if a language has any zero first-person/nonzero third-person inflections, they will be found in the possession of kin terms. In these cases, the class of words containing markedness reversals is a subclass of a larger class of words bearing the normal markedness pattern, and it appears that in many languages the local markedness pattern simply does not exist.

One phenomenon that has already been described in detail in this volume, word-order harmony, displays typological features that closely resemble the phenomena described in this chapter. Harmony, unlike dominance, is a correlation between grammatical values in different categories: for example, AN word order is harmonic with DemN word order. Harmony also appears to undergo a markedness reversal: while AN is harmonic with DemN, NDem is harmonic with NA. This is represented in table 3.1, in which two general harmonic patterns are described, each the opposite of the other. Finally, although structural and behavioral markedness do not apply to word order, the frequency data found in the tetrachoric tables for word-order universals do imply that harmonic combinations are unmarked. In virtually all cases, the harmonic combinations of word-order types are far more frequent than the attested disharmonic combinations.

6.4 **More complex interactions**

Prototypes – clusters and complementary (reverse) prototypes – represent typological patterns that tend to pervade the grammatical systems of languages. For example, the transitivity prototype covers virtually all of the grammatical features of clauses, and as a consequence is quite manifest in the grammars of human languages. However, individual grammatical features can interact with other features in quite different ways. No grand pattern emerges, but each pattern is typologically valid and requires explanation.

6.4.1 *Place of articulation*

An example of the complex interaction of typological patterns is found in the typology of place of articulation, described in 5.4. Gaps in segment inventories have been used to propose a hierarchy for voiceless ejectives of velar < dental/alveolar < bilabial, so that the least marked place of articulation is the most back one (velar) and the most marked place of articulation is the most front one (bilabial).

Examining the same type of cross-linguistic evidence (inventory gaps) for voiced implosives, one observes almost the opposite effect:

(xiii) A language with any implosives or laryngealized stops has /ɓ/ and /ɗ/. 36/42 85.7%

(xiv)   If a language has /ʄ/ it has /ɠ/. 3/4 75.0% (Maddieson 1984:121)

The opposite hierarchy is found: the most front position is least marked, and the most back position is the most marked. This is a typical markedness reversal.

Examining the same evidence for plosives and nasals, however, leads to rather different hierarchies. Voiceless plosives might be expected to behave like ejectives (so that the labial end of the hierarchy is most marked), and voiced plosives like implosives (so that the velar end of the place hierarchy is most marked). Maddieson's evidence reveals a slightly different pattern:

(xiii) If a language has /p/ then it has /k/, and if it has /k/ then it has /*t/ (4 counterexamples in the UPSID sample).

(xiv) If a language has /g/ then it has /*d/, and if it has /*d/ then it has /b/ (3 counterexamples in the UPSID sample). (Maddieson 1984:40)

The data supports the presence of the place hierarchy for voiced stops, but not for voiceless stops, which supports a ranking dental/alveolar< velar<labial. If we turn now to (voiced) nasals, we find the following generalizations:

(vi) A language with any nasals has /*n/. 304/307 99.0%

(vii) The presence of /m/ implies the presence of /*n/. 297/299 99.3%

(viii) The presence of either /ŋ/ or /*ɲ/ in a language implies the presence of both /m/ and /*n/. 197/200 98.5% (Maddieson 1984:69)

These universals, which are very strongly confirmed in the UPSID sample, suggest a place of articulation hierarchy for nasals of dental/ alveolar<labial<velar.[19]

Thus, the place hierarchy that applies for glottalized consonants and voiced plosives does not apply to voiceless plosives or nasals. However, it is not the case that the voiceless plosives and nasals do not display any hierarchical pattern with respect to place of articulation. There are hierarchical patterns for the latter two consonant types; but they are not the same as the place hierarchy that is found with the other consonant types and that basically reflects the front-to-back order of place of articulation. These data do not invalidate the front-to-back place hierarchy; they indicate that the ranking of places of articulation on the hierarchy is related to the manner of articulation of the consonant.

To summarize, the following patterns are found:

Voiced implosives and plosives: bilabial < dental/alveolar < velar
Voiceless ejectives: velar < dental/alveolar < bilabial
Voiceless plosives: dental/alveolar < velar < bilabial
Nasals: dental/alveolar < labial < velar

Instead of a global hierarchy of place of articulation, there are purely "local" hierarchies relating to specific cross-cutting phonetic features. This means that any explanation for the existence of the typological hierarchy (presumably phonetic) will have to be specific to the particular manner of articulation in question.

6.4.2   *Person*

The discussion of animacy (including person) in 4.3.3, 5.3.3, 6.2.1 and 6.3.2 should make the reader aware that typological behavior of animacy is extremely complex. It should not be surprising, therefore, to discover that animacy interacts with still other grammatical properties in different ways.

We have observed that the person hierarchy, the "top end" of the animacy hierarchy, is ranked 1,2 < 3 when it interacts with the GR hierarchy (A acting on P; 6.3.2). However, in 4.3.3, it was pointed out that frequency counts for subject verb-forms indicated a person hierarchy of 3 < 1 < 2 (Greenberg 1966b:44–5), and zero-marked verb forms (including zero verb-agreement forms) follow this hierarchy.[20] Even there, in hortatory and imperative forms second person is the least marked: 2 < 1,3 (Greenberg 1966b:44).

A glance at pronominal systems and verb inflections reveals that different hierarchies result depending on which cross-cutting parameter is used to determine the markedness of person. With respect to the category of number, the first person is least marked, followed by second and third person; that is 1 < 2 < 3 (data in Ingram 1978:243–5). Modern English is an exception; a safer statement is 1 < 2,3. With respect to the category of gender, the third person is generally the least marked, followed by second and third person; that is 3 < 2 < 1. Again, there are some exceptions in which second person but not third has gender distinctions; Greenberg's Universal 44 (1966a:96) gives the more cautious 3,2 < 1. Finally, an unsystematic survey of politeness distinctions suggests a hierarchy 2 < 3 < 1. We may summarize the typological patterns as follows (using "? <" again for a less-certain ranking of values):

> *GR hierarchy*: 1, 2 < 3
> *Non-imperatives*: 3 < 1 < 2
> *Imperatives*: 2 < 1,3
> *Number*: 1 < 2? < 3
> *Gender*: 3? < 2 < 1
> *Politeness*: 2 < 3 < 1

It is important to reiterate that there is consistency across languages for each feature against which the markedness of person is calculated. One does not find one set of languages treating first person as marked with respect to number and another set treating first person as unmarked with respect to number. Instead, the hierarchy (markedness patterns) varies depending on the cross-cutting category involved: case, number, gender, politeness, non-imperative verb agreement and imperatives or hortatives. As in the case of the place of articulation hierarchies, the explanation for the different hierarchies will have to be based on the relationship between person and each grammatical category (for example, the high frequency of hortatory verb forms directed at the addressee is probably the reason for the unmarked status of second person in imperatives).

In studying the cross-linguistic patterns of phonological and morpho-syntactic phenomena, typology has had to proceed far beyond the original concepts of markedness proposed by the Prague School and the simple implicational universals first proposed by Greenberg. Many of the markedness patterns given at the end of chapter 4 have turned out to be multivalued hierarchies (as was already indicated there in some cases). Binary features and hierarchies have been found to cluster into typological prototype patterns. The interactions between grammatical categories and constructions have turned out to involve clusters, complementary prototypes and highly specific correlations between categories. It is likely that many of the markedness patterns described in chapter 4 will turn out to be more complex than current typological research has indicated, and perhaps all of the absolute, global markedness patterns will be found to have local markedness reversals or correlations. The extensive research on case, animacy, definiteness and number described in chapters 4–6 has indicated just how complex, yet universal, those patterns can be.

6.5 Typology and syntactic analysis

In the past four chapters, we have described the major typological patterns and interactions among those patterns that have been discovered in the world's languages. Before proceeding to the extension of typological analysis to functional and diachronic domains, it is worth re-examining some issues raised in chapter 1 on the relationship of typology to the syntactic analysis of single languages.

In 1.2, the method of syntactic argumentation in structural and generative analysis was illustrated by a set of English sentences, repeated here:

Case marking:	He congratulated him/*he.
Verb agreement:	Teresa likes/*like horses.
NP deletion:	
in nonfinite forms:	Jack wants -∅ to leave.
in imperatives:	∅ Take out the garbage.
in coordination:	John found a ring and ∅ took it home with him.

These sentences represent "five independent pieces of evidence for identifying the immediately preverbal NP as the 'subject' of the sentence" (see the discussion of examples 3–7 in section 1.2). These are transparent cases of syntactic argumentation. Although they have typological consequences, more challenging argumentation is required when the various pieces of grammatical evidence do not converge on a single category. This is clearly true in the case of "subject" in "ergative" languages. In "ergative" languages, case marking and/or agreement patterns splits English-style "subjects" (S+A) and instead combines S with English-style "objects" (P). The existence of this pattern lays doubt on the universality of the concept "subject." A common strategy to reassert the universality of fundamental grammatical concepts such as "subject" is represented by Stephen Anderson's analysis of "subject" in "ergative" languages (1976). Anderson argues that, although case marking and agreement follow the ergative (A vs. S+P) pattern in many languages, in almost all of those languages the NP-deletion processes described above follow a nominative–accusative pattern, so that A+S is deleted, not S+P. For example, in Basque, a language which displays ergative–absolutive case marking and verb agreement, the deleted NP in nonfinite complements is A+S (Anderson 1976:12):

(48) nahi dut   ∅ joan
     desire I.have.it (I) go.INF
     'I want to go.'
(49) nahi dut   -∅ egin
     desire I.have.it (I) do.INF
     'I want to do it.'

Anderson then argues that case marking and verb agreement are "morphological" rather than "syntactic" indicators of ergativity, and so languages like Basque display **morphological ergativity,** but **syntactic (or deep) accusativity** (terms that have come into widespread use since Anderson's article). Thus, Basque is essentially an "accusative" language, with the same notion of subject that English has, and therefore the universality of "subject" (i.e. A+S) is preserved.

Anderson's strategy (followed by many other grammarians faced with conflicting or variable grammatical evidence) captures only a small part of the universal properties of "subjects." Subjecthood, taken from a typological perspective, does display a large range of universal patterns. However, most of these patterns are patterns of variation, and in the case of subjects, patterns of great complexity. The patterns that Anderson's strategy essentially ignores, the "morphological" phenomena of case marking and agreement,[21] have turned out to be sensitive to a wide array of interacting hierarchies, particularly animacy and case. Nevertheless, they have revealed a pair of complementary prototypes, roughly high-animacy agents and low-animacy patients, which probably represent the universal categories of "subject" and "object" respectively.

There is another reason not to set aside grammatical evidence that does not support an unrestricted-universal view of a grammatical concept: the fact that certain types of evidence do not fit the presupposed universal pattern may itself represent a typological pattern. For instance, it is well known that case marking is the most highly variable grammatical phenomenon associated with the grammatical relations of "subject" and "object." Agreement tends to follow an accusative pattern more frequently. For example, in Georgian, an accusative agreement pattern is found in the aorist-tense series (traditionally described as "Series II") combined with an active case-marking pattern (Harris 1982:293):

(50) Vano -m   gamozarda   3ma
      Vano -ACTIVE 3SBJ.3OBJ.grow.II brother.NOM
      'Vano raised his brother.'

(51) bavšv -ma   iṭira
      child -ACTIVE 3SBJ.cry.II
      'The child cried.'

(52) Rezo   gamoizarda
      Rezo.NOM 3SBJ.grow.II
      'Rezo grew up.'

The existence of such languages alongside of more "consistent" systems suggests the following implicational universal:

> If the case-marking pattern in a language is nominative–accusative (if case marking of S, A and P exists), then the verb agrees with its NP arguments in a nominative–accusative pattern in that language, if agreement exists.

As Anderson notes, the various NP-deletion patterns are far more uniform typologically, although there are exceptions. Another phenomenon, not discussed by Anderson, NP accessibility in relative clauses, sometimes patterns as an ergative–absolutive system, though that is less common than ergative–absolutive agreement patterns. Finally, NP deletion on an ergative/absolutive basis in sentence co-ordination is extremely rare, found in, for example, Dyirbal (though see Heath 1979 for an alternative analysis). On the basis of the data offered in Anderson's article and elsewhere, one may propose the following implicational hier-

archy, in which the unmarked (high) end of the hierarchy indicates "least
subject to ergative–absolutive pattern" (see Croft, forthcoming; also
Cole *et al.* 1980 for a diachronic perspective):

co-ordination < relative clause < verb agreement < case marking

One may look to correlations between ergativity/accusativity and
specific grammatical constructions. For instance, Dixon (1979:112)
argues that all imperative constructions follow an accusative pattern.
Each of these correlations may have specific external explanations. For
instance, by nature of the meaning of imperatives, imperative subjects
must have control over the action described by the verb, otherwise the
issuing of the command is unacceptable, or at least infelicitous; thus,
imperative subjects must include most As and some Ss.[22] Similar arguments apply to the nonfinite clauses of complement verbs.

Thus, even the pattern of "confirming" and "disconfirming" evidence
for an unrestricted universal definition of "subject" fits into general typological patterns. In general, the method of argumentation in structuralist-
generative syntax is fundamentally different from the method of argumentation in typology. In the former, a group of constructions are used
to argue for a grammatical concept that has universal import, and constructions that do not fit the concept must be explained away in some
fashion. In the latter, the very constructions that support *and disconfirm*
a structuralist-generative analysis are themselves studied, in order to
find universal patterns of cross-linguistic variation. The patterns of variation are as universally valid and at least as interesting as the relatively
small set of unrestricted universals that can be expressed regarding concepts such as "subject."

The preceding discussion has compared structuralist-generative and
typological styles of argumentation for putatively universal grammatical
concepts. In 1.2, we also raised the issue of what typology can contribute
to the description of a single language. In that section, it was argued
that it is important to distinguish what is language-specific from what
is universal in human languages. Since virtually all of the significant
universals are (ultimately) implicational in form, it is worth examining
how they would interact with a particular language analysis. Consider
the following English sentence:

(53)   I was beaten by him twice.

In this sentence we can observe the operation of the following typological universals (references to relevant sections are in brackets):

(1) Word order:
  (a) dominant pattern: SV (3.3);
  (b) VO-harmonic patterns: AuxV, Prep NP (3.3);
  (c) order of arguments matches case hierarchy (subject < oblique) (5.3.2).
(2) Markedness, hierarchies and prototypes:
  (a) marked status of definite/animate nonsubjects (oblique *him*) (6.2.1);
  (b) correlation of animacy and case hierarchy (first-person subject, marked passive construction with *-en*) (6.3.2);
  (c) correlation of individuals with referring function (unmarked pronouns), actions with predicating function (adjective-like passive form marked by presence of *be*) (6.3.3);
  (d) marked status of plurality (necessary presence of time adverbial *twice*) (4.3.1);
  (e) unmarked status of lower numerals (inflectional *once, twice, thrice* vs. syntactic *four, five*, etc., *times*) (4.3.2.1; 4.3.3).

The list indicates the extent to which the morphological and syntactic structures of the sentence can be treated as instances of general typological patterns described in chapters 3–6. These patterns are universal, and therefore are part of the grammatical description of any language. Language-specific facts involve the degree to which typological universals are conventionalized in a particular language; e.g. what cut-off point in the animacy hierarchy is used to structurally and behaviorally mark direct objects. In the following two chapters, we will examine external explanations for the typological patterns and some of the interactions among external motivations and conventionalized constraints of particular languages.

7
External motivation and the typology of form–function relations

7.1 Introduction

In the last four chapters, we have described a large class of cross-linguistic patterns, including implicational universals, markedness, hierarchies and prototypes. All of these patterns represent asymmetrical implicational relationships among grammatical parameters, and define and limit possible variation in human languages. We also argued that they were almost all founded on basically the same kinds of linguistic evidence, which was first introduced in chapter 4 as evidence for markedness. This family of cross-linguistic patterns basically corresponds to typology in the third sense described in chapter 1, the "standard" sense of typology as a subdiscipline of linguistics. In this chapter, we will discuss the relationship between typology and external explanation, or more precisely, external **motivation**, for language structure. This brings us to typology in the fourth sense, the functional-typological approach to linguistic theory and explanation.

The relationship between typology and functionalism, as it is seen by the practitioners of the functional-typological approach to language, can be summarized quite simply at the broadest level. Functionalism seeks to explain language structure in terms of language function. It assumes that a large class of fundamental linguistic phenomena are the result of the adaptation of grammatical structure to the function of language. In grammatical basics, the function of language is universal across cultures: roughly, language is the general-purpose communication device.[1] As a consequence, functionalism ought to try to account for those facts about language that are universal across all languages. Typology is a primary source for those universals, particularly those universals which are not unrestricted.

The patterns described in the preceding four chapters are cross-linguistic patterns of linguistic structure. The only reference to external parameters so far has been in cross-linguistic comparability, which is the basis for the discovery of typological patterns (see 1.3). The next section of this chapter (7.2) will discuss external motivation for those patterns, in particular how they apply to markedness. However, direct confrontation of the relationship between linguistic form and linguistic function, under the name **iconicity**, has led to the discovery of another class of cross-linguistic patterns, the typology of form–function relations; these will be discussed in 7.3. Sections 7.4 and 7.5 will describe the interaction of different motivations, both in competition and in conspiracy.

This chapter does not discuss functionalism *per se*, that is the model of language function and adaptation that must necessarily be the foundation of a functional-typological approach. The purpose of this chapter is to describe how linguistic form, as manifested by various cross-linguistic patterns, has been linked to linguistic function by linguists who consider themselves practitioners of the functional-typological approach.

7.2 Markedness and economic motivation
7.2.1 Frequency
In the preceding three chapters we have described a large class of typological patterns that pervade the expression of all grammatical categories and phonological features. Simple markedness, hierarchies and prototypes all appear to be manifested in the various grammatical criteria described in chapter 4: structural expression, inflectional and distributional behavior and frequency, as well as possibly certain kinds of "neutral values." The convergence of these grammatical criteria must now be accounted for.

Greenberg (1966b:65–9) argues that in the case of morphosyntax, textual frequency is the source of the other markedness criteria. The most frequent grammatical value has zero or minimal expression (the structural criterion), because it is the most common form, and the uncommon form (marked value) is given a distinctive mark. The hidden assumption for the connection between frequency and zero expression is the principle that people will shorten the linguistic expressions that are used most commonly for economy, that is to simplify their linguistic utterances. This principle is sometimes called "Zipf's Law," after the linguist who popularized it: "High frequency is the cause of small magnitude" (Zipf 1935:29). John Haiman has called it **economic motivation** or **economy** (Haiman 1985), and he argues that it pervades grammatical expression. Most markedness patterns can be analyzed as economically motivated, and economic motivation probably plays a role in other aspects of grammar and typology.

If Greenberg, Haiman and the others who have made a causal connection between frequency and zero expression via economic motivation are correct, then one should be able to account for behavioral markedness via economy as well. How to do this is not so obvious. The inflectional behavioral criterion states that the unmarked value will express more cross-cutting inflectional categories. That would appear to be uneconomical, since the language user has to retain more forms. However, we may turn the expression of inflectional behavior around by saying the marked value will express *fewer* cross-cutting inflectional categories. One must begin by assuming that a language (that is, its speakers) has chosen to express a certain number of inflectional categories. It will be more difficult for the speakers to retain cross-cutting distinctions in marked categories since the forms are used less often, and so those forms will be regularized, disappear or never arise in the first place. This reasoning may be illustrated by a hypothetical example. In a typical language, the singular will be much more frequent in discourse than the plural. The frequency of the singular may be so great that singular nominatives and singular accusatives are each as frequent as plural nominatives and accusatives put together, as the following imaginary figures illustrate:

% Total	Nominative	Accusative	Total
Singular	40	25	65
Plural	20	15	35
Total	60	40	100

If this is the correct state of affairs, as the markedness patterns of case and number suggest, then it would be just as economic to have distinct nominative singular and accusative singular forms as to have a single plural form. In fact, when combinations of unmarked features are taken into consideration, much greater differences in frequency occur, and "such enormous disparities must surely have an effect in that such a highly infrequent formation must follow analogically other parts of the system, while only a fairly frequent form can preserve irregularities" (Greenberg 1966b:68–9; see also Bybee 1985a).

Haiman, following Meillet (Haiman 1985:157), offers another suggestion for the origin of cross-cutting categories in unmarked rather than marked values. Frequent combinations tend to be "run together" and eventually phonologically fused – that is, frequent expression is economized by being physically shortened. This may occur only for the most frequent – that is unmarked – values in a paradigm, hence the greater inflectional versatility of unmarked forms. This is essentially a diachronic account of markedness, and will be discussed further in chapter 8.

The economic motivation for inflectional unmarkedness, particularly inflectional irregularities, may account for some discrepancies between certain unmarked values and the "prototypical" members of those categories. In general, the prototypical members of a category in the cognitive-psychological sense are the most commonly referred to by human beings, and therefore they are the most frequent in texts. In some cases, however, other members of a category are extremely frequent for independent reasons, and in those cases the frequent members have the characteristics of the unmarked values. For example, in many languages the least-marked verbs by inflectional behavior include the verbs "be" and "have": in English, for example, these two verbs have the largest inflectional paradigms. Neither "be" nor "have" may be considered to be prototypical verbs, since they are stative. The verbal inflections which are used to define unmarked verbal categories are characteristic of the discourse category of predication, not (just) the semantic category of verbs. Both "be" and "have" are extremely frequent predications in human languages, by virtue of their use as auxiliaries and as copulas and their use in the expression of physical and mental states. Also, we have observed that, with respect to nominal categories, the least-marked members are not "prototypical" nouns but rather personal and demonstrative pronouns. Again, pronouns are by far the most frequent noun phrases – that is, referring expressions – in texts, and therefore the inflectional categories associated with reference will tend to demonstrate that pronouns are the least-marked NP type.

The distributional-behavioral criterion may be accounted for by a similar argument. A larger array of linguistically distinguished construction types is likely to be found for the unmarked value, just as a larger array of inflectional distinctions is likely to be found for the unmarked value. However, the connection of distribution to frequency is more tenuous, since the ability for a value, marked or unmarked, to occur in a construction is often constrained semantically. In cases of semantic neutralization, however, one would expect the otherwise more frequent value by economy simply because it is the one "most easily available" to the speaker.

The final criteria for markedness are typological frequency and typological distribution (dominance). The typological-frequency criterion is relatively simple to account for: if a grammatical/semantic category is very infrequent, it simply will not be expressed as a distinct grammatical category in as many languages. Typological distribution is more problematic. There does not seem to be a general explanation in terms of economy, or any other functional motivation for that matter. In the case of dominant word order, it does not appear that economic motivation can play any role, and the "preferred word order" (other things being equal) presumably has to do with factors such as the heaviness of the constituent (see Hawkins 1983) and the pragmatics of word order (see 7.4). Both of these may be functionally motivated, but not by economy. However, explanations of preferred word order will not help to explain the "preference" for number inflection manifested in the universal "If nouns inflect for gender, then they inflect for number."

It appears that economic motivation can easily provide a functional explanation of morphosyntactic markedness for the structural, typological frequency and the inflectional behavioral criteria, using text (discourse) frequency as the causal source. It may also account for the distributional-behavioral criterion. However, it does not account for the typological-distributional criterion. In itself, this does not question the validity of the latter two criteria as criteria of markedness. But it does suggest that markedness is more than just one manifestation of economic motivation.

In the case of phonology, Greenberg considered frequency as well as other markedness criteria to be derivative. Higher frequency was due to the tendency of certain historical phonological processes to produce unmarked phonological segments. However, Schwartz (1980) notes a fallacy in Greenberg's argument. Greenberg's argument only demonstrated that a greater range of phonological contexts may allow the unmarked value, since the historical processes he referred to tend to eliminate the marked value or convert it to the unmarked one. However, that is logically independent of the text frequency of the phoneme. The argument is exactly analogous to the argument we presented for the independence of the textual-frequency criterion and the distributional-behavioral criterion of markedness in chapter 4. We will use another imaginary example to illustrate it here. Consider the three environments word-initial, word-medial and word-final, and a language in which final devoicing has eliminated word-final voiced stops. It may still be the case that voiced stops are more frequent overall, as in the following imaginary text count:

	Word-initial	Word-medial	Word-final	Total
Voiceless stops	10	10	10	30
Voiced stops	25	25	–	50

This imaginary example demonstrates that voiceless stops can be found in a larger number of contexts and yet be less frequent. This demonstrates that behavior cannot determine frequency, and that the two criteria are logically independent. Thus, the empirical evidence in both phonology and morphosyntax demonstrates that frequency accounts for the behavioral criteria, at least to a significant degree.

7.2.2 *Other external explanations for markedness patterns*

Frequency is generally considered to be an external factor to the grammatical system. It is not part of the system *per se*, but instead a property of speech, that is, actual utterances. Nevertheless, it imposes considerable constraints on possible human languages, as the preceding chapters demonstrate.

Of course, one need not stop here in analyzing external explanations. First, not all markedness patterns are directly associated with frequency. Second, even if frequency is the immediate cause of markedness patterns, it is worth investigating in turn the cause of the frequency of certain grammatical values and combinations in speech. One may ask, for example, why the singular category is more frequent in discourse, that is why singular entities are more spoken about than plural collections of those entities. In other words, the functionally oriented typologist may seek justification of the prominence or salience of particular semantic categories to human beings: "those constructions that involve less formal [structural] markedness linguistically correspond to those extralinguistic situations which – in fact or in our conceptualizations – are more expected" (Comrie 1986:104; cf. Witkowski & Brown 1983:570). On the other hand, all that is necessary for invoking economic motivation to explain linguistic markedness is reliable frequency data. Only in the case of prototypes does there appear to be enough independent psychological evidence to make it worth venturing farther afield in the functional justification of typological patterns. We will therefore restrict ourselves to discussing some proposed external explanations of the patterns found in chapter 6 in the typological literature.

In describing the cluster of animacy and definiteness (6.2.1), we noted that agreement and case marking gave conflicting markedness assignments to direct objects. Direct objects that are high on the animacy and/or definiteness hierarchies are case-marked, and therefore marked; but the same direct objects trigger agreement, which should indicate unmarked status. This conflict can be resolved by developing separate functional accounts for agreement and case marking (Croft 1988).

In addition to being associated with high animacy and definiteness, agreement is also associated with high rank on the case hierarchy (5.3.3). All of these point to agreement as an indicator of high salience or topicality (Givón 1976). Topics are associated with definite noun phrases, as is agreement; and highly animate (especially human) referents are the most topical, other things being equal, so it is not surprising to see the topicality of animates conventionalized by rules of agreement. The central arguments of a clause, representing the central participants of an event, are also highly topical. Givón supplements this circumstantial evidence with examples of languages in which topicalization of an argument (by shifting it to the front of the sentence) triggers agreement in case when the untopicalized argument would not (examples from Givón 1976):

Swahili
(1) ni-   li-   vunja kikopo
    1SG.SBJ- TNS-   break cup
    'I broke a cup.'
(2) kikopo ni-   li-   ki-   vunja
    cup   1SG.SBJ- TNS   3SG.OBJ- break
    'The cup, I broke it.'

Amharic
(3) Almaz bet -u -n bä-   mäträgiya -w tärräga -cc
    Almaz house -the -OBJ with- broom   -the swept   -she
    'Almaz swept the house with the broom.'
(4) bet   -u -n Almaz bä-   mäträgiya -w tärräga -cc **-ɨw**
    house -the -OBJ Almaz with- broom   -the swept   -she **-it**
    'The house, Almaz swept it with the broom.'

Zakho dialect of Eastern Neo-Aramaic
(5) baxta qam yaw -a -le aw hammash ta dan   gure
    woman PAST gave -she -it that book   to those men
    'The woman gave the book to those men.'
(6) an   gure baxta qam yaw -a **-lu**   aw hammash
    these men woman PAST gave -she **-them** that book
    'The men, the woman gave them the book.'

Case marking, in contrast to agreement, suggests complementary prototypes for subjects and objects. This pattern has attracted much attention in the literature, and several explanations have been put forward.

The association of animacy in the broad sense (including person, NP type and animacy proper) with case – high animacy with subjects and low animacy with objects – was first explained in terms of "natural agency": "This hierarchy [the animacy hierarchy] expresses the semantic naturalness for a lexically-specified noun phrase to function as agent of a true transitive verb, and inversely the naturalness of functioning as patient of such" (Silverstein 1976:113; cf. Dixon 1979:86). This explanation thus turns the issue of animacy to verbal semantics: verb meanings are such that the agents are typically higher in animacy and patients are lower in animacy. This is certainly true for the human–nonhuman distinction, and is borne out by frequency data (Greenberg 1974b:25).[2] However, it does not suffice to account for differences in the person hierarchy, particularly for personal pronouns. It is common for third-person pronouns to refer to humans, just as first- and second-person pronouns do, and humans do not differ from each other in natural agentivity (Wierzbicka 1981).[3]

DeLancey, focusing on the person hierarchy in case marking and on the interaction of aspect with case marking, proposed an account based on deixis and a spatial metaphor. The distinction between first/second person and third person is one of spatial orientation: towards (or at) the speech event vs. away from the speech event. The agent–patient relation can be represented metaphorically as motion from the agent to the patient (i.e. transmission of force from the agent to the patient; see Lichtenberk 1985; Langacker 1987b; Croft, forthcoming). Likewise, perfective (completive) aspect focuses on the end-point of the event and its effect on the patient, while imperfect focuses on the activity of the agent rather than its outcome. DeLancey (1981) draws these together by identifying the correlation (repeated here) as representing the speaker's viewpoint on the event: moving from agent to patient in the event is metaphorically interpreted as moving away from the speech situation:

> 1st/2nd person → 3rd person
> subject (A) → object (P)
> imperfective → perfective

Both DeLancey's and Silverstein's analyses explain much, but not all, of the complex data surrounding animacy and case. DeLancey's data account for the phenomena related to the person hierarchy, but do not account for NP type of "true" animacy-hierarchy interactions with the case hierarchy. Nor does it account for the marked status of obliques relative to both subjects and objects. Silverstein's analysis, in terms of the "natural" or "typical" type of participant playing a (case) role in the clause, can account for the human–nonhuman animacy–case interactions, and can be extended to obliques, to account for the "natural" unmarkedness of place terms in locatives, human artifacts in the instrumental, and other oblique cases. However, it does not account for the person–case interactions, which are the most common. Finally, neither explanation accounts for (or is intended to account for) the closely related definiteness–case hierarchy interactions. It appears that there is some truth in all of the analyses, but no unified account has appeared at this time.

The other major typological prototype associated with clause structure is transitivity. Hopper and Thompson's original article (1980) does more than present the typological evidence, which is extremely consistent, in favor of a prototype interpretation of transitivity. They also examine narrative texts for the distribution of transitive and intransitive clauses. In their study, the presence of transitive clauses correlates with **foregrounding**, the presentation of information that carries the narrative along. The presence of intransitive clauses correlates with **backgrounding**, the presentation of information that elaborates or modifies the basic narrative line without carrying it forward.

Hopper and Thompson then argue that the foregrounding–backgrounding distinction is the explanation for the grammatical transitive prototype. That is, "transitive" encodes the foregrounding of information, and "intransitive" encodes the backgrounding of information. The remaining correlations follow because foregrounded information tends to be telic, punctual, volitional, etc., and backgrounded information tends to be stative, durative, nonvolitional, etc. However, the correlation of foreground with "high transitivity" and background with "low transitivity" is not complete (DeLancey 1987:55), and there appears to be no reason to posit the foreground–background distinction as causally prior to the other properties that make up the transitivity prototype.

The primary difference between foregrounding–backgrounding and the other properties is that the former is a discourse function, discovered through text analysis, and the latter are semantic categories, discovered through interpretation of the meaning of grammatical categories. Hopper and Thompson argue that the discourse function is causally prior to the cluster of semantic properties (and many functional-typologically oriented grammarians have followed them). DeLancey, on the other hand, argues that neither the clustering of semantic grammatical properties nor the correlation of the prototype with discourse properties is causally prior: both are derived from human cognition. The semantic properties cluster together because they represent a cognitively salient type, *à la* Rosch: "the various transitivity parameters [properties] cohere in the way that they do because they code aspects of a coherent semantic prototype" (DeLancey 1987:55). The correlation with foregrounding can be explained by cognitive salience: "transitivity in morphosyntax is associated with foregrounding in discourse because events which approximate the transitive prototype are more likely to be of interest, and thus inherently more likely to constitute foregrounded information" (DeLancey 1987:55). Of course, "cognitive salience" must be defined and psychologically confirmed before DeLancey's explanation can be accepted. However, as DeLancey correctly points out, one cannot assert the causal priority of discourse function over semantic structure without a virtually perfect correlation (DeLancey 1987:55, citing an unpublished paper by Russell Tomlin).[4]

Markedness patterns, and the closely related hierarchies and prototypes, are only part of the typological patterns that exist (albeit the most explored part). Markedness, particularly structural markedness, is an example of what Haiman calls **syntagmatic** or **discourse** economy: the gradual shift to shorter utterances to express (frequent or typical) concepts. Haiman distinguishes syntagmatic economy from **paradigmatic** economy: minimization of the inventory of signs within a system (Haiman 1985:158). Haiman argues that these two types of economy relate to another external motivation, iconicity, in very different ways, as we will see in the next section.

7.3 Iconicity

The other major type of external motivation for linguistic structure is **iconicity**. The intuition behind iconicity is quite simple: the structure of language reflects in some way the structure of experience, that is to say, the structure of the world, including (in most functionalists' view) the perspective imposed on the world by the speaker. The structure of language is therefore motivated or explained by the structure of experience to the extent that the two match. As we have already seen, there are other motivations which destroy the parallelism between linguistic structure and external structure in the name of economy: an unmarked concept often has no corresponding linguistic entity referring to it. The interaction between economic and iconic motivation will arise in this and the following section.

Iconicity of linguistic structure to external or experiential structure can be divided into two aspects: the correspondence of parts and the correspondence of relations between parts. Haiman calls these "isomorphism" and "motivation." This is an unfortunate selection of terms, since in mathematics "isomorphism" refers to correspondence of elements and relations (that is, includes what Haiman calls "motivation"), and "motivation" includes all kinds of motivation, such as economic motivation. We will use Haiman's term **"isomorphism"** in quotes, and refer to **iconic motivation** rather than "motivation" alone.

7.3.1   *"Isomorphism" and polysemy*

Haiman interprets "isomorphism" as referring to the hypothesis of "one form, one meaning." This is the correspondence of parts of the linguistic structure (including the linguistic construction as a whole) to parts of experience, and represents an unrestricted universal of human language. Haiman observes this requires the explanation of four types of exception or "mismatch" (Haiman 1985:21):

1   one form to zero meaning: empty morphemes;
2   zero form to one meaning: zero morphemes;
3   many forms to one meaning: synonymy;
4   one form to many meanings: homonymy (including polysemy).

Haiman has "nothing useful to say about empty morphemes," and indeed they pose a problem, albeit a relatively minor one, for the "isomorphism" hypothesis. It is true that many so-called "empty" morphemes are not that empty, given closer attention to the semantics and pragmatics of their contexts of use, and that all empty morphemes can be traced back to contentful morphemes where historical evidence is available (see chapter 8).[5]

The phenomenon of zero morphemes is for the most part a consequence of economic, not iconic, motivation, particularly with respect to markedness. Haiman observes that the correspondence of a single form (i.e. a form with zero morpheme[s]) to several concepts (the root plus the unmarked concept[s]) is an indication of familiarity, not conceptual simplicity (Haiman 1985:167–8). This is a clear example of the interaction of two distinct functional motivations that conflict, that is **competing motivations**. Zero morphemes for unmarked categories contrast with an iconically motivated paradigm in which every value, including the unmarked value, is expressed by a distinct nonzero morpheme. We will defer discussion of competing motivation until 7.4.

This brings us to synonymy and homonymy. Haiman echoes the hypothesis by Bolinger (1977) that synonymy *per se* does not exist, and that every distinction of form in every language is used and interpreted by speakers as a distinction in meaning (semantic or pragmatic). In typological terms, this is an unrestricted universal, and so does not involve any uniquely typological method or form of argumentation. But Haiman contrasts synonymy and homonymy and does bring in typology in a crucial way in discussing homonymy.

Haiman points out an essential difference between synonymy and homonymy: although neither is iconic, homonymy but not synonymy is economic. Homonymy represents paradigmatic economy: minimizing the number of morphemes, by giving them several meanings.[6]

Homonymy is particularly common with morphemes that occur very frequently in utterances, especially "grammatical" morphemes (which might be expected, given the existence of syntagmatic economy). Homonymy is also commonly found in grammatical constructions, such as inversion in English, which is used for various purposes. But many cases of homonymy among grammatical morphemes and constructions signify more than just economizing with forms. Economizing with form is motivated by the relationships between meanings subsumed under a single form. For example, the English morpheme *to* is used to indicate direction towards some location, the recipient of a verb of possession or transfer, and the hearer in verbs of speaking:

(7) I drove to Chicago.
(8) I gave/sent the package to you yesterday.
(9) I told the story to my brother.

There is a clear metaphorical relationship between transfer of possession of an object and transfer of information, and a frequent associational relationship between change in location and transfer of possession (the link is provided by verbs of physical transfer: *I took the sofa to the Salvation Army*). The patterns of related meanings for a given word are called **polysemy**. Polysemy is iconic as well as economic: *"recurrent similarity of form must reflect similarity in meaning"* (Haiman 1985:26; italics original).

The question is, how do we distinguish accidental homonymy, such as *two*, *to* and *too*, from iconically motivated polysemy, such as the directional and recipient meanings of *to*? The answer in most cases is provided by cross-linguistic – typological – comparison: if many diverse languages independently have the same pattern of "homonymy," then the meanings are closely related. Haiman has used this typological method to demonstrate the semantic relatedness of grammatical categories that have otherwise been thought to be widely separated (Haiman 1974, 1976, 1977, 1978a, 1978b, 1985). We will present one example of his work here.

Much of Haiman's work has been devoted to complex sentences, particularly conditional sentences and their relationships to other complex-sentence types (Haiman 1978a, 1978b, 1985). The dominant English conditional construction uses the conjunction *if*, while a construction involving subject–verb inversion is more restricted (usually to counterfactual conditionals):

(10) If it had been otherwise, I would have told you.
(11) Had it been otherwise, I would have told you.

Both of these constructions are also used with polar questions: *if* with polar question complements, and inversion with standard polar questions (Haiman 1985:27):

(12) Mary doesn't know if it will rain today.
(13) Will it rain today?

This coincidence in itself suggests some functional (semantic/pragmatic) connection between conditionals and polar questions. But it is the typological evidence that confirms this suggestion beyond a reasonable doubt. Haiman provides a number of examples that illustrate this recurrent polysemy: Russian *esli* 'if' is derived from *est* 'be (3sg.)' and *li* 'whether,' the polar-question marker; the Turkish conditional suffix *-se* can be replaced in colloquial registers by *-mi*, the polar-question marker; and the Hua conditional suffix can in certain conditions be replaced by *-ve*, a highly polysemous morpheme whose "typical" use is with polar questions (Haiman 1985:28–9). Haiman also demonstrates that the concessive conditional and the "non-hypothetical conditional" (in which the protasis, or antecedent, is factual) are also closely related to the "normal" causal and hypothetical conditional. Haiman argues that the protasis of a conditional functions more like a topic or background state of affairs against which the apodosis (consequent) is evaluated (Haiman 1985:33–4; see also Haiman 1978b). This functional argument is in turn supported by typological evidence that conditional markers are polysemous with topic markers, evidence that we have alluded to in chapter 1. For example, in Turkish, the aforementioned conditional marker *-se* is used for contrastive topics; in Tagalog the conditional morpheme *kung* is also used for contrastive topics; in Korean, the conditional copula *-(i)myen* can replace the topic marker-*(n)un*; in Vietnamese, the topic particle *thì* is also used to indicate the protasis, and so on (Haiman 1985:34–5). Haiman concludes his analysis by arguing (following Jespersen and other linguists) that topics, and also conditionals *qua* topics can be introduced by questions (Haiman 1985:38, examples 36 and 37):

(14) A: You know Max, the barber?
B: (silence = "yes")
A: Well, he died yesterday

(cf. 'Max died yesterday.')

(15) A: Is he coming?
B: (silence = "yes")
A: Then I'll stay

(cf. 'If he's coming, then I'll stay.')

The recurrent polysemy of polar question, topic and conditional protasis reflects the abbreviation of this pragmatic strategy by taking B's assent for granted (or not allowing B to object), and linking the two turns of A.

Another example of typological polysemy leading to analyses of functional similarity is the relationship between focus of a noun phrase, relativization, information ("WH") questions and constituent negation. The typological similarity between focus constructions and (restrictive) relative clauses was described by Schachter (1973); the following examples illustrate ordinary declaratives, relative clauses and focus constructions:

Akan
(16) mìhúú àbòfrá/nò
I.saw child/him
'I saw a child/him.'
(17) àbòfrá áà míhúù nó
child that I.saw him
'a child that I saw'
(18) àbòfrá nà míhúù nó
child that I.saw him
'It's a child that I saw.'

Hausa
(19) sū gayà̀ wà yārò̀
they told the child
'They told the child.'
(20) yārò̀ dà sukà gayà̀ masà/wà
child REL they.REL told him
'the child that they told'
(21) yārò̀ nē sukà gayà̀ masà/wà
child REL they.REL told him
'It was the child that they told.'

Ilonggo
(22) nag- dala ang babayi sang bata
AGT.TOP- bring TOP woman NONTOP child
'The woman brought a child.'

(23)   babayi nga nag-   dala sang   bata
       woman that AGT.TOP- bring NONTOP child
       'the woman that brought a child'
(24)   ang babayi ang nag-   dala sang bata
       TOP woman   TOP AGT.TOP- bring the child
       'It was the woman who brought a child.'

In Akan, the relative clause and the focus construction are similar
in that both involve positioning the relativized/focused NP before the
verb and the use of a special anaphoric pronoun form *nó* (high tone
instead of low tone). In Hausa, both relative clause and focus constructions use a special subject pronoun form (*suka*). In Ilonggo, the "agent
topic" construction (with the prefix *nag-*), one of several constructions
available in the ordinary declarative, is required in the relative clause
and focus constructions, and the relativized/focused NP is placed before
the verb.

Schachter argues that since there is a parallelism in form between
focus constructions and relative clauses, there must be some semantic
or pragmatic similarity between the two forms. Schachter proposes that
the out-of-focus/relative-clause construction had the effect of backgrounding the information contained therein. In a focus construction,
the focused NP rather than the predicate is the prominent or foregrounded piece of information that the speaker is communicating, and
the information in the out-of-focus clause is secondary (in fact, usually
already given information in the discourse). Likewise, the head of the
relative clause is the prominent piece of information, that is the participant in the main clause, while the description in the relative clause is
functionally as well as syntactically subordinate to the assertion in the
main clause.

Information questions and constituent negation also commonly use
the same construction as focus and/or relativization. For example, in
Makua all constructions share a distinct set of aspect suffixes, and all
but the relative clause have in common the postverbal position of, and
low tones on, the foregrounded NP (Stucky 1979:362–4; Stucky
1981:186):[7]

       Ordinary declarative
(25)   hín-Sepété áhó-   han -á   níváka
       Sepete   SBJ.TNS- forge -ASP spear
       'Sepete forged a spear.'

Focus
(26) hín-Sepété aa-   han   -ílé   nivaka
     Sepete   SBJ.TNS- forge-PERF spear
     'It's a spear that Sepete forged, . . .'

Constituent negation
(27) kʰáá-   han -ílé   ihipa
     NEG.SBJ.TNS- forge -PERF hoe
     '. . . it wasn't a hoe that he forged.'

Question
(28) hín-Sepété aa-   han -ílé   -ni
     Sepete   SBJ.TNS- forge -PERF -what
     'What did Sepete forge?'

Relative clause
(29) niváká aa-   han -ílé   hín-Sepété -(ńné)
     spear   SBJ.TNS- forge -PERF Sepete   -DEM
     'the spear that Sepete forged'

This polysemy is compatible with Schachter's foreground–background analysis. In information questions, the questioned element is the foregrounded piece of information by virtue of its being the focus of the question, and the other information is frequently presupposed. Likewise, answers to information questions are generally focus constructions as well (and indeed are preferred or required in Makua and Quiché). In constituent negation, the negated element is the most prominent piece of information, while the rest of the clause is frequently presupposed. In addition, focus or foregrounding constructions across languages have common structural characteristics: the foregrounded element, usually an NP, is structurally separated from the backgrounded rest of the clause, and the rest of the clause is distinctively marked (special verb form, complementizer, special pronominal/agreement forms). Thus, the focus sentence structure mirrors the sentence function, by separating the foregrounded element and marking the backgrounded clause. This is an example of iconic motivation: grammatical structure reflects conceptual structure (see 7.3.2).

One can even provide phonological analogues to the typological polysemy phenomenon. One frequently finds that different phonological segments or features are associated in a particular way in phonological rules across a wide variety of languages. The phonological counterpart of the "similar form implies similar function" hypothesis is "similar phonological behavior implies similar phonetic reality." In many cases, this fact has already been captured through the distinctive-feature system. However, occasionally there are instances in which there are similarities in phonological behavior which are not fully captured by the distinctive-feature system. For example, a typological survey of phonological processes involving [w] reveals that [w] has both labial and velar relationships. Ohala and Lorentz (1977:581) note the following [w]–labial–velar relationships:

1   Morphophonemic alternations between [w] and either labial or velar obstruents or both (Nguna, Berber, Mende, Vai, Loma, Fulani, Zuni, Hausa, Nunggubuyu, Esako, and Chamorro, among others);
2   Historical processes by which labial or velar obstruents developed labial offglides and then changed to [w] (Indo-European, Solomon Islands Melanesian);
3   Allophonic labial offglides after labial and velar consonants (Berber);
4   Greater frequency of labialization on velar, uvular and labial consonants, as opposed to dental, alveolar and palatal consonants (study of 706 languages by Ruhlen 1976).

The typological survey thus reveals a pattern of similarity between labials, velars and [w] that would not be evident from a single language such as English – a similarity which Ohala and Lorentz go on to exploit for phonetic explanation.

7.3.2   *Iconic motivation*

Haiman's narrow use of the term (iconic) "motivation" is defined by him as the parallelism between the relations among parts in linguistic structure and relations among parts in the structure of what is signified (Haiman 1985:11). The distinction between "isomorphism" and iconic motivation is not entirely clear, as we will see from the following illustrations of iconic motivation. Before we turn to these illustrations, we must take up two general points: the structure of what is signified, and the typological perspective on iconic motivation.

The primary difficulty in evaluating arguments in favor of iconicity is that the structure of what is signified, "experience" as we put it above, is not well established. The first question that comes to mind is, should the structure of language be compared to the structure of physical reality or the structure of human conceptualization of that reality? Since language is a human faculty, the general assumption on the part of functional linguists has been that the structure of language should be compared to human conceptualization of the world (see, for example, Langacker 1987b: chapter 1). Thus, the iconically minded typologist should turn his or her attention to psychology. At this point, one faces the primary difficulty in evaluating hypotheses of iconic motivation in language: the shortage of firm evidence for the structure of experience outside of language itself. Although we have many powerful intuitions about the organization of experience, the functional linguist cannot turn to a large body of psychological evidence giving us theories of the cognition of events, for example, that are justified independently of language. In fact, psychological and especially philosophical models of the world and experience are very strongly influenced by the structure of language, and so iconicity may be a self-fulfilling hypothesis unless (or until) non-linguistic means of obtaining psychological evidence are developed and refined.

However, this argument can be turned on its head. The iconicity of human language is a hypothesis that can be used to propose hypotheses of cognitive structure that can be tested and confirmed or rejected by cognitive psychological research. This is actually a reasonable way to proceed, because language provides the most explicit and most easily observed facet of cognitive behavior, and therefore is better suited to be the producer rather than the verifier of hypotheses regarding cognitive structure. The adoption of iconicity as a working hypothesis need not be self-fulfilling, because the effect of doing so is to study some aspect of language that would not otherwise be studied. If the study yields interesting cross-linguistic generalizations, then the working hypothesis will have been useful – at least to typology – even if it turns out to be ultimately an unsatisfactory explanation.

The typological study of iconicity essentially boils down to the typology of grammatical **structure**. This contrasts sharply with the kinds of cross-linguistic patterns that we have discussed so far. Those patterns characterize various asymmetries and irregularities of grammatical **behavior** for the most part.[8] The typology of grammatical structure requires an explicit reference to the external basis of cross-linguistic comparison, since the typological patterns found so far have to do with what kinds of grammatical structures express what cognitive concepts.

The typology of grammatical structure is not as far advanced as the typological study of grammatical behavior described in the preceding chapters. Much of the existing research has involved comparisons of a small number of languages, usually one or two languages whose expressions of concepts differ considerably from that of English. Thus, the results so far (with a few exceptions) indicate certain extreme points of variation, not the range and pattern of variation; it is the latter that is the essence of typological research. Nor has much of the research gone beyond typological classification to typological generalizations.

Also, current research has involved very basic questions of grammatical structure. Nevertheless, the typology of grammatical structure has indeed produced a number of cross-linguistic patterns that are interesting in themselves and are worth investigating from a cognitive perspective.

There are three very general aspects of grammatical structure that can be, and have been, studied from a typological perspective. Each of these has its corresponding hypothesis for iconic motivation.

1 *Simple vs complex expressions*. One can study what concepts are expressed cross-linguistically by simple grammatical structures – single morphemes, single words, single clauses – as opposed to what concepts are expressed by complex structures – multiple morphemes, compound words, complex sentences. One also finds concepts that are expressed sometimes by simple morphemes, sometimes by complex ones (this is where attention has been focused so far). This already represents a proto-type structure: prototypically simple concepts are universally expressed as single morphemes, prototypically complex concepts are universally expressed as complex linguistic structures, and intermediate concepts vary cross-linguistically. Ideally, one would also find typological dependencies among the intermediate concepts that would yield implicational relations or hierarchies, but research has not advanced to this point yet. The iconicity hypothesis would propose that the concepts which are always, or frequently, expressed by simple grammatical structures are cognitively primitive and those expressed by complex structures are cognitively complex.

2 *Categorization*. One can study what concepts are placed into the same grammatical category. This resembles the typological notion of poly-semy: in this instance, the assignment of concepts to the same gram-matical category (e.g. "auxiliary") implies conceptual similarity or relatedness. Two general classifications will concern us here. The first is the classification of concepts into specific grammatical categories – noun, verb, adverb, etc. The iconicity hypothesis would propose that the concepts that fall into the same grammatical category are cognitively similar in some respects. The second question is the more general classifi-cation of concepts into two types of grammatical categories: either a closed-class, usually bound-morpheme "function-word" category or an open-class, usually free-morpheme "content-word" category. The icon-icity hypothesis would propose not only that the concepts falling into each of these two categories are cognitively similar but that the distinction

in grammatical structure and behavior corresponds to some cognitive distinction.

3 *Structural isomorphism.* One can study the range of structures (types or strategies) used for the expression of complex concepts across languages, looking for similarities and regularities in the types used. The iconicity hypothesis would propose that (to the extent that structures are universal) the structure of a grammatical construction will reflect the structure of the complex concept it expresses.

The study of any one grammatical structure frequently involves more than one of these aspects. The examples used here will therefore sometimes illustrate two or three of these aspects at once.

7.3.2.1 Conceptual distance and constituent structure

We will begin by describing Haiman's primary example of iconic motivation: linguistic distance between constituents implies conceptual distance between the concepts signified by those constituents. This is an example of what we have called (following the more common mathematical use of the term) **structural isomorphism**: the structure of the utterance reflects the structure of the (complex) concept. As expected, the definition of linguistic distance is considerably easier to come by than a definition of conceptual distance (Haiman 1985:105, example 88; see Bybee 1985a:12):

> Diminishing linguistic distance between X and Y
> a. $X \# A \# B \# Y$
> b. $X \# A \# Y$
> c. $X + A \# Y$
> d. $X \# Y$
> e. $X + Y$
> f. Z [= fusion of X and Y into single form]

Haiman describes conceptual distance in terms of conceptual closeness:

> Two ideas are conceptually close to the extent that they
> a. share semantic features, properties or parts;
> b. affect each other;
> c. are factually inseparable;
> d. are perceived as a unit, whether factually inseparable or not.
>   (Haiman 1985:106–7).

We may construct the following implicational universal to describe the typological facts that would support the iconic motivation of linguistic distance:

If a language has two near-synonymous constructions which differ structurally in linguistic distance, they will differ semantically in (among other things) conceptual distance in a parallel fashion.

Haiman proceeds to give examples from co-ordination, causation, transitivity, possession and other domains to demonstrate that across languages, this implicational universal holds (Haiman 1985: section 2.2; cf. also Haiman 1983). We will discuss one example, the distinction between alienable and inalienable possession.

Inalienable possession refers to a permanent relationship between two entities. The most conspicuous examples are parts, such as body parts ("head," "hand" and sometimes abstract attributes like "name," "spirit") and kinship relations ("mother," "son" and sometimes social relations like "chief," "enemy"). Alienable possession refers to a relationship that can be temporary, such as personal belongings. It is intuitively clear that inalienable possession is a conceptually closer relation than alienable possession, and Haiman lists a large number of languages in which the linguistic expression of inalienable possession is lower on the scale of linguistic distance than the expression of alienable possession. For example, compare the patterns of relationships in Mekeo, an Austronesian language (Haiman 1985:131):

X # Y: alienable possession
eʔu/emu/aʔa ngaanga 'my/your/his canoe'

X + Y: inalienable possession
aki -u/-mu/-ʔa 'my/your/our (incl.) younger brother'

A more interesting example provided by Haiman is Kpelle. In Kpelle, the possessive constructions differ for pronominal vs. nominal possessors:

Pronominal possessors:
X # Y: alienable
nga pérɛi 'my house'
X + Y: inalienable
m-pôlu 'my back'

Nominal possessors:
X+A Y: alienable
ʔkaloñg nc pérɛi 'chief's house'
X # Y: inalienable
ʔkaloñg pôlu 'chief's back'

The interesting fact here is that the construction X # Y is used for inalienable possession for nominal possessors, but alienable possession for pronominal possessors. This apparent anomaly renders it impossible to generalize over the linguistic expression of the alienable–inalienable distinction in Kpelle except in terms of relative linguistic distance (Haiman 1985:132). The correct generalization here is that in each subclass of possessors, the linguistically more distant construction is used for the conceptually more distant possession relation (alienable possession).[9]

The iconicity of distance has also been applied to the ordering of affixes within the noun and the verb complexes. Bybee (1985a:24–5) argues that the linguistic distance inside the word corresponds iconically to the degree that the semantics of the affix affects the meaning of the word and does not refer to any other constituent (i.e. any other component of the described situation). Greenberg's original paper contains two universals relevant to the iconicity of distance. His Universal 28 states that "If both the derivation and inflection follow the root, or they both precede the root, the derivation is always between the root and the inflection" (Greenberg 1966b:93). This generalization seems to be very largely correct, and supports Haiman's conceptual-distance hypothesis. Derivational morphology alters the lexical meaning of the root, sometimes drastically, whereas inflectional morphology only adds semantic properties or embeds the concept denoted by the root into the larger linguistic context.

Greenberg's Universal 39 states, "Where morphemes of both number and case are present and both follow or both precede the noun base, the expression of number almost always comes between the noun base and the expression of case" (Greenberg 1966a:95). In other words, the linguistic distance between the noun and case marking is greater than the linguistic distance between the noun and number. In this case, application of the number affix affects the semantics of the referent because it determines the cardinality (number) of the group of entities referred to. However, the addition of the case affix does not affect the semantics of the referent, because the meaning of the case affix (to the extent that it has meaning) describes the relationship between the noun referent and the verbal event, not anything about the noun referent itself. Hence, Greenberg's universal can be accounted for by the iconic-distance hypothesis, using Bybee's criterion.

The paper of Bybee's just referred to is a typological investigation of the iconic-distance hypothesis for verbal affixes indicating valence, voice, aspect, tense, modality, person and number. Bybee considered linguistic distance to be defined in terms of the ordering of affixes, as with the Greenberg universals, and in terms of the lexical, derivational or inflectional expression of the category (cf. the lower end of Haiman's scale of conceptual distance). As with nominal affixes, conceptual distance is defined as the degree to which the meaning of the affix affects the meaning of the verb and does not affect the meaning of the rest of the sentence (what Bybee calls "relevance" to the verb). Bybee argues that the ranking of conceptual closeness of inflectional affixes to the verb is as follows (leftmost = conceptually closest):

valence < voice < aspect < tense < mood < person/number agreement

The arguments for conceptual distance are rather uncertain in several cases. Valence (that is, transitivity) alternations clearly affect the meaning of the verb quite drastically, and determine other syntactic properties of the clause, and so may be considered the most relevant to the verb. Voice, in Bybee's definition, characterizes the "perspective" taken on the event, and so combines deictic differences such as *buy/sell* with active, passive and middle voice "proper." Bybee states "It is not surprising, then, that voice may be morphologically coded on the NPs of the sentence, on the verb or both" (Bybee 1985a:14), but then appears to conclude that voice is highly relevant to the verb.

Aspect covers a large semantic range. Aspect alternations such as stative vs. inchoative (e.g. Latin *caleō* 'I am warm [stative]' vs. *calescō* 'I get warm [inchoative]'; Bybee 1985a:15) significantly change the meaning of a verb. Other alternations such as perfective vs. imperfective (e.g. Spanish *dormí* 'I slept [preterit]' vs. *dormía* 'I was sleeping [imperfective]') do not change the meaning of a verb as much. In fact, completive/durative aspect alters the status of the direct object. In the latter case, aspectual distinctions are often expressed in the direct-object noun-phrase, as in English durative/habitual *I drank wine* vs. completive *I drank the wine* (see also the Finnish partitive/accusative case distinction illustrated in 6.2.2, which serves the same purpose). This aspectual distinction is less relevant to the verb because it actually applies to the verb phrase. Also, Hopper (1979) argues that some inflectional distinctions that have been labelled "aspect" actually signal discourse status of the utterance as a whole, and so are even less relevant to the verb. Bybee observes that the stative/inchoative aspectual type is the one type most likely to be expressed lexically rather than inflectionally (1985a:100–2).

Tense and modality semantically apply to the clause (proposition) as a whole, and so are less relevant than any of the verbal categories discussed so far. Bybee argues that tense is more relevant to the verb than modality because tense denotes a point in time (past, present, future), and verbs, unlike nouns, are generally transitory events. Therefore, tense is more likely to be associated with verbs than nouns, since the objects denoted by nouns usually exist before and after the event as well as during it. Finally, agreement categories, unlike all of the categories discussed so far, do not refer to the event at all, but to its participants, and so are the least relevant to the event.

Valence, voice and (a subset of) aspect are expressed lexically and derivationally as well as inflectionally across languages, thus confirming that part of Bybee's ranking of inflections by conceptual closeness. Number is sometimes expressed lexically and derivationally, thus apparently violating the ranking of conceptual closeness. However, derivational and lexical number appears to alter the meaning of the verb, in particular to add distributive or collective meanings: "when plurality is a derivational (and perhaps a lexical) category, its meaning extends beyond pure agreement with the arguments of the verb" (Bybee 1985a:36). This is true for example in Kwakwalla (Kwakiutl), in which there are several plural verb forms (Boas 1947:246):

mɛdɛ'lqwɛla	'it is boiling (sg.)'
meʔmɛdɛ'lqwɛla	'they are boiling (pl. subject)'
maʔɛ'mdɛ'lqwɛla	'it is boiling in all its parts (pl. extensive)'
mɛdɛ'lxumɛdɛ'lqwɛla	'it is boiling repeatedly (pl. action)'

Thus verbal number, like aspect, demonstrates that linguistically more close expressions entail conceptually more intimate semantic relations.

Bybee used a fifty-language sample to determine order of inflectional affixes. After excluding cases in which the inflectional category did not exist, Bybee analyzed pairwise comparisons of the inflectional categories in which the linguistic distance from the verb differed. This resulted in the following ranking:

$$\text{(inflectional) aspect} < \text{tense} < \text{mood ?} < \text{person/number}[10]$$

The results confirmed the majority of Bybee's conceptual rankings for the ranking from inflectional aspect onward. One anomaly was that in cases in which object agreement occurred together with subject agreement, object agreement was closer to the verb, indicating greater relevance; but object agreement is less frequent than subject agreement, indicating lesser relevance (Bybee 1985b:38). In sum, although there are some problems with both the data and the definition of conceptual closeness for verbal affixes, it appears that the order of affixes on both nouns and verbs generally supports the iconic-distance hypothesis.

Bybee introduces the aforementioned essay with a summary of the iconic-distance hypothesis applied to syntactic constituent structure:

It has often been observed that the proximity of elements in a clause follows some natural (iconic) principle whose result is that elements that go together semantically tend to occur close together in the clause [footnote cites Vennemann 1973 and Behaghel 1923–32]. Following this principle, we would expect that elements whose position is defined in terms of the position of the noun would have meanings that modify or relate to the meaning of the noun or noun stem, while elements whose position is defined in terms of the position of the verb would have meanings that modify or relate in some way to the meaning of the verb or verb stem. Similarly, elements whose position is determined with respect to the whole clause would have the entire proposition in their semantic scope. (Bybee 1985a:11)

If this hypothesis is valid, then the iconic-distance hypothesis could account for almost all of constituent structure (that is, constituency and contiguity, not word order) in one stroke. Indeed, under most semantic analyses of nominal and verbal modifiers and of sentence modifiers, the iconic-distance hypothesis as applied to syntactic constituent structure is generally corroborated in the languages of the world. However, there are several important exceptions, which an iconic-distance hypothesis would have to accommodate in some way or another. First, a relatively small number of languages appear to allow discontinuous noun phrases. In one well-known example, Russian, nouns can be fronted independent of their modifiers in certain constructions (Fowler 1987:97):

(30) knig -∅   ja   kupil pjat'
     book -GEN.PL 1SG.NOM bought five
     'I bought five books.'

In this case, pragmatic factors determining word order compete with the iconic-distance principle in determining linguistic structure (see 7.4). Other examples of discontinuous noun phrases, particularly among Australian languages, may not be amenable to such an explanation, since in those languages discontinuity is not associated with a special position for the "moved" modifier, for example in Nunggubuyu (Heath 1980:510):

(31) Baḷamumu   wuː=wali-ɲ ruŋgal
     (tribal name) they.arrived big
     'The Balamumu tribe arrived, lots of them.'

However, in these cases it may be that the "discontinuous noun phrases"

are actually independent noun phrases that refer to the same entity
(Heath 1984:498), as Heath's translation suggests.[11]

A second problem is that there appears to be a great deal of cross-
linguistic variation of certain verbal modifiers as to whether their position
is defined with respect to the verb or with respect to the clause as a
whole. Steele's (1975) typological survey of auxiliary elements, which
usually incorporate modal and aspectual concepts, for example, shows
that in some languages the auxiliary is located next to the verb, while
in other languages it is located in first, second or final positions in the
clause (the usual positions for elements syntactically defined by the
clause). Nevertheless, tense and modality are generally agreed to modify
the proposition as a whole, and aspect and even voice are considered
by some to apply to the verb phrase, not the verb (see above, and also
Keenan 1979; Bach 1980). In sum, the iconic-distance hypothesis will
have to be modified to account for (or exclude) the aberrant verbal
modifiers; but better semantic analyses are required to provide independent supporting or disconfirming evidence for iconic distance.[12]

Nevertheless, the general cross-linguistic support for iconic distance
is very strong: almost all languages have well-defined noun phrases,
most languages place verbal modifiers contiguous to the verb, and sentential modifiers are frequently placed in sentence-first, -second or -final
position. Some exceptions are clearly accounted for by other principles
that compete with iconicity of constituent structure (word-order pragmatics, isomorphism; see 7.4 for an example).

Conceptual distance in syntax has been explored in detail for verbal-
complement constructions by Talmy Givón. Givón (1980b) provides
grammatical evidence for a **binding hierarchy** of complement types. He
ranks complement types on a semantic scale in terms of three semantic
criteria:

1   *Binding*: "The stronger the influence exerted over the agent of the
    complement clause by the agent of the main-clause verb, by whatever
    means, the higher is the main-clause verb on the binding scale."
2   *Independence*: "The higher a verb is on the binding scale, the less
    is the agent of its complement clause capable of acting indepen-
    dently."
3   *Success*: "The less independence possessed by the embedded-clause
    agent, and the higher the main-clause verb on the binding scale,
    the more is the intended manipulation likely to succeed." (Givón
    1980b:335)

Givón's semantic criteria lead to the following rough scale of complement types, from most distant to least: direct speech; indirect speech; verbs of belief, knowledge and doubt; emotive verbs; verbs of attempt or of manipulation of others (commands, requests, etc.); and causative or successful outcome verbs ("finish," "succeed," etc.).

Givón also ranks complement types on a grammatical (syntactic) scale, based on the degree to which a complement clause is syntactically coded as an independent/main clause (Givón 1980b:337):

1 "The higher a verb is on the binding scale, the less is the agent in its complement/embedded clause likely to exhibit the case-marking characteristics of subjects/agents/topics."
2 "The higher a verb is on the binding scale, the less is the verb of its complement clause likely to exhibit the tense–aspect–modality markings characteristic of main clauses."
3 "The higher a verb is on the binding scale, the more is the verb in its complement clause likely to be predicate-raised, i.e. lexicalized as one word with the main verb." (Givón 1980b:338)

The typological pattern that Givón discovered is as follows:

If a point on the semantic hierarchy of binding is coded by a certain syntactic coding device, then a semantically higher point cannot be coded by a syntactically lower point. Rather, it will be coded either by the same coding point, or by a higher coding point on the syntactic coding scale. (Givón 1980b:370)

He then proceeds to demonstrate a correlation between the semantic scale and the syntactic scale, for English, Krio, Bemba, Spanish, Finnish, Hebrew, Palestinian Arabic, Ute, Persian and Sherpa. For example, in Sherpa, verbs of saying require finite-clause complements, whereas all other verbs require nominalized complements, lacking syntactic properties 1 and 2 (Givón 1980b:367):

(32) ti -la   nyee   wa   -up -ti   ca   -no
      he -DAT my.POSS come -INF -NOM know -PERF
      'He knew that I came. He knew of my having come.'
(33) ti -gi   ŋ lagha kyaa -yin   si   -no
      he -ERG I work do   -PERF say -PERF
      'He said: "I have worked."'

Modern Hebrew displays a broad range of morphosyntactic complements that divide the semantic binding scale fairly evenly (Givón 1980b:353–4). The causative complement is fully fused with the causal form, which is a causative prefix:

(34) Miryam he- exil -a   et   Yoram
      Miriam CAUS- eat -PAST-she ACC.DEF Yoram
      'Miriam fed Yoram. Miriam made Yoram eat.'

Strong emotive verbs which entail the truth of the complement use an infinitive form:

(35) Miryam hixrixa   et   Yoav le- exol
Miriam force.PAST.she ACC.DEF Yoav INF- eat
'Miriam forced Yoav to eat.'

Verbs of suggestion, summons, etc., allow either an infinitive complement or a subjunctive complement that encodes the subject; not surprisingly, the latter is less "strong" than the former (note also the difference in the English glosses):

(36) Miryam amra   lo   le- exol
Miriam   tell.PAST.she to.him INF- eat
'Miriam told him to eat.'
(37) Miryam amra   lo   she- yexol
Miriam   tell.PAST.she to.him COMP- he.eat.MODAL
'Miriam told him that he should eat.'

Finally, verbs that merely express emotions allow only the subjunctive complement, but in addition require the subject to be in the complement clause instead of in the main clause:

(38) Miriam ratsta   she- Yoav yoxal
Miriam want.PAST.she COMP- Yoav he.eat.MODAL
'Miriam wished that Yoav would eat.'

The correlation between the semantic scale and the syntactic one is a function of iconic distance: the semantic relationship between the main verb and the complement clause is reflected by the syntactic relationship between the main verb and its complement.

If the iconic-distance principle motivates unrestricted universals of constituent structure, then it should also reveal intermediate cases in which there is cross-linguistic variation. One such example of a conceptually intermediate category is directional phrases, found in sentences that express motion along a path relative to an object. In these sentences, the path is conceptually linked to the action, because motion involves change in location; but it is also conceptually linked to the object, since the path is defined relative to the object ("in," "out of," "to," etc.). Typologically, this is manifested in variation as to whether the directional phrase forms a prepositional phrase with the object noun, or an adverb or directional affix with the verb:

Directional # NP: English
(39) Minnie walked slowly **into** the room.

Directional + NP: Hungarian (Whitney 1944:20)
(40)   Szabó úr   kiszáll   a   vonat **-ból**
       Szabo Mr. get.out the   train **-out.of**
       'Szabo got out of the train.'

Directional # V: Mandarin (Li & Thompson 1981:400)
(41)   wǒ bǎ tā tuī **dǎo** zài shāfa shang
       1SG ACC 3SG push **down** at sofa on
       'I pushed her/him down onto the sofa.'

Directional + V: Kinyarwanda (Kimenyi 1980:89)
(42)   umugóre y-   oohere -jé -ho isóko umubooyi
       woman 3SGF- send   -ASP -LOC market cook
       'The woman sent the cook to the market.'

In sum, the iconicity of constituent structure hypothesis, combined
with the typological principles of word order described in chapter 3 (see
also chapter 8), provide the basis for a functional-typological theory
of syntactic structure; though at the present, it remains more a promise
than an accomplishment.

7.3.2.2   Syntactic categories, objects and events

For nouns and adjectives, the question of simple vs. complex
expression can be studied in terms of simple roots vs. compounds. Typological research pertaining to this question can be found in ethnobotany
and ethnozoology, the cultural classification of living things. Berlin
(1978) summarizes cross-cultural study of taxonomic classification and
observes that there are generally three (sometimes more) distinct levels
of classification that are linguistically expressed. Berlin calls the highest
level the **life-form**, the most important intermediate level **generic** and
the usual lowest level the **specific** level. Life forms in English include
tree, *grass*, *fish*, *bird*, *animal* and *bug*. The generic level of classification
for trees includes *oak*, *pine*, *cedar* and *maple*. Specific-level terms in
the same domain include *tan oak*, *blue oak*, *sugar pine*, *incense cedar*,
red cedar, *bigleaf maple*, *vine maple*. In English, the specific-level terms
are very commonly compounds of the generic-level term and some modifier. This pattern is quite common cross-linguistically; the following
examples are from Aguaruna (Berlin 1978:20):

Generic:	ipák	'achiote (*Bixa orellana*)'
Specific:	beeŋ ipák	'kidney achiote'
	čamíŋ ipák	'yellow achiote'
	hémpe ipák	'hummingbird achiote'
	šiŋ ipák	'genuine achiote'

Interpreted iconically, this pattern suggests two things: first, the generic-level concepts are more basic than the specific-level concepts, since the latter are expressed by compounds; second, the structure of the compound used for the specific-level term mirrors the structure of the classification: each species is a special case of the genus. This assumes that the modifier–head structure reflects a daughter–parent structure of the taxonomy.[13]

Berlin's results represent one of the few cases in which the psychological research has been done to fill in the other side of the equation between linguistic structure and cognitive structure. Eleanor Rosch (Rosch 1978) has demonstrated that there is a "basic level" of categorization that corresponds to Berlin's generic level, and that the higher (life-form) and lower (specific) levels are conceptually more complex. Rosch argues that the basicness of the generic level is due to perceptual characteristics of that taxonomic level. Rosch and Berlin both argue that the distinction between two objects belonging to different generic categories is perceptually greater than the distinction between two objects belonging to different specific categories of the same genus. Conversely, the similarity between two objects in the same generic-level category is perceptually much greater than the similarity between two objects in the same life-form (higher)-level category but different generic-level categories. Hence, the generic level is perceptually very well defined: a generic-level category has high internal homogeneity but is also highly distinct from other generic-level categories. Linguistically, the compounds used for the specific-level terms can be argued to reflect both the derived nature of the specific category (the compound) and the lack of interspecific distinguishability (the specific terms all share the same head noun). The linguistic features of the higher-level terms are somewhat more difficult to explain in iconic terms. The higher-level terms are usually simple roots, but they are frequently missing in languages; perhaps that can be explained by the lack of internal homogeneity of a category leading to its lack of explicit categorization by the granting of a name. The cross-linguistic pattern of simple vs. compound nouns illustrates a domain in which both linguistic and nonlinguistic cognitive evidence can be compared to each other.

The domain of verbs and verblike words is more complex. With verbs, cross-linguistic variation has been emphasized more than unrestricted universals. The studies we will cite are mainly comparisons of single languages or a small number of languages with English; for that reason, any typological extrapolation can only be tentative. The first aspect of the typology of grammatical structure that we will address is the categor-

ization issue. There is a considerable amount of variation in the assignment of concepts to the category "verb" as opposed to other categories
such as adverb, adjective, adposition and auxiliary. English represents
a highly differentiated system in which there are several distinct categories:

Finite verb:	He **ran**.
Nonfinite verb:	She asked him **to run**.
Preposition:	He ran **across** the field.
Particle:	He ran **away**.
Adverb:	He ran **slowly**.
Auxiliary:	He **was** running. (aspectual)
	She **made** him run. (causative)

A single sentence can include many of these categories:

(43)   He **was running away slowly across** the field.
　　　AUX V　　　 PRT　ADV　　PREP

The other extreme is represented by Lahu, in which the concepts
expressed by these various categories in English would all be found
in the category "verb." Compare the English sentence to the following
examples from Lahu (Matisoff 1969:82, 70):

(44)　(a)　ğa　　　qɔ̀ʔ　　phô ʔ　　lɔ̀　　 **câ**
　　　(b)　get　　return　gather　　beg　eat
　　　(c)　OBLIG　again　together
　　　(d)　AUX　　ADV　　ADV　　　　　VINF
　　　(e)　'have to beg together to eat, again'

(45)　(a)　ŋà-hɨ　ğa　　qɔ̀ʔ　　**chî**　tɔ̂ʔ　　 pî　　 ve
　　　(b)　we　　get　　return　lift　come.out　give　NOM
　　　(c)　　　　OBL　　again　　　 out　　　 for
　　　(d)　　　　AUX　ADV　　　 PRT　　　 PREP
　　　(e)　'We had to lift (it) out again for (them).'

(46)　(a)　ŋà-hɨ　tạ　　 **yù**　qai　cɨ　　 cɔ̂　　　 ve　　 lâʔ
　　　(b)　We　　begin　take　go　　send　be.correct　NOM　INTERR
　　　(c)　　　　　　　　　away　CAUS　EVAL
　　　(d)　　　　　VINF　PRT　AUX　AUX
　　　(e)　'Should we make (them) begin to take (it) away?'

(Line (a) in each example gives the Lahu original. Line (b) gives
the gloss of each lexical item as a verb. Line (c) provides glosses of
Lahu "verbs" that serve a function filled by English categories other
than a verb; line (d) gives the English category for those words. Line
(e) provides the translation.)

Presumably, other languages fall in between these two extreme cases. Without doing a typological study, it is impossible to be certain; but one may guess that some cross-linguistic pattern of category membership would be found, for example a hierarchy of verbhood, so that if spatial concepts (adpositions) were categorized as verbs, then so are property concepts (adjectives). Such a pattern would then have to be accounted for by iconic motivation, by arguing that property concepts resembled actions (prototypical verbs) in some cognitive or perceptual features more than spatial concepts did.

The expression of events by verbs and other categories in Lahu and English also touches on the matter of simple vs. complex expression and the structure of the expression. The Lahu words that do not translate as verbs in English are not heads of their compound verbal expressions. When they are not heads, they represent aspectual, modal, evidential and other modifications of "content" verb meaning, not their full verb meaning (Matisoff 1969:104; cf. English *have* as verb and as auxiliary):

(47) **lɔ̂**   chê
      be.there beg
      'beg to be there'

(48) lɔ̂   **chê**
      be.there beg
      'is begging'

(49) ğa   **kì**
      get   be-
            .busy
      'must be busy'

(50) **ğa** kì
      get be.busy
      'be busy getting'

Looking at it this way, similarities between Lahu and English arise which appear to be shared in other languages. In both languages, the head of the clause (or VP, if such a category exists) is the word which is always identified as belonging to the category "verb." In both languages, the heads express the same class of concepts, which, for want of a better term, we will call the "content" of the action, and the non-heads (which we will call **satellites**, after Talmy 1985) also express the same class of concepts across languages – aspect, direction, modality and verbal properties ("adverbs").[14] In both languages, then, events

are structured as single grammatical units (hence the head–satellite structure), albeit complex ones (hence the multimorphemic expression). The
only difference is in the categorization of the satellites.

If Lahu and English are representative, then it appears that events
in their causal–aspectual–directional–modal totality cannot be primitive
concepts in natural languages; they are always expressed by complex
structures (except in the case of irregular suppletive forms). But the
separate concepts in these structures are themselves temporally simulta-
neous and are definitely parts of the event (assuming that events are
structured in time). Therefore (goes the iconic-motivation argument)
the grammatical unit is a single structure.

The head–satellite structure also indicates the primacy of some event
feature, the one chosen as the head. We have suggested that that element
is generally the same across languages: it is the "contentful" element,
not the aspectual–modal–directional–(secondary) causal one. However,
research in verbal dependencies, mostly the work of Leonard Talmy
(1972, 1974, 1985), has revealed that there is some typological variation
in heads. Talmy analyzed motion events as having two chief components:
manner (the "contentful" component) and path (direction). Languages
vary as to which of these two conceptual components is expressed as
the head of the verb phrase (not to mention what category the dependent
element is):

English
(51) He **ran** into the cave. (manner = head)

Russian (Talmy 1985:105)
(52) Ja vy- **bežal** iz doma
I out- ran from house.GEN (manner = head)
'I ran out of the house.'

Spanish (Talmy 1985:111)
(53) **Entró** corriendo a la cueva
enter.3SG.PAST run-PART to the cave (path = head)
'He ran into the cave.'

Nez Perce (Talmy 1985:110)[15]
(54) hi- ququ.- **láhsa** -e
3SG- galloping- go.up -PAST (path = head)
'He galloped uphill.'

In languages in which head verb and satellite are not distinguished
by grammatical category, this means that one cannot determine on typo-

logical grounds (or sometimes even on language-internal grounds) which is the head:[16]

> Mandarin Chinese (Li & Thompson 1981:58)
> (55) tāmen pǎo chū lái   le
>   3PL   run exit come PERF
>   'They came running out.'
>   (cf English *They came out*, *They ran out*, *They exited*)

The Mandarin example illustrates another component of motion events (and other events as well): **deixis**, that is, the direction of motion with respect to the speaker, represented by *lái* 'come.' The deictic component can also be either head or satellite cross-linguistically:

> Kiowa (Watkins 1984:179)
> (56) ɔːpàl sép **cándé** -ą̀ː   nɔ̀   pàhį̀ː   bà-thːį́dáy
>   nearer rain reach -come and.DS clearly 2pl-get.wet.PERF
>   (path = head)
>   'THE RAIN IS **coming** closer and it is clear we will get wet.'
>   (deixis = head)
>   English
> (57) Harriet came running out.   (deixis = head)

Thus, the manner, deictic and directional elements may be the head of a verbal unit representing an event, and therefore presumably have some common conceptual structure lacking in satellites that never are the head cross-linguistically.

In the examples we have discussed so far, the primitive components that have made up events have been relatively uniform across languages (though they are categorized differently in different languages). There are also more radical decompositions of events found in some languages, particularly in New Guinea; the examples here are from Kalam (Pawley 1987:329,340):

> (58) mnek   am mon pk d   ap   ay-a-k
>   next.morning go wood hit get come he.placed
>   'Next morning he gathered firewood.'
> (59) kab añañ ap   yap pk-e-k   pag-p   ok
>   stone glass come fall it.having.hit.DS it.has.broken that
>   'A stone broke the glass.'

(60) kty am kmn pak dad apl   nb   okok   ad
     they go game kill carry having.come.ss there around bake
     ñbelgpal
     they.used.to.eat
     '...they used to cook (and eat) in places around there the game
     they killed/...they used to hunt game.'

In this dimension, Kalam appears to represent the opposite extreme
to English, in which such actions are described by single roots, "gather,"
"break" and "hunt." However, looking at other examples reveals a
pattern that applies at least to English and Kalam. There are a number
of actions that are expressed by single clauses in both Kalam and English,
representing what Pawley calls "a core of conceptual events," including
concepts such as "take," "cut," "split," "go" and "give." We might
suggest speculatively that concepts representing actions could be divided
into three types with respect to expression in a single clause: (1) those
that are always expressed in single clauses; (2) those that sometimes
are expressed in single clauses; and (3) those that never are expressed
in single clauses. This is the simple vs. complex expression phenomenon
manifested at the clause level rather than the lexical level. The iconic-
motivation hypothesis would use a typological analysis based on this
distribution to propose a ranking of event types by conceptual complexity
that could be tested for cognitive generality.

The relationship between verbal structures and the conceptual structure
of events is perhaps the most thoroughly explored area of the typology of
grammatical structure. However, most of the studies do not have the necessary breadth of a typological sample, and, as we have indicated, there
are important gaps in our knowledge. We have only been able to note
what appears to be universal and what appears to be variable. This
is only the first step in the typology of form–function relations for verbs.

7.3.2.3 Other universals of linguistic structure

There is a further way to categorize grammatical morphemes
other than by syntactic and inflectional category: a general distinction
between "lexical" and "grammatical" morphemes. The precise definition of this distinction has eluded linguists, chiefly because "lexical"
and "grammatical" are both prototype concepts. Three structural criteria
have been proposed to distinguish the two:

1 Lexical morphemes are prototypically **free**, while grammatical morphemes are prototypically **bound** (affixed to another word). A possible
intermediate category is that of a clitic: an unstressed morpheme whose

position is syntactically rather than lexically determined (e.g. suffixed to the first constituent in a clause).

2 Lexical categories are **open-class**, that is they may absorb new elements easily. The standard examples are nouns, verbs and adjectives. Grammatical categories are **closed-class**, that is they rarely absorb new members, and that only slowly. For example, English only slowly has gained a number of auxiliary verbs, and even those (*ought to, going to, have to, better*) have not yet been integrated into the auxiliary-verb category (or **paradigm**, as it is usually called). Openness of class is a matter of degree; for example, the English auxiliary category is being expanded, while the category of nominal number does not appear to be about to admit any new members.

3 Lexical modifiers are optional, while grammatical inflections or modifiers are obligatory (heads of constructions, usually obligatory for other reasons, are excluded from this criterion). Of course, obligatoriness can be conditional – for instance, noun phrases except for subjects and objects require prepositions in English, so the category "preposition" in English is conditionally obligatory.

As we mentioned above, these three criteria do not entirely coincide, and the two syntactic criteria appear to be gradient. Prepositions in English are fairly closed-class, but they are free morphemes. Nouns in noun-incorporating languages are open-class, but they can appear as bound forms (e.g. indefinite objects). However, in the majority of cases, these three criteria cluster, so that the prototypical grammatical element is bound, relatively closed-class and obligatory, and the prototypical lexical element is free, relatively open-class and optional (when not a syntactic head).

There is a functional-typological pattern to the lexical–grammatical distinction. Grammatical morphemes (closed-class and/or bound morphemes) tend to express the same concepts across the world's languages. These are, of course, the standard inflectional and "function-word" categories, including comparison and degree for adjectives; number, size, gender (including classifiers), and spatial and grammatical relations for nouns; tense, aspect, modality, evidentiality, formality, transitivity, and speech-act type for verbs and/or clauses. To put it in implicational terms: if a language expresses a concept as a member of a bound, closed-class and/or obligatory (nonhead) category, then that concept belongs to the aforementioned small set, which we will call **grammatical concepts**.

There are a number of questions that this pattern raises for the functionally-oriented typologist. The first question is whether or not there is something conceptually in common among grammatical concepts. This is the question that has occupied most linguists interested in the problem. A non-answer to this problem is to say that grammatical concepts are "abstract." Some of the cognitive linguists (Talmy 1978, 1988; Morrow 1986) have suggested that the grammatical elements function to structure or conceptualize human experience for the purpose of linguistic expression. Without going into particular detail, it appears that there is some plausibility to this claim, though in fact little attention has been directed to it.

The second question that could be raised is what is the precise typological pattern involved? It would seem that some concepts are more likely to be expressed grammatically than others. In fact, Greenberg (1966a) proposed several universals that reveal that one is not dealing with a simple dichotomy between lexical and grammatical elements. Universal 30 ("If the verb has categories of person–number or if it has categories of gender, it always has tense–mode categories") indicates that tense–aspect and modality are more basic grammatical categories than agreement in person–number and gender. Universals 32 ("Whenever the verb agrees with a nominal subject or nominal object in gender, it also agrees in number") and 36 ("If a language has the category of gender, it always has the category of number") indicate that number is a more basic grammatical category than gender. Finally, Universal 29 ("If a language has inflection, it always has derivation") indicates that the various concepts expressed in derivational categories are more basic grammatical elements than concepts expressed in inflectional categories. These universals alone suggest the following hierarchy of grammatical concepts:

derivational concepts < tense–aspect–modality < number < gender

In addition to such universals, which certainly could be added to, there might be relationships between the specific structural criteria and particular subclasses of grammatical concepts. As with many other grammatical questions, the typology of the phenomenon remains to be explored.

Finally, one may raise the question of how the ranking of concepts along this scale is related to the structural expression of grammatical concepts as closed-class, bound, obligatory grammatical elements. The following reasoning is suggested, based on the assumption that grammatical concepts are used to structure or conceptualize human experience for the purpose of communication. On this assumption, it would seem quite obvious that grammatical concepts would be expressed obligatorily, since any time one utters a sentence, one must use those concepts to organize the content of the sentence. Also, grammatical concepts would make up tightly integrated sets (i.e. closed classes or paradigms), since the structuring of experience necessarily involves the simplification and ordering of indefinitely complex phenomena (see Lakoff 1977). Finally, the fact that grammatical concepts are bound would follow from syntagmatic economy, since they would be used in virtually every sentence.[17]Although this is highly speculative, on the basis of the preceding illustrations of iconic motivation, it is equally worth investigating.

There are many other aspects of syntactic structure that remain to be explored with respect to a typology of form–function relations. For example, little research has been done on the typology of how various modification relations (demonstrative, numeral, possessive, adjectival, etc.) in the noun phrase are expressed in the world's languages, not to mention the typology of complex sentence structures (for a fine study of comparative constructions and chaining co-ordinate constructions, see Stassen 1985). A more thorough examination of grammatical structure from the perspective of how that structure expresses conceptual structure would result in considerably more typological generalizations and also shed light on the iconic-motivation hypothesis.

7.4 Competing motivations

In the preceding sections, we have discussed various examples of competing motivations, in which economy competed with iconicity in various ways. One example was the paradigmatic-economic motivation to minimize vocabulary, opposed to the iconic motivation of having a distinct word for every distinct concept. In this case, the resolution of the conflict gave rise to the phenomenon of polysemy. It is important to note that the competition between economy and iconicity has different possible resolutions; that is, it allows for cross-linguistic variation. Either polysemy occurs, signalling the predominance of economy; or separate forms for each concept occur, signalling the predominance of iconicity. The competing-motivation model of economy and iconicity excludes one logically possible type: the uneconomic and un-iconic presence of more than one form for a given concept. This is synonymy, whose existence Haiman, Bolinger and other linguists have argued against. Thus, competing motivations provide an important class of explanations for both typological variation and constraints on that variation.

A competing-motivation analysis also underlies markedness patterns, at least structural markedness. In chapter 4, we emphasized that markedness is not an unrestricted universal. The structural criterion allowed two of three logical possibilities: the marked category was expressed by more morphemes than the unmarked category (usually one morpheme to zero), or both categories were expressed by the same number of morphemes. The third possibility, for the marked category to be expressed by fewer morphemes than the unmarked category, is excluded by markedness. By analogy with the previous example, it should be clear that the first allowable type corresponds to the predominance of economy (ideally, no morpheme for the more frequent value), and the second allowable type corresponds to the predominance of iconicity (ideally, one morpheme per value, for both the unmarked and the marked values). The excluded type is the one in which uneconomically, the more frequent value is assigned an "extra" morpheme, while uniconically the other value, the marked one, is expressed by no morpheme.[18]

These two examples demonstrate that competing-motivation analyses can exclude certain logically possible types, and therefore are not vacuous explanations. This criticism has been applied to all analyses of competing motivations, and while it does apply to some competing-motivation analyses, it does not apply to those described in the preceding paragraph. Another example of a nonvacuous competing-motivation analysis is Greenberg's analysis of dominant and harmonic word order, described in chapter 3. In that analysis, one logically possible type was excluded: the type in which the two word orders were disharmonic and both recessive. This type is, of course, the one type excluded by the implicational statement of the word-order pattern. In general, we may characterize a nonvacuous competing-motivation model as one in which:

1 satisfaction of both motivations simultaneously is logically impossible (hence the competition between the two);
2 some allowed logically possible type(s) can be attributed to satisfaction of one motivation;
3 the other allowed logically possible type(s) can be attributed to satisfaction of the other motivation;
4 the prohibited logically possible type(s) represent the satisfaction of neither motivation.

At this point, the value for typology of nonvacuous competing-motivation analyses should be clear: they allow for universal characterization of typological variation. All languages, and therefore all human beings, can have both motivations attributed to them. A particular language at a particular historical stage has conventionally resolved the competing motivation in one of the several possible acceptable ways, just as a particular language resolves hierarchical scales and prototypes in some acceptable way. Moreover, languages can change over time through the shift in predominance of one motivation over the other (see chapter 8). Nevertheless, certain possible types are excluded by virtue of satisfying no motivation. Thus, nonvacuous competing-motivation analyses satisfy the theoretical goal of limiting possible language types (see 3.1).

The difference between a vacuous and a nonvacuous model of competing motivations is that condition 4 above does not apply, because every logically possible type is allowed. In other words, one could reach the same explanatory goal simply by stating that every logically possible type is actually possible. Most linguists would select the latter explanation over a vacuous competing-motivation analysis because the latter is simpler. It must be pointed out that the latter explanation is really a non-explanation. Also, the fact that a competing-motivation analysis does not exclude any possible types does not mean that the analysis is wrong (assuming all the possible types are attested). The real problem is the lack of corroborating evidence to support the analysis, such as would be provided by the predicted exclusion of unattested language types. For this reason, functionally oriented typologists usually attempt to refine a vacuous competing-motivation analysis so that some logically possible language type is indeed excluded by the analysis, and is indeed empirically unattested. We will illustrate this with two examples.

A number of linguists have proposed a set of universal pragmatic principles, or at least motivations, for word order. These principles have a long history in functionalism, and the three most important ones are listed here, as presented by Haiman (1985; cf. Behaghel 1923–32, vol. IV; Jespersen 1909–49, vol. VII:54; Tomlin 1986, Mithun 1987):

1　What is old information comes first, what is new information comes later, in an utterance.
2　Ideas that are closely connected tend to be placed together.
3　What is at the moment uppermost in the speaker's mind tends to be first expressed.
　(Haiman 1985:237–8)

Principle 1 is iconic: the temporal order of elements in the utterance reflects the temporal order of the introduction of information into the discourse. Principle 2 is also iconic; we have already discussed it in detail in 7.3.2.1. Principle 3 appears also to be iconic, though in a metaphorical rather than direct fashion: the order of elements in the utterance reflects the order of importance in the speaker's mind. The significant problem is that new information is generally "what is at the moment uppermost in the speaker's mind" and old information is not. By principle 1, new information should follow old information. By principle 3, new information should precede old information.

Principles 1 and 3 appear to provide a classic vacuous competing motivation for the ordering of old and new information in utterances.[19] Haiman, however, focuses his argument on the fact that principle 3 is in conflict with principle 2 as well. Fronting of uppermost information often splits up otherwise conceptually close constituents. Thus, principle 2 will tend to place certain constituents together, and principle 3 will tend to separate them, other things being equal. This is again a classic case of vacuous competing motivation, since no possibility is excluded.

Haiman's argument against vacuity is applied to one word-order phenomenon: WH movement in information questions and relative clauses. Haiman identifies principle 3 with linguistic focus, which is generally "new" information, and most likely uppermost in the speaker's mind. He argues that principle 3 applies to information questions only: the questioned element is in focus, and will therefore move to the focus position (if focus is indicated by a special position).[20] Haiman predicts that relative pronouns will behave differently from interrogative pronouns, even though they are usually analyzed to be the same kind of syntactic element as interrogative pronouns. Principle 3 does not apply, since they are not in focus (and, apparently, principle 1 does not apply either). Instead, principle 2 applies: they are attracted to the head noun of the relative clause. In other words, for information questions, focusing – generally governed by principle 3 – overrides conceptual closeness, while for relative pronouns focusing does not apply, and so principle 2 is free to apply. Typologically that means language types in which the relative pronoun is not fronted should not exist, even if the question word (allegedly the same constituent type) is not fronted.

Haiman's conjecture is confirmed by his survey, with one exception (Luganda). The crucial test cases are those languages in which focused elements are not fronted. An example of this language type is Hungarian, in which relative pronouns consist of the definite article *a* combined with the interrogative pronoun. In Hungarian, focused elements are placed immediately before the verb (a common phenomenon in SOV languages, though whether Hungarian is SVO, SOV or neither is controversial). Relative pronouns are moved next to the head noun, which precedes the relative clause. The crucial examples are those in which the question word is not initial, thus demonstrating that it is in preverbal, not sentence-initial, position:

(61) a   lova -t   ki   hozta   haza?
      the horse -ACC who   brought home
      'Who brought the horse home?'

and those in which the relative pronoun is separated from the verb, thus demonstrating that the relative-pronoun position is sentence-initial, not preverbal (Haiman 1985:244):

(62) az   újság   amit   Pista   végig   olvasott
      the newspaper which   Stephen to.the.end read
      'the newspaper which Stephen read to the end'

Haiman has demonstrated that principles 2 and 3 exist and operate independently in the ways that a competing-motivation analysis would predict.[21]

Another example of the refinement of a vacuous competing-motivation analysis is DuBois' analysis of ergative and accusative patterns (DuBois 1985, 1987). DuBois argues, following most other linguists, that accusative patterns represent the conventionalization of the prototypical agent–topic type, manifested by the subject of an intransitive verb (S) and the subject of a transitive verb (A). DuBois proposes a novel interpretation of ergative patterns based on discourse structure. He notes that the vast majority of clauses in naturally occurring language have zero or one nominal argument (subject or object) only, and very few clauses have two nominal arguments (cf. Lambrecht 1987; Mithun 1987; and Haiman 1985:244, citing Behrens 1982:161). More specifically, DuBois observes that the one nominal argument usually found with transitive verbs is almost always the transitive object. The reason for this, DuBois hypothesizes, is that transitive subjects are almost always the continued topic and are therefore pronominal. New participants, that is nominal arguments, are almost always introduced as intransitive subjects or transitive objects. DuBois proposes a "preferred argument structure" of verb + absolutive NP. This structure is the motivation for the existence of ergative patterns: leave the NPs that occurred most commonly, that is, the absolutive NPs, unmarked (cf. economy and markedness).

This analysis leaves DuBois with motivations for accusative and for absolutive patterns, which leads to a vacuous competing-motivation analysis.[22] In order to avoid this state of affairs, DuBois refines his analysis to account for split-ergative patterns. Following DeLancey (1981), DuBois notes that accusative–ergative splits divide speech-act participants (first and second person) from nonparticipants (third person), and the speech-act participants are marked accusatively, nonparticipants ergatively (see 6.3.2). DuBois argues that speech-act participants are inherently given, and so can never be new participants. Therefore his discourse motivation for ergative patterning does not apply, and instead the accusative pattern always applies.

Thus, DuBois' analysis predicts that no languages exist in which a split-ergative pattern occurs so that first and second person are marked ergatively, and third person accusatively. This is confirmed empirically. More precisely, DuBois' analysis makes the stronger claim that in all languages, first and second person are marked accusatively, while third person can be marked either ergatively or accusatively. The stronger claim is false (for example, first/second person A argument NPs are marked with ergative case in Basque and Eskimo, and trigger ergative agreement in Tzotzil and in the perfect in Hindi). Also, there is the additional problem (for DuBois and also DeLancey, as we observed in 6.3.2) that some languages split lower on the animacy hierarchy than first/second person vs. third person. Although there are significant empirical problems for DuBois' analysis, it is nevertheless not an example of vacuous competing motivations.

7.5   Typological conspiracies and communicative motivation

This section will illustrate another kind of interaction among language types that appears to have a functional basis. This is essentially the typological version of a rule conspiracy, in which two logically independent typologies are related.

The first example is of a conspiracy between accessibility in relative-clause formation and "promotion" of oblique noun phrases to direct object and direct object to subject (Givón 1975b; 1979: chapter 4). In chapter 5, we pointed out the discovery by Keenan and Comrie that accessibility in relative-clause formation obeys the case hierarchy. That is, we may construct a typological classification of languages as follows:

1   languages that allow relativization of subjects only;
2   languages that allow relativization of subjects and direct objects only;
3   languages that allow relativization of subjects, objects and oblique NPs.

The second typological classification, that of promotion, involves the existence of verbal derivations that have the effect of expressing as direct objects noun phrases that are normally oblique (in transformational terms, the "promotion" of an oblique noun phrase to direct-object status). The term that is used for this class of derivative verbal forms is **applicative**. Promotion also involves the existence of verbal derivations that have the effect of expressing as subjects noun phrases that are normally direct objects or obliques. This category includes, of course, the passive; it also includes the verbal derivational forms, found in some Austronesian languages (notably the Philippine languages), that have the effect of expressing "normally" oblique noun phrases as subjects. Thus, we may propose a typological classification based on promotion, that is whether a language has **object-creating** applicative verbal derivatives and whether a language has **subject-creating** verbal derivatives.

Givón discovered the following relationship between relativization types and promotion types:

> If a language allows relativization of subjects only, then it has subject-creating verbal derivatives. If a language allows relativization of subjects and direct objects only, then it has applicative verbal derivatives.[23]

The aforementioned Austronesian languages, which are the only languages of type 1, all have the subject-creating verbal derivatives (Givón 1979:152). Givón uses Indonesian and various Bantu languages to illustrate type 2; all of these languages have applicative (object-creating) verbal derivatives. Givón also observed additional constraints on languages of type 2, summarized in his Typological Condition IV:

Only languages in which (a) the accusative object is unmarked, (b) the promotion of non-accusative objects results in loss of their case-marking, and (c) that promotion results in verb-coding of the semantic case of the nonaccusative, will have the direct-object-only constraint on the relativization of object arguments. (Givón 1979:181)

The explanation for the "conspiracy" between relativization type and promotion type of a language is twofold. First, the conspiracy satisfies the functional communicative requirement that it be possible to relativize any noun-phrase argument of a relative clause. If there is a restriction on relativization such that a direct object and/or an oblique cannot be relativized directly, then the language has a verbal derivation that allows the direct object or oblique to be "promoted" to a higher position on the case hierarchy that *can* be relativized (see Keenan & Comrie

1977:88–9). In the Philippine languages, nonsubject noun phrases can be promoted to subject position and then be relativized. In the Bantu languages, oblique noun phrases can be promoted to direct-object position and then be relativized.

This typological pattern does not represent the operation of economic or iconic motivation; the interactions involved do not make utterances more economical or more iconic. Their functional motivation is more basic: they make the communication of certain combinations of concepts possible, period. We will call this **communicative motivation**, the need to provide some grammatical means to express virtually any concept or complex structure of concepts. Given a typological pattern that constrains expression of certain concepts in certain languages, such as the accessibility (grammatical relations) hierarchy, the examination of the alternative grammatical structure for the "prohibited" concept will frequently yield typological conspiracies due to communicative motivation. Communicative motivation, like economic and iconic motivation, also limits the range of possible language types. For example, it excludes languages in which relativization is restricted to subjects only but there are no subject-creating verbal derivations.

Verbal derivation also satisfies the hearer's communicative functional requirement to figure out what grammatical relation the relativized noun phrase originally had in the relative clause. That is, the presence of a verbal derivational affix and its meaning will indicate the original grammatical relation that the relativized noun had in the relative clause. This condition Givón calls **case recoverability**. The operation of this second functional requirement is supported by evidence from languages that do not satisfy Givón's Typological Condition IV, or do not have restrictions on relativization. Typological Condition IV states in essence that if the language does not code the original grammatical relation of a promoted oblique by a nonzero verbal derivation, then the language will not have the direct-object constraint on relativization, because one cannot recover the original grammatical relation that the direct object had from the verbal form. Languages of this type discussed by Givón are English, Hebrew and Sherpa. All of these languages use different relativization strategies from the ones illustrated by languages of types 1 and 2. Significantly, the relativization strategies allow case recoverability by different means than verbal derivational affixes. Hebrew uses an anaphoric pronoun strategy, in which the anaphoric pronoun retains its original position and case marking in the relative clause (Givón 1979:183):

(63) ha- ish she raiti et- ha- isha shel -o
     the- man that- I.saw ACC- the- wife of   -him
     'the man whose wife I saw'

English uses two strategies. One is a relative-pronoun strategy, in which the grammatical relation is indicated by the prepositions associated with the relative pronoun:

(64)   the student to whom I offered the book

English also uses a gap strategy in which the original position is left empty, except for a stranded preposition (if required) that, along with the empty position, indicates the original grammatical relation of the relativized noun phrase:

(65)   the student who I offered the book to ___

Case recoverability is not an absolute communicative functional requirement. Keenan and Comrie distinguish what they call [+case] and [−case] strategies (1977:65). A [+case] relative-clause strategy indicates the case relation of the relativized NP, via anaphoric pronouns or relative pronouns marked for case; a [−case] strategy does not indicate the case relation in this way. A language such as English that uses a [−case] strategy for more than one position on the case hierarchy therefore does not allow perfect case recoverability (*the man that Mary met, the man that met Mary*). However, a survey of Keenan and Comrie's data demonstrates some striking facts. The primary relativization strategy tends to be a [−case] strategy, and is, of course, restricted to the upper end of the case hierarchy. However, many languages have a secondary relativization strategy that is used for those case relations that the primary strategy cannot apply to, and they are [+case] strategies. This was illustrated in 5.3.2 for Toba Batak and Tamil; in table 7.1 we present some of Keenan and Comrie's data (1977:77–9; + = applies; − = does not apply).

These examples suggest that secondary, [+case] relativization strategies are associated with the lower end of the case hierarchy (here extended to nonverbal case relations of genitive and object of comparison). This is not surprising from the point of view of markedness, since a [+case] strategy generally consists of an additional morpheme (the one that encodes the case relation), and case marking is also associated with the lower end of the case hierarchy. The significant fact for this section is that the secondary [+case] relativization strategies fill in the

Table 7.1 *Distribution of [−case] and [+case] relativization strategies*

	Sbj	DO	IO	Obl	Gen	Ocomp
Kera						
−case	+	−	−	−	−	−
+case	−	+	+	+	+	+
Welsh						
−case	+	+	−	−	−	−
+case	−	−	+	+	+	+
Roviana						
−case	+	+	+	−	−	−
+case	−	−	−	+	+	−
Turkish						
−case	+	+	+	+	−	−
+case	−	−	−	−	+	+?

communicative gap, namely relative clauses, that the primary strategy is prohibited from expressing.[24]

Thus, different relative-clause strategies, and the interaction of constraints of accessibility with derived verb forms, anaphoric pronouns and relative pronouns all have the effect of allowing relativization of virtually any NP, and (to a lesser extent) of maintaining case recoverability.[25]

A second example of a conspiracy that has the effect of satisfying communicative functional needs is described by Heath (1975). He compares the degree of differentiation of third person pronominal forms in Choctaw, Turkish, Basque, English, Arabic and Nunggubuyu, and ranks the languages by degree of pronominal differentiation as follows:

1 Choctaw: one form
2 Basque, Turkish: two forms (singular and plural)
3 English: four forms (three singular gender forms and one plural)
4 Arabic: six forms (singular, dual and plural masculine and feminine)
5 Nunggubuyu: ten forms (masculine and feminine singular and dual forms, human plural and five nonhuman classes)

Heath then compares the languages with respect to "identification rules," that is rules that indicate the coreferentiality and non-coreferentiality of noun phrases. Identification rules vary considerably, some referring to simple clauses (as in *He killed himself*), as opposed to complex clauses (*I want to ɸ go home*), while others are less strictly defined in their conditions of application (*I wanted to kill him*). Heath then ranks the same languages by the number and degree of use of identification rules, resulting in exactly the reverse ranking: Nunggubuyu, Arabic,

English, Basque and Choctaw. Again, there is a typological "conspiracy" linking the two types of rules, and Heath argues that the reason for this is communicative function. In order to maintain "referential clarity" and minimize ambiguity, one may use either a variety of distinct pronominal forms, or encode coreference relations in syntactic constructions. The more a language uses one strategy, the less it uses the other, since both have the same communicative function.

Of course, communicative motivation also excludes an enormous range of possible language types that grossly violate communicative function, for example languages in which there are fewer than one hundred lexical items or languages without constructions that serve the function of questions. The typological conspiracies described by Givón and Heath represent more subtle and complex examples of communicative motivation, pertaining to relatively specific typological classifications of human languages. Communicative motivation certainly plays a fundamental role in constraints of form–function relations across languages.

7.6 Conclusion

In this chapter, we have examined external explanations for typological patterns, focusing chiefly on economy, iconicity and communicative function. The principle of economy provides an explanation for those many aspects of markedness patterns (including hierarchies and prototypes) that can be traced to frequency. The principle of iconicity, including "isomorphism" and iconic motivation, along with the principle of communicative function can be used to account for the typology of form–function relations. The empirical study of cross-linguistic patterns of form–function relations is basically in its infancy, although we have described several studies in this chapter that lend support to the operation of iconicity and communicative function in grammatical structure. This area is currently attracting considerable attention in typological research, as is the topic of the next chapter, diachronic typology.

8
Diachronic typology

8.1 Introduction

Languages do not occur in static or stable states. All languages exhibit some degree of grammatical variation, and they change over time – in fact, much synchronic variation represents language change in progress. Changes in linguistic structure are changes in the grammatical properties that enter into one or more of the cross-linguistic patterns described in the preceding chapters. This fact suggests two extensions of typology. First, if linguistic types fall into universal cross-linguistic patterns, then it is worth investigating if the cross-linguistic patterns also govern changes in linguistic type. Second, it should be possible to classify typologically linguistic changes themselves, and look for relationships among linguistic processes in the same way that typologists seek relationships among linguistic states. This latter process has been especially fruitful and has led to a considerable effort to study a family of associated language processes called "grammaticalization."

8.2 The dynamicization of synchronic typology

Let us return to the foundations of synchronic typology in order to see its consequences for language change. Synchronic typology is founded on the typological classification of logically possible linguistic types (see chapter 2). Once this is established, one then takes a language sample in order to determine which of the logically possible linguistic types are actually attested in the languages of the world, and formulates universals (implicational universals, markedness, hierarchies, form–function relations, etc.) that restrict human languages to the actually occurring types. These universals are then explained in some fashion (e.g. in external terms).

The first application of typology to language change was the hypothesis that a reconstructed protolanguage state has to be of the same type as an attested language state. That is, one could not violate the constraints that synchronic typology imposes on current languages in the postulation of a reconstructed protolanguage. This constraint was first proposed by Jakobson (1958), with respect to the reconstructed voiced aspirate series of Indo-European. In that reconstruction, the labial voiced aspirate /bʰ/ was quite common in reconstructed forms, but the voiceless aspirate counterpart /pʰ/, one of the least-marked phonological segments according to the place of articulation hierarchy, was absent. In the past twenty years, various proposals have been made to alter the reconstructed consonant system so that the series with the labial gap in the Proto-Indo-European phoneme inventory has a manner of articulation in which a gap in the labial position is expected (see Collinge 1985:259–69 for a summary of current proposals). In other words, the Proto-Indo-European stop system was overhauled in order to accommodate this typological constraint and render it more "typologically natural."

The "typological naturalness" constraint proposed by Jakobson, like all of the constraints that synchronic typology imposes on language change, is actually a byproduct of a hypothesis of diachronic typology. In this case, the hypothesis is **uniformitarianism**:[1] languages of the past (at least, those that we can reconstruct or find records of) are not different in nature from languages of the present. Therefore, the typological universals discovered in contemporary languages should also apply to ancient and reconstructed languages. The uniformitarian hypothesis is actually implicit in some typological work, in that language samples occasionally include ancient languages such as Latin, Greek, Hittite or Classical Nahuatl (Aztec) without special justification. The uniformitarian hypothesis, like other hypotheses of diachronic typology, is a general assumption about the nature of language and language change that can be considered a defining characteristic of diachronic-typological theory, in the same way that the innateness hypothesis of generative grammar (that most linguistic competence is biologically innate) is a general assumption that can be only quite indirectly verified or falsified.

The observation of ancient languages such as Latin and their modern descendants indicates another commonplace fact about language change, namely that languages can change type. For example, Latin's highly flexible SOV word order changed to French's rigid SVO order, and the inflectional morphological structure of Old English changed to the isolating structure of modern English. This fact points to a fundamental shift in the view of language types from synchronic to diachronic typology. Instead of viewing language types as states that languages are *in*, in the diachronic view language types are viewed as stages that languages *pass through*. In diachronic typology, synchronic language states are reanalyzed as stages in the process of language change. The focus of attention, as a consequence, shifts from the language states themselves to the transitions from one state to another.

The reinterpretation of language states as stages leads to another set of hypotheses of diachronic typology. The first hypothesis is **connectivity**: within a set of attested language states defined by a given typological classification, a language can (eventually, and possibly indirectly) shift from any state to any other state. For example, consider the typological classification covered by the implicational universal "AN word order implies NumN word order":

   1   AN & NumN
   2   NA & NumN
   3   NA & NNum

The connectivity hypothesis asserts that a language can change from any one of these three types to any other of the types. The connection need not be direct; for example, it probably is the case that AN & NumN languages cannot change directly into NA & NNum languages, but must go through an intermediate NA & NumN stage (see below).

It is worth considering what the state of affairs would be if the connectivity hypothesis were false. If it were false, there would exist autonomous linguistic types, including perhaps "eternal" types that never changed. Demonstration of the genetic relatedness of languages of different types supports connectivity. If two languages of different types are genetically related, then they would have a common ancestor; the common ancestor's type would be connected to both daughter languages' types, and so the three types would be partially connected.

The argument from genetic relatedness only partially supports connectivity. It demonstrates that there is a one-way historical connection between the ancestor's linguistic type and the daughter languages' types; it does not show that any linguistic type can change into any other type. For example, consider the hypothesis that Proto-Indo-European was SOV (one of the major competing hypotheses for the word order of Proto-Indo-European). The existence of daughter languages that are SVO and VSO demonstrates that SOV can change to SVO and VSO, which, following historical linguistic practice, we will notate SOV > SVO and SOV > VSO. However, it does not demonstrate the opposite direction of change, namely that SVO > SOV and VSO > SOV. Thus, it does not demonstrate that there exists a way to change from SVO to VSO or vice versa. Nor does it demonstrate a connection between daughter-language types, in this case SVO to VSO or vice versa. However, let us consider what would be the case if it were indeed true that the only changes in word-order type are the one-way changes SOV > SVO and SOV > VSO. Over time, there would be an increase in the number of SVO and VSO languages, leading to the gradual extinction of the SOV type. (And, of course, the SVO and VSO types would be "eternal" language states.) This state of affairs is not generally accepted to occur by diachronic typologists (though see Givón 1979:275–6). The connectivity hypothesis as we have phrased it has as a corollary that a language can both enter any language state and exit any language state.

The connectivity hypothesis was suggested by Greenberg (1978b) in a discussion of the diachronic interpretation of synchronic universals, or as he calls it, the **dynamicization** of typology.[2] In the same paper, Greenberg introduced two additional concepts that are relevant for the dynamic interpretation of language states as stages: stability and frequency (Greenberg 1978b:75).

Stability represents the likelihood that a language will exit a language state, that is, change out of a language state once it is in it. Hawkins' (1983) mobility principle for word-order universals (see 3.3) is a measure of stability. The mobility principle ranks word orders on their likelihood to shift from one order to its opposite, so that, for example, adjective–noun order is more unstable (mobile) than numeral–noun order. That is, an adjective is more likely to change position from one side of the noun to the other than a numeral is. Another example of an unstable linguistic type is nasal vowels: they tend to change to oral vowels (losing the nasal feature) quite rapidly relative to other phonological changes.

Frequency, on the other hand, represents the likelihood that the linguistic type is to occur, that is how likely a language will enter a state involving that type. Nasal vowels can be used to illustrate a frequent type: languages tend to evolve nasal vowels quite rapidly relative to other phonological features.

Stability and frequency are logically independent characteristics of language states. There are linguistic phenomena that illustrate all possible combinations of stability and frequency.[3] Linguistic phenomena that are frequent and stable tend to be areally widespread, and common in genetically closely related languages. Examples include front unrounded vowels, adpositions and possibly the major word orders SVO and SOV.[4] Frequent but unstable phenomena will be widespread but relatively sporadic within genetic groups; examples include nasal vowels and definite articles. Phenomena that are stable and infrequent will be relatively scarce in the world's languages but common in the genetic groups in which they occur. Examples include vowel harmony and verb-initial word order (though the latter tends to shift to SVO word order). Finally, unstable and infrequent linguistic phenomena will be both scarce and sporadic; examples include velar implosives, possessive classifiers and object-initial word orders OVS and OSV (if the latter exists). As can be seen, areal–genetic distribution is a good clue to the frequency and stability of linguistic phenomena. Frequency corresponds to how widespread the phenomenon is, both genetically and geographically: if it arises frequently, then it can arise in any genetic group in any geographical region. Stability corresponds to how concentrated in genetic groups or geographic areas the type is: if it is stable, then it is likely to have been a property of the parent language of a genetic group, or to have diffused and stayed in geographically contiguous languages.

Stability and frequency can have a significant role in typological analysis in two ways. First, from a purely methodological point of view, the choice of a language sample can be influenced by the stability of the phenomenon to be investigated. In the discussion of language sampling in 1.4, the possibility was raised that even a widely distributed sample might not represent independent cases of the phenomenon in question. This possibility is directly linked to the degree of stability of the phenomenon. For example, in 1.4 we gave the example of SVO order in Congo–Kordofanian languages as an example of probably historically related cases of word-order type. The comments in the previous paragraph suggest that SVO order is fairly stable, and so a sample including truly independent cases will have to be very widespread but also rather small, with only a few languages from each areal/genetic group. In 1.4, we also gave the example of the reflexive morpheme acquiring "middle voice" uses as an example of a phenomenon in which a cognate morpheme underwent independent changes. This is an example of an unstable linguistic type: reflexives tend to rapidly acquire middle voice uses (Hatcher 1942; Kemmer 1988). In this case, the problem of independence of cases is not nearly so acute.[5]

Above all, however, stability and frequency combine with other typological concepts to produce a diachronic typological analysis that accommodates "exceptions" to synchronic universals (see Givón 1979: chapter 6), and may even be used to account for the frequency distribution of linguistic types across languages. This implies that synchronic universals, exceptionless or not, are a byproduct of general diachronic principles. Implicational universals and markedness patterns (including, of course, hierarchies and prototypes) have a dynamic interpretation in which the synchronic typological patterns are attributable to "deeper" diachronic patterns.

Let us return to the example of the implicational universal "AN word order implies NumN word order." In chapter 3, we pointed out that this implicational universal is a generalization over the pattern of attested word-order types such that the type AN & NNum does not exist. Following the Greenberg–Hawkins analysis, one would account for this pattern by means of the concepts of dominance (heaviness) and harmony (we will begin by using Greenberg's version). Greenberg proposed a rule relating dominance and harmony so that dominant word orders could occur at any time, but recessive word orders could occur only if they were harmonic with some other (dominant) order (see 3.3). This rule can be dynamicized for word-order universals as follows: "The dominant order can shift away from a harmonic word order, but a recessive order can shift only in harmony with some existing (dominant) order."[6] Now let us examine the word-order types predicted by the synchronic universal:

1 AN & NumN
2 NA & NumN
3 NA & NNum
4 *AN & NNum

Types 1 and 3 are harmonic patterns, while type 2 has the dominant word orders for both adjective–noun and numeral–noun. Type 4, the type with both of the recessive word orders, is excluded. The dynamic rule says essentially that a language can shift from one harmonic order to the other only through the dominant orders. That is, a language can go from type 1 to type 3 only by a shift of adjective to its dominant NA order, that is by passing through type 2. Conversely, a language can go from type 3 to type 1 only by a shift of the numeral to its dominant NumN order, that is by passing through type 2. A language could not get into type 4, because that would imply that moving from type 1, the numeral shifted to its recessive order without there being a harmonic order for it to follow, and a similar line of reasoning excludes the transition from type 3 to type 4. Thus, type 4 can never come to exist, and so we have the synchronic distribution of language types that led linguists to the synchronic universal to begin with.

This argument has an implicit assumption about language change.

Why couldn't a language shift directly from type 1 to type 3? The assumption that prohibits this possibility is that language change is (more or less) **gradual**. Languages do not change several grammatical features at once, overnight. The term "gradual" must be taken with a grain of salt. In the example we have been using, there are three discrete linguistic types that are attested. In our example (which is a simplification of the facts in many ways), a "gradual" change is a change of one word order at a time, instead of both at once. In fact, word-order change can be even more gradual than that: for example, a language may change from AN to NA order by going through a stage in which both AN and NA orders are grammatical alternatives, or a stage in which AN order is used for one construction and NA order is used for another construction. In fact, the gradualness of language change forces us to abandon the view of language processes as a sequence of discrete stages (see the following section). However, this does not invalidate the basic concepts of the dynamicization of typologies presented in this section.

If one examines the actual frequency distribution of languages among the three allowed types – dominant but not harmonic, as in type (2), and the two harmonic types, for example types 1 and 3 – one discovers that the harmonic types are more frequent than the type which is disharmonic but has both dominant patterns. This is, in fact, generally true of all of the word-order universals in which dominance and harmony play a role, as a brief perusal of Greenberg 1966a and Hawkins 1983 indicates.[7] This suggests that in general, harmonic patterns are more stable than disharmonic patterns, when the latter are allowed to occur. Although violations of harmony occur (attributable to the competing motivation of dominance), disharmonic patterns are relatively unstable, and eventually shift to harmonic patterns.[8]

More interesting, however, is that type 4, the type excluded by the synchronic implicational universal, does exist, though it is very rare and of much lower frequency than type 2. The existence of these "exceptions" cannot be explained by dominance and harmony alone (though dominance and harmony should at least account for its very low frequency). However, it can be accounted for by the higher mobility (stability) of adjectives with respect to numerals, that is, the relative instability of adjective–noun order. The diachronic prediction is that type 4 could only arise from type 3, NA & NNum. Type 3 would either change into type 2 by the shift of the numeral to its dominant NumN position, or into type 4 by the shift of the more mobile adjective order. Type 1 can shift to type 2 by the dominant and more mobile adjective shifting to its dominant NA order; but type 1 cannot shift to type 4 since numerals are less mobile than adjectives and NNum order is recessive. The reason that type 4 is possible is that adjective–noun order is more unstable than numeral–noun order, and so the adjective might shift before the numeral does even if the adjective's shift is to its recessive order. Presumably, the extremely low frequency of type 4 is due to its being highly unstable, since it is disharmonic and both adjective and numeral are in their recessive orders.

This prediction must be borne out by empirical investigation of languages of type 4 in order to determine that they actually have evolved from languages of type 3 and not languages of type 1. We may nevertheless note that there is other evidence that adjective–noun order is quite unstable, and that we have not invoked instability as an *ad hoc* explanation to account for the exception. Hawkins' mobility hierarchy, which is based on a wide range of word-order patterns of noun modifiers, ranks adjective–noun order as quite mobile (i.e. unstable). Turning to word orders outside the noun phrase, there is also evidence for the mobility of adjective–noun order. Greenberg originally classified languages into twenty-four types based on major word order (VSO, SVO, SOV), adposition (prep.–postp.), genitive and adjective order. Four of the fifteen types attested are far more frequent than any other type (Comrie 1981a:89; the numbering is Greenberg's):

1 VSO/Prep/NG/NA [generalized by Hawkins to V-initial/Prep/NG/NA]
9 SVO/Prep/NG/NA
23 SOV/Postp/GN/AN
24 SOV/Postp/GN/NA

If we set aside verb–subject order (SV order appears to be so dominant in the world's languages that V-initial order is rare and often alternates with SVO), then we see that the most frequent orders are the harmonic orders, with one exception. We would expect the harmonic orders to be very stable and thus very common, on the basis of the evidence presented before. The exceptional order is SOV/Postp/GN/NA, which is harmonic except for adjective–noun order, which has shifted to its disharmonic but dominant position. The fact that the only common disharmonic type that is at all common involves NA order suggests that adjective–noun order is less stable than the other three word orders. If genitive–noun order or verb–object order were as unstable as adjective–noun order, for example, then we would expect to find SOV/Postp/NG/AN or SVO/Postp/GN/AN orders to be as frequent as SOV/Postp/

GN/NA; but they are not. If subject–verb order were as unstable as adjective–noun order, not only would SVO/Prep/NG/NA be common but so would OVS/Postp/GN/AN; but it is not.

Thus, a diachronic model of the competing motivations of dominance (heaviness), harmony and stability (mobility) can account for the frequency distribution of noun–adjective and noun–numeral word-order types across languages. It appears that all three of these principles have a far-ranging significance for word-order patterns, so that our explanation for adjective and numeral order is not *ad hoc*, though it requires more empirical investigation of actual word-order changes for verification. This goes far beyond a simple synchronic implicational universal.

The diachronic argumentation illustrated in the preceding paragraphs represents an important shift in the interpretation of synchronic universals. In the preceding chapters, the focus has been on accounting for **possible** and **impossible** language states. Here, the focus has shifted to accounting for **more probable** vs. **less probable** language states. Returning to the example of adjective–noun and numeral–noun order: types 1 and 3 are predicted to be the most probable (i.e. typologically most frequent) language states, type 4 the least probable, and type 2 in between. Implicit in this shift of focus is a shift of goals: instead of seeking universals that constrain possible language types, diachronic typology attempts to discover universals that predict the frequency of actual language types. Of course, the two goals converge in the limiting case: if the frequency of a language type is zero, and so its probability is zero, then the goals of diachronic typology are equivalent to those of synchronic typology (and contemporary synchronic linguistic theory in general). However, the diachronic typological approach represents a different perspective on synchronic "exceptions": they represent extremely low-probability language states that may be explainable by diachronic principles. This shift in goals represents an important difference in functional-typological and structuralist-generative approaches to explanation in grammatical theory (see chapter 9).

In the adjective/numeral word-order example, the introduction of a fundamentally diachronic concept, stability, led to a plausible account for the synchronically "exceptional" word-order type. We now turn to another example, which illustrates both the value of making synchronic universals more precise (as Hawkins has argued; see chapter 3) and how a diachronic interpretation can account for the apparent exceptions. The universal in question is the logical equivalence Prep ≡ NG (and its logically equivalent contrapositive, Postp ≡ GN). The logical equivalence allows two types, the two harmonic types, but disallows the two disharmonic types:

1 Prep. & NG
2 *Prep. & GN
3 *Postp. & NG
4 Postp. & GN

However, as both Greenberg and Hawkins noted, there are exceptions to this universal: both types 2 and 3 exist, although they are extremely rare. These "exceptions" are actually expected in the diachronic view, because of the gradualist hypothesis. If only types 1 and 4 existed, then the shift of a language from type 1 to type 4 or vice versa would involve the change of both genitive order and adposition order at once. If only one order changed at a time, as the gradualist hypothesis would suppose, then types 2 and 3 would both have to exist, although they would be unstable. If the language sample was large enough, cases of types 2 and 3 would appear in the sample. This is an example of **transitory** language states: synchronically "exceptional" language states may come to exist (and reveal themselves in large samples) because they represent diachronic transitions from one well-attested and well-explained state to another.[9] The reason that these transitional states, unlike the state NumN & NA in the adjective–numeral example, are synchronic "exceptions" is that there are no clear dominance patterns for adposition and genitive orders, and so dominance does not predict the existence of type 2 or type 3. Since only harmony and stability are operating in this example, a very high-frequency (probability) distribution for types 1 and 4, and a correspondingly very low frequency of types 2 and 3, are predicted.

Now the question is, how does that change occur? Both Greenberg and Hawkins modified the universals to accommodate an additional fact, that languages of types 2 and 3 had a consistent adjective–noun order that was harmonic with the genitive order but not with the adposition order:[10]

(a) Prep ⊃ (GN ⊃ AN)
(b) Postp ⊃ (NA ⊃ NG)

Either formulation has the effect of asserting that the genitive–noun order can be disharmonic with the adposition order only if it is harmonic with the adjective–noun order. A diachronic (dynamic) interpretation of this would be that the adjective–noun order would shift away from the adposition order first (adjective–noun order being less stable than genitive–noun order), then genitive–noun order would shift away from adposition order and finally adposition order would shift, yielding the opposing harmony. The sequence of languages states – all allowed by the revised universal, of course – is illustrated here for (a):

Prep & NG & NA→ Prep & NG & **AN**
$\qquad\qquad\qquad$ → Prep & **GN** & **AN** → **Postp** & **GN** & **AN**

Greenberg illustrated exactly this sequence of changes, in greater detail, for the revised universal (a) in Ethiopian Semitic languages and also for certain Iranian languages (Greenberg 1980; see 8.3). In both cases, the process of change was begun by a change in major word order to SOV (in the Ethiopian case, due to contact with surrounding SOV languages); the adjective was the first to change its order, and the genitive and adposition followed as expected. Thus the conditions added to the synchronic universal, along with the gradualist hypothesis, led to a diachronic interpretation that was empirically validated in at least two cases.

The preceding examples have illustrated the dynamicization of implicational universals, or rather the dominance-harmony principles underlying them, and the addition of essentially dynamic concepts, such as stability (mobility), frequency of occurrence and transitory language states, to account for otherwise exceptional synchronic phenomena. The grammatical criteria for markedness, hierarchies and prototypes (correlations) – structure and behavior – also lend themselves to a diachronic interpretation that can account for otherwise exceptional synchronic phenomena. A dynamic interpretation of markedness will refer to the origin and loss of a grammatical asymmetry instead of to its presence:

	Origin	*Loss*
Structure	A nonzero morpheme to indicate a marked value (or correlation) will arise first	A nonzero morpheme to indicate a marked value (or correlation) will be lost last
Behavior (cross-linguistic)	An unmarked value will arise as a grammatical category first	An unmarked category will be lost as a grammatical category last
Behavior (other)	A grammatical distinction will arise in the unmarked (or correlated) value of a cross-cutting category first	A grammatical distinction will be lost in the unmarked (or correlated) value of a cross-cutting category last

Diachronic typology

Let us return to the first example of number used to illustrate the structural markedness of plural over singular in chapter 4. The structural criterion allowed only three language types:

1   zero singular & zero plural markers (i.e. no number inflection)
2   zero singular & nonzero plural markers
3   nonzero singular & nonzero plural markers
4   *nonzero singular & zero plural markers

The dynamicization of the structural criterion states that a language will (more accurately, can) acquire a nonzero plural marker first, and then a nonzero singular marker – making the gradualist assumption that a language cannot change directly from type 1 to type 3.[11] This would prevent type 4 from arising during the development of number inflection in a language. Conversely, the criterion states that a language will lose a nonzero singular marker before it would lose a nonzero plural marker; this prevents type 4 from arising during the loss of number inflection.

The dynamicization of the cross-linguistic behavioral criterion involves the origin and loss of grammatical categories such as the dual and the plural. The origin and loss of marked and unmarked values for grammatical categories involve the existence of a grammatical distinction, however it is marked. For example, the hierarchy singular < plural < dual, interpreted dynamically, implies that languages will acquire the singular-plural distinction before they acquire the dual–plural distinction. This will be true independent of how the singular–plural distinction and the dual–plural distinction are expressed; how they are expressed is determined by the structural criterion. For example, the dual and plural may both be expressed by a single unanalyzable morpheme, thus telling us nothing about the structural markedness of dual and plural.

Finally, a cross-cutting grammatical distinction will (can) arise in the unmarked category first, and be lost in the unmarked category last. For example, a number distinction often arises in the less marked gender (masculine, human, animate) before it arises in the more marked gender, if it arises there at all. This example is very common and also very important because it explains an apparent markedness paradox. Consider the following paradigm for number agreement in the verb for third-person forms in Lakhota:

	Singular	*Plural*
Animate	-ϕ	-pi
Inanimate	-ϕ	-ϕ

From a purely synchronic point of view, this contains a markedness paradox. Although it is clear on behavioral grounds that the animate is less marked than the inanimate, as expected, the structural and behavioral criteria for number appear to conflict. Structurally, the plural is marked because it is a nonzero form for animates, but behaviorally it appears to be marked because it displays an animate–inanimate distinction. The appearance of being unmarked is a side-effect of the development of a number distinction, for animates specifically the development of a nonzero plural morpheme, that has not come to be used for inanimates. The clue that leads us to this interpretation is that the three forms "animate singular," "inanimate singular" and "inanimate plural" are identical. In fact, they are just the unmarked "singular" form, which is still used for the "inanimate plural" because the grammatical distinction "singular–plural" does not exist for inanimates. The same phenomenon can be found in Ngandi for the dual–plural distinction, found only in masculine forms, in which the less-marked form is expressed by a nonzero morpheme *ba-* (illustrated here with the forms for human nouns; Heath 1978b:35):

	Dual	Plural
Masculine	bari-	ba-
Feminine	ba-	ba-

Here, the presumed historical scenario is that the dual morpheme *-ri-* is added to the plural *ba-* only in the unmarked masculine value. This phenomenon can also be found in situations in which the new cross-cutting distinction arises through the substitution rather than the addition of the new morpheme, as has apparently occurred with the plural *ki-* in Quiché:

	Singular	Plural
Animate	r-	ki-
Inanimate	r-	r-

The common pattern in all of these examples is that the cross-cutting grammatical distinction arises through the entry of a new nonzero morpheme for the marked member of the cross-cutting category (plural in Lakhota and Quiché, dual in Ngandi) into the unmarked value of the category in question (animate in Lakhota and Quiché, masculine in Ngandi). In these examples, the diachronic interpretation involves an additional prediction: the new morpheme expresses the marked value of the cross-cutting category. For instance, it is assumed that in Lakhota *-pi* originated as a (nonzero) marker of the category "plural" that is restricted to the animate class, not a marker of the category "animate"

215

that is restricted to the plural number. If it were the latter case, that would violate the markedness pattern of both number and animacy (gender). Needless to say, this prediction would have to be confirmed by historical work on Lakhota. However, it illustrates the importance of determining what the morpheme denotes (or denoted in its evolution) in deciding how to apply the structural and the behavioral criteria of markedness.

Since language change is gradual, one would expect to be able to find the same process in an earlier stage in its evolution. In Quiché, inanimate nouns usually do not have any inflection for number, but they may be preceded by a particle *taq* that indicates plurality (with connotations of distributivity). This leads to a "paradigm" as follows:

Singular	*Plural*
NP	NP *or* taq NP

Again, it would appear that the plural is structurally more marked (because it has a construction with a nonzero morpheme), but behaviorally less marked (because it has two alternative plural constructions compared to one for the singular). Again, the clue that indicates the genuine state of affairs is that one of the alternative plural constructions is identical to the singular construction. The difference between this example and the earlier examples is that it represents an "intermediate" stage between the absence of a singular–plural distinction and the obligatory expression of a singular–plural distinction.

An example of a synchronic "exception" to markedness patterns is the genitive plural in Slavic (Greenberg 1969:185–9). Most modern Slavic languages divide nouns into gender classes and have a set of suffixes that indicate the case and number of the noun to which they are affixed. The markedness patterns described in chapter 4 predict that if any suffix is zero, it will be the nominative singular. In fact, many nouns have nonzero nominative singular affixes and zero genitive plural forms, e.g. standard Czech *žen-a* 'woman (nom. sg.)' vs. *žen-ø* 'of the women (gen. pl.)'. The origin of this exception to the markedness of number and case is due to competing motivation from a completely independent source: the loss of the short high vowels ("jers") of Common Slavic, including the short vowel that formerly marked the genitive plural in some declensions. In fact, since the phonological system of a language is quite independent of the syntactic–semantic system, conflicts in externally motivated processes between the two systems are rather common in languages, and hence lead to synchronic "exceptions." The interest in this example, however, is the evidence that some of the daughter languages are restructuring the nominal declensions in such a way that the languages are shifting to the predicted markedness pattern. The nonzero genitive plural endings that survived in minor declensions have spread to other declensions at the expense of the zero ending in almost every Slavic language, while the zero nominative singular ending has also spread at the expense of the nonzero nominative ending of the feminine *a*-stems in West Slavic, particularly Upper Lusatian and Slovak (Greenberg 1969:188–9). As Greenberg puts it: "Synchronic regularities are merely the consequence of [diachronic] forces. It is not so much again that 'exceptions' are explained historically, but that the true regularity is contained in the dynamic principles themselves" (Greenberg 1969:186).

The example of the restructuring of nominal declensions in Slavic demonstrates that markedness governs more drastic diachronic changes than the simple addition of a morpheme indicating a marked category to an unmarked member of the root. Bybee (1985a) has explored these diachronic changes constrained by markedness (i.e. text frequency) in some detail.[12] Bybee discusses two phenomena beyond those described in chapter 4 that are associated with markedness: the restructuring of paradigms using the least-marked form as the basic form, and the survival of irregularity in the least-marked form(s) of a paradigm. Both of these phenomena have been associated with markedness patterns, but have not figured prominently in typological discussions of markedness. Both can be illustrated here with a single example, the development of the preterit in Provençal (Bybee 1985a:55; cf. Bybee & Brewer 1980). The Old Provençal preterit had the following forms:

1sg	améi	1pl	amém	'love'
2sg	amést	2pl	amétz	
3sg	amét	3pl	améren	

These forms, as with most Romance verb forms, involve fusion of subject person and number with verbal tense/aspect. One restructuring of the Old Provençal preterit that illustrates Bybee's analysis is the modern Charente dialect:

1sg	cantí	1pl	cantétem	'sing'
2sg	cantétei	2pl	cantétei	
3sg	cantét	3pl	cantéten	

The Charente dialect altered the second-person singular and all the plural forms so that the base form on which they were formed is the third-person singular; only the first-person singular is distinct, and hence

217

irregular. Typologically, the third-person singular verb form is the least marked, followed by first-person singular (see 4.3.3 and 7.2.1). In the Charente dialect, the restructuring of the preterit paradigm has made the third-person singular form not only the least-marked form, but the base form for the other inflections (apart from first-person singular); this has "corrected" the markedness pattern from Old Provençal by analogical change rather than the addition of new plural and second-person forms.[13] The one form that resisted restructuring was the first-person singular, which is the next least-marked form. Bybee explains this in terms of a psychological model of storing word forms based on frequency, so that the higher frequency/less marked a form is, the more likely it is to remain irregular (i.e. resist restructuring) and/or be used as the base (zero) form for the restructuring of less-frequent/more-marked forms (Bybee 1985a: chapter 5). Bybee's model gives a psychological account of frequency effects and also of analogical restructuring and irregularity, and provides an important link between the "natural salience" explanations of frequency discussed in 7.2 and the specific grammatical manifestations of markedness.[14]

8.3 From states to processes

In the last section, language states, represented by linguistic types in a synchronic typological classification, were reinterpreted as stages of language change, in order to demonstrate how synchronic typology defines constraints on language changes. We assumed a model of language change in terms of transitions from one language state (stage) to another. In the process, we introduced several concepts that are essentially diachronic in character: stability, frequency of occurrence, transitory stages, the origin and loss of grammatical markers and grammatical distinctions and gradualness. A closer examination of this last assumption, the gradualness of language change, will lead us away from the state–transition view of language change to one that more directly focuses on the change itself.

Most of the implicational universals and markedness patterns involve binary distinctions along the grammatical parameters that are being connected: a language is either DemN or NDem; a language either uses a nonzero morpheme for the plural or it doesn't. Some implicational universals and, of course, hierarchies and prototypes involve a larger number of values on a given grammatical parameter. However, in most cases, the values are all discrete.

As anyone who has worked closely with actual languages knows quite well, languages do not fall into such discrete, well-defined types. For instance, let us take a simple binary distinction, presence of articles vs. absence of articles. Since genetically closely related languages can differ in this feature (e.g. Russian and Bulgarian), it is clear that languages can go from one state to another: that is, languages can gain articles and lose articles. This is in itself not a very useful generalization. However, closer examination suggests that one ought to distinguish intermediate stages in both the gain and the loss of articles. For example, many languages do not have articles proper, but do have a category called **anaphoric demonstratives**: anaphoric demonstratives differ from "true" (**deictic**) demonstratives in that they may refer to an object previously mentioned in the discourse, but they differ from "true" definite articles in that they are not used to refer to uniquely identifiable objects not previously referred to (as in *I found a jar and unscrewed the lid*). An example of an anaphoric demonstrative is found in Nguna (Schütz 1969:5; the relevant form is glossed "before-mentioned"):

> (1)   Maa te   toropusi na-vasua ni m̃aleoputo raki na-anoai
>   but she kept   piece   of middle   for man
>   p̄ota wanogoe
>   other before-mentioned
>   '. . . but she kept the middle piece for the man.'

Still closer examination reveals even more intermediate cases: languages in which the demonstrative has both deictic and anaphoric uses; languages in which there is a demonstrative with only deictic use which alternates with another demonstrative with both deictic and anaphoric uses; languages with both anaphoric demonstratives (which may or may not have deictic uses) and definite articles, so that the definite article competes with the anaphoric demonstrative in anaphoric use; and so on.

The difficulty is that there is no end to the possibility of distinguishing "intermediate" stages. The division of a language process into discrete stages yields an apparently infinite regress. The way to avoid the infinite regress is to examine the process directly. This shift in perspective solves two other problems simultaneously. The first problem is what to do with synchronic variation in language; this was discussed in 2.2. As we indicated in that chapter, the problem can generally be avoided by referring to the "basic" linguistic type of a language as the language type. This cannot always be done; sometimes one cannot identify which of two linguistic types is "basic." At any rate, this is an oversimplification of the actual synchronic state of a language, and in idealizing away from that variation, one loses an important empirical fact that needs to be explained, namely the nature of synchronic variation and its role in grammar. But, if we examine more fine-grained "intermediate" stages, a good deal of synchronic variation finds its place, since that variation is actually a language change in progress.[15]

There is a second problem encountered in treating historical change as a sequence of states. Consider again the case of articles. A simplified view of the relevant language states would be as follows:

1 languages with no articles;
2 languages with anaphoric demonstratives;
3 languages with definite articles.

Typological and historical research (Greenberg 1978c, 1981) has indicated that the sequence of articles states for the evolution of definite articles is as follows:

no articles → anaphoric demonstratives → definite articles

The stage-by-stage description of the process does not tell us the most important fact of this process: what linguistic construction in the "no articles" stage became the anaphoric demonstratives in the next stage, and what linguistic construction became the definite article(s) in the last stage. In other words, the stage-by-stage description does not indicate what has changed from one stage to the next; and that is what forms the basic data of diachronic typology (notwithstanding the value of the dynamicization of synchronic typology). The shift from the study of language states to that of language processes focuses directly on how languages change from one stage to the next.

This problem is clearer in the case of a syntactic change than in the case of the evolution of a grammatical category. The discussion of the sequence of changes adjective–noun, genitive–noun and adposition order is too abstract without a more precise description of *how* NA order changes to AN, NG to GN and Prep to Postp (see below). Such an account, in fact, would go far to confirm or disconfirm the role of harmony and stability in the explanation of that particular constraint on language change.

In sum, the stage-by-stage view of diachronic processes cannot independently define discrete stages, especially when synchronic variation is taken into consideration, and it cannot describe the actual change in linguistic elements or constructions that leads to the change in linguistic type represented by the transition from one stage to the next.

The switch from viewing language change as a sequence of stages to viewing it as a process does raise some new problems, however. The chief problem is a new version of the problem of cross-linguistic comparability described in chapter 1. Two processes that appear to be identical from an abstract view of the process turn out to differ in possibly crucial details across languages. For example, the change $s>h$ is attested in many languages, and many analysts have considered each example of the change as an instance of the same phenomenon. But examination of the way the change $s>h$ spread through phonological contexts reveals differences across languages. For example, s changed to h in word-initial and intervocalic positions first in Greek; but s changed to h first in word-final position, then preconsonantal position in Spanish, and is now spreading to intervocalic and initial positions (Ferguson 1978:416). One cannot be certain that the Spanish and Greek changes can be thought of as instances of the same process. It can be said in favor of combining them that the significant fact to be explained here is that s changes to h but h does not change to s; both Spanish and Greek have the same overall directionality of change. Nevertheless, the Spanish and Greek changes may be in the same direction but for different reasons or motivations, and so any general explanation of $s>h$ without taking the specifics into account may ultimately be fallacious. It should be emphasized that this is not necessarily the case: it may be that the differences in details of otherwise similar diachronic processes may not be significant for the overall explanation of their directionality.

Diachronic typology is closely related to certain trends in modern historical linguistics. In fact, diachronic typology is essentially typological historical linguistics. Historical linguistics involves more than the specifics of the study of ancient languages through philological materials and the reconstruction of Indo-European or other language families, just as synchronic linguistics involves more than the specifics of the study of modern languages and the grammatical analyses of those language. In the same way that synchronic linguistics, including typology, seeks universals of language structure, historical linguistics seeks universals of linguistic processes. Diachronic typology is historical linguistics using a typological method.

The marriage of typology and historical linguistics requires the mutual adaptation of different methods developed for somewhat different purposes. The dynamicization of synchronic typology discussed in 8.2 describes the adaptation of typological concepts to a diachronic perspective. In the remainder of this section, we will present a brief discussion

221

of the adaptation of historical-linguistic methods for typological purposes.

A typological analysis of historical language processes involves the sampling of (more or less) independent cases of the linguistic features in question and a comparison of how those features evolve. The comparison will reveal which of the logically possible changes in the linguistic features are actually attested, typological universals can be constructed to limit the logically possible change and explanations (possibly of a functional character) can be sought for those universals.

The simplest adaptation of historical-linguistic method to typology is the use of direct historical records for particular cases of a linguistic process such as word-order change. In this case, diachronic typologists are simply using already-established evidence in the same way that synchronic typologists use evidence from informants or grammatical descriptions for synchronic research. However, the lack of direct historical records is even more dramatic than the lack of good synchronic descriptions. One must instead extrapolate from existing languages that are presumed to be related what the original protolanguage was and what changes led from that protolanguage to the contemporary languages.

This leads to a chicken-and-egg problem regarding the relationship between diachronic typology and historical reconstruction (or indeed, language comparison for the purposes of genetic classification). The diachronic typologist may use reconstructed language changes to support his or her hypotheses. The historical linguist interested in reconstruction, given two genetically related languages which represent two different linguistic types, let us say (A) anaphoric demonstratives and (B) definite articles, has to decide which type the protolanguage is: type A, type B or some other type, C. The historical linguist makes this decision by choosing the linguistic type of the protolanguage that makes the changes of type from the protolanguage to the daughter languages "plausible" or "reasonable." However, the constraints on "plausible" or "reasonable" language changes should, in theory, be provided by diachronic typology. This appears to be a vicious circle.

Fortunately, synchronic language states are extremely variable and include a great deal of variation that is actually language change in progress. From these variable synchronic language states, the language change itself can be extrapolated with a good degree of confidence, either for the purposes of reconstruction or for the purposes of constructing a typology of language changes.

An example of a standard sort of comparative–historical method used for typological purposes is what Greenberg (1969) calls **intragenetic comparison**, comparison of related languages in the same genetic group. The comparative–historical linguist interested in reconstruction of a protolanguage will examine all of the daughter languages with respect to the feature being reconstructed. The hypothesis that historical linguists (including diachronic typologists) use in this task is that the variation across daughter languages represents different stages in the evolution of the feature from the protolanguage. For example, the aforementioned evidence for the sequence of changes adjective–noun order > genitive–noun order > adposition order (Greenberg 1980) was obtained through a combination of direct historical evidence and intragenetic comparison. Greenberg examined several Ethiopian Semitic languages that differed in their word-order properties, and arranged them in an order that presumably represented the order of evolution of those properties (see table 8.1).

Table 8.1 *Evolution of word order in Ethiopian Semitic languages*

Language	Major order	Adj–N order	Nominal genitive	Pronominal genitive	Adposition
Ge'ez	free (VSO)	NA/ an	NG/ N zä-G/ zä-G N	N-Poss	Prep
Tigre	SOV/vso	AN/ NA	NG/ N nay-G/ nay-G N	N-Poss	Prep
Tigrinya	SOV	AN (na)	NG/ nay-G N/ N nay-G	N-Poss/ nay-Poss N	Prep, bə S məknəyat "because S"
Amharic (14c)	SOV	AN	N yä G/ yä G N	N-Poss/ yä-Poss N	Prep N Postp/ ?ə N Postp/ N Postp
Amharic	SOV	AN	yä G N	N-Poss/ yä-Poss N	Prep N Postp/ ?ə N Postp/ N Postp
Old Harari	SOV	AN	GN/ zi G N/	Prn N-Poss/ N-Poss	Prep N Postp
Harari	SOV	AN	GN/ G N-Poss	Prn N-Poss/ N-Poss	Postp, ta-N-bah, takil N, miša N

Poss = possessive pronoun; Prn = independent pronoun. X/Y means X is more commonly found than Y. X/y means y is much less common than X. X,y means y is a single example of a type not represented by X. In Ge'ez, word order is free, but the commonest order is VSO. In Tigrinya, the minor order "na" is cited in an 1871 grammar, but not in modern grammars. For fourteenth-century Amharic and Old Harari, only the significant differences from the modern languages were cited by Greenberg; I assume the other features are the same.
Source: Table based on data presented in Greenberg 1980.

In Ge'ez, the classical Ethiopian language, basic word order was free although VSO was the most frequent order. However, AN order also occurs as a minor alternative to NA order, and the third most frequent genitive type, using the preposition *zä*, has GN order. In Tigre, SOV and AN orders are dominant, though NG order remains dominant over GN. In Tigrinya, the prepositional genitive construction using GN order is more frequent than its NG counterpart, although overall the old NG construction is most common. Also, the prepositional genitive also comes to be used for pronominal possession as well, and there is a complement-izer which "brackets" the clause with a prepositional and a postpositional element. In Amharic and other South Ethiopic languages, GN order for nominal possession has taken over (contrast fourteenth-century Amharic to modern Amharic), while NG order still dominates for pro-nominal possession; and prepositions of a more general meaning are supplemented by postpositions with a more specific meaning (these are called **circumfixes** or **circumpositions**). Finally, in modern Harari, the preposition in the genitive and adpositional constructions has been dropped, except in two or three fossilized prepositional constructions, and in fact a new genitive construction has developed, using the possessed form of the head noun.

There are two important observations to be made from this example of real data supporting a diachronic typological generalization. The first is that every language in the sample has internal variation on at least one of the word-order parameters. This is the situation that made it difficult to assign a particular language as a whole to a structural type in 2.2, which posed potential difficulties for the synchronic generaliza-tions of chapters 3–7. The advantage of this situation for diachronic typology is that it produces a whole host of "intermediate" language states for diachronic analysis. These states differ from each other in small enough ways that the actual historical process can be perceived, just as motion is perceived in a sequence of stills from a movie.

In historical reconstruction, this method can be used to determine the word-order type of the parent language and the changes that the daughter languages underwent as they evolved. From the point of view of diachronic typology, the comparative–historical method provides one example (or a family of related examples) of a particular historical pro-cess that can then be compared to other historical processes. Since the diachronic typologist is not concerned with reconstruction for its own sake, however, this method can be extended to the comparison of un-related or more distantly related languages. One can compare language states in their full range of internal variation and, if the data are orderly, rank them in a sequence representing gradual linguistic change. Imagine, for example, that Ge'ez, Tigre, etc. were not all South Ethiopic languages, but instead were a language sample scattered across the world. Each language represents a different language state, taking all the internal variation into consideration. They can be ranked, as has already been done, in an order which is intended to reflect the historical sequence of events from a prepositional language to a postpositional one.

It should be clear that this is simply the dynamicization of synchronic typology taken to its logical conclusion. Instead of comparing idealized language types like "AN & NG & Prep" and "AN & GN & Postp," one compares real language types like "AN/na & NG/N Prep-G/Prep-G N & N-Poss & Prep" and "AN & Prep G N & N-Poss/Prep-Poss N & Prep N Postp/Prt N Postp/N Postp." The complexity of real language types that caused so much difficulty in constructing synchronic universals is a godsend for discovering diachronic universals. The chief danger of tackling the dynamicization of synchronic typology in its full detail is that the data may not be so orderly as the data from a single language family. In a single language family, we can be reasonably certain that all the languages represent different stages of a single historical process.[16] In a large cross-linguistic sample, the complex language states that would be found may represent several different historical processes in progress.

The second important observation that can be made from the Ethiopian Semitic example is that there are different kinds of synchronic variation which have different implications for diachronic typology. The different kinds of synchronic variation were described in 2.2 from a synchronic perspective; here we will briefly review their significance for diachronic typology. One can distinguish four different types of variation.

The first is **simple alternation**, illustrated, for example, by Tigre SOV/ vso: there are two word orders without any significant structural differences. One order is most likely a historically earlier order than the other. Although in the contemporary language there may be a difference in semantic/pragmatic function or a sociolinguistic stratification of use, it is often the case that one word order is in the process of displacing the other (in Ethiopic, SOV is displacing VSO).

The second type is **constructional alternation**, in which two different constructions are used for the same grammatical phenomenon (again, with possible functional or sociolinguistic differentiation). An example of this is the alternation between suffixation of the possessive pronoun to the head noun and use of the oblique suffix with *yä-* for pronominal possession in Amharic (Greenberg 1980:236):

(2) bet   -e
    house -my
    N   POSS
    'my house'

(3) yä- na   bet
    of- me   house
    POSS   N
    'my house'

As with simple alternation, the assumption is that one construction is newer and may displace the other as the basic construction of the language, leading to a change in type. This appears to be happening in Ethiopic as NPoss gives way to Prep-Poss N.[17] From the historical point of view, this represents **replacement**.

The third type is called, loosely here, **polysemy**: a single construction (or morpheme) is used for two or more grammatical functions. The grammatical functions are assumed to be related in some fashion (usually semantically or pragmatically, but also possibly by structural analogy), and one function is considered to be an extension of the other – if not synchronically, then diachronically. An example of this is the use of the aforementioned prepositional genitive for both nominal and pronominal genitives in Tigrinya. The diachronic assumption is that the construction spread from one function to another, in this case that the prepositional genitive construction spread from nominal genitives to pronominal genitives – and, ultimately, to adpositions. The fact that the same construction is used for NG, NPoss and PrepN order accounts for their harmonic pattern and, in fact, constructional polysemy may account for many of the harmonic patterns (see Aristar 1987; Bybee 1988:353–4).

A corollary type to polysemy is a case of phonological similarity between forms with related uses. For example, Russian has a reflexive pronoun *sebja* that is declined for various cases. It also has a verbal suffix *-sja/-s'* that is used for various middle-voice and other uses that can be demonstrated to be semantically related to the reflexive (Faltz 1985; Croft, Shyldkrot & Kemmer 1987; Kemmer 1988). These are essentially two different versions of the same morpheme that co-exist in Russian, with a concomitant division of functional labor.[18] Presumably, one form can be derived from the other; this will be discussed in 8.5.2.

The fourth type is called by historical linguists **reinforcement**: two morphemes with independent historical sources are used in the same construction. This is illustrated here by the circumpositions (circumfixes) in Amharic. The postpositional elements in the circumfixes are historically independent developments that were simply added to the prepositions without replacing them (at least at first). In fact, this is perhaps the most interesting part of the historical sequence. The postpositions were nouns indicating spatial relations such as "front" or "back," and the Prep N Postp construction is really an instance of the Prep G N construction, where "N" is the relational noun and "G" is the object of the preposition plus relational noun (Greenberg 1980:233):

(4) bä- bet   wəst
     in- house interior
     'inside the house'

This is exactly analogous to English *in front of the house*; in fact, if the correct English were *in the house's front*, the situation would be identical to Amharic. Consequent to the reinforcement, there was a **reanalysis** of the Prep G N construction as a Prep N Postp construction. The concept of reanalysis is a central one to diachronic typology, especially in the area of syntactic change. For example, the harmony relation between genitive–noun order and adposition order is due primarily to the reanalysis of genitive constructions as adpositional constructions.

Thus, the diachronic typologist comparing real language states, either within a language family or across a broad typological sample, can use internal variation of different kinds to extrapolate historical language processes. The methods described here and in the preceding sections allow us to determine paths of language change by means of discovering sequences of historically related language states. However, they tell us little about the most important constraint on language change: directionality of the change. Recent work in diachronic typology has addressed this problem, and revealed a large class of grammatical changes in which the directionality of change appears to be quite clear.

8.4 Directionality of change

Let us return to the idealized situation that was illustrated by the Ethiopic example. In that situation, there are four language types, arranged in a sequence so that each differs from the next one in the sequence by one word-order parameter:

NA & NG & Prep
AN & NG & Prep
AN & GN & Prep
AN & GN & **Postp**

This sequence was then presumed to represent a historical process. The Ethiopic example illustrated that the process can proceed in one direction: a change in adjective order leads to a change in genitive order which leads to a change in adposition order. However, there are no attested cases of the reverse direction of change: a change in adposition order leads to a change in genitive order which leads to a change in adjective order. This particular sequence of changes appears to occur only in one direction, that is, it is **unidirectional**.

Discovering that a linguistic process is unidirectional is significant for diachronic typology because it imposes a major constraint on possible language changes. In fact, it cuts out half of the logically possible language changes, and thus dramatically restricts the number of types of language change. More important, most deeper explanations for language changes can account for only one direction of language change. For example, heaviness or dominance can account for a language change from RelN to NRel, but not vice versa. In the Ethiopian example, genitive–noun order changes in harmony with adjective–noun order, and then adposition order changes by the gradual replacement of the original adpositions by new adpositions derived from the new genitive construction by reanalysis. The harmony and reanalysis explanation works only in one direction. For this reason, a major focus of research in diachronic typology is the discovery of unidirectional language processes.

Actually, it may be that more language processes are unidirectional than one may think at first. On closer examination, language processes that appear to be bidirectional often turn out to represent two distinct unidirectional changes that involve different mechanisms of language change or involve different intermediate language states. For example, it is true that languages change from RelN to NRel and also vice versa. The change from RelN to NRel is motivated by heaviness or dominance, while the change from NRel to RelN is motivated by harmony – it occurs only after other modifiers have shifted to prenominal position (Hawkins 1983; see also 7.4). The change from RelN to NRel is probably a relatively autonomous process, but the change from NRel to RelN is (in theory) only a part of a larger shift of noun modifiers from the position after the noun to a position preceding the noun. Another example, a phonological one, is offered by Ferguson (1978). The changes $ð > d$ and

$d > \eth$ are both possible, indicating an apparently bidirectional change. However, $\eth > d$ is an instance of the more general change of interdentals to dentals, as found in some modern American English dialects, and so is associated with $\theta > t$. The change $d > \eth$, on the other hand, is an instance of the change of stops to fricatives, as found in Spanish, and so is associated with $b > \beta$ and $g > \gamma$. A single language change must be put in the context of other related changes going on at the same time in the language in order to discover its underlying motivation.

In fact, it may even be the case that all language changes are ultimately unidirectional; that is, that for any apparent bidirectionality of change between type A and type B, the mechanism underlying the change from A to B will be different from the mechanism for the change from B to A. At this point, however, there has been too little research on apparently bidirectional language changes to support the hypothesis that all language changes are unidirectional.

Unquestionably unidirectional language processes pose a slight dilemma for the hypothesis of connectivity, that it is possible to get from any language state to any other language state. If the change from type A to type B is unidirectional, then it would appear that there is no way to get from type B to type A, and eventually all languages will become type B, which is contrary to the general view of language change. This is, in fact, what the dynamic interpretation of nineteenth-century morphological typology, as expounded by August Schleicher, implied: languages went from isolating to agglutinative to inflectional, but not the other way around. The solution to this problem is a simple one: language processes that are unidirectional are also **cyclic** when viewed as changes from one language state to another. The "endpoint" of the sequence of changes is the beginning stage, arrived at through a different process. For example, Greenberg (1978c, 1981) demonstrates that the evolution of articles continues to the point that "articles" are found on every noun (for example, the suffix *-tl* that is found on every Classical Nahuatl noun formerly was probably an article); at that point the language has "lost" its articles and is at the beginning state.[19] Schleicher's dynamic interpretation of morphological typology – isolating to agglutinative to inflectional – is now considered to be two-thirds correct. The missing third is the final stage of the process, the shift from inflectional to isolating via the loss of inflections (the occurrence of this in modern French and English in fact disturbed Schleicher). In fact, the strong unidirectionality hypothesis described in the preceding paragraph simply states that bidirectional processes are, in fact, the simplest form of unidirectional cyclic processes: type A can change to type B by one mechanism and type B can change (back) to type A by a different mechanism.

We now turn to a large and important class of correlated unidirectional cyclic processes that have been strongly confirmed across a wide range of languages.

8.5 Grammaticalization

Diachronic typology, like synchronic typology, involves not just putting constraints on logically possible types but also discovering relationships among otherwise independent grammatical parameters. The major type of constraints found on diachronic language processes are twofold. First, sequences of language states have been found to represent a step-by-step language process (e.g. adjective order change → genitive order change→ adposition change). Unattested synchronic states are excluded because they do not adhere to the sequence of changes entailed by the step-by-step process. Second, many such processes are unidirectional; the reverse sequence is impossible, and return to the original state is effected by a different process (cyclicity). The next step, then, is the discovery of relationships among otherwise logically independent unidirectional sequences of language changes.

There is one major class of correlated unidirectional changes that has emerged from diachronic typological (that is, typological historical-linguistic) research: **grammaticalization**. Grammaticalization is the process by which full lexical items become grammatical morphemes. This process is unidirectional and cyclic, in the senses of those terms given above: grammatical morphemes originate from lexical items, disappear through loss and reappear when new words become grammatical morphemes. Phonological, morphosyntactic and functional (semantic/pragmatic) changes are correlated: if a lexical item undergoes a certain kind of morphosyntactic change, it implies corresponding functional and phonological changes. The correlation of phonological changes brings the nineteenth-century morphological typology back into consideration in modern typology. The pattern of correlated phonological, grammatical and functional changes allows grammaticalization to be defined in such a way that it covers the evolution of virtually every type of grammatical morpheme, from tense inflection to case marker to complementizer.

8.5.1 *Correlated grammaticalization processes*

Two recent surveys of grammaticalization attempt an overall classification of the linguistic processes involved in grammaticalization.[20]

The two surveys use different parameters to classify the processes involved. Heine and Reh (1984) use a tripartite classification into phonological, morphosyntactic and functional changes, that is changes in phonological substance, grammatical behavior and semantic/pragmatic shifts. Lehmann (1981, 1985) uses a classification based on paradigmatic and syntagmatic grammatical processes. Paradigmatic processes involve alterations to the morpheme itself or in contrast with other morphemes which could be substituted for it in the same slot. Syntagmatic processes involve changes in the relationship between the morpheme in question and its grammatical context. These two classifications complement each other: phonological, morphosyntactic and functional processes can all be syntagmatic or paradigmatic. Our presentation will combine the two classifications (with certain modifications to be noted).

8.5.1.1 Phonological

The phonological process of grammaticalization involves the syntagmatic **coalescence** and paradigmatic **attrition** of a morpheme (Lehmann's terms). The syntagmatic process of coalescence begins with two independent words which over time eventually become one. Heine and Reh divide the process of coalescence into several stages: compounding, cliticization, affixation and fusion. The first three processes involve the "reduction" of a word boundary to a word-internal morpheme boundary.[21] The distinction between **compounding** and **cliticization/affixation** is a fine one, in the way that Heine and Reh define them. Compounding involves the combination of two morphemes which are both roots or both nonroot, whereas cliticization/affixation involves the combination of a root morpheme and a nonroot morpheme (Heine & Reh 1984:32). Yoruba *kɔ́wĕ* "study" is an example of the compounding of two root morphemes (from *kɔ́* "learn" and *iwé* "book"; Rowlands 1969:29), and colloquial English *outta* is an example of the compound of the two nonroot morphemes *out* and *of*. An example of affixation is found in the Kituba examples (5) and (6) below, in which the subject pronoun and auxiliary become affixed to the verb. It is difficult, however, to maintain the distinction between compounding and affixation in examples such as the English contractions *I'm*, *I'll*, *he's*, etc., in which the stress falls on the pronoun though the auxiliary is more of a lexical root in the usual sense. This distinction may be an artificial one.

Cliticization precedes affixation, though defining the difference between the two is extremely difficult and is also artificial from a diachronic perspective (Heine & Reh 1984:32–5). It is better to conceive

231

of coalescence as a whole representing a continuum from independent words to outright fusion. The last stage, **fusion**, involves the loss of the word-internal morpheme boundary, which leads two morphemes to become one. For example, Ewe *nɛ̂* 'to him' evolved from *ná* 'dative' + *e* '3sg.obj.' (Heine & Reh 1984:26); and French *du* 'of the (masc. sg.)' evolved from *de* 'of' + *le* 'the (masc. sg.).'

On the paradigmatic side of phonological grammaticalization, Heine and Reh divide the process into erosion and loss. Phonological **erosion** is the shortening of a morpheme in length. Erosion can be quite irregular phonologically, not being directly comparable to regular phonological processes such as assimilation, etc. Erosion reduces a polysyllabic morpheme to a monosyllabic one, a monosyllabic morpheme to a single phoneme and possibly a single phoneme to a suprasegmental or internal alternation. An example of accelerated phonological erosion is found in Kituba, a pidginized variety of Kikongo (Heine & Reh 1984:21–2):

> Two generations ago
> (5) munu lenda ku- sala
> I   may   INF- work
> 'I may work.'

> Present generation
> (6) mu- le-   sala
> I-   may- work
> 'I may work.'

The final stage of an erosional process is phonological **loss**. Heine and Reh define loss as a phonological process, but there is also a morphosyntactic process of loss distinct from the phonological one. That is, loss may result from phonological reduction, or it may result from a morphosyntactic simplification of the construction with little or no phonological erosion involved – that is, the morpheme may just drop out suddenly. For example, the loss of the infinitive prefix in the Kituba example in (6) may involve morphological, not phonological, loss.

Heine and Reh describe a fourth process of phonological grammaticalization that covers both syntagmatic and paradigmatic processes. Phonological **adaptation** is any sort of phonological alteration of a morpheme to its environment. In the vast majority of cases, phonological adaptation is assimilation, but adaptation could also be dissimilation or some other phonological process. Heine and Reh note that an effect of phonological adaptation is an increase in allomorphy (1984:17). Phonological adaptation is syntagmatic, in that a phonological process may be triggered by the phonological environment of a contiguous morpheme; but it is also paradigmatic, in that the same process may also result in the erosion of the morpheme. For example, the adaptation of the preposition *ní* to *l'* in Yoruba *l'ówó* 'Prep-money' is triggered by the syntagmatic combination with a following nonhigh vowel, but also involves the erosion of the one-syllable preposition to a single consonant phoneme (with a shift of its tone to the first vowel of the root).

8.5.1.2 Morphosyntactic

Morphosyntactic grammaticalization processes can also be divided into syntagmatic and paradigmatic types. There are two major syntagmatic processes. The first is **rigidification** of word order (called "fixation" by Lehmann). Heine and Reh use the rather odd term "permutation" to represent the rigidification of a particular word order. Sometimes the rigidified word order differs from the "normal" syntactic order, as in the case of the positioning of object clitics in French before the verb, unlike full NP objects, which follow the verb (*Je l'ai lu* 'I read it' vs. *J'ai lu le livre* 'I read the book'). In these cases, "permutation" is an appropriate description. However, the types of phenomena that Heine and Reh describe include the fixing of the position of an element which formerly was free. In this case, it is not accurate to speak of permutation of a word order, but rather the rigidification of an already existing word order. The general phenomenon is the establishment of the word in some position, which may or may not have been an acceptable position for the element before rigidification took place. Heine and Reh follow Simon Dik's (1981) model of word-order patterns for describing what factors determine position in rigidification. The first factor is "analogy," which Heine and Reh describe as "an attempt at placing constituents which have the same functional specification in the same structural position" (1984:28). This factor is essentially a version of harmony (see 3.3). The second factor is "thematic," that is the use of certain positions, such as clause-initial or clause-final, for thematic (pragmatic) functions such as topic, focus, and new information. The discourse significance of clause positions is based on research dating back at least to the functional sentence perspective of the Prague School. The third factor is Dik's "Language-Independent Preferred Order of Constituents" (LIPOC), that is overall preferences for the position of syntactic elements. This appears to be a version of dominance and/or heaviness – for example, "pronominal constituents tend to precede nominal constituents" (Heine & Reh 1984:31; cf. Greenberg's Universal 25). The final factor is a novel one, **verbal attraction**, describing the common process in which various dependents on the verb – adverbs, auxiliaries, pronominal subjects and objects, etc. – move to a position next to the verb (and often ultimately become affixed to it). Heine and Reh illustrate verbal attraction with examples of adpositions being affixed to verbs (a very common process; see the discussion of the syntactic position of directionals in 7.3.2.1). In Dholuo, topicalization of a benefactive noun results in the benefactive preposition ("for") being moved and affixed to the verb (Heine & Reh 1984:51):

(7) Jon   nego   diel ne Juma
     John is.killing goat for Juma
     'John is killing a goat for Juma.'
(8) Juma Jon   nego   -ne diel
     Juma John is.killing -for goat
     'John is killing a goat for *Juma*.'

    The second syntagmatic morphosyntactic grammaticalization process is called **condensation** by Lehmann. Condensation is the process by which the morpheme undergoing grammaticalization becomes the syntactic sister of a smaller constituent. For instance, in English one can say *inside of the box* or *inside the box*. In the former, *inside* is the sister of a prepositional phrase (though this depends on one's analysis), but in the latter, more grammaticalized, construction, *inside* is the sister of the noun phrase, a smaller constituent than the prepositional phrase. The logical endpoint of condensation is that the two syntactic sisters are single words, and may ultimately coalesce into a single word.

    The paradigmatic grammaticalization processes are more complex. Two processes discussed by Lehmann, paradigmaticization and obligatorification, occur earlier in the grammaticalization process than several other processes described by Heine and Reh and Greenberg. **Paradigmaticization** is the integration of a former lexical item into a closed class of grammatical elements, or from a large closed class to a smaller one. For example, the case endings of Russian and other Slavic languages make up a small class (six cases in Russian), and thus a tightly organized paradigm, whereas the prepositions in those same languages, numbering a few dozen, make a very loose paradigm. The case endings are therefore more paradigmaticized than the prepositions.

    The process of **obligatorification** involves the transition from an optional or variable element in the construction to an obligatory one. For example, the Latin prepositions are optional elements in the argument phrase, since the case endings alone can perform certain functions; but the modern French descendants of those prepositions are obligatory in the same functions, the case endings having disappeared. Likewise, the different negative emphatic forms found in earlier stages of French have given way almost entirely to *pas* – which has also become an obligatory instead of an optional element in negative sentences.

There are (at least) four possible ways for a morpheme to end its morphosyntactic life (Greenberg 1981, to appear). First, it can simply disappear; this is **grammatical loss**, which was distinguished above from phonological loss. The second possibility is **fossilization** (as Heine and Reh call it), the loss of productive use of a morpheme. Certain morphemes or phonological alternations cease to be the standard means of forming a grammatical category or construction. Instead, they become restricted chiefly to a limited specified class of words or constructions. For example, most locatives in Yurok are formed in -(V) ɬ: e.g. *cpegaʔr-oɬ* 'ear (loc.)' (Robins 1958:24). However, there is a less common locative in *-i(k),* found (not surprisingly; see 6.3.4, 8.2) on nouns denoting places: e.g. *ʔoʔlep-ik* 'house (loc.)' (Robins 1958:25).

An extreme case of fossilization is the random retention of a former morpheme on lexical items. In this case, the element is reinterpreted as part of the lexical root, that is, fused to it. For example, there is a prefix *k*(V)- found in Nilo-Saharan that Greenberg (1981) hypothesized came originally from a definite article and, ultimately, a demonstrative (Greenberg 1978c). Cognates from distinct branches of Nilo-Saharan display random appearance of the *k*(V)- formative (Greenberg to appear):

Nile Nubian		Bari	
guar	'ant'	**ki**-gwur-te	'ant'
ur	'head'	ur-et	'crown'
aru	'rain'	**k**-are	'river'
gu-mur	'neck'	mur-ut	'neck'

The third possibility is that the morpheme will spread onto every lexical item of the relevant type. In Classical Nahuatl, there is a noun marker *-tl* found on every nominal root, e.g. *coyo-tl* 'coyote,' *cihua-tl* 'star.' Presumably it had the same history as Nilo-Saharan *k*(V)-, except that it spread to all noun roots. This is actually obligatorification taken to the extreme: a grammaticalized morpheme becomes obligatory in all constructions, without any more meaning than the general indication of the construction type. Finally, however, a morpheme that has lost its original function can be appropriated for a different function entirely (**regrammaticization**; Greenberg to appear). For example, in some Nilo-Saharan languages the $k(V)$- formative, having lost its demonstrative-article function, has been regrammaticized as a prefix deriving verbal nouns, such as Ngambay Mundu k-*usa* 'act of eating' from *usa* 'eat' (found on vowel-initial stems only; Greenberg 1981:108).

8.5.1.3 Functional

Regrammaticization is as much a functional process as a mor-phosyntactic one; in fact, fossilization, grammatical loss and complete obligatorification all involve **functional loss**. In fact, it is difficult to keep morphosyntactic and functional grammaticalization processes separate, as our summary of the latter will demonstrate. Here we will begin by discussing the paradigmatic processes.

The most important functional grammaticalization process is called **desemanticization** by Heine and Reh. This is the process by which lexical meanings shift to the meanings of grammatical items. A typical example of "desemanticization" is found in the evolution of reflexives: by compar-ative-historical evidence, the Dinka reflexive marker *rɔ* is derived from a word meaning "body" (cf. Kanuri *rô*; Kemmer 1988:269–70).

The term "desemanticization" implies that the process involves a loss of meaning. This is really not an accurate assessment of what goes on in grammaticalization, since the grammatical elements do have meanings of their own (up to the end, as described in the last paragraph). A number of researchers, notably Elizabeth Traugott (1982, 1985, 1988), have analyzed various processes of semantic change in grammaticaliz-ation and have attempted to replace concepts like "loss of meaning," "from concrete meaning to abstract meaning" or "from lexical meaning to grammatical meaning" with something more substantive. The general phenomenon that Traugott and others are trying to capture is the very well-attested unidirectional shift in semantic/pragmatic function of the use of lexical items in grammaticalization. The question is, can the shifts of lexical items from their original meanings to the wide variety of "gram-matical" meanings or functions be subsumed under a single general pro-cess? Traugott (1988) has proposed that the semantic change involves a shift from meanings defined in terms of the described situation, such as objects, properties and actions, to meanings based on the utterance situation, such as deictic categories, epistemic meaning and evaluative terms. This problem is the diachronic analogue to the problem of distinguishing "lexical" from "grammatical" elements in synchronic analysis (see 7.3.2.3). It remains to be seen whether the unification of the various shifts from lexical to grammatical meaning will succeed, and for now we will continue to use scare quotes around the term "desemanticization" in order to alert the reader to its misleading implications.

Heine and Reh describe two other paradigmatic functional grammaticalization processes: expansion and simplification. Morphemes that undergo grammaticalization tend to broaden the range of meanings that they encompass, so that a grammaticalized morpheme is very polysemous. Heine and Reh call this **expansion**. For them expansion involves the addition of a grammatical function to a grammatical unit, whereas "desemanticization" involves the addition of a grammatical function to a lexical unit (1984:39). Expansion can be illustrated with the verbal directional suffix *-da* 'up' in Mokilese, which has come to indicate a variety of verbal derivatives (Harrison 1976:198, 230; Harrison & Albert 1977):

> Direction: *aluh-da* 'walk up' (*alu* 'walk'), *wah-da* 'carry up' (*wa* 'carry');
> Repeated activity, possibly towards a goal: *doakoah-da* 'stab repeatedly' (*doakoa* 'lunge, stab'), *pwukul-da* 'make random holes in' (*pwukul* 'poke a hole in');
> Activity directed towards goal: *audoh-da* 'fill up' (*audo* 'fill'), *jaun-da* 'stoke up (a fire)' (*jaun* 'stoke');
> Creation or bringing into being: *lemeh-da* 'to recall, come into mind' (*leme* 'think'), *diar-da* 'find' (*diar* 'look for').

"Desemanticization" and expansion appear to be very similar. A crucial difference not mentioned by Heine and Reh, however, is that in "desemanticization" the lexical meaning is eventually lost, whereas in expansion the old grammatical meanings are often kept, resulting in morphemes that end up being ubiquitous, such as English *that*, Spanish *a*, Classical Nahuatl *in*, Indonesian *-nya*, etc. This distinction should perhaps not be overstated, since many "desemanticized" elements retain their lexical meaning and many grammatical units lose their former grammatical meanings rather than expand. But it appears that there are two distinct processes, one of semantic or functional shift, and another of functional expansion, which may have different end results.

The process of **simplification**, in which there is a loss of cross-cutting paradigmatic distinctions – for example, the loss of tense in the English modal auxiliary verbs – is considered by Heine and Reh to be a functional process.[22] Their argument in favor of this position is that simplification is a variant of expansion: one linguistic form is extended to cover the whole paradigm. This is certainly the case, because in the vast majority of instances the new form that covers the whole paradigm is one of the several original paradigm forms (usually the unmarked form; see 8.2). However, simplification involves the loss of a grammatical distinction which is still present semantically. For example, the loss of a gender distinction in pronouns in pidgin Hausa such that Hausa *yā* 'he' is now used for 'he or she' (Heine & Reh 1984:42) does not mean that sex is semantically irrelevant; it is only grammatically irrelevant. Thus, simplification may be better described as a morphosyntactic process rather than a functional one. The same argument could be applied to many of the examples of extension, where polysemous grammatical elements are defined as having a single, general meaning: the former differences in meaning are not lost, they are simply no longer relevant grammatically. This problem demonstrates the thin line between morphosyntax and function, just as the reduction in word boundaries demonstrated the thin line between phonology and morphosyntax.

Finally, there is **functional loss**. Functional loss may occur through grammatical loss, fossilization or complete obligatorification, as was stated above. Functional loss is not solely a consequence of these morphosyntactic processes, however. Heine and Reh discuss functional loss in a separate section of their monograph, titled "Other processes" (1984:46–50). An element may lose its function because it is **replaced** by another element which comes to have the same function. Replacement results in the eventual loss of the old element, or its fossilized retention, such as the *-en* plural in *ox-en*, *brethr-en* and *childr-en* in English, replaced by the productive *-s* plural. An old element may also be **reinforced** by a new element, so that both elements occur together, at least for a while. For example, French *ne* is reinforced by *pas*; the former has lost its negative meaning on its own, while the latter has lost its emphatic meaning, and has now been extended to virtually all negative contexts. Reinforcement usually involves the spread of the old element to all contexts, and often its loss (for example, French *ne* is being lost in colloquial speech). However, a fossilized form can be reinforced by another form; the *-r* plural in *child-r-en* is reinforced by *-en* (which is itself fossilized now).

The one syntagmatic functional grammaticalization process is merger (Heine & Reh) or **idiomaticization**. Merger is defined by Heine and Reh as follows: "the meaning or function of two linguistic units merges into one new meaning/function which is different from that of the combined units" (1984:44–5). Merger is basically the same as idiomaticization, where the meaning of the whole is not a simple semantic composition of the meanings of the parts. This is another gradual process, like cliticization/affixation, where some meaning combinations are more transparently derivable from the meanings of the parts than others. Heine and Reh give several examples from standard Ewe involving compounds with *ga* 'metal, money' (1984:45):

zĕ	'pot'	ga-zĕ	'metal pot, kettle'
sɔ́	'horse'	ga-sɔ́	'bicycle'
-tɔ́	'owner'	ga-tɔ́	(1) 'somebody owning money, rich person'
			(2) 'prisoner'
mí	'excrement'	ga-mí	'rust'
χɔ	'house'	ga-χɔ	'prison'

The compounds (including the two meanings of *ga-tɔ́*) are ranked in approximate order of idiomaticization, from least to most idiomatized, as suggested by Heine and Reh. Idiomaticization can also lead to functional loss. Heine and Reh give the example of Krongo (Kordofanian) *óob-íy* 'close-eyes,' meaning 'sleep,' as a case of idiomaticization (in their terminology, "merger"; 1984:44). In examples such as these, the two separate parts lose their independent meanings and function as a whole with a different meaning.

We may now summarize the processes of grammaticalization. The paradigmatic phonological process of attrition, the erosion of the phonological size of the morpheme, ends in phonological loss. The syntagmatic phonological–syntactic process of coalescence (compounding and affixation of morphemes) ends in fusion (loss of morpheme boundary), which again may result in loss. The syntagmatic processes of condensation (smaller syntactic constituent structure) and rigidification of word order generally lead to phonological coalescence (loss of word-external morpheme boundary). The paradigmatic morphosyntactic processes of paradigmaticization (shift to a closed-class element) and obligatorification (obligatory presence in a construction) are generally accompanied by the paradigmatic functional processes of semantic shift ("desemanticization") and spread (expansion of meaning); the morphosyntactic and functional processes seem to reinforce each other. Finally, the loss of function of an element, which may occur by itself but can also occur through replacement, reinforcement and idiomatization, results in complete morphosyntactic obligatorification, fossilization or loss (and also phonological attrition, fusion or loss).

8.5.2 *Some issues in grammaticalization*

A large amount of research in diachronic typology has gone into grammaticalization, as the rather detailed discussion in the last section should indicate. Not surprisingly, many specific grammaticalization processes have been discovered and documented. Christian Lehmann's monograph contains a summary of grammaticalization processes (1981:26–120), and Heine and Reh's volume ends with an index of grammaticalization processes, organised both by function of grammatical morpheme and by type of source lexical item (1984:269–82).

As in all the other examples of diachronic processes that we have described in this chapter, grammaticalization processes are frequently manifested in synchronic language states.[23] In fact, many of the examples in the preceding section contrasted more grammaticalized with less grammaticalized elements in specific languages. And, as is the case with other diachronic phenomena that are manifested in synchronic variation, one can determine which of two competing forms, or two related forms, is the more grammaticalized. From this information one can then infer which is the newer form (which consequently may ultimately displace the older form). If the generalizations provided by grammaticalization theory are correct, the various symptoms should all point to the same form as being the more grammaticalized form.

Determining which form is the newer depends on whether the forms are related to each other as cognates or not. If the forms are related to each other, then the more grammaticalized form is the newer form, because it represents a later stage in the evolution of the same morpheme (with a proviso to be noted below). For example, the Russian verbal suffix *-sja/-s'* is more grammaticalized than the reflexive *sebja:* the suffix *-sja/-s'* is phonologically more eroded; it changes form due to phonological context (adaptation); it is affixed to the verb (coalescence), and is part of the verb, not the verb phrase (condensation); it does not decline (simplification); and its meaning is "less concrete" ("desemanticization") and covers a wider range of uses (expansion). It is cognate with *sebja*; therefore it represents a later stage in the evolution of the reflexive form and so is the newer form.

If, on the other hand, the two forms are not related as cognates, then the less grammaticalized form is the newer form, since its relative lack of grammaticalization indicates its more recent evolution to a grammatical morpheme. For example, the English obligative construction *have to* is less grammaticalized than the obligative auxiliary *must: have to* is two more or less separate morphemes (not yet coalesced); it inflects for person, number and tense (not simplified); and it is part of a large class of verbs with *to* + infinitival verb-phrase complements (not paradigmaticized), and therefore includes a (nonfinite) clause boundary (not condensed).[24] It is not cognate with *must;* therefore it represents a more recently evolved competitor to *must* and so is the newer form.

In some cases it is difficult to tell whether a more grammaticalized form is the later stage of the less grammaticalized form, or a different form from it. For example, in Kanuri, a Nilo-Saharan language spoken in northern Nigeria, we find the following deictic demonstratives (Hutchison 1981:50–1):

	Singular	*Plural*
Proximal	ádə̀	ànyì
Distal	túdù	túnyì

These forms can be used anaphorically as well, though in the anaphoric demonstrative function the proximal singular *ádə̀* 'this' can be used for any form. In addition, there is a suffix *-də̀* which can be used as an anaphoric marker and also more generally on "topic" nouns. *-də̀* is also used as a relativizer and a complementizer.

If we compare *ádə̀* to *-də̀*, it is clear that *-də̀* is the more grammaticalized form: it is phonologically more eroded; it is a suffix; and it has a much wider range of grammatical functions in which it is the only possible form or only one of two forms. It also appears to be a historical continuation of *ádə̀*, in which case it is the newer (i.e. further evolved) form. However, it may not be a continuation of the morpheme *ádə̀*. The reason for doubt is that *ádə̀* may be a **reinforcement** of *-də̀*. That is to say, rather than *-də̀* being historically derived from *adə̀* through the phonological loss of *á-*, it may be that *adə̀* is derived from *-də̀* by the addition of a morpheme *á-*. Examination of the demonstrative forms suggests that there exists a morpheme *á-:* one can analyze *á-/à-* proximal vs. *tú-* distal and *-də̀* singular (allowing for vowel harmony in the distal) vs. *-nyí* plural. If *ádə̀* is a reinforcement of *-də̀*, then *-də̀* is not the historical continuation of *ádə̀* but its predecessor, and is thus the older form. Thus, sometimes reinforcement of a grammatical morpheme might be confused with a less-eroded version of the same morpheme. In general however, the possibility of confusion is rather rare and even in the Kanuri case, the morphological analysis of the demonstratives makes it seem fairly clear that reinforcement has occurred.

Examples of synchronic variation based in grammaticalization patterns are pervasive in the grammars of human languages. Careful examination of almost any grammatical domain in any language will reveal variant forms whose phonological structure, grammatical behavior and semantic/pragmatic range of functions differ along one or more of the parameters of grammaticalization. Typological patterns of grammaticalization are manifested in individual languages to a great degree. Grammaticalization is another example of the high degree of interpenetration of language processes in synchronic language states, and raises the question of the relationship of diachronic explanation to synchronic structure, to be discussed in chapter 9.

Grammaticalization represents a correlation of a set of unidirectional grammatical processes not unlike the correlations of synchronic grammatical properties that were described for transitivity, agreement, etc., in chapter 6. Unlike the synchronic correlations, grammaticalization represents a correlation of processes over time, which raises a new question: how precisely are the various processes in grammaticalization synchronized? The strongest hypothesis would be that for each process, one can (roughly) identify a sequence of stages, so that a morpheme that has reached a certain stage in one of the grammaticalization processes will also have reached the corresponding stage in the other grammaticalization processes. Weaker hypotheses would allow for greater or lesser degrees of synchronization for various parameters.

The strongest hypothesis is empirically unacceptable for at least some grammaticalization phenomena, even with fairly loose definitions of stages. The evolution of pronouns to agreement (indexation) markers involves roughly three stages of morphosyntactic evolution:

1 the morpheme is optional, found only in certain contexts, often discourse-determined;
2 the morpheme is obligatory, found in every finite clause, but does not co-occur with independent NP arguments;
3 the morpheme is obligatory and does co-occur with independent NP arguments (at this stage, it is generally no longer called a pronoun but instead an agreement marker).

To this are correlated phonological changes, which can also be simplified to three stages:

(a) independent morpheme;
(b) clitic;[25]
(c) affix.

The strongest hypothesis would imply the existence of only the following types, illustrated by attested examples:

1(a) Independent, optional pronoun: Salt-Yui (Irwin 1974:52, 55)

(9) (**ni**) buku irai makena ene?
(you) book that where did.you.put
'Where did you put the book?'

2(b) Obligatory pronominal clitic: French object clitics

(10) je **le lui** dirai
I it him tell.FUT
'I'll tell him.'

3(c) Agreement affix: Lenakel subject markers (Lynch 1978:45):

(11) ka(t) -lau **ki-** m- ia- vɨn apwa i- paat
IINCL -DU IINCL- PAST DU- go LOC LOC- shore
'We (you and I) went towards the shore.'

However, a number of other combinations occur (the examples of independent obligatory pronouns and agreement markers may not be all that independent phonologically):

2(a) Obligatory independent pronouns: English pronouns

(12) I found **it**.

3(b) Agreement clitics: Woleaian subject markers (Sohn 1975:145)

(13) Yaremat laal **ye** be mas
man that **3SG** will die
'That man will die.'

2(c) Obligatory pronominal affixes: Kinyarwanda (Kimenyi 1980:179; the third-person singular emphatic is required after *ná* "also" and refers to the subject)

(14) n- a- guz -e igitabo na Yôhaani ná we
ISG.SBJ- PAST- buy -ASP book and John also 3SG.EMPH
y- a- **ki-** guz -e
3SG.SBJ- PAST- **3SG.OBJ**- buy -ASP
'I bought a book, and John also bought one.'

The examination of intermediate stages also illustrates "out-of-sync" changes:

2/3(c) Obligatory affixes that may or may not allow doubling: Kanuri subject and object affixes (Hutchison 1981:139)

(15) **nzú-** rú -kɔ́ -nà
2SG- see -ISG -PERF
'I saw/have seen you.'

(16) nyí -à   rú -kɔ́ -nà
    2SG -ASSOC see -1SG -PERF
    'I saw/have seen you.'

(17) nyí -à   **nzú-** rú -kɔ́ -nà
    2SG -ASSOC 2SG- see -1SG -PERF
    'I saw/have seen you.'

It may be that the English, Woleaian and Kinyarwanda examples represent unstable states, and Kanuri represents an exceptional pattern "correcting itself" over time, just as the exceptional GN & Prep languages represented unstable transitory states between two predicted and widespread "normal" states. However, the gradualness hypothesis that accounted for the existence of the GN & Prep languages does not help here: there is no explanation of how the grammaticalization process got "out of sync" in the first place.

Thus it appears that the strongest hypothesis of grammaticalization – that the correlated diachronic processes associated with grammaticalization are always "in sync" – will have to be weakened somewhat. It may turn out that some grammaticalization processes are always synchronized, or that additional conditions may constrain the number of possible "out of sync" states. Nevertheless, the hypothesis of grammaticalization represents a degree of generalization comparable to that underlying hierarchies and prototypes in synchronic typology. A large number of diachronic linguistic phenomena have been subsumed under a single very general concept.

8.6 Conclusion

Diachronic typology, like external motivation, represents a reinterpretation of the results of "classical" synchronic typology and an extension of typological analysis to a new domain. External motivation represents synchronic cross-linguistic patterns as due to factors external to the linguistic system, including language function. By bringing language function onto the scene, a new area of typological analysis, the typology of form–function relations, arose. Likewise, diachronic typology reinterpreted synchronic patterns as the result of the interplay of dynamic factors. By expanding the scope of typology to language change, the typology of diachronic linguistic processes began to be explored, particularly in the area of grammaticalization.

The developments in typological research described in the last two chapters have occurred in the past two decades, and are associated with the functional-typological approach to linguistic analysis. The final chapter will describe how the practitioners of the functional-typological approach have attempted to draw together the disparate strands of typological analysis, in particular the relationship of synchronic language structure to language function and language change.

9
Linguistic explanation in the dynamic paradigm

9.1 Introduction

In this chapter, we will describe the nature of linguistic explanation in the functional-typological approach to language. The extension of typological analysis to form–function relations and to language change described in chapters 7 and 8 led to a rethinking of the nature of linguistic explanation on the part of many typologists that brought about an alternative approach to understanding the nature of grammar and human language.

The functional-typological approach is inevitably compared to the generative approach – more accurately, the structuralist-generative approach, since generative grammar took over much of the method of analysis of American structuralism. Nevertheless, as we remarked in chapter 1, the functional-typological approaches and the structuralist-generative approaches have much in common. Both approaches take as their primary object of study the structure of individual languages. In this respect both approaches are descendants of early twentieth-century structuralism (see, for instance, the comments in 2.2). Typology has broadened its object of study by including the semantic and pragmatic function of language structures, and also by including textual data; the reasons for this will be discussed below. Both approaches consider the primary question of linguistics to be, what is a possible human language? The universalist scope that this question implies marks an important departure from American structuralism for the generative approach as well as the typological approach. Finally, both approaches seek answers for these questions in psychology (for typology, also in sociology and anthropology) and, ultimately, in biology. The willingness to look for deeper explanations also represents a major shift from American structuralism.

Some differences in the two approaches involve the method, not the nature of linguistic explanation. The functional-typological approach uses an empiricist method to answer the question of "what is a possible human language?" by determining what is an attested human language. This differs considerably from the rationalist postulation of universal grammatical structures found in most generative grammatical studies. The empiricist method gives the popular view that the most salient feature of typology is that it involves the study of many languages. It also focuses greater attention on the problem of cross-language comparability, discussed in 1.3. The solution to the problem of comparability taken by the functional-typological approach is a functional one: universal definitions of categories must be based on function, or more precisely, the relationship between function and form (structure).[1] Thus, external or functional factors enter into the typological method at its very root, the construction of the data sample, and not surprisingly, functional considerations continue to play a major role in typological explanations.

9.2 Description, explanation and generalization

A good deal of debate between the two approaches has centered on the relationship between description and explanation. In the more polemical discussions (e.g. Smith 1982; Givón 1979: chapter 1), each approach claims that its analysis constitutes an "explanation" and the other approach's analysis is merely a "description." In the case of Smith, an "explanation" involves the postulation of **abstract** structures and rules that relate those abstract structures to the actually-existing "surface" structures of language. Typological analysis, by making generalizations over "surface"-structure facts of languages, can only be "taxonomic" (Smith 1982:255–6).

For Givón, on the other hand, an "explanation" requires reference to one or more of the following "natural explanatory parameters": propositional content; discourse pragmatics; the processor; cognitive structure; world-view pragmatics; ontogenetic development; diachronic change; and phylogenetic evolution (Givón 1979:3–4). These parameters are those that we have called "external" explanations. Any analysis that does not refer to these parameters, in particular a formal model of abstract structures, is not an "explanation," in his view:

a formal model *by itself* could not be "a theory" of a complex, organismic behavior, since in the realms of complex organisms a theory without explanation is not a theory ... To the extent that a linguistic theory makes no reference to the natural explanatory parameters of language, it remains perforce a higher level of formalism. (Givón 1979:6–7; his emphasis)

Although the views of Smith and Givón represent the standard way

247

in which the lines are drawn in the debate between the two approaches, each side misinterprets the other to some extent. The generative approach finds its foundation in psychology and biology, in innate internal mental structures, even if those structures are discovered without direct reference to external parameters. And, as we have observed throughout this book, although typology begins with "surface"-structure generalizations like implicational universals, it has moved quickly to more abstract concepts, such as dominance, prototypes and grammaticalization. Both approaches include abstraction and external explanations, to a greater or lesser extent. Therefore, it should be easier to compare them more directly, using a more general framework for characterizing the notion of explanation in terms of **generalization** (Greenberg 1968, 1979; cf. Bybee 1988).

Instead of using the dichotomy of "description" vs. "explanation," one can describe grammatical analysis (or any sort of scientific analysis, for that matter) with a scalar concept of degrees of generalization. The basic concept is that a more general linguistic statement can be said to explain a more specific one, though it may itself be explained by a yet more general statement. Thus, any given statement is an explanation for a lower-level generalization, but a description in comparison to a higher-level generalization. Greenberg illustrates this point with a low-level linguistic example:

If, for example, a student who is just learning Turkish is told that the plural of *diş* (tooth) is *dişler* while that of *kuş* (bird) is *kuşlar*, he may ask why the first word forms its plural by adding *-ler* while the second does so by adding *-lar*. He may then be told that any word whose final vowel is *-i* takes *-ler*, while one in which the final vowel is *-u* takes *-lar*. This may be considered an explanation, insofar as further interrogation has to do with classes of words that have *-i* or *-u* as their final vowel rather than with the individual forms *diş* and *kuş*. If he asks about these two classes, he may be given a still more general statement ... Pressing still further, he will finally receive a full statement of the vowel harmony system of Turkish. (Greenberg 1968:180–1)

The shift from one level to a higher (more general, or more explanatory) is indicated by the shift in the phenomenon under investigation, from individual words to words ending in particular vowels, from words ending in particular vowels to words ending in vowels with particular features (front and back), from the particular suffix *-lar/-ler* to all suffixes with the *a/e* alternation, and so on. In general, we may say that we have succeeded in explaining some phenomenon (to a relative extent), when we have shifted analysis from that phenomenon to another one

– from a more specific to a more general or abstract concept, or from an internal phenomenon to an external one. A successful generalization shifts the kinds of questions that are asked to a higher plane. To the extent that the lower-level questions are not asked any more, one can say that the lower level of phenomena has been explained.

Given this view of scientific explanation, one can impose boundaries so that generalizations below the boundary are "descriptions" in some absolute sense and those above the level are "explanations" in an absolute sense. For example, one might decide that any generalization that covers less than the whole language, for example less than the whole system of vowel-alternating suffixes in Turkish, cannot constitute an "explanation." Or one might decide that any generalization that does not involve the shift from internal, structural phenomena to external phenomena cannot constitute an "explanation." These may be taken to be the generative and typological definitions of "explanation" respectively.

In linguistics, we may distinguish three levels of generalization that are significant for approaches to human languages. The first level is the lowest, the level of observation, that is what constitutes the basic facts of language. There is essential agreement on the level of observation between the generative and typological approaches: both begin with basic facts of linguistic structure.[2] The second level is actually a set of levels, the levels of internal generalization. The third level is that of external generalization, at which the linguist invokes concepts from psychology, biology and other realms outside the structure of the language. Finally, there is a cross-cutting level of generalization that plays a role in linguistic explanation, diachronic generalization. We will take up each of these levels in the following sections.

9.3 Internal generalizations: language-internal and cross-linguistic

Not all internal generalizations are directly commensurable, and this figures importantly in the distinction between generative and typological approaches. For example, given a phenomenon to analyze such as relative-clause structure in English, one could generalize in several directions. One could compare relative-clause structure with other complex sentence structures in English and generalize over complex sentence structures in English; this is the classic structuralist-generative approach. Alternatively, one could compare relative-clause structure in English with relative-clause structure in other languages and generalize over relative clauses in human languages; this is the classic typological approach.[3] In general, one can say that the typologist begins with cross-linguistic comparisons, and then compares typological classifications of different structural phenomena, searching for relationships. In contrast, the generative linguist begins with language-internal structural generalizations and searches for correlations of internal structural facts and only then proceeds to cross-linguistic comparison. The reasoning for the typological predilection to cross-linguistic comparison is that the linguist should move directly to generalizations that hold of human languages in general, in order to be certain of making language-universal generalizations (see 1.2 and 6.5 for more detailed discussion).

In the long run, it appears that different sequences of generalizations should in principle ultimately lead to the same result. The generative linguist who has discovered generalizations over complex sentence structures in English will eventually have to compare complex sentence structures in other languages. The typologist who has discovered generalizations over relative-clause structures will eventually have to compare relative-clause typology to the typology of other complex sentence types. In the meantime, however, the nature of the explanations or generalizations offered differs considerably.

First, as we have noted in 1.3 and 9.1, cross-linguistic comparison brings in external (semantic and pragmatic, or phonetic) considerations in the effort to find a common denominator for comparison. Thus, the constitution of the level of observation, the basic data, is changed from just linguistic structures to linguistic structures plus their function. Since the external elements are the basis of comparison, it is almost inevitable that they play a role in cross-linguistic generalization, as we have seen throughout this volume. On the other hand, external factors can be avoided more easily in single-language structural analysis.[4]

Second, and equally important, the comparison of grammatical phenomena across languages before relating phenomena together within languages requires the accommodation of typological variation more directly. As we stated in 3.2, there are relatively few unrestricted universals compared to restricted universals, that is universals which allow typological variation but constrain it in some fashion. However, restricted universals, and the abstract typological concepts such as dominance that underlie them, are manifested only in cross-linguistic comparison. This has two consequences for the typologist pursuing cross-linguistic generalizations as opposed to the structuralist or generative linguist constructing language-internal generalizations. First, while typological generalizations constrain variation, they do not completely account for which attested type a language belongs to. For example, the implicational universal AN ⊃ DemN can "explain" why in English the recessive order AN is accompanied by the harmonic, dominant order DemN, that is why English is not AN and NDem. However, it does not "explain" why English is AN & DemN instead of NA & DemN or NA & NDem. That is, relationships between grammatical phenomena cannot be "completely" explained because they are not completely deterministic. In a structuralist-generative analysis of a single language as a whole, on the other hand, each grammatical structure is explained as completely as possible through abstract patterns of relationships with other structures.

However, there is a trade-off: in the cross-linguistic comparison, one discovers immediately which relationships between grammatical phenomena are language-universal and which are idiosyncratic to particular languages. As we noted in 1.2 with respect to the example of definite and indefinite articles in English and French, a single-language analysis is an amalgamation of universal and language-particular patterns, and in fact an abstract language-internal generalization may be based on what is a coincidental relationship from a typological perspective. For example, Carlson's (1977) subsumption of the "generic" and "existential" bare (articleless) plural noun phrases under a single semantic generalization rests on the more-or-less coincidental expression of the two types in English (examples repeated from chapter 1):

(1) **Birds** have wings.
(2) **Dogs** were playing in the garden.

This is not found in French, where the "generic" is expressed by a plural definite article (most of the time), but the "existential" is expressed by a partitive plural:

(3) **Les oiseaux** ont des ailes.
(4) **Des chiens** jouaient dans le jardin.

Thus, it should be clear that the order of generalization will emphasize (or, if one prefers, reveal) different sorts of abstractions, and thus different sorts of concepts that will be accounted for by external generalizations. The functional-typological approach focuses on language-universal, restricted generalizations, and abstract concepts based on them. The structuralist-generative approach focuses on either unrestricted language universals or complex patterns of generalizations based on language-universal and language-specific relationships among grammatical features without necessarily distinguishing the two.

9.4   External generalizations: language and biology

In comparing the functional-typological and structuralist-generative approaches to linguistic explanation, most commentators focus on the invocation of external factors (meaning, discourse, etc.) on the part of the former as opposed to the invocations of abstract structures distinct from the "surface" structures on the part of the latter (see, for example, the passages quoted above from Givón 1979). Nevertheless, one of the major innovations of generative grammar over (American) structuralism is the placement of structural analysis on a psychological, and ultimately biological, foundation. Whereas the American structuralists were reluctant to impute any "psychological reality" to their analyses, the generative grammarians have always argued that their syntactic analysis must have an internal mental reality. Moreover, the mental representations of syntactic structures are ultimately innate, and therefore part of the biological make-up of the human organism. However, continuity with structuralist methods of analysis is maintained, in that the mental representations of language are revealed through analysis of the internal structure of a language. The psychological connection is made via the grammaticality judgment of the informant, an introspective act on the informant's own mental processes.

Functional-typological explanations are also based on psychology – but also sociology and anthropology, since most linguists of this persuasion are convinced of the central role of interpersonal interactions and cultural values in determining language structure. Again, however, biology is the foundation, since social and cultural behavior, like psychological make-up, are ultimately the product of biological evolution. The primary difference is that psychosocial (and biological) considerations play a much more direct role in functional-typological explanations than they do in generative explanations. The central concept is the evolutionary biological one of **functional adaptation**: language structure has evolved as an adaptation to language function:

The biologist . . . strives for a systematic understanding of the relation between structure and function in living organisms . . . Ultimately, the biologist is bound to ponder some more fundamental questions, such as the functional, adaptive, or evolutionary reasons for the seeming paucity of diverse types of structures performing the same or similar functions, or the seeming restrictions upon the typological variety of entire organisms. In a broad way, the [functional-typological] study of syntax is rather similar to the study of anatomy-cum-physiology. (Givón 1984:30)[5]

Therefore, language structure can be explained to the extent that it can be demonstrated that it maximizes functional adaptation within the constraints of human beings and the medium of expression.

The basic analogy is that language structure evolved just as biological organisms evolved, as an adaptation to the organism's environment. The various parts of a biological organism (and their integration) can be explained in part as an adaptation to a particular function, subordinated to the general function of survival and reproduction.[6] In particular, the primary function of language is to communicate information (though the sociolinguists and anthropologists would hasten to include a number of other functions, e.g. the reaffirmation of intimacy or solidarity, the maintenance of social distinctions, etc.). For this reason, psychology (and sociology and anthropology) must be studied in order to produce legitimate functional-typological explanations. Closer to linguistics proper, semantics and pragmatics provide the direct connection between language structure and the aforementioned disciplines that are functionally related to linguistics (see Givón 1984:30–2). The medium of expression is a linear string of sounds, and the primary constraint of human beings is their cognitive-processing abilities, from neuromuscular articulatory control and auditory perception to inferential abilities from past experience and current context. (Next in importance as a constraint on human beings are sociocultural constraints on interpersonal interaction.) Thus a proper functional-typological explanation accounts for a particular typological universal as the best means of encoding, transmitting and decoding information in a linear medium by human beings in real time.

The view of external explanation as biological adaptation can be further divided into two parts. The first part is simply performing the relevant function successfully. The linguistic side of the analogy is the constraint that a possible human language must be able to satisfy the basic range of communicative needs. This is communicative motivation (see 7.5). To provide substance to this type of explanation, the functional-typological linguist must map out what the basic range of communicative needs are. For example, why exactly do human beings need to relativize direct objects and obliques? It is intuitively obvious that a language in which one cannot relativize direct objects has a communicative gap, but a precise characterization of the communicative need (the communicative function of relative clauses, of direct objects and the

253

relation between the two) is necessary to demonstrate the existence of the gap.

The second part of the adaptation analogy corresponds to the normal interpretation of biological adaptation: the performance of the function in an efficient manner, given the constraints imposed by the structural medium and the environment. Both economy (7.2) and iconicity (7.3) are manifestations of efficient adaptation. In linguistics, efficient adaptation goes under the name of **processing** considerations.

Economy is transparently a processing phenomenon: "simplification is necessary because life is short and human memory finite" (Haiman 1985:11). Syntagmatic economy is most straightforwardly a processing consideration, as was implied in 7.2. Processing efficiency for both speaker and hearer is increased by shortening the most common forms (structural unmarkedness), and simplifying the less-used forms (behavioral markedness). Paradigmatic economy also reflects processing efficiency. Minimizing the number of distinct linguistic forms that must be acquired and retained presumably minimizes the load on memory.

Iconicity is also ultimately a processing consideration. Assuming that human beings must master the structure of experience, it is more efficient that language parallel that structure as much as possible. First, it minimizes the kinds of information structures a human being must acquire by not requiring a completely different information structure for language than for the world. Second, it minimizes the conversion process from the structure of information as we perceive and use it nonlinguistically to the structure of information as we comprehend and express it linguistically. Givón calls this the "iconicity meta-principle": "All other things being equal, a coded experience is easier to *store, retrieve* and *communicate* if the code is maximally isomorphic to the experience" (Givón 1985:189; his emphasis).[7]

Without this processing consideration, and its adaptive function, there is no *a priori* reason for language structure to be maximally iconic rather than not so: "the whole raison d'être for iconicity in language is thus grounded in the need to facilitate processing within real time" (Givón 1985:198). Nor is there any *a priori* reason for it to be economic, for the same reason. Thus, both economy and iconicity are basically different manifestations of processing efficiency. The external explanations of the functional-typological approach cannot cease with economy and iconicity, but must be based ultimately on the hypothesis of language structure as an adaptive response to functional pressures, in particular functional adequacy and functional efficiency.

For this reason, a central requirement for plausible functional-typological explanations is a model of how human beings experience the world and interact with it (including interaction with other human beings). The functionally related disciplines provide such models, though not always with the unanimity and firm empirical foundations that would provide comfort to the linguist seeking to explain typological generalizations by them. Certainly, a greater effort to use psychological, sociological and anthropological models of cognitive processing and human behavior would improve the quality of functional explanations found in the typological literature. On the other hand, linguistic evidence, taken from a functional perspective, has legitimate value of its own in confirming or disconfirming hypotheses of cognitive processing and human behavior generated in other disciplines. Generalizations about language structure are easier to confirm and disconfirm than many generalizations about mental processes, social mores or cultural values. A functional-typological linguistic analysis can be used to evaluate hypotheses as much as it can itself be judged by psychological, sociological and anthropological models.

The parallels between functional-typological analysis and evolutionary biology go considerably beyond the notion of functional adaptation in explaining structure. In fact, it might be said that just as generative grammarians consider linguistics to be a branch of psychology (or even mathematics), functional-typological linguists might consider the discipline as they view it as a branch of evolutionary biology.[8] The most basic parallel is methodological, namely, the method of observation of a wide variety of organisms (languages) and their comparison in terms of function (Mayr 1982:30–2).[9] In both evolutionary biology and the functional-typological approach, the focus of attention is on variation, both within populations (languages) and across them, and the search for constraints on the patterns of variation. There are also closer parallels in functional adaptation that have not been pursued by functional-typological linguists. In evolutionary biology, there exist complex adaptations, in which various parts of an organism which seems autonomous operate together to adapt to some function. This may be compared to typological conspiracies such as that between relative-clause accessibility and "promotion rules" (see 7.5). It has also been observed that not all variation is adaptive; in particular, some apparently non-adaptive traits arise because they are part of a complex adaptation of separate parts whose development is centrally controlled genetically. There are constant trade-offs, where a change in the organism to improve one function must be balanced by a loss in another function. This may be compared to competing motivations, such as the competition between economic and iconic motivation. There is no such thing as "perfect adaptation"; ecosystems are unstable even when external conditions do not change dramatically. This leads to the most important parallel between evolutionary biology and the functional-typological approach: systems change, and the structure of the system is partly explainable by its history.

9.5   Diachronic explanations and synchronic grammar

Perhaps one of the most distinctive characteristics of functional-typological explanation is the major role given to historical explanations. This is manifested in the work of many functional-typological linguists, including Comrie, Givón, Hopper, Bybee, Traugott, C. Lehmann, Heine, Hawkins and, of course, Greenberg. We have described some of their work in chapter 8. The appeal of diachronic explanation is obvious, since it provides an account of otherwise exceptional synchronic generalizations, and gives the most "natural" explanations of many linguistic phenomena (see chapter 8 for examples).

This development represents a reversal in the attitude towards diachrony and synchrony that has prevailed in linguistics since the advent of structuralism, however. Saussure (1959 [1915]) presented a firm separation of synchrony and diachrony on the basis of his theory of synchronic structure. A language at a given stage represents a system of relationships among parts regardless of the historical origins of those parts, and in fact independent of the historical origins of those parts. The psychological and cognitive orientation of modern (post-Chomskyan) theories of language has strengthened the importance of the Saussurean system. On this view, what a speaker knows is the synchronic language system. The speaker does not know the historical development of the parts of the system (although a good historical linguist can consciously figure it out in many cases). Thus, historical explanations can have nothing to do with explaining the nature of language *as a system that a speaker knows*.

This argument still appears to hold if one adopts the functional perspective described in the preceding section: language structure is shaped by contemporary functional adaptation, and again history appears to have no place. This does not fit the biological model adopted by Givón and others, however. The biological model is not a static one, in which an organism possesses a perfect adaptation to a stable niche inside an ecosystem in equilibrium.[10] The static biological view of adaptation is not tenable in the face of empirical evidence of non-adaptive variation and competing adaptive motivations of organisms, the difficulty, if not impossibility, of defining discrete niches, and the realization that ecosystems go through "natural" processes. Taking into account variation and change in organisms and their environment, the biologist actually speaks of approximate adaptations to constantly shifting niches (to the extent that they are definable) in dynamic ecosystems.

Some functional-typological linguists who have used historical explanations, particularly Givón, have developed an alternative interpretation of language structure and function that mirrors the current biological view of adaptation of organisms as described in the preceding paragraph. It is based on two general principles. The first is that the synchronic language system is not as stable, uniform and perfectly adapted as the Saussurean view implies. A language in a community at any given time is highly variable, as we noted in describing the difficulties in defining a language type in chapter 2 and in arguing that most languages represent "transitional types" in chapter 8. A great deal of the variation involves the uses of different structures for the same or similar functions, so that the iconic principle of "one form, one meaning" discussed in chapter 7 is constantly in a state of flux:

language – within the minds of speakers, rather than as some abstract system of *langue* – is always in the middle of change in lexicon/meaning, syntax, morphology and phonology. Language as a cognitive map is thus not only a system of coding knowledge, but perhaps primarily a system of re-coding, modifying and re-structuring existing knowledge and integrating into it newly-acquired knowledge. (Givón 1982a:112)

The parenthetical comment in Givón's statement represents the second general principle: that language *change* is a cognitive-psychological activity (and also a social one), as much as synchronic language structure is at heart cognitive-psychological (and also social). To put it aphoristically: languages don't change; people change language. Processes such as grammaticalization and reanalysis are psychological processes that language speakers undergo during the course of the history of the language. The argument that follows from these two principles is straightforward. The higher-level explanation for a historical–dynamic generalization, such as those described in chapter 8, must be psychological (and also sociological/cultural). But speakers are constantly involved with a dynamic, unstable system, not a fixed, static one. Therefore, speakers have cognitive competence of dynamic processes – not static arrangements – by which they comprehend the variation in the language they use, and influence it so that, over time, the language changes.

Other linguists in the functional-typological approach present essentially the same argument in different words, focusing on the "microevolutionary" aspect of language structure, function and change. John Haiman, in describing what he calls the "functional theories of grammar," characterizes them diachronically:

> [The functionalists'] chief insight [is] that all change originates as a violation of preexisting "rules." The focus of this kind of investigation is on the nature of these mistakes, and the factors which motivate them constantly, throughout the evolution of all languages ... [T]he "grammar of mistakes" ... is no less significant than the grammar of "correct speech." Perhaps it is even more significant, since it attests directly to the dynamic forces which cause language change, while the grammar of correct speech at any time may be no more than an agglomeration of fossils. (Haiman 1985:259)

Since much of grammar is fossilized, preserved through the inertia of social convention (hence the relevance of "historical" explanations), recent attention by diachronically oriented typologists has shifted to how new grammatical constructions arise: "Indeed we may suggest that it is largely the need to consistently resolve the competition between diverse external motivations that leads in the first place to the existence – as a fixed structure – of grammar itself" (DuBois 1985:360). Paul Hopper has given the name "emergent grammar" to this view:

> The notion of Emergent Grammar is meant to suggest that structure, or regularity, comes out of discourse and is shaped by discourse as much as it shapes discourse in an on-going process ... [Grammar's] forms are not fixed templates, but are negotiable in face-to-face interaction in ways that reflect the individual speakers' past experience of these forms, and their assessment of the present context, including especially their interlocutors, whose experiences and assessments may be quite different. Moreover, the term Emergent Grammar points to a grammar which is not abstractly formulated and abstractly represented, but always anchored in the specific concrete form of an utterance. (Hopper 1987:142)[11]

The effect of the argument by Givón, Haiman, Hopper and others is to reduce synchrony to diachrony through the analysis of intralinguistic as well as cross-linguistic variation. The synchronic system is in a constant state of flux, and what the speaker knows about his or her language are the dynamic principles that govern the flux (and, of course, the language-specific conventions that represent stabilizing factors in the synchronic situation). This is the heart of what may turn out to be a new linguistic paradigm, the **dynamic paradigm**, in which the study of all types of linguistic variation – cross-linguistic (typology), intralinguistic (sociolinguistics and language acquisition) and diachronic (historical linguistics) – are unified. What all these "subdisciplines" have in common is that they study linguistic variation, rather than abstracting away from it. As such, they represent a reaction to structuralist idealization and its primary dependence on "unrestricted universals" (though it has, of course, benefited from a century of structuralist research, as we have indicated in a number of places in this volume). The dynamic paradigm proceeds on the assumption that the underlying factors in all types of linguistic variation are fundamentally the same; in particular, that external factors of all types play a major role in linguistic explanations.

The dynamic paradigm is very new, as the recency of the publications just cited indicates, and it remains to be seen how (or if) it will develop. The unification of subdisciplines studying variation described in the preceding paragraph does not yet exist in theory or in practice, except in the coming together of much historical and typological work.[12] In its reaction to certain aspects of structuralist thought, its advocates have revived the work of nineteenth- and early twentieth-century linguists of a functional and/or historical persuasion, such as Karl Brugmann (1906–11), Hermann Paul (1880), Philipp Wegener (1885), Charles Bally (1965), Henri Frei (1929), Karl Bühler (1934), Otto Behaghel (1923–32), Wilhelm Havers (1931), Carl Meinhof (1936), Sir Alan Gardiner (1935), George Zipf (1935) and Otto Jespersen (1909–49). What is perhaps distinctive of the contemporary manifestation of the dynamic paradigm compared to its precursors is the strong typological dimension to the modern work (which itself has historical roots in the Prague School). It seems clear that if the dynamic paradigm continues to develop into a fruitful approach to the nature of language, it will continue to be strongly influenced by typology.

NOTES

1 Introduction

1 It is important to note that functionalism and typology (*qua* subdiscipline) are not *a priori* related. Many functionalists develop their hypotheses with little or no cross-linguistic data, and some typologists – not to mention most structuralist and generative linguists – explain the cross-linguistic patterns they discover in nonfunctional terms.

2 This position is even taken by a number of typologists themselves. For example, Leon Stassen states at the end of the introduction to his cross-linguistic study of comparative constructions that "my general approach should be conceived of as being *model neutral*" (Stassen 1985:21; italics original). This statement comes, ironically, at the end of a chapter which is one of the more lucid and complete explications of typological theory and method in the literature. It is clear from the context of the quotation, however, that Stassen means neutral to any current generative model of linguistic theory, involving the use of abstract representations of structure and operations on those representations. Likewise, Mallinson and Blake (1981:35–6) defend "model-neutrality" in their textbook on language typology, but it is also clear from their examples that by "model" they mean some version of transformational grammar.

3 On rare occasions, the data is published elsewhere. The data for Keenan and Comrie's study on the Noun Phrase Accessibility Hierarchy (Keenan & Comrie 1977; see chapter 5) was eventually published in another journal (Keenan & Comrie 1979), and the data from Maxwell's study on linearization (Maxwell 1984) was published by a linguistics department (Maxwell 1985).

4 Zero article forms are also found in this function in English: *She went to school/to college.*

5 In fact, one may attribute the difference to the partitive marker *de.* But if we turn to still other languages – and that is the point of this section – such as Rumanian (Farkas 1981:40–5), which distinguish the two uses solely by the presence vs. absence of the article, then we will not be able to invoke such an alternative.

6 This is an area in which more interaction between generative theory and typological theory would be quite fruitful. Generative syntactic argumentation has produced an enormous number of cross-construction correlations in English and other languages which ought to be surveyed more systemati-

cally in the world's languages by typologists. Typologists, on the other hand, have concentrated on the cross-linguistic patterns of single constructions, which in turn could be taken into consideration by generative linguists. There is a largely complementary distribution of the types of relations among morphosyntactic phenomena examined by typological and generative research whose filling out might lead to a more constructive dialogue between these two approaches to linguistic theory.

7 The lack of an objective form for *you* is an apparent exception which also may be due to a general pattern, namely the "markedness" of plural forms (see chapter 4; *you* was originally the second-person plural form).

8 To the extent that they can be; see chapter 9.

9 See also Downing (1978:377–80), and in more general terms, Stassen (1985:14).

10 The cross-linguistic identification of verbs and nouns is discussed in chapter 6.

11 The auxiliary "be" as well as the third-person plural subject-indexing form is usually suffixed onto the first constituent in the sentence (Givón 1980a:52).

12 This section cannot be a survey of all of the issues involved in the construction of typological samples; for an excellent discussion, see Bell 1978.

13 I am grateful to John Myhill for pointing out this fact.

14 Ian Maddieson has discussed the problem, though not yet in print (Matthew Dryer, p.c.).

15 This is not an uncontroversial position; Heine and Reh (1984:186–214) argue that SVO is the original order, whereas Givón (1975a) and Hyman (1975) argue for SOV as the original order.

16 Bell writes: "I think that a case can be made that such research [on language universals] can properly be conceived as sampling language changes, not languages themselves" (Bell 1978:46).

17 Another reason for obtaining a geographically and genetically distributed sample is the apparent phenomenon of **drift**, the seemingly parallel development of related or nearby languages in the same direction towards similar structure (Sapir 1921). Drift may be an epiphenomenon of contact or it may represent general principles of unidirectional change; but unless or until we can safely "explain it away," a broad distribution of languages is necessary for typological research.

18 In addition to the rigid word-order types defined by Greenberg (SOV, SVO, etc.), one must include "free" or "discourse-determined" word-order types, such as Papago (Payne 1987) and Mohawk (Mithun 1987).

2 Typological classification

1 "Concord" is sometimes also used for all types of agreement; we will avoid that usage.

2 However, we should point out that the pronominal possessive construction is by far the more common one, and for that reason perhaps should be treated as more "basic" by this second criterion.

3 Not all the factors are entirely logically independent; for example, if the construction does not use an additional morpheme, then all of the other

"additional morpheme" features are irrelevant. In general, structural analysis does not entirely lead to purely independent features. However, the point is that a good structural analysis will allow one to carefully enumerate *all logically possible* construction types.

4 Sometimes the individual structural features are called **devices** for expressing the construction type in question, but the distinction between a "strategy" and a "device" is not entirely clear and at any rate is not maintained in the literature.

5 This section is based largely on the discussion in Greenberg 1954, 1974b.

6 On the other hand, by postulating a structural unity to language in which "everything holds together" – "tout se tient" in Meillet's phrase – the "organic unity" view of language persists.

3 Implicational universals

1 In fact, the greatest problem facing typological research is that the number of living languages, most of which are poorly described at best, is decreasing so rapidly that there may indeed be such a reduction of the data base that the resulting typological generalizations will be less secure.

2 There are a number of basic logic textbooks that illustrate the truth tables and other basic logical concepts used in this chapter, e.g. Allwood, Anderson and Dahl 1977. The logical symbols employed here are: P & Q "P and Q"; P v Q "P or Q"; P ⊃ Q "If P, then Q"; P ≡ Q "P if and only if Q"; ~P "not P."

3 This is not an exceptionless universal; there are languages that are SOV and prepositional, and (more rarely) VSO languages that are postpositional. Also, Greenberg did not include any VOS, OVS or OSV languages in his sample.

4 This still leaves the disharmonic relation between adposition order and adjective–noun order to be explained however. Hawkins' complex implicational universals numbers III – Prep ⊃ (NA ⊃ NG) – and IV – Postp ⊃ (AN ⊃ GN) – explicitly lay out the dominance-recessive pattern (Hawkins 1980:201–3, 1983:66–9). That is, if a language is prepositional, then only if it is NA can it also be NG (i.e. disharmonic with Prep but harmonic with NA; III), and if it is postpositional, only if it is AN can it also be GN (IV).

5 See Comrie (1981a:89–94) for a critique of the harmony-only approach, associated chiefly with Winfred Lehmann and Theo Venneman.

6 This may explain why adjective–noun order can be disharmonic with adposition order, as in Greenberg's dominance-harmony analysis described above. The adjective is more mobile, so it moves away from the harmonic pattern defined by adposition–noun and object–verb order, and then genitive–noun order shifts in harmony with the new adjective–noun order (see 8.3).

7 A good critique of semantic proposals, mostly by Theo Venneman, for explaining harmony can be found in Hawkins (1983:31–9, 43–50). Hawkins also expounds a basic modifier–head analysis not unlike the one described here (Hawkins 1983:93–8).

8 This example was provided to me by Paul Wu.

4 Markedness in typology

1 See Greenberg (1966b:11), who notes related concepts in the work of Hjelmslev and Trnka.

2 This statement is not entirely accurate. In a number of languages, including Classical Arabic, Shilluk and Russian, a subclass of nouns refer to a group or plurality in their root form, and singular reference is accomplished by the addition of a nonzero "singulative" morpheme (Greenberg 1977:287–93). However, the singulative form generally also has a marked plural form, and the root "plural" is really a collective that is found on a particular semantic subclass of nouns (see 6.3.4).

3 These statements are qualified by "at least as ... " or a synonymous expression in order to indicate that the possibility of the marked and unmarked values might not differ in the given parameter.

4 This analysis of Greenberg's properties of markedness into four general criteria was briefly presented in Croft 1984, 1986, 1988.

5 As usual, a few qualifications are in order. The "animate" classes, masculine and feminine, are somewhat arbitrary in their classification. Also, the inanimate classes, usually characterized by the prefixes *gu-* and *mu-*, can sometimes allow zero verb-agreement (in the third-person singular, of course).

6 Instead, the presence of irregular forms is related to markedness patterns in a slightly different way; see 4.3.2.1 and chapter 7.

7 One cannot appeal to abstract underlying analyses here, because markedness patterns are based on "surface" morphosyntax, and it would be circular to selectively utilize abstract underlying forms in markedness arguments only when we need or want to. (In fact, adherents of the functional–typological approach eschew "abstract" analyses entirely, since their goal is to account for universal patterns of surface structure in functional terms, not abstract structural terms.) This is not to exclude the possibility of a "surface" nonlinear phonological representation that might actually allow us to state that a linearly represented ablaut relationship is actually the addition of a morpheme on a different tier. Until we have a principled means for an autosegmental phonetic representation, however, we must be conservative and treat ablaut in the same way as suppletion.

One possibility for defining markedness patterns in ablaut alternations without reference to underlying representations would be to use the markedness of the phonemes which alternate: the morphosyntactically marked form is the one with the more marked phoneme alternant. This would only be applicable to internal alternations of a single phoneme.

8 This is not without its exceptions. In some dialects of Spanish, gender distinctions are found in the first and second plural forms but not in the singular: *nosotros/nosotras* 'we (masc.f.),' *vosotros/vosotras* 'you (pl. masc./f.),' but *yo* 'I' and *tú* 'you (sg.).' This phenomenon has a historical explanation: the plural forms were originally *nos* and *vos*, but the adjective *otros/otras* 'others,' with its masculine and feminine forms, was added to the plural. Nevertheless, it is surprising that the historical process did not follow markedness constraints in this case.

9 Greenberg calls this a case of defectivation, since the inflectional category *qua* inflection is "missing" (Greenberg 1966b:30).

10 Also, the pronouns have case distinctions (except for *you* and *it*) and the nouns do not, another piece of behavioral evidence that pronouns are less marked.

11 Again, there is the issue of how to restrict oneself to a surface-based phonological analysis, the proper domain for typological markedness patterns.

12 For a detailed discussion of markedness and distribution, see Gundel, Houlihan and Sanders (1986).

13 The use of abstract underlying forms frequently regularizes phonotactic irregularity, and so should not be used in determining phonological markedness.

14 Indeed, the only way in which stative predicates can occur in the progressive is if they are "coerced" into (reinterpreted as) process predicates: *She is resembling her mother more and more* (= she is coming to resemble her mother more and more); *He is being a boor* (= he is acting like a boor).

15 Unless they too are coerced into nouns denoting kinds or varieties: e.g. *the wines of France.*

16 This corresponds to Gundel, Houlihan and Sanders' "typological markedness" (1986:108).

17 There may also be a correlation between plurality and indefiniteness involved here: the third-person plural pronoun (or verb form) is often used for impersonal constructions or unspecified agents in passive-like constructions.

18 On the basis of these types of examples, another putative criterion for markedness has arisen in the literature: the form which has the wider semantic range is the unmarked form. This criterion is not acceptable because (morphosyntactic) markedness is not a property of specific forms in specific languages, but of grammatical categories across languages. Nevertheless, it illustrates a widespread confusion, or at least difference of opinion, as to whether markedness is a property of specific linguistic forms or a property of cross-linguistic categories. The consistent typological position is the latter.

19 It is not clear if this is correct cross-linguistically; problems arise in Slavic and other Indo-European languages, for example. In Slavic languages, the perfective is derived from the imperfective through the addition of a prefix for many verbs. However, different prefixes can often be added to the same imperfective verb root (analogous to the English verb-particle constructions as in *shut up, shut down, shut out*), and from those perfective verbs structurally marked imperfectives can be derived.

20 Second-person imperatives represent a markedness paradox: structurally, they are often the least marked members of the verbal system; behaviorally, however, they are highly defective compared to declarative verb-forms.

21 The markedness reversal between vowels/sonants and consonants will be discussed in 6.3.1.

5 Grammatical hierarchies

1 Many linguists also use the notation singular > plural > dual. We will continue to use the less-than sign to indicate "less marked than ... " for mnemonic reasons, some of which will be more apparent below.

2 Not all of it was: Trubetzkoy considered text frequency, for example (Greenberg 1966b:14).

3 There is a noteworthy parallel between the reinterpretation of markedness in terms of scalar values here and the reinterpretation of morphological types by Greenberg also as scalar values.

4 The example "noun" is used here, but this classification can also be used for the category of number as expressed in personal pronouns, demonstrative pronouns, adjectives, verbs or any grammatical category in which number is expressed.

5 Some of the excluded types are highly dysfunctional: there would be a severe communicative impairment if a language had only a dual form for nouns, for instance.

6 This method also implies that frequency is more basic to the concept of markedness than the other criteria, a matter which we will return to in chapter 7.

7 The terms S, A and P for intransitive and transitive verbs were first used by Comrie (1978) and Dixon (1979; Dixon uses "O" instead of "P"). The terms T and G are proposed here (the variation in object marking for which these terms are proposed is described in detail in Dryer 1986, but he does not propose any analogous terms). The terms in scare quotes are the mnemonic names for the letters; except for S(ubject), they are taken from semantic case (thematic-role) analysis. However, one should not take the abbreviations to indicate semantic values. In particular, there are many transitive verbs which would better be described as taking T(heme) and G(oal) arguments. Not surprisingly, their case marking is closely related to that for T and G arguments in ditransitive clauses.

8 Of course, G can also be expressed as an unmarked noun phrase immediately following the verb: *Joan sent Paul a package.* In this sentence, G rather than T resembles P. This is exactly the phenomenon that we will describe shortly.

9 I do not know of any language that belongs to the type "zero case-marking for subject, object and oblique (including indirect object)." In those languages that allegedly have zero case-marking for "indirect objects," the "indirect objects" are actually primary objects.

There are a small number of exceptions. In some Indo-European languages, e.g. Icelandic and Old French, the subject case-ending is nonzero while the nonsubject case-ending is zero. This may be accounted for by the general breakdown of the case system in those languages. However, there are language families in which nonzero subject marking appears quite robust: in the Yuman languages, e.g. Hualapai (Watahomigie, Bender and Yamamoto 1982) and Maricopa (Gordon 1986), and in some Cushitic languages (Dixon 1979:77), the direct object is unmarked, but the subject – both transitive and intransitive – is expressed with a nonzero subject morpheme.

10 Dryer (1986:816–17) gives a number of exceptional cases (Khasi, Lahu, Kokborok) in which the primary object has a nonzero case-marking but the secondary object is zero-marked. However, the original sources for Khasi (Rabel 1961:76) and Lahu (Matisoff 1973:155–8) make it clear that the non-

zero form is highly variable in its distribution, a fact which Dryer describes in another language, Kham (Dryer 1986:817). It may be the case that these examples can be attributed to the more general phenomenon that more animate and definite objects, whether P or G, tend to be case-marked (see 5.3.3), since all of Dryer's examples are of animate Ps, and this is common in languages of the South Asian area. For Dryer's Nez Perce example (1986:817), see note 12.

11 DuBois (1987:819) reports a text count in Sacapultec with 264 (58 percent) intransitive clauses, 179 (39 percent) transitive clauses and 13 (3 percent) equational clauses; Payne (1987:793) reports a text count in Papago with 523 (69 percent) intransitive clauses and 236 (31 percent) transitive and ditransitive clauses. I found no text counts of ditransitive clauses in the literature. A count of approximately 180 clauses in a Nganytjarra text (Glass & Hackett 1979: text 1) revealed no ditransitives. A count of 144 clauses in a Quiché text (Mondloch 1978:192–203) included 75 (52 percent) intransitive, 51 (35 percent) transitive, 16 (11 percent) ditransitive and 2 (1 percent) equational clauses. Larger samples are necessary to confirm these figures, since the nature of the texts influenced the percentage of each clause type.

12 There are few languages that have both the ergative/absolutive distinction and the primary/secondary object distinction. One exception is Tzotzil, along with some other Mayan languages (Aissen 1983), in which the absolutive argument (indicated by verb agreement) is S+P+G. Another exception is Nez Perce (Rude 1982, cited in Dryer 1986:817). In Nez Perce, however, it is the secondary object, not the primary object, that is zero-marked. This seeming exception can be accounted for by examining frequency. The nonzero ergative case is restricted to third person As (see 5.3.3); this will be indicated by A3. The nonzero "object" case is P+G. The zero-marked case, including the first-/ and second- person As, is S + T + A1/2. The zero-marked case is almost certainly the most frequently occurring class.

13 It is extremely difficult to find cases of languages that agree with indirect objects (viz. G, as opposed to P+T). In the vast majority of cases, T is third person, which is conveniently zero-marked, so that three affixes never appear, e.g. Georgian (Comrie 1981b:216) or Chickasaw (Munro & Gordon 1982). A number of languages (e.g, Maltese; Borg & Comrie 1984) use pronominal affixes indicating G on the verb if a G argument NP is absent, but not if it is present; hence, there is no agreement *per se*. Indexation of more than two pronominal arguments is found in some Bantu languages, e.g. Kinyarwanda (Dryer 1983:137), and some Northwest Caucasian languages, such as Abaza (Allen 1956:139) and Abkhaz (Hewitt 1979). The maximum number of indexed arguments found is four: A, T, G and either a benefactive (Kinyarwanda) or a causer in a causative form:

Kinyarwanda

Umugóre	a-	ra-	bi-	yí-	mu-		he	-er	-a
woman	she-	PRES-	it(T)-	it(G)-	him (BEN)-		give	-BEN	-ASP

'The woman is giving it (food) to it (the dog) for him.'

Abaza

aláɡaʒ^w áčʸkʷəncʷakʷa llá aphʷə́spa **y-** **gʸ-** **y-** **z-** **d-**
boys old.man dog girl 3SGNH- NEG- 3-PL- POT- 3SGH-
m- l- r- ətxd
NEG- 3SGF- CAUS- gave

'The old man couldn't make the boys give the girl her dog back.'

However, the pronoun sets for each argument are identical (Kinyarwanda) or nearly identical (Abaza, Abkhaz).

14 In all of the languages in which the verb agrees with the absolutive only, the verbal agreement pattern is based on gender/number, not on person. True indexation (cross-reference) systems by person either fit a subject/object pattern, or agree with both the ergative and absolutive argument, as in Quiché.

15 As with indirect objects, it is extremely difficult to find clear cases of languages that agree with secondary objects. Languages such as Kinyarwanda (Kimenyi 1980) use pronominal affixes on the verb if a T argument NP is absent from the clause.

16 Unfortunately, by this argument the many ergative languages that are SOV would have the order Erg-Abs-V, which violates the frequency criterion.

17 Mandarin Chinese, in which oblique phrases usually precede the verb but unmarked objects follow, is a notable exception.

18 Hawkins lists several word orders in which oblique phrases precede objects (both T and G; Hawkins 1983:137). All of these languages are SOV languages in which neither objects nor obliques can follow the verb. German displays a similar pattern, but is not fully SOV (it is verb-second in main clauses, but if an auxiliary verb occupies second position, as often happens, the "main" verb is final). The objects may follow the obliques in these languages due to their syntactically and semantically more intimate connection to the verb; see chapter 8 for further discussion.

19 Keenan and Comrie also include NPs that are not directly related to the verb, such as the possessor of the subject, in their hierarchy. Lehmann (1986:668) argues that although NP types other than verbal grammatical relations also belong in the accessibility hierarchy, the other NP types form special subhierarchies.

20 Keenan and Comrie do not address the issue of how the indirect object is encoded, and posit a separate level on the hierarchy for it.

21 The existence of this type hinges on the ability to define the category "subject" in these languages, a most difficult problem even given the qualifications discussed in this section (see, for instance, Schachter 1976, 1977; Lawler 1977; Durie 1988). However, many languages including English have non-finite forms (participles) that function as relative clauses which allow only subject NP heads, as in *the child playing in the bedroom*.

22 The antipassive construction has the effect of expressing the P argument as an oblique phrase, such as the dative *yabu-gu* "mother" in (30). The antipassive appears to be a sort of "converse" of the passive construction, which has the effect of expressing the A argument of a transitive verb as an oblique phrase, hence the name "antipassive."

23 The animals *pəlaŋəmwani* 'dog.' *tajamini* 'dingo' and *muani* 'goanna' are included in the human class.

24 Proper names are included between pronouns and common nouns (see Dixon 1979:85), though most grammatical descriptions do not include information on proper names.

25 For more discussion of Silverstein's analysis of animacy, see below and chapter 6.

26 Lichtenberk goes on to say: "Although the Manam may derogatively speak of certain mainlanders as 'wild,' grammatically they nevertheless always treat them as higher animals."

27 As usual, the situation is somewhat more complex than the illustrative examples here indicate. Foley notes that if the use of the ligature is optional for a modifier type on the hierarchy, it may also be optional on modifier types lower on the hierarchy (Foley 1980:175). Optional alternative constructions are not illustrated here. For full details on the qualifications to the hierarchy, see Foley (1980:178–95).

28 The symbol "*t" is used by Maddieson to indicate dental or alveolar place of articulation. The numbers following the generalizations refer to the proportion of verifying cases, in numerical and percentage terms.

29 Maddieson also notes, "(vi) If a language has ć or q́ it also has p̓, *t̓ and k̓. 15/19 78.9%" (Maddieson 1984:120). This ordering seems to be based on the rarity of palatal and uvular consonants in general, rather than the hierarchy of ejectives described here (see Lindblom and Maddieson's (1988) concept of "basic" vs. "elaborated" articulations in their analysis of consonant segment inventories).

30 This formulation is from Hooper (1976:196); however, this hierarchy dates back at least to the early part of this century (Lass 1984:263–4).

6 Prototypes and the interaction of typological patterns

1 Actually, there are certain special noun and verb forms which tend to be at least as unmarked as the forms just described. The **vocative** noun form, which is used to call to someone, is at least as unmarked as the nominative (if a language has a distinct vocative form). For example, Yurok has vocative forms for kin terms that are less marked than the invariant form used for other grammatical functions, e.g. *picowos* 'grandfather,' voc. *pic; kokos* 'mother,' voc. *kok* (Robins 1958:23). For verbs, the imperative, used for commands, is often as unmarked as or less marked than the third singular present indicative. For example, Wikchamni uses the "reduced base" of a verb for the imperative: *kʰam̓* 'dance!' (from normal root *kʰam̓* 'to dance'; Gamble 1978:64); this is the least marked verb form in Wikchamni.

2 There are, however, several exceptions to this pattern, in which low-definiteness objects are marked. For example in West Greenlandic Eskimo indefinite objects take the instrumental case (Sadock 1980:306):

angut -ϕ   arna   -mik untaavoq
man   -ABS woman -INST beat.ANTIPASS.INDIC.3SG
'The man beat a woman.'

However, all such cases occur in ergative languages and involve the derivation of the antipassive (intransitive) verb form, so that in effect the "object" becomes an oblique.

3 Intransitive subjects (S in the terminology of 5.3.2) also incorporate. Incorporation is obligatory if S is an inanimate common noun, and prohibited if S is animate or a proper name. Thus, low animacy–definiteness Ss are prone to incorporation; this pattern is common in other languages as well.

4 For more discussion of incorporation, see Mithun (1984, 1986) and Sadock (1980, 1986).

5 An exception to this pattern is Hindi. In Hindi, definite/animate direct objects are marked with a postposition *ko*. In the past tense, the verb will agree with the direct object in gender if it is not marked with *ko*. This appears to be due to an independent factor: NPs marked with postpositions are oblique, and Hindi verbs do not agree with oblique arguments.

6 The agreement examples suggest that definite-animate direct objects are less marked, since agreement is possible with them, while the case-marking patterns suggest that definite-animate direct objects are more marked, since they require nonzero case markings. This is an example of a markedness reversal, and will be discussed further below.

7 Unfortunately for this analysis, (1) and (2) are often in direct conflict because the "special accusative case marker," e.g. *ko* in Hindi, is often identical to an oblique marker (in this case, the dative). This can lead to paradoxes if the special accusative case for a high-transitivity object is also used to make a low-transitivity object into an oblique. For example, in Russian, human masculine P's take a special accusative marker, e.g. *Marija ubila Ivan*-**a** (Mary killed Ivan-"acc.") 'Mary killed Ivan,' and therefore are indicators of high transitivity. Also, objects that are only partly affected are placed into an oblique case: *Ivan el xleb*-**a** (Ivan ate bread-"Obl.") 'Ivan ate some bread,' and therefore are indicators of low transitivity. But the "accusative" case is actually the genitive, and the "oblique" case is also the genitive (for many nouns; some nouns take a special partitive case in *-u).*

8 There is evidence that the correct feature controlling the markedness reversal of the place of articulation hierarchy among glottalized consonants is voicing, not airflow (ingressive for implosives, egressive for ejectives). It is possible to articulate voiceless implosives, and they are found in Mayan languages (Pinkerton 1986); but the voiceless implosives appear to pattern like the voiceless ejectives, not like the voiced implosives.

9 The phenomenon of complementary prototypes is not unique to linguistic typology. Rosch noted that prototypes tend to be as contrastive as possible with adjacent prototypes (Rosch 1978:37).

10 For example in Tangut, the verb always agrees with the object (P+G) in such cases (Kepping 1979:267; see also Comrie 1980). The "focus" voice of Quiché, used when an absolutive argument is focused, questioned, negated or relativized, is used only when at least one of the arguments is third person; if the arguments are first or second person, the simple voice is used and

the verb agrees with both arguments (Mondloch 1978:71–4). Nocte takes the elegant way out by using first person plural if A is first person and P is second person; see Greenberg 1988 for discussion of the combination "first person and second person."

11 DeLancey argues that the primary animacy distinction governing the correlation of animacy and case is the person hierarchy, i.e. first/second person vs. third person (DeLancey 1981:644). However, "split ergative" systems do exist in which other animacy distinctions play the central role, especially if the animate–definite direct-object cluster is included (Croft 1983, 1988).

12 Thus, passive differs from the direct–inverse constructions (e.g. Cree). The voice alternation active–passive allows a potential mismatch between morphosyntactic subject–object and semantic agent–patient. In direct–inverse systems, however, there is a direct correlation between animacy and agent–patient. Of course, the passive voice of English and other languages involves something more than a violation of morphosyntactic and semantic ranking: passive forms represent the result of the action and the agent is actually not one of the verb's arguments. Support for this analysis is lent by the absence of agents in most passive sentences and the outright prohibition against agents in passive constructions in many languages (see Shibatani 1985).

13 In some languages, this is an outright violation of grammaticality (e.g. Quiché; Mondloch 1978:59).

14 Some linguists include the category "adposition" among the major lexical categories. However, unlike nouns, verbs and adjectives, they are never open-class categories. Even adjectives are open-class categories in many languages. Most of the noun-like and verb-like behavior of adpositions that have led them to be called "major category words" is based on the fact that adpositions are historically derived from nouns and verbs; see chapter 8.

15 This analysis is based on Croft (1984, forthcoming). Hopper and Thompson have also proposed a typological analysis of the syntactic categories "noun" and "verb" (Hopper & Thompson 1984). Although a number of their criteria are identical to those described here, most of their criteria and almost all of their theoretical discussion actually define the concept of **categoriality,** that is the concept of a lexical root as an independent syntactic unit (see also Myhill 1988). Their criterion for categoriality is the degree to which a lexical root is presenting a new, salient piece of information in the discourse (participants in the case of nouns, events in the case of verbs). The typological pattern is that of a cluster prototype, not unlike their transitivity prototype. The less categoriality a root has (e.g. one denoting a nonreferential noun phrase, or a dependent clause), the more likely it is to appear both without any structural mark and without any inflections. Thus, they resemble imperatives and vocatives (described in note 1 of this chapter), and not marked/unmarked categories, in that both absence of structural mark and of grammatical behavior pattern together. Hopper and Thompson's study strongly

suggests that this pattern – bare root expression – has cross-linguistic significance,though it is not as common as patterns based on markedness criteria.

16 The prefixes are fused gender-number markers.

17 In some languages, marked plurals are derived from singulatives; these are
called **pluratives** (Dimmendaal 1983:233). The unmarked correlation here,
as with the other patterns described in this chapter, is only the typological
manifestation of a fascinating complex of grammatical and semantic phenomena.

18 As in Lakhota, the inflection of kin terms for possession is morphologically
somewhat irregular. Also, the regular possessive suffixes may also be used,
and the kin term possessive prefixes for second and third person may be
dropped, especially when those suffixes are used (Heath 1978b:38).

19 Gamkrelidze (1978:14–17) claims that a place hierarchy exists for fricatives
also, which is not generally confirmed in the UPSID sample (Maddieson
1984:47–9).

20 One must distinguish between zero-marked verb agreement and absence
of agreement. For example, in Quiché, the verb agrees with the absolutive
(S + P + T), but the third person singular form is zero; on the other hand,
the verb does not agree with the indirect object (G), period. The ability
to agree is a behavioral property, and so inability of a verb to agree with
an argument indicates markedness. Zero-marked agreement, on the other
hand, is a structural indicator of unmarkedness. This is a subtle but extremely
important distinction. Absence of agreement with a direct object indicates
the markedness of the direct object relative to the subject; but zero-marking
of third person singular subjects indicates the unmarkedness of third person
and singular number.

21 Anderson's characterization of case marking and verb agreement as "only
morphological" is at best misleading: both are subject to conditions dependent on the syntactic relationship between the verb and its noun-phrase arguments. Developments in generative syntactic theory since Anderson's article
have tended to reanalyze case assignment and verb agreement as "syntactic"
phenomena and treat phenomena such as passive and control of nonfinite
complements as lexical phenomena, further conflating the distinction between
the two.

22 If anything, imperatives follow an active–stative pattern, since stative commands are unacceptable: *Resemble Fred! *Be old!* This further illustrates
that a division of grammatical phenomena into (universal) "accusative" and
(sporadic, superficial) "ergative" is oversimplistic.

7   External motivation and the typology of form–function relations

1 This is not to say that some facets of linguistic structure are not culture-
dependent: an obvious example is kinship systems. But even patterns of
kinship terminology obey typological universals, that is universal constraints
of variation (Greenberg 1966b: chapter 5).

2 Qualifications must be made for the T and G arguments of ditransitive verbs,

of course: the former are almost never human, and the latter are. Data on objects must carefully separate T and G patterns.

3 Perhaps the fact that third-person pronouns do not *always* do so will suffice to explain the ranking $1, 2 < 3$.

4 Essentially the same comments apply to Hopper and Thompson's analysis of nouns and verbs in terms of the discourse functions "discourse-manipulable participant" and "reported event." However, those "discourse functions" contain semantic definitions as well, namely "participant" and "event."

5 The "isomorphism hypothesis," at least in a dynamic (historical) form, would assert that empty morphemes will disappear once they lose their content entirely – or else gain a new function (see Greenberg, forthcoming).

6 Haiman uses a nice analogy: homonymy is like having a map in which the color orange is used for more than one country, as long as they are not contiguous; synonymy is like having a map in which countries or elevations etc. are indicated in either blue or orange without any difference in significance (Haiman 1985:21–2).

7 In Quiché, the focus, WH-question, negation and relative-clause constructions all have in common the fronting of the foregrounded NP (in a normally verb-initial language), a special verbal voice form for transitive verbs (the "Voice 5" form), and an animacy-based agreement pattern for the same verbs (see 5.3.3).

8 The main exceptions to this are word order and the structural criterion of markedness; but the latter is, however, a product of economy, not iconicity.

9 Seiler argues for a more subtle gradation of 'inherence' of possession based on different types of grammatical constructions for possession:

N N < N conn N < N class N < N case N < N w.o./loc./exist./dir./def. N < N V N [Here conn stands for connective, class for classifier, w.o. for word order, loc. for location, exist, for existence, dir. for directionality, and def. for definiteness] (Seiler 1983:72)

However, Seiler's scale conflates predication of possession and possessive modification, and does not quite follow the iconic pattern Haiman is describing (see Seiler 1983:72–5).

10 For mood < person/number, there were five exceptions out of eighteen cases.

11 However, this analysis then presents a problem for the isomorphism principle, since two separate linguistic expressions refer to the same individual. Incidentally, this is an instance of a similar problem with agreement: in agreement, two morphemes (the agreement morpheme and the NP) refer to the same entity. One possible argument in favor of an iconic analysis is that there is a pragmatic function associated with double reference, e.g. emphasis, or "afterthought" (Hyman 1975), which is not incompatible with iconicity.

12 An advocate of the iconicity of constituent structure hypothesis will have to account for the surface discontinuities found in complex syntactic constructions in which constituents "go with" more than one other constituent in different ways. For example, in *John is easy to please*, the noun phrase *John* "goes with" *please* as well as *be easy*, and conceptual distance will have

to be defined more precisely in order to determine whether this construction (and its cross-linguistic distribution) supports or disconfirms the iconicity hypothesis. This represents another instance of iconic distance competing with isomorphism: a construction such as * *John is easy to please John* violates isomorphism, since two NPs (*John*) refer to the same individual (and moreover neither is reduced to a pronoun, as occurs in some languages).

13 Not surprisingly, the simple–compound distinction in folk taxonomies is rather complex. Generic forms are sometimes themselves compounds headed by a higher-level form (e.g. *pine tree*). Specific-level entities are sometimes named by the same name as the generic entity; Berlin notes "the monomials [simple forms] will invariably refer to a taxon of major cultural importance" (Berlin 1978:21) – i.e. the simpler lexical form corresponds to a more salient object.

14 A qualification must be made for nonfinite verbal forms. These often contain the "content" of the action, and so are verbal forms; but the "main" verb represents concepts expressed as satellites in other languages. This situation is often reanalyzed historically so that the "main" verb becomes an auxiliary (see e.g. Heine & Reh 1984).

15 This example is given in morphophonemic notation; the surface form is *hiqqoláhsaya*.

16 In fact, Li & Thompson call these directional verbal **compounds** avoiding the headedness issue (assuming they intend to refer to exocentric compounding).

17 Support for this explanation would be establishment of the following universal: "If an element is expressed by a bound category, then it is obligatory in all appropriate contexts."

18 This analysis, however, requires that we return to the classic concept of markedness as zero vs. one morpheme. It would have to be altered considerably to be compatible with the generalized concept of fewer vs. more morphemes that was used in chapter 4.

19 Actually, it is not entirely clear that principle 3 is always in conflict with principle 1, since the topic, or given information, may be uppermost in the speaker's mind because that is what the sentence is about. True evaluation of the effects of principle 3 requires a better definition of "uppermost in the speaker's mind."

20 Actually, since focus position can be sentence-initial, preverbal or even postverbal, Haiman is arguing that information questions apply to whatever principle is relevant for focus, including principle 3.

21 One problem with Haiman's analysis is that anaphoric, as opposed to relative, pronouns do not move to the head; instead they stay in their "normal" position. Haiman argues that the normal position of anaphoric pronouns is maintained due to analogy with main clauses. This does not, however, explain why anaphoric pronouns are not attracted to their heads in main clauses.

22 Actually, it is not entirely vacuous, since it excludes patterns in which transitive subject and transitive object are marked alike as against intransitive subject. However, most linguists invoke a different principle – mark potentially confusable constituents distinctly – to account for this (see Comrie 1978).

23 No correlation is found with languages that allow relativization of subjects, objects and obliques.

24 This description necessarily involves a considerable simplification of the facts; for fuller details, see Givón 1975b; Keenan and Comrie 1977; Maxwell 1979; and Comrie & Keenan 1979. In particular, it is worth noting that there are cases of "overlap," in which the case relation at the change-over point from primary to secondary relativization strategy actually can use either strategy for relative-clause formation.

25 Givón (1979: chapter 4) also argues that case recoverability also governs passivization in those languages that allow passivization of obliques via promotion to direct object.

8 Diachronic typology

1 This term is borrowed from geology and biology.

2 Greenberg's phrasing of the hypothesis permitted certain autonomous language types, and has been corrected here, reflecting his original intention (Greenberg, personal communication).

3 The phonological examples in this paragraph are Greenberg's (1978b:76).

4 Although basic word order has changed significantly in Indo-European, a wider examination of language families suggests that SOV and SVO orders are quite stable.

5 Frequency serves merely to indicate the relationship of the sample size to the total population: for very infrequent phenomena, a good sample will probably be the total population.

6 Or, to put it in Hawkins' terms, a heavy constituent can move after the noun or a light one before the noun against a harmonic pattern, but not vice versa.

7 Unfortunately, there are no frequency data for numeral–noun and adjective–noun orders. Also, dominant patterns will have stability and frequency values associated with them. For example, the dominant orders subject–object and subject–verb are presumably high in stability and/or frequency, since verb-initial languages are quite rare (see figures in Tomlin 1986:22).

8 Note that the term "eventually" represents a major promissory note on the part of diachronic typology. "Relatively unstable" language states may persist for a long time, perhaps centuries (see, for example, the case of the zero-marked genitive plural in Slavic below). Stability is also controlled by non-linguistic forces (other than the external ones described in chapter 7), such as the enforcement of a written standard. For more discussion, see chapter 9.

9 An analogy to this situation can be made in physical theory. It is a physical law that ice melts at zero degrees centigrade at standard pressure. However, anyone who has lived on the inside edge of the snowbelt can observe that the temperature may go above zero degrees centigrade for several days before the snow and ice all melt away. Melting takes time, and the existence of ice above zero degrees centigrade for several days is not a counterexample to the physical law.

10 I have used a logical equivalent to Hawkins' and Greenberg's versions to illustrate the diachronic point better. Note that the logical form does not automatically predict historical sequence; for example, Prep ⊃ (GN ⊃ AN) is equivalent to (Prep & GN) ⊃ AN and also GN ⊃ (Prep ⊃ AN), suggesting quite different historical scenarios.

11 Of course, it may be that a language would never acquire either a nonzero plural or singular marker. There is no imperative to change imposed by diachronic typology, just a constraint on possible language changes. This applies to the dynamicization of implicational universals also, of course.

12 Bybee refers to them as frequency-determined phenomena, but frequency is the source of most markedness patterns (see 7.2.1).

13 This is the same sort of data that Tiersma uses to argue for "local markedness" patterns, that is markedness reversals (Tiersma 1982, discussed in 6.3.4).

14 Bybee's analysis can be applied to syntactic constructions as well. For example, the English negative imperative for verbs is formed by the auxiliary *do + not: Don't jump* (cf. the positive *Jump).* The negative imperative for adjectives was formed by the auxiliary *be + not: Be not afraid* (cf. the positive *Be courageous).* The negative imperative for adjectives was restructured to *Don't be afraid,* which uses the positive as the base form (due to the unmarkedness of positive polarity) and the verbal imperative pattern *Jump/Don't jump* as the base (due to the unmarkedness of the verbal form).

15 Not all synchronic variation represents historical change in progress. Some variation is stable, representing uniform social stratification of some type (Labov 1966).

16 This may not necessarily be the case. If one examines two closely related languages and finds them to be SVO and VSO, it may be that the proto-language is something different, e.g. SOV, which led to the SVO and VSO daughter languages by different paths. This problem can be mitigated by looking at a larger number of daughter languages, when they exist, or looking at a wider language family that includes the family originally examined.

17 Or in some languages, PossPrn N-Poss. The effect is the same N Poss order shifts to Poss N order.

18 There may also be sociolinguistic differences between phonologically related forms in a given language.

19 More frequently, a new diachronic cycle of article formation has begun before the old one has "ended," leading to multiple "layers" of articles; see 8.5. In fact, this has occurred in Classical Nahuatl, the new article being *in.*

20 The surveys, both outgrowths of research at the Cologne universals project, also describe or list the attested cases of grammaticalization; the reader is directed to those works for an inventory of typical grammaticalization processes (Lehmann 1981: chapter 3; Heine & Reh 1984:269–81).

21 For this reason, Heine and Reh classify them as morphosyntactic processes; but they represent the phonological coalescence of words, for the most part. Most of the properties that distinguish different kinds of morpheme boundaries are phonological, though the syntactic property of word order/morpheme position also plays a role.

22 Lehmann includes simplification ("loss of inflection," Lehmann 1985: 307)

with attrition – note that he does not separate phonological, morphosyntactic and functional processes in his classification.

23 This point is emphasized in Lehmann 1985, whose title is "Grammaticalization: synchronic variation and diachronic change."

24 Actually, compared to most other *to* + infinitive forms, *have to* is more grammaticalized: it is pronounced [hæftə], and, taking this phonological coalescence into consideration, fits in a paradigm with *gotta, wanna, oughta, gonna, musta, shoulda* and *useta.*

25 A (phonological) clitic is informally defined here as an element that never can be stressed.

9 Linguistic explanation in the dynamic paradigm

1 Analogously, universal definitions of phonological categories must be based on (external) phonetic characteristics. It is worth noting that the notorious difficulties in defining "noun," "verb," "sentence," "main clause," and "subject" are matched by the difficulties in defining "segment," "consonant," "vowel," "syllable" and "word" in phonetic terms.

2 The differences in data – the role of meaning and use in typological data – are attributable to differences in the kinds of generalizations typologists make at higher levels.

3 One could also compare relative-clause structure in English with relative-clause structures in earlier stages of English, Germanic and Indo-European, generalizing over the structures to yield a historical process – the only legitimate "explanation" in nineteenth-century historical linguistics. We return to this in 9.5.

4 Though it need not be, as for example Bolinger (1977), Kuno (1987) and others demonstrate.

5 DuBois (1985:273) calls this the 'ecology of grammar'.

6 They are also explained in part by the retention of historically earlier forms that may have lost their primary adaptive value but have survived for various reasons; see Frazzetta 1975. This is of central importance to the relationship between synchronic and diachronic linguistics (see 9.6).

7 For this reason, Givón uses the term "iconicity" to describe all processing considerations, both iconicity proper and economy (see also Givón 1984:30). We will continue to use "processing" to cover both iconicity proper and economy.

8 This observation of a distantly related field may seem irrelevant to the justification of an approach to language, but as Laudan (1976) has pointed out, part of the plausibility of a scientific paradigm is its theoretical coherence with more established scientific paradigms in related fields.

9 It is worth quoting part of this section, in which Mayr compares experiment with the comparative-observational method:

Each science demands its own appropriate methods ... Progress in many branches of science depends on observations made in order to answer carefully posed questions. Modern evolutionary, behavioral and ecological biology have demonstrated conclusively that these largely observational sciences are anything but descriptive . . . Mere observation, however, is not sufficient. It was not until late in the eighteenth century that a method was first seriously employed which is peculiarly suitable for the study of diversity; it is the comparative method. (1982:30–1)

10 The metaphor of a language as a perfectly adapted "organic" system was prominent in early structuralist writing and, as we have noted, in contemporary functionalist work.

11 See LePage and Tabouret-Keller 1985, chapters 5–6 for a similar statement in the context of pidgin and creole studies.

12 It is worth noting that Greenberg, Givón, Haiman, Hopper and Traugott are all historical linguists as well as typologists, and Givón has devoted some efforts to pidgins and creoles (e.g. Givón 1982b).

REFERENCES

Abraham, R. C. 1959. *The language of the Hausa people*. London: University of London Press.

Aissen, Judith 1983. Indirect object advancement in Tzotzil. In *Studies in Relational Grammar*, Vol. 1, ed. David Perlmutter, 272–302. Chicago: University of Chicago Press.

Allen, Barbara, Donna B. Gardiner and Donald G. Frantz 1984. Noun incorporation in Southern Tiwa. *International Journal of American Linguistics* 50:292–311.

Allen, W. Sidney 1956. Structure and system in the Abaza verbal complex. *Transactions of the Philological Society*, 1956:127–76.

1964. Transitivity and possession. *Language* 40:337–43.

Allwood, Jens, Lars-Gunnar Andersson and Östen Dahl 1977. *Logic in linguistics*. Cambridge: Cambridge University Press.

Andersen, Henning 1968. IE *s* after *i, u, r, k* in Baltic and Slavic. *Acta Linguistica Hafniensa* 11:171–90.

1972. Diphthongization. *Language* 48:11–50.

Anderson, Stephen 1976. On the notion of subject in ergative languages. In *Subject and topic*, ed. Charles Li, 1–24. New York: Academic Press.

Aristar, Anthony 1987. On the diachronic source of linguistic universals. Paper presented to the annual meeting of the Linguistic Society of America, San Francisco, California.

Bach, Emmon 1980. In defense of passive. *Linguistics and Philosophy* 3:197–341.

Bally, Charles 1965. *Linguistique générale et linguistique française* (4th edition). Berne: Editions Franke.

Battistella, Edwin Forthcoming. *Markedness*.

Behaghel, Otto 1923–32. *Deutsche Syntax*, vols. I–IV. Heidelberg: Carl Winter.

Behrens, Leila 1982. *Zur funktionalen Motivation der Wortstellung: Untersuchungen anhand des Ungarischen*. Publication of the Finno-Ugric seminar, University of Munich, C-13.

Bell, Alan 1978. Language samples. In *Universals of human language*, vol. 1: *Method and theory*, ed. Joseph H. Greenberg, Charles A. Ferguson and Edith A. Moravcsik, 123–56. Stanford: Stanford University Press.

Berlin, Brent 1978. Ethnobiological classification. In *Cognition and categorization*, ed. Eleanor Rosch and B. B. Lloyd, 9–26. Hillsdale, N.J.: Lawrence Erlbaum Associates.

Biligiri, H. S. 1965. *Kharia phonology, grammar and vocabulary*. Poona: Deccan College.

Boas, Frans 1947. *Kwakiutl grammar, with a glossary of the suffixes*. Transactions of the American Philosophical Society, vol. 37, Part 3.

Boas, Frans and Ella Deloria 1941. *Dakota grammar*. Washington, D.C.: National Academy of Sciences.

Bolinger, Dwight 1977. *Meaning and form*. London: Longmans.

Borg, A. J. and Bernard Comrie 1984. Object diffuseness in Maltese. In *Objects*, ed. Frans Plank, 109–26. New York: Academic Press.

Brugmann, Karl 1906–11. *Grundriss der vergleichenden Grammatik der indogermanischen Sprachen* (2nd edition). Strassburg: K. J. Trübner.

Buechel, Eugene 1939. *A grammar of Lakota*. Rosebud, S. Dak.: Rosebud Educational Society.

Bühler, Karl 1934. *Sprachtheorie: die Darstellungsfunktion der Sprache*. Jena: Fischer.

Bybee, Joan L. 1985a. *Morphology*. Amsterdam: John Benjamins.

　1985b. Diagrammatic iconicity in stem–inflection relations. In *Iconicity in syntax*, ed. John Haiman, 11–48. Amsterdam: John Benjamins.

　1988. The diachronic dimension in explanation. In *Explaining language universals*, ed. John A. Hawkins, 350–79. Oxford: Basil Blackwell.

Bybee, Joan L. and Mary Alexandra Brewer 1980. Explanation in morphophonemics: changes in Provençal and Spanish preterite forms. *Lingua* 52:271–312.

Campbell, Lyle, Terrence Kaufman and Thomas C. Smith-Stark 1986. Mesoamerica as a linguistic area. *Language* 62:530–70.

Carlson, Greg N. 1977. A unified analysis of the English bare plural. *Linguistics and Philosophy* 1:413–57.

Catford, Ian 1977. Mountain of tongues: the languages of the Caucasus. *Annual Review of Anthropology* 6:283–314.

Chambers, J. K. and Peter Trudgill 1980. *Dialectology*. Cambridge: Cambridge University Press.

Chung, Sandra 1976. *Case marking and grammatical relations in Polynesian*. Austin: University of Texas Press.

Churchward, C. Maxwell 1940. *Rotuman grammar and dictionary*. Sydney: Australasian Medical Publishing Company.

　1953. *Tongan grammar*. Nuku'alofa, Tonga: Taulua Press.

Cole, Peter, Wayne Harbert, Gabriella Hermon and S. N. Sridhar 1980. The acquisition of subjecthood. *Language* 56:719–43.

Collinge, N. E. 1985. *The Laws of Indo-European*. Amsterdam: John Benjamins.

Comrie, Bernard 1978. Ergativity. In *Syntactic typology*, ed. Winfrid Lehmann, 329–94. Austin: University of Texas Press.

　1979. Definite and animate objects: a natural class. *Linguistica Silesiana* 3:13–21.

　1980. Agreement, animacy and voice. In *Wege zur Universalien Forschung; Sprachwissenschaftliche Beiträge zum 60. Geburtstag von Hansjakob Seiler*, ed. Gunter Brettschneider and Christian Lehmann, 229–34. Tübingen: Gunter Narr.

References

1981a. *Language universals and linguistic typology*. Chicago: University of Chicago Press.

1981b. *The languages of the Soviet Union*. Cambridge: Cambridge University Press.

1982. Grammatical relations in Huichol. In *Studies in transitivity* (Syntax and Semantics, 15), ed. Paul Hopper and Sandra Thompson, 95–115. New York: Academic Press.

√ 1983. Review of Mallinson and Blake 1981. *Language* 59:908–11.

? 1986. Markedness, grammar, people and the world. In *Markedness*, ed. Fred R. Eckman, Edith A. Moravcsik and Jessica R. Wirth, 85–196. New York: Plenum Press.

Comrie, Bernard and Edward Keenan 1979. Noun phrase accessibility revisited. *Language* 55:649–64.

Cowell, Mark 1964. *A reference grammar of Syrian Arabic*. Washington, D.C.: Georgetown University Press.

Crazzolara, J. P. 1955. *A study of the Acooli language* (2nd impression, revised). London: Oxford University Press.

? Croft, William 1983. Grammatical relations vs. thematic roles as universals. In *Papers from the nineteenth regional meeting of the Chicago Linguistic Society*, ed. by A. Chukerman, M. Marks and J. Richardson, 76–94. Chicago: University of Chicago Linguistics Department.

1984. Semantic and pragmatic correlates to syntactic categories. In *Papers from the parasession on lexical semantics, twentieth regional meeting of the Chicago Linguistic Society*, ed. D. Testen, V. Mishra and J. Drogo, 53–71. Chicago: University of Chicago Linguistics Department.

1988. Agreement vs. case marking in direct objects. In *Agreement in natural language: approaches, theories, descriptions*, ed. Michael Barlow and Charles A. Ferguson, 159–80. Stanford: Center for the Study of Language and Information.

? forthcoming. *Syntactic categories and grammatical relations: the cognitive organization of information*. Chicago: University of Chicago Press.

Croft, William, Hava Bat-Zeev Shyldkrot and Suzanne Kemmer 1987. Diachronic semantic processes in the middle voice. In *Papers from the seventh international conference on historical linguistics*, ed. Ann Giacolone Ramat, Onofrio Carruba and Giuliano Bernini, 179–92. Amsterdam: John Benjamins.

Davies, John 1981. *Kobon*. (Lingua Descriptive Studies, 3.) Amsterdam: North-Holland.

Dayley, Jon 1985. *Tzutujil reference grammar*. (University of California Publications in Linguistics, 107.) Berkeley and Los Angeles: University of California Press.

DeLancey, Scott 1981. An interpretation of split ergativity and related patterns. *Language* 57:626–57.

1982. Aspect, transitivity and viewpoint. In *Tense and aspect: between semantics and pragmatics*, ed. Paul Hopper, 167–84. Amsterdam: John Benjamins.

1987. Transitivity in grammar and cognition. In *Coherence and grounding in discourse*, ed. Russell Tomlin, 53–68. Amsterdam: John Benjamins.

Derbyshire, Desmond 1977. Word order universals and the existence of OVS languages. *Linguistic Inquiry* 8:590–9.

Derbyshire, Desmond and Geoffrey Pullum 1981. Object-initial languages. *International Journal of American Linguistics* 47:192–214.

Dik, Simon 1981. *Functional grammar*. Dordrecht: Foris.

Dimmendaal, Gerrit Jan 1983. *The Turkana language*. Dordrecht: Foris.

Dixon, R. M. W. 1977. Where have all the adjectives gone? *Studies in Language* 1:19–80.

1979. Ergativity. *Language* 55:59–138.

Dodds, R. W. 1977. *Malay*. Sevenoaks: Hodder and Stoughton.

Dorian, Nancy 1981. *Language death*. Philadelphia: University of Pennsylvania Press.

Downing, Bruce T. 1978. Some universals of relative clause structure. In *Universals of human language*, vol. IV: *Syntax*, ed. Joseph H. Greenberg, Charles A. Ferguson and Edith A. Moravcsik, 375–418. Stanford: Stanford University Press.

Dryer, Matthew 1983. Indirect objects in Kinyarwanda revisited. In *Studies in relational grammar*, vol. I, ed. David Perlmutter, 129–40. Chicago: University of Chicago Press.

1985. Object–verb order and adjective–noun order: dispelling a myth. Paper presented at the annual meeting of the Linguistic Society of America, Seattle, Washington.

1986. Primary objects, secondary objects and antidative. *Language* 62:808–45.

1988. Object–verb order and adjective–noun order: dispelling a myth. *Lingua* 74:185–217.

DuBois, John A. 1985. Competing motivations. In *Iconicity in syntax*, ed. John Haiman, 343–66. Amsterdam: John Benjamins.

1987. The discourse basis of ergativity. *Language* 64:805–55.

Durie, Mark 1988. The so-called passive of Achenese. *Language* 64:104–13.

England, Nora 1983. *A grammar of Man, a Mayan language*. Austin: University of Texas Press.

Faltz, Leonard M. 1978. Indirect objects in universal grammar. In *Proceedings of the fourteenth regional meeting of the Chicago Linguistic Society*, ed. Donka F. Farkas, Wesley M. Jacobsen and Karol W. Todrys, 76–87. Chicago: University of Chicago Linguistics Department.

1985. *Reflexivization: a study in universal syntax*. New York: Garland.

Farkas, Donka 1981. *Intensionality and Romance subjunctive relatives*. (Ph.D dissertation, University of Chicago.) Bloomington: Indiana University Linguistics Club.

Ferguson, Charles A. 1966. Assumptions about nasals: a sample study in phonological universals. In *Universals of language*, ed. Joseph H. Greenberg, 53–60. Cambridge, Mass.: MIT Press.

1978. Phonological processes. In *Universals of human language*, vol. II: *Phonology*, ed. Joseph H. Greenberg, Charles A. Ferguson and Edith A. Moravcsik, 403–42. Stanford: Stanford University Press.

Foley, William. 1980. Toward a universal typology of the noun phrase. *Studies in Language* 4:171–99.

References

✓ Fowler, George 1987. The grammatical relevance of theme/rheme position. In *Papers from the twenty-third annual regional meeting of the Chicago Linguistic Society*, ed. Barbara Need, Eric Schiller, and Anna Bosch, 93–104. Chicago: University of Chicago Linguistics Department.

Fox, B. J. 1979. *Big Nambas grammar.* (Pacific Linguistics, B60.) Canberra: Australian National University.

Frazzetta, T. H. 1975. *Complex adaptations in evolving populations.* Sunderland, Mass.: Sinauer Associates.

Frei, Henri 1929. *La Grammaire des fautes.* Paris: Geuthner.

von der Gabelentz, Georg 1972 [1901]. *Die Sprachwissenschaft: ihre Aufgaben, Methode und bisherige Ergebnisse.* Tübingen: Tübinger Beiträge zur Linguistik.

Gamble, Geoffrey 1978. *Wikchamni grammar.* (University of California Publications in Linguistics, 89.) Berkeley and Los Angeles: University of California Press.

Gamkrelidze, Thomas V. 1978. On the correlation of stops and fricatives in a phonological system. In *Universals of human language*, vol. II: *Phonology*, ed. Joseph H. Greenberg, Charles A. Ferguson and Edith A. Moravcsik, 9–46. Stanford: Stanford University Press.

Gardiner, Sir Alan 1935. *The theory of speech and language* (2nd edition). Oxford: Oxford University Press.

Gildersleeve, B. L. and Gonzalez Lodge 1895. *Latin grammar.* London: Macmillan.

Givón, Talmy 1975a. Serial verbs and syntactic change: Niger–Congo. In *Word order and word order change*, ed. Charles Li, 47–112. Austin: University of Texas Press.

1975b. Promotion, accessibility and case marking: towards understanding grammars. *Working Papers in Language Universals* 19:55–126.

1976. Topic, pronoun and grammatical agreement. In *Subject and topic*, ed. Charles Li, 149–89. New York: Academic Press.

1979. *On understanding grammar.* New York: Academic Press.

1980a. *Ute reference grammar.* Ignacio, Colo.: Ute Press.

1980b. The binding hierarchy and the typology of complements. *Studies in Language* 4:333–77.

1982a. Logic vs. pragmatics, with natural language as the referee: towards an empirically viable epistemology. *Journal of Pragmatics* 6:81–133.

1982b. Tense–aspect–modality: the creole proto-type and beyond. In *Tense and aspect: between semantics and pragmatics*, ed. Paul Hopper, 115–66. Amsterdam: John Benjamins.

1984. *Syntax: a functional-typological introduction.* Amsterdam: John Benjamins.

1985. Iconicity, isomorphism and nonarbitrary coding in syntax. In *Iconicity in syntax*, ed. John Haiman, 187–220. Amsterdam: John Benjamins.

Glass, Amee and Dorothy Hackett 1979. *Nganyatjarra texts.* Canberra: Australian Institute of Aboriginal Studies.

Goodwin, William W. 1892. *A Greek grammar.* Boston: Ginn.

Gordon, Lynn 1986. *Maricopa morphology and syntax.* (University of California

References

Publications in Linguistics, 108.) Berkeley and Los Angeles: University of California Press.

Greenberg, Joseph H. 1954. A quantitative approach to the morphological typology of language. In *Method and perspective in anthropology*, ed. R. F. Spencer, 192–220. (Reprinted in *International Journal of American Linguistics* 26:178–94, 1960.)

1959. Africa as a linguistic area. In *Continuity and change in African cultures*, ed. W. R. Bascom and M. J. Herskovits, 15–27. Chicago: University of Chicago Press.

1966a. Some universals of grammar with particular reference to the order of meaningful elements. In *Universals of grammar*, ed. Joseph H. Greenberg (2nd edition), 73–113. Cambridge, Mass.: MIT Press.

1966b. *Language universals, with special reference to feature hierarchies*. (Janua Linguarum, Series Minor, 59.) The Hague: Mouton.

1968. *Anthropological linguistics*. New York: Random House.

1969. Some methods of dynamic comparison in linguistics. In *Substance and structure of language*, ed. Jan Puhvel, 147–203. Berkeley and Los Angeles: University of California Press.

1970. Some generalizations concerning glottalic consonants, especially implosives. *International Journal of American Linguistics* 36:123–45.

1974a. *Language typology: a historical and analytic overview*. (Janua Linguarum, Series Minor 184.) The Hague: Mouton.

1974b. The relation of frequency to semantic feature in a case language (Russian). *Working Papers in Language Universals* 16:21–47.

1977. Numeral classifiers and substantival number: problems in the genesis of a linguistic type. In *Linguistics at the Crossroads*, ed. Adam Makkai, Valerie Becker Makkai and Luigi Heilmann, 276–300. Padua: Liviana Editrice.

1978a. Some generalizations concerning initial and final consonant clusters. In *Universals of human language*, vol. II: *Phonology*, ed. Joseph H. Greenberg, Charles A. Ferguson and Edith A. Moravcsik, 243–80. Stanford: Stanford University Press.

1978b. Diachrony, synchrony and language universals. In *Universals of human language*, vol. I: *Method and theory*, ed. Joseph H. Greenberg, Charles A. Ferguson and Edith A. Moravcsik, 61–92. Stanford: Stanford University Press.

1978c. How does a language acquire gender markers? In *Universals of human language*, vol. III: *Word structure*, ed. Joseph H. Greenberg, Charles A. Ferguson and Edith A. Moravcsik, 47–82. Stanford: Stanford University Press.

1979. Rethinking linguistics diachronically. *Language* 55:275–90.

1980. Circumfixes and typological change. In *Papers from the fourth international conference on historical linguistics*, ed. Elizabeth Traugott, Rebecca Labrum and Susan Shepherd, 233–41. Amsterdam: John Benjamins.

1981. Nilo-Saharan movable *k-* as a Stage III article (with a Penutian typological parallel). *Journal of African Languages and Literature* 3:105–12.

References

1984. Some areal characteristics of African languages. In *Current approaches in African Linguistics*, ed. Ivan Dihoff, 3–21. Dordrecht: Foris.

1988. The first person inclusive dual as an ambiguous category. *Studies in Language* 12:1–18.

forthcoming. The last stages of grammatical elements: degrammaticalization and regrammaticalization. In *Grammaticalization*, ed. Elizabeth Closs Traugott and Bernd Heine. Amsterdam: John Benjamins.

Greenberg, Joseph H. and Chris O'Sullivan 1974. Frequency, marking, and discourse styles with special reference to substantival categories in the Romance languages. *Working Papers in Language Universals* 16:47–73.

Gregores, Emma and Jorge A. Suárez 1967. *A description of colloquial Guaraní*. The Hague: Mouton.

Gundel, Jeannette K., Kathleen Houlihan and Gerald A. Sanders 1986. Markedness and distribution in phonology and syntax. In *Markedness*, ed. Fred R. Eckman, Edith A. Moravcsik and Jessica R. Wirth, 107–38. New York: Plenum Press.

Haiman, John 1974. Concessives, conditionals, and verbs of volition. *Foundations of Language* 11:341–59.

1976. Agentless sentences. *Foundations of Language* 14:19–53.

1977. Connective particles in Hua; an essay on the parts of speech. *Oceanic Linguistics* 16:53–107.

1978a. Conditionals are topics. *Language* 54:564–89.

1978b. A study in polysemy. *Studies in Language* 2:1–34.

1980. The iconicity of grammar: isomorphism and motivation. *Language* 54:565–89.

1983. Iconic and economic motivation. *Language* 59:781–819.

1985. *Natural Syntax*. Cambridge: Cambridge University Press.

Hale, Kenneth 1983. Warlpiri and the grammar of nonconfigurational languages. *Natural Language and Linguistic Theory* 1:5–47.

Harning, Kerstin Eksell 1980. *The analytic genitive in the modern Arabic dialects*. Göteborg: Acta Universitatis Gothoburgensis.

Harrell, Richard S. 1962. *A short reference grammar of Moroccan Arabic*. Washington, D.C.: Georgetown University Press.

Harris, Alice C. 1982. Georgian and the unaccusative hypothesis. *Language* 58:290–306.

Harrison, Sheldon P. 1976. *Mokilese reference grammar*. Honolulu: University Press of Hawaii.

Harrison, Sheldon P. and Salich Albert 1977. *Mokilese–English dictionary*. Honolulu: University Press of Hawaii.

Hatcher, Anna Granville 1942. *Reflexive verbs: Latin, Old French, Modern French* (The Johns Hopkins Studies in Romance Literatures and Languages, 43). Baltimore: The Johns Hopkins Press.

Havers, Wilhelm 1931. *Handbuch der erklärenden Syntax*. Heidelberg: Carl Winter.

Hawkins, John A. 1980. On implicational and distributional universals of word order. *Journal of Linguistics* 16:193–235.

1983. *Word order universals*. New York: Academic Press.

Heath, Jeffrey 1975. Some functional relationships in grammar. *Language* 51:89–104.

1978a. *Linguistic diffusion in Arnhem Land.* Canberra: Australian Institute of Aboriginal Studies.

1978b. *Ngandi grammar, texts and dictionary.* Canberra: Australian Institute of Aboriginal Studies.

1979. Is Dyirbal ergative? *Linguistics* 17:401–63.

1980. *Nunggubuyu myths and ethnographic texts.* Canberra: Australian Institute of Aboriginal Studies.

1981. A case of intensive lexical diffusion: Arnhem Land. *Language* 57:335–67.

1984. *Functional grammar of Nunggubuyu.* Canberra: Australian Institute of Aboriginal Studies.

1986. Syntactic and lexical aspects of nonconfigurationality in Nunggubuyu (Australia). *Natural Language and Linguistic Theory* 4:375–408.

Heine, Bernd 1980. Determination in some East African languages. In *Wege zur Universalien Forschung: Sprachwissenschaftliche Beiträge zum 60. Geburtstag von Hansjakob Seiler*, ed. Gunter Brettschneider and Christian Lehmann, 180–6. Tübingen: Gunter Narr.

Heine, Bernd and Mechthild Reh 1984. *Grammaticalization and reanalysis in African languages.* Hamburg: Helmut Buske Verlag.

Henderson, Eugénie A. J. 1965. The topography of certain phonetic and morphological characteristics of South East Asian languages. *Lingua* 15:400–34.

Hewitt, B. G. 1979. *Abkhaz.* (Lingua Descriptive Studies, 2.) Amsterdam: North-Holland.

Holisky, Dee Ann 1987. The case of the intransitive subject in Tsova-Tush (Batsbi). *Lingua* 71:103–32.

Hooper, Joan Bybee 1976. *An introduction to natural-generative phonology.* New York: Academic Press.

Hopper, Paul 1979. Aspect and foregrounding in discourse. In *Discourse and syntax* (Syntax and Semantics, 12), ed. Talmy Givón, 213–41. New York: Academic Press.

1987. Emergent grammar. In *Proceedings of the thirteenth annual meeting of the Berkeley Linguistics Society*, ed. Jon Aske, Natasha Beery, Laura Michaelis and Hana Filip, 139–57. Berkeley: University of California at Berkeley.

Hopper, Paul and Sandra A. Thompson 1980. Transitivity in grammar and discourse. *Language* 56:251–99.

(eds.) 1982. *Studies in transitivity* (Syntax and Semantics, 15). New York: Academic Press.

1984. The discourse basis for lexical categories in universal grammar. *Language* 60:703–72.

Hutchison, John P. 1981. *The Kanuri language: a reference grammar.* Madison: University of Wisconsin African Studies Program.

Hyman, Larry 1975. On the change from SOV to SVO: evidence from Niger–Congo. In *Word order and word order change*, ed. Charles Li, 113–47. Austin: University of Texas Press.

Ingram, David 1978. Typology and universals of personal pronouns. In *Univer-*

References

sals of human language, vol. III: *Word structure,* ed. Joseph H. Greenberg, Charles A. Ferguson and Edith A. Moravcsik, 213–48. Stanford: Stanford University Press.

Irwin, Barry 1974. *Salt-Yui grammar.* (Pacific Linguistics, B35.) Canberra: Australian National University.

Jakobson, Roman 1958. Typological studies and their contribution to historical and comparative linguistics. In *Proceedings of the eighth international congress of linguists,* ed. Eva Sivertsen, Carl Hj. Borgstrøm, Arne Gallis, and Alf Sommerfelt, 17–25. Oslo: Oslo University Press.

1984a [1932]. Structure of the Russian verb. In *Russian and Slavic grammar: Studies, 1931–1981* (Janua Linguarum, Series Maior 106), ed. Linda R. Waugh and Morris Halle, 1–14. The Hague: Mouton. (Originally published as "Zur Struktur des russischen Verbums," *Charistera Guglielmo Mathesio,* 74–84, Prague, 1932.)

1984b [1939]. Zero sign. In *Russian and Slavic grammar: Studies, 1931–1981* (Janua Linguarum, Series Maior 106), ed. Linda R. Waugh and Morris Halle, 151–60. The Hague: Mouton. (Originally published as "Signe zéro," in *Mélanges de linguistique offerts à Charles Bally,* Geneva, 1939.)

Jespersen, Otto 1909–49. *A modern English grammar on historical principles,* vol. I – VII. London: Allen and Unwin.

Keenan, Edward 1979. Passive is phrasal, not sentential or lexical. In *Lexical grammar,* ed. T. Hoekstra, H. Hulst and M. Moortgat, 181–215. Dordrecht: Foris.

Keenan, Edward and Bernard Comrie 1977. Noun phrase accessibility and universal grammar. *Linguistic Inquiry* 8:63–99.

1979. Data on the noun phrase accessibility hierarchy. *Language* 55:333–51.

Kemmer, Suzanne 1988. The middle voice: a typological and diachronic study. Ph.D dissertation, Department of Linguistics, Stanford University.

Kepping, Ksenia Borisova 1979. Elements of ergativity and nominativity in Tangut. In *Ergativity,* ed. Frans Plank, 262–78. New York: Academic Press.

Kimenyi, Alexandre 1980. *A relational grammar of Kinyarwanda.* (University of California Publications in Linguistics, 91.) Berkeley and Los Angeles: University of California Press.

Kisseberth, Charles and Mohammad Imam Abasheikh 1977. The object relationship in Chi-Mwi:ni, a Bantu language. In *Grammatical relations* (Syntax and Semantics, 8), ed. Peter Cole and Jerrold Sadock, 179–218. New York: Academic Press.

Kraft, C. H. and A. H. M. Kirk-Greene 1973. *Hausa.* London: English Universities Press.

Kroeber, A. L. 1904. The languages of the coast of California south of San Francisco. *University of California Papers in American Archaeology and Ethnology* 2:29–80.

Kuno, Susumu 1972. *The structure of the Japanese language.* Cambridge, Mass.: M.I.T. Press.

1987. *Functional syntax: anaphora, discourse and empathy.* Chicago: University of Chicago Press.

Labov, William 1966. *The social stratification of English in New York City.* Washington, D.C.: Center for Applied Linguistics.

Lakoff, George 1977. Linguistic gestalts. In *Papers from the thirteenth regional meeting of the Chicago Linguistic Society*, ed. Woodford A. Beach, Samuel E. Fox and Shulamith Philosoph, 236–87. Chicago: University of Chicago Linguistics Department.

Lambrecht, Knud 1987. On the status of SVO sentences in French discourse. In *Coherence and grounding in discourse*, ed. Russell Tomlin, 217–62. Amsterdam: John Benjamins.

Langacker, Ronald 1987a. Nouns and verbs. *Language* 63:53–94.

1987b. *Foundations of cognitive grammar*, vol. 1: *Theoretical prerequisites.* Stanford: Stanford University Press.

Larsen, Thomas and William Norman 1979. Correlates of ergativity in Mayan grammar. In *Ergativity*, ed. Frans Plank, 347–70. New York: Academic Press.

Lass, Roger 1984. *Phonology.* Cambridge: Cambridge University Press.

Laudan, Larry 1976. *Progress and its problems: towards a theory of scientific growth.* Berkeley and Los Angeles: University of California Press.

Lawler, John 1977. *A* agrees with *B* in Achense: a problem for relational grammar. In *Grammatical relations* (Syntax and Semantics, 8), ed. Peter Cole and Jerrold Sadock, 219–48. New York: Academic Press.

Lazdiņa, Terēsa Budiņa 1966. *Latvian.* London: English Universities Press.

Lee, Kee-dong 1975. *Kusaiean reference grammar.* Honolulu: University Press of Hawaii.

Lehmann, Christian 1981. *Thoughts on grammaticalization: a programmatic sketch, Vol. 1.* (Arbeiten des Kölner Universalien-Projekts, 48.) Cologne: Institut für Sprachwissenschaft.

1985. Grammaticalization: synchronic variation and diachronic change. *Lingua e Stile* 20:303–18.

1986. On the typology of relative clauses. *Linguistics* 24:663–80.

LePage, R. B. and Andrée Tabouret-Keller 1985. *Acts of identity.* Cambridge: Cambridge University Press.

Leslau, Wolf 1968. *Amharic textbook.* Berkeley and Los Angeles: University of California Press.

Lewis, G. L. 1967. *Turkish grammar.* Oxford: Oxford University Press.

Li, Charles and Sandra A. Thompson 1981. *Mandarin Chinese: a functional reference grammar.* Berkeley and Los Angeles: University of California Press.

Lichtenberk, Frantisek 1983a. Relational classifiers. *Lingua* 60:147–176.

1983b. *A grammar of Manam.* (Oceanic Linguistics Special Publication, 18.) Honolulu: University of Hawaii Press.

1985. Multiple uses of reciprocal constructions. *Australian Journal of Linguistics* 5:19–41.

Lindblom, Björn and Ian Maddieson 1988. Phonetic universals in consonant systems. In *Language, speech and mind: studies in honour of Victoria A. Fromkin*, ed. Larry M. Hyman and Charles N. Li, 62–78. London: Routledge.

References

Lynch, John 1978. *A grammar of Lenakel*. (Pacific Linguistics, B55.) Canberra: Australian National University.

Mace, John 1962. *Modern Persian*. London: English Universities Press.

Maddieson, Ian 1984. *Patterns of sounds*. Cambridge: Cambridge University Press.

Mallinson, Graham and Barry Blake 1981. *Language typology*. Amsterdam: North-Holland.

Masica, Colin 1976. *Defining a linguistic area: South Asia*. Chicago: University of Chicago Press.

Matisoff, James 1969. Verb concatenation in Lahu: the syntax and semantics of "simple" juxtaposition. *Acta Linguistica Hafniensa* 12:69–120.

1973. *The grammar of Lahu*. (University of California Publications in Linguistics, 75.) Berkeley and Los Angeles: University of California Press.

Maxwell, Daniel 1979. Strategies of relativization and NP accessibility. *Language* 55:352–71.

1984. A typologically based principle of linearization. *Language* 60:251–85.

1985. *A crosslinguistic data sample in support of a principle of linearization*. Bloomington: Indiana University Linguistics Club.

Mayr, Ernst 1982. *The growth of biological thought: diversity, evolution, inheritance*. Cambridge, Mass.: Belknap Press.

Meinhof, Carl 1936. *Die Entstehung flektierender Sprachen*. Berlin: Reimel.

Merlan, Francesca 1983. *Ngalakan grammar, texts and vocabulary*. (Pacific Linguistics, B89.) Canberra: Australian National University.

Mithun, Marianne 1984. The evolution of noun incorporation. *Language* 60:847–94.

1986. On the nature of noun incorporation. *Language* 62:32–7.

1987. Is basic word order universal? In *Coherence and grounding in discourse*, ed. Russell Tomlin, 281–328. Amsterdam: John Benjamins.

Mondloch, James 1978. *Basic Quiché grammar*. Albany: State University of New York Institute for Mesoamerican Studies.

Moravcsik, Edith A. 1974. Object–verb agreement. *Working Papers in Language Universals* 15:25–140.

Morrow, Daniel G. 1986. Grammatical morphemes and conceptual structure in discourse processing. *Cognitive Science* 10:423–55.

Munro, Pamela and Lynn Gordon 1982. Syntactic relations in Western Muskogean: a typological perspective. *Language* 58:81–115.

Myhill, John 1988. Categoriality and clustering. *Studies in Language* 12:261–97.

Newman, Stanley 1944. *Yokuts language of California*. (Viking Fund Publications in Anthropology, 2.) New York: Viking Fund.

Nichols, Johanna 1984. Direct and oblique objects in Chechen-Ingush and Russian. In *Objects*, ed. Frans Plank, 183–209. New York: Academic Press.

Ohala, John and Lorentz 1977. The story of [w]. In *Proceedings of the Third Annual Meeting of the Berkeley Linguistics Society*, ed. Kenneth Whistler, Robert D. Van Valin *et al.*, 577–99. Berkeley: University of California at Berkeley.

Osborne, C. R. 1974. *The Tiwi language*. Canberra: Australian Institute of Aboriginal Studies.

288

Paul, Hermann 1880. *Prinzipien der Sprachgeschichte* (8th edition). Tübingen: Max Niemeyer.

Pawley, Andrew 1987. Encoding events in Kalam and English: different logics for reporting experience. In *Coherence and grounding in discourse*, ed. Russell Tomlin, 329–60. Amsterdam: John Benjamins.

Payne, Doris 1987. Information structuring in Papago narrative discourse. *Language* 63:783–804.

Payne, John R. 1980. The decay of ergativity in Pamir languages. *Lingua* 51:147–86.

Pinkerton, Sandra 1986. Quichean (Mayan) glottalized and nonglottalized stops: a phonetic study with implications for phonological universals. In *Experimental phonology*, ed. John J. Ohala and Jeri J. Jaeger, 125–39. New York: Academic Press.

Pitkin, Harvey 1984. *Wintu grammar.* (University of California Publications in Linguistics, 94.) Berkeley and Los Angeles: University of California Press.

Poppe, Nicholas 1974. *Grammar of written Mongolian.* Wiesbaden: Otto Harrassowitz.

Press, Margaret L. 1979. *Chemehuevi: A grammar and lexicon.* (University of California Publications in Linguistics, 92.) Berkeley and Los Angeles: University of California Press.

Pullum, Geoffrey 1977. Word order universals and grammatical relations. In *Grammatical relations* (Syntax and Semantics, 8), ed. Peter Cole and Jerrold Sadock, 249–77. New York: Academic Press.

1981. Languages with object before subject: a comment and a catalogue. *Linguistics* 19:147–55.

Rabel, Lili 1961. *Khasi, a language of Assam.* Baton Rouge: Louisiana State University Press.

Raz, Shlomo 1983. *Tigre grammar and texts.* (Afroasiatic Dialects, 4.) Malibu, Calif.: Undena Press.

Reed, Irene, Osahito Miyaoka, Steven Jacobson, Paschal Afcan and Michael Krauss 1977. *Yup'ik Eskimo grammar.* Anchorage: University of Alaska, Alaska Native Language Center.

Rehg, Kenneth L. 1981. *Ponapean reference grammar.* Honolulu: University Press of Hawaii.

Robins, R. H. 1958. *The Yurok language: grammar, texts, lexicon.* (University of California Publications in Linguistics, 15.) Berkeley and Los Angeles: University of California Press.

Rood, David and Allan R. Taylor 1976. *Beginning Lakhota*, vol. 1. Boulder, Colo.: University of Colorado Lakhota Project.

Rosch, Eleanor 1978. Principles of categorization. In *Cognition and categorization*, ed. Eleanor Rosch and B. B. Lloyd, 27–48. Hillsdale, N.J.: Lawrence Erlbaum Associates.

Rowlands, E. C. 1969. *Yoruba.* Sevenoaks: Hodder and Stoughton.

Rude, Noel 1982. Promotion and topicality of Nez Perce objects. In *Proceedings of the eighth annual meeting of the Berkeley Linguistic Society*, ed. Monica Macaulay, Orin Gensler *et al.*, 463–83. Berkeley: University of California at Berkeley.

References

Ruhlen, Merritt 1976. *A guide to the languages of the world.* Stanford: Stanford Language Universals Project.

1987. *A guide to the world's languages,* vol I: *Classification.* Stanford: Stanford University Press.

Sadock, Jerrold 1980. Noun incorporation in West Greenlandic: a case of syntactic word formation. *Language* 56:300–19.

1985. The Southern Tiwa incorporability hierarchy. *International Journal of American Linguistics* 51:568–71.

1986. Some notes on noun incorporation. *Language* 62:19–31.

Sandfeld, Kr. 1930. *Linguistique balkanique: problèmes et résultats.* (Collection linguistique publiée par la Société Linguistique de Paris, 31.) Paris: Champion.

Sapir, Edward 1921. *Language.* New York: Harcourt, Brace and World.

1922. Takelma. In *Handbook of American Indian languages, part 2,* ed. Franz Boas, 1–296. Washington, D.C.: Bureau of American Ethnology.

Saussure, Ferdinand de 1959 [1915]. *Course in general linguistics* (translated Wade Baskin). New York: McGraw-Hill.

Scatton, Ernest A. 1983. *A reference grammar of Modern Bulgarian.* Columbus, Ohio: Slavica.

Schachter, Paul 1973. Focus and relativization. *Language* 49:19–46.

1976. The subject in Philippine languages: topic, actor, actor-topic, or none of the above. In *Subject and topic,* ed. Charles Li, 491–518. New York: Academic Press.

1977. Reference-related and role-related properties of subjects. *Grammatical relations* (Syntax and Semantics, 8), ed. Peter Cole and Jerrold Sadock, 279–306. New York: Academic Press.

Schmalstieg, William R. 1976. *Old Church Slavonic.* Columbus, Ohio: Slavica.

Schmid, Annette 1985. The fate of ergativity in dying Dyirbal. *Language* 61:378–98.

Schütz, Alfred 1969. *Nguna texts.* (Oceanic Linguistics Special Publication, 4.) Honolulu: University of Hawaii Press.

Schwartz, Linda 1980. Syntactic markedness and frequency of occurrence. In *Evidence and argumentation in linguistics,* ed. Thomas Perry, 315–33. Berlin: Walter de Gruyter.

Seiler, Hansjakob 1983. *Possession as an operational dimension of language.* Tübingen: Gunter Narr.

Shackle, C. 1972. *Punjabi.* London: English Universities Press.

Siewierska, Anna 1984. *The passive: a comparative linguistic analysis.* London: Croom Helm.

Silverstein, Michael 1976. Hierarchy of features and ergativity. In *Grammatical categories in Australian languages,* ed. R. M. W. Dixon, 112–71. Canberra: Australian Institute of Aboriginal Studies.

Skalička, Vladimir 1941. *Vývoj české deklinace; studie typologická.* (Studie Pražského linguistického Kroužko, 4.) Prague: Jednota českých matematiků a lysiků.

Smith, Neil 1982. Review of Comrie 1981. *Australian Journal of Linguistics* 2:255–61.

Sohn, Ho-min 1975. *Woleaian reference grammar*. Honolulu: University Press of Hawaii.

Stassen, Leon 1985. *Comparison and universal grammar*. Oxford: Basil Blackwell.

Steele, Susan 1975. On some facts that affect and effect word order. In *Word order and word order change*, ed. Charles Li, 197–268. Austin: University of Texas Press.

  1978. Word order variation: a typological study. In *Universals of human language*, vol IV: *Syntax*, ed. Joseph H. Greenberg, Charles A. Ferguson and Edith A. Moravcsik, 585–624. Stanford: Stanford University Press.

Stucky, Susan 1979. Focus of contrast aspects in Makua: syntactic and semantic evidence. In *Proceedings of the fifth annual meeting of the Berkeley Linguistic Society*, ed. Christine Chiarello *et al.*, 362–72. Berkeley: University of California at Berkeley.

  1981. Word order variation in Makua: a phrase structure grammar analysis. Ph.D dissertation, Department of Linguistics, University of Illinois at Champaigne-Urbana.

Talmy, Leonard 1972. Semantic structures in English and Atsugewi. Ph.D dissertation, Department of Linguistics, University of California, Berkeley.

  1974. Semantics and syntax of motion. In *Syntax and Semantics*, vol. IV, ed. John Kimball, 181–238. New York: Academic Press.

  1978. The relation of grammar to cognition. In *Proceedings of TINLAP-2*, ed. David Waltz. Urbana, University of Illinois Coordinated Science Laboratory.

  1985. Lexicalization patterns: semantic structure in lexical forms. In *Language typology and syntactic description*, vol. III: *Grammatical categories and the lexicon*, ed. Timothy Shopen, 57–149. Cambridge: Cambridge University Press.

  1988. The relation of grammar to cognition. In *Topics in cognitive linguistics*, ed. Brygida Rudzka-Ostyn, 165–205. Amsterdam: John Benjamins.

Thomas, David D. 1971. *Chrau grammar*. (Oceanic Linguistics Special Publication, 7.) Honolulu: University of Hawaii Press.

Tiersma, Peter Meijes 1982. Local and general markedness. *Language* 58:832–49.

Tomlin, Russell 1986. *Basic word order: Functional principles*. London: Croom Helm.

Traugott, Elizabeth Closs 1982. From propositional to textual and expressive meanings: some semantic-pragmatic aspects of grammaticalization. In *Perspectives on historical linguistics*, ed. Winfred P. Lehmann and Yakov Malkiel, 245–71. Amsterdam: John Benjamins.

  1985. On regularity in semantic change. *Journal of Literary Semantics* 14:155–73.

  1988. Pragmatic strengthening and grammaticalization. In *Proceedings of the fourteenth annual meeting, Berkeley Linguistics Society*, ed. Shelley Axemaker, Annie Jaisser and Helen Singmaster, 406–16. Berkeley: University of California at Berkeley.

References

Trubetzkoy, Nicholas 1931. Die phonologischen Systeme. *Travaux du Cercle Linguistique de Prague* 4:96–116.

1969 [1939]. *Principles of phonology*. (Translation of *Grundzüge der Phonologie*, Prague, 1939). Berkeley and Los Angeles: University of California Press.

Vennemann, Theo 1973. Explanation in syntax. In *Syntax and semantics*, vol. II, ed. John Kimball. New York: Academic Press.

Watahomigie, Lucille J., Jorigine Bender and Akira Y. Yamamoto 1982. *Hualapai reference grammar*. Los Angeles: UCLA American Indian Studies Center.

Watkins, Laurel J. 1984. *A grammar of Kiowa*. Lincoln: University of Nebraska Press.

Wegener, Philipp 1885. *Untersuchungen über die Grundfragen des Sprachlebens*. Halle: Max Niemeyer.

Whitney, Arthur 1944. *Colloquial Hungarian*. London: Routledge and Kegan Paul.

Whorf, Benjamin Lee 1956. *Language, thought and reality*. Cambridge, Mass.: M.I.T. Press.

Wierzbicka, Anna 1981. Case marking and human nature. *Australian Journal of Linguistics* 1.43–80.

1985. Oats and wheat: the fallacy of arbitrariness. In *Iconicity in syntax*, ed. John Haiman, 311–42. Amsterdam: John Benjamins.

1986. What's in a noun? (or: how do nouns differ in meaning from adjectives?). *Studies in Language* 10:353–89.

Williams, C. J. 1980. *A grammar of Yuwaalaraay*. (Pacific Linguistics, B74.) Canberra: Australian National University.

Witherspoon, Gary 1977. *Language and art in the Navajo universe*. Ann Arbor: University of Michigan Press.

Witkowski, Stanley R. and C. H. Brown 1983. Marking reversals and cultural importance. *Language* 59:569–82.

Wolfart, H. Christoph and Janet F. Carroll 1981. *Meet Cree: A guide to the Cree language* (2nd edition). Lincoln: University of Nebraska Press.

Wurm, Stephen and Shiro Hattôri 1981. *Language atlas of the Pacific area*. (Pacific Linguistics, C66.) Canberra: Australian National University.

Zipf, George 1935. *The psychobiology of language: An introduction to dynamic philology*. Cambridge, Mass.: M.I.T. Press.

MAP OF LANGUAGES CITED

A map of the location of the languages referred to in the text follows, giving the genetic classification of those languages. Languages and language groups cited are in bold-face type; languages in parentheses are extinct. Numbers following the names of the languages identify their location on the map; the numbers identify the approximate location of the traditional use of the language (generally, prior to European colonization). The classification is based on Ruhlen 1987; some subgroupings have been slightly simplified, and Greenberg's Eurasiatic proposal is included. In general, the Ruhlen–Greenberg classification represents the avant-garde rather than the consensus position in genetic classification; higher-level genetic groupings that are not widely accepted are in italics.

NIGER–KORDOFANIAN
Kordofanian: Kadugli: Eastern: **Krongo 1**
Niger–Congo:
  Mande: Northern–Western:
    Northern: Vai–Kono: **Vai 2**
    Southwestern: **Kpelle 3, Mende 4, Loma 5**
  Niger–Congo Proper: West Atlantic:
    Northern: Senegal: **Fula 6**
  South Central Niger–Congo:
    Western:
      Nyo: Yi: Volta–Comoe: Central: **Akan 7**
      Togo: **Ewe 8**
    Eastern:
      Yoruba–Northern Akoko: Yoruba: **Yoruba 9**
      Edo: **Esako 10**
      Lower Niger: Igbo: **Igbo 11**
      Benue–Zambesi: Nyima: Wel: Bantoid: Broad Bantu: Narrow Bantu:
        Zone G: Swahili: **Swahili 12**
        Zone H: **Kituba (pidginized Kikongo) 13**
        Zone J:
          Nyoro–Luganda: **Luganda 14**
          Rwanda–Rundi: **Kinyarwanda 15**
        Zone M: **Bemba 16**
        Zone P: **Makua 17**

Map of languages cited

EURASIATIC
Indo-Hittite:
  Anatolian: **(Hittite 50)**
  Indo-European:
    Indo-Iranian:
      Indic: Northern India: Central: **Punjabi 51, Hindi 52, Gujarati 53**
      Iranian:
        Eastern: Northeast: East Scythian: Pamir: **Bartangi 54**
        Western: Southwest: Persian: **Persian 55**
    Albanian 56
    Greek: **(Classical Greek 57), Modern Greek 58**
    Italic: Latino-Faliscan:
      (Classical Latin 59)
      Romance: Continental:
        Eastern: North: **Rumanian 60**
        Western: Gallo-Ibero-Romance:
          Gallo-Romance: **(Old French 61), French 62, (Old Provençal 63), Modern Provençal, Charente dialect 64**
          Ibero-Romance: **Spanish 65**
  Celtic: Insular: Brythonic: **Welsh 66**
  Germanic:
    North: West; **Icelandic 67**
    West:
      Continental: East: **German 68**
      North Sea: **English 69, Frisian 70**
  Balto-Slavic:
    Baltic: East: **Latvian 71**
    Slavic:
      East: North: **Russian 72**
      West:
        Central: **Upper Lusatian 73**
        South: **Czech 74, Slovak 75**
    South:
      (Old Church Slavic 76)
      East: **Bulgarian 77**
Uralic–Yukaghir: Uralic: Finno-Ugric:
  Ugric: **Hungarian 78**
  Finnic: North Finnic: Baltic Finnic: **Finnish 79**
Altaic:
  Turkic: Common Turkic: Southern: **Turkish 80**
  Mongolian–Tungus: Mongolian: **(Classical Mongolian 81)**
Korean–Japanese-Ainu:
  Korean 82
  Japanese–Ryukuan: **Japanese 83**
Eskimo–Aleut: Eskimo:
  Inuit: **West Greenlandic 84**
  Yupik: Alaskan: **Central Alaskan Yup'ik 85**

Map of languages cited

Remote Oceanic:
    Micronesian: Micronesian Proper:
        Kosraean/Kusaiean 112
        Ponapean–Trukic:
            Ponapeic: **Mokilese 113, Ponapean 114**
            Trukic: **Woleaian 115**
    Southeast Solomons 116
    Central & Northern New Hebrides:
        Malekula Interior: **Big Nambas 117**
        NE New Hebrides–Banks Islands:
            Epi: **Bierebo, Baki, Mari, Biera, Lewo 118**
        Central New Hebrides: **Nguna 119**
    Central Pacific:
        Rotuman–Fijian: **Rotuman 120**
        Polynesian:
            Tongic; **Tongan 121**
            Nuclear Polynesian: Samoic Outlier: **Samoan 122**

INDO-PACIFIC

Trans-New Guinea: Main Section: Central & Western: East New Guinea Highlands:
    Kalam: Kalam–Kobon: **Kobon 123, Kalam 124**
    East–Central: **Hua 125**
    Central: **Salt-Yui 126**

AUSTRALIAN

Nunggubuyu 127
Tiwi 128
Gunwinyguan: **Ngandi 129, Ngalakan 130**
Pama–Nyungan:
    Dyirbalic: **Dyirbal 131**
    Wiradhuric: **Yuwaalaraay 132**
    South-West Wati: **Nganyatjarra 133**

NA-DENE

Continental Na-Dene: Athabaskan-Eyak: Athabaskan: Apachean: **Navajo 134, Chiricahua 135**

AMERIND

Northern Amerind
  Almosan–Keresiouan

Map of languages cited

Almosan:
Algic:
Ritwan: **Yurok 136**
Algonquian: Algonquian Proper: **Cree 137**
Mosan: Wakashan: Northern: **Kwakwalla/Kwakiutl 138**
Keresiouan:
Siouan-Yuchi: Siouan: Siouan Proper: Mississippi Valley: **Lakhota 139**
Iroquoian: Northern: Five Nations: Mohawk–Oneida: **Mohawk 140**
Penutian:
Oregon:
Takelman: **Takelma 141**
Coast: **Coos 142**
Plateau:
Klamath 143
Sahaptin–Nex Perce: **Nez Perce 144**
California:
Wintun: **Wintu 145**
Maiduan: **Maidu 146**
Yokuts; **Yokuts, Wikchamni dialect 147**
New Mexico: **Zuñi 148**
Gulf: Natchez–Muskogean: Muskogean: Western: **Choctaw 149, Chicka-saw 150**
Mexican:
Mayan:
Yucatecan: **Yucatec 151**
Greater Tzeltalan: Tzeltalan: **Tzotzil 152**
Eastern:
Greater Mamean; Mamean: **Mam 153**
Greater Quichean: Quichean: **Quiche 154, Tzutujil 155, Sacapultec 156**
Hokan:
Northern: Pomo: **Eastern Pomo 157**
Salinan–Chumash: **Chumash 158**
Seri–Yuman: Yuman:
River: **Maricopa 159**
Pai: **Hualapai 160**
Central Amerind:
Tanoan:
Kiowa–Towa: **Kiowa 161**
Tewa–Tiwa: **Southern Tiwa 162**
Uto-Aztecan:
Numic:
Western: **Ute 163**
Southern: **Chemehuevi 164**
Pimic: Piman; **Papago 165**
Corachol: **Huichol 166**
Aztecan: Aztec Proper: **(Classical Nahuatl 167)**

Equatorial–Tucanoan:
  Equatorial:
    Jivaroan: **Aguaruna 168**
    Kariri-Tupi: Tupi: Tupi-Guarani: Group I: Tupi: **Guaraní 169**
Ge–Pano-Carib:
  Macro-Carib: **Carib languages 170**
  Ge—Pano: Macro-Panoan: Pano-Tacan: Panoan: **Cashinawa 171**

CREOLES

English-Based: **Krio 172**

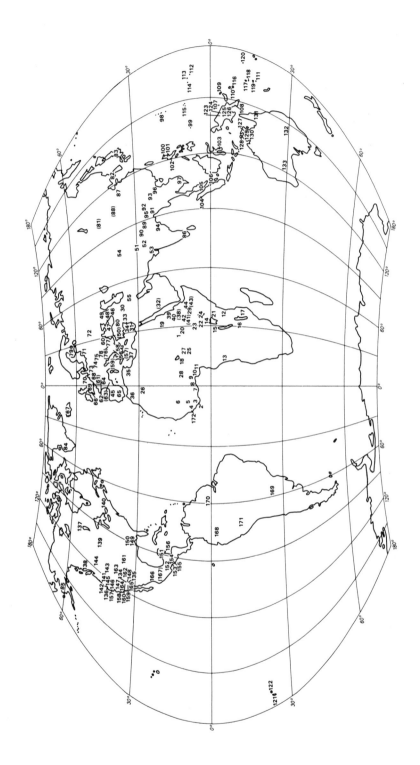

AUTHOR INDEX

Author index

LANGUAGE INDEX

Language index

SUBJECT INDEX

ablaut, 74, 75
absolutive, 102, 104–8, 110, 112, 124, 131,
    132, 133, 137–8, 266, 267, 270
accusative, 20–1, 124, 133, 137–8, 143, 144,
    151–2, 157, 177, 196–8, 271
adaptation, 232, 240
adjective, 13, 52–3, 54, 56, 57, 65, 69, 73,
    85–7, 92–3, 119, 139–43, 183, 192,
    205–6, 208–13, 220, 223–8, 230, 251,
    262, 265, 275
adposition, 10, 11, 13–16, 20–1, 30, 33, 36,
    37, 49, 51, 56, 59–61, 68, 73, 182, 185,
    190, 206, 220, 234, 262, 270
    and case marker, 24
    and genitive, 55, 59–61, 211–13, 223–8,
        230, 244
adverb, 56, 173, 182, 185, 186
affixal languages, 39
affixation, 29, 31, 37, 38, 231, 234, 239,
    240, 242–4
agent, 13, 102, 161–2, 169, 180, 196, 270
agglutinative languages, 39–40, 42, 229
agreement, 8, 13–16, 30–1
    adjectival (concord), 30, 37
    and animacy, 114, 129–30
    verbal (indexation), 14–15, 30, 31, 32,
        37, 38, 88, 101, 105–7, 114, 129–30,
        131, 149, 150, 160–1, 176–8, 197,
        242–4, 266–7, 271, 272
    with possessed item, 30
allomorphy, 232
analytic languages, 40, 41
anaphoric demonstrative, 219–20
animacy, 74, 124, 126, 132, 143
    and case marking, 9, 127–8, 136–9,
        160–4, 270
    and definiteness, 115, 127–30, 154, 160,
        266, 269
    hierarchy, 111–17
    hierarchy of features, 116
    noun number, 111–12
    verb agreement, 112
antipassive, *see* voice

applicative, 198
articles, 4–7, 21, 118, 195, 207, 219–20,
    229, 235–6, 251, 260, 276
aspect, 74, 83, 93, 132, 133, 139, 143, 162,
    163, 176–8, 180–1
aspiration, 93, 204
attested language types, 44–5, 68, 70, 78,
    194
attrition, 231, 239, 276
augmentative, 92
auxiliary, 80, 158, 173, 180, 185, 190, 231,
    237, 240, 261, 275
backgrounding, 163, 169–70
basic type, 34–6, 219
benefactive, 130, 234
bound morphemes, 189, 192, 273
case marking, 8, 11, 13–14, 20–1, 29, 30,
    32, 37, 39, 78, 79, 99–100, 101–5, 114,
    117, 124, 126, 136–9, 143, 149, 150,
    157, 176, 187, 190, 230, 234, 264, 265,
    271
    and adpositions, 24
    and animacy, 9, 127–8, 160–4
    and grammatical relations, 104
case recoverability, 199–201, 274
categoriality, 270–1
causation, 175, 181, 187
circumpositions, 61, 224
classification
    noun classes, 15–16, 190
    numeral classifiers, 31
    possessive classifiers, 31, 37, 207
clause-chaining, 24
clitic, 189, 231, 239, 242, 276
closed-class (vs. open-class), 140, 173,
    190–2, 239
coalescence, 231, 232, 239, 240, 276
comparability, cross-linguistic, 11–18, 69,
    155, 221, 247
comparative, 19, 24, 28, 56, 69–70, 73–4,
    92, 190
comparison, cross-linguistic, 1, 4–11, 47,
    70, 166, 250–1